Contraceptive Diplomacy

ASIAN AMERICA
A series edited by Gordon H. Chang

The increasing size and diversity of the Asian American population, its growing significance in American society and culture, and the expanded appreciation, both popular and scholarly, of the importance of Asian Americans in the country's present and past—all these developments have converged to stimulate wide interest in scholarly work on topics related to the Asian American experience. The general recognition of the pivotal role that race and ethnicity have played in American life, and in relations between the United States and other countries, has also fostered the heightened attention.

Although Asian Americans were a subject of serious inquiry in the late nineteenth and early twentieth centuries, they were subsequently ignored by the mainstream scholarly community for several decades. In recent years, however, this neglect has ended, with an increasing number of writers examining a good many aspects of Asian American life and culture. Moreover, many students of American society are recognizing that the study of issues related to Asian America speak to, and may be essential for, many current discussions on the part of the informed public and various scholarly communities.

The Stanford series on Asian America seeks to address these interests. The series will include works from the humanities and social sciences, including history, anthropology, political science, American studies, law, literary criticism, sociology, and interdisciplinary and policy studies.

A full list of titles in the Asian America series can be found online at www.sup.org/asianamerica

Contraceptive Diplomacy

REPRODUCTIVE POLITICS AND
IMPERIAL AMBITIONS IN THE
UNITED STATES AND JAPAN

Aiko Takeuchi-Demirci

STANFORD UNIVERSITY PRESS
STANFORD, CALIFORNIA

Stanford University Press
Stanford, California

© 2018 by the Board of Trustees of the Leland Stanford Junior University. All rights reserved.

This book has been partially underwritten by The Susan Groag Bell Publication Fund in Women's History. For more information on the fund, please see www.sup.org/bellfund.

No part of this book may be reproduced or transmitted in any form or by any means, electronic or mechanical, including photocopying and recording, or in any information storage or retrieval system without the prior written permission of Stanford University Press.

Printed in the United States of America on acid-free, archival-quality paper

Library of Congress Cataloging-in-Publication Data

Names: Takeuchi-Demirci, Aiko, author.
Title: Contraceptive diplomacy : reproductive politics and imperial ambitions in the United States and Japan / Aiko Takeuchi-Demirci.
Description: Stanford, California : Stanford University Press, 2017. | Series: Asian America | Includes bibliographical references and index. |
Identifiers: LCCN 2017028676 (print) | LCCN 2017030895 (ebook) | ISBN 9781503604414 (electronic) | ISBN 9781503602250 (cloth : alk. paper) | ISBN 9781503604407 (pbk. : alk. paper)
Subjects: LCSH: Birth control—United States—History—20th century. | Birth control—Japan—History—20th century. | United States—Population policy—History—20th century. | Japan—Population policy—History—20th century. | Sanger, Margaret, 1879-1966. | Katō, Shizue, 1897-2001. | United States—Relations—Japan. | Japan—Relations—United States.
Classification: LCC HQ766.5.U6 (ebook) | LCC HQ766.5.U6 T35 2017 (print) | DDC 363.9/60973—dc23
LC record available at https://lccn.loc.gov/2017028676

Typeset by Motto Publishing Services in 11/14 Adobe Garamond Pro

Contents

Figures and Tables ix
Acknowledgments xi
Abbreviations xiii
Note on Japanese Names and Words xv

Introduction 1

1. The Women Rebels: Transnational Socialism, Feminism, and the Early Birth Control Movement 19
2. Spreading the Gospel of Birth Control: The Limits of International Women's Activism 55
3. Danger Spots in World Population: The Eugenic and Imperial Struggles in the Pacific 83
4. Between Democracy and Genocide: US Involvement in Population Control in Occupied Japan 117
5. Re-producing National Bodies: Promoting Eugenic Marriages in Postwar Japan 151
6. Birth Control for the Masses: Technological Imperatives for Global Population Control 181

Epilogue 211

Notes 223
Bibliography 285
Index 311

Figures and Tables

FIGURES

0.1	Population and birth rates in Japan and the United States, 1880–2014	17
1.1	Portrait of Margaret Sanger and her son Grant	39
3.1	Map of California showing the "dark sections occupied by Orientals"	93
4.1	Poster comparing the average numbers and rate of childbirths among city dwellers, teachers, and farmers	134
4.2	Crawford F. Sams, head of the Public Health and Welfare Section of SCAP	148
5.1	Declining birth rates and population of each imperial power	161
5.2	Rates of contraception and induced abortion in Japan, 1950–2000	179
6.1.	A drawing satirizing the four Japanese delegates attending the 1952 Third International Conference on Planned Parenthood	185

TABLES

5.1	Rate of contraception use in Japan, 1950–2000	175
6.1	Percentage of use of contraceptive methods in Japan, 1950–2000	208

Acknowledgments

This book embodies the support of all the kind and brilliant people I met throughout my years at the University of Tokyo, Brown University, and Stanford University. First and foremost, my mentors at Brown University, Robert G. Lee, Naoko Shibusawa, Lundy Braun, and Kerry Smith, have helped guide this project from its inception. My former adviser at the University of Tokyo, Notoji Masako-sensei, also continued to inspire me in many ways. Gordon Chang has been a true advocate of my work through the revision and publication processes. I am grateful to Shelley Fisher Fishkin for adding me to the editorial team of the *Journal of Transnational American Studies*, an opportunity that has also helped me evaluate my own contribution to the field. My intellectual journey has been shaped by the invaluable input and support of many other colleagues at Brown and the University of Tokyo: Sarah Wald, Gillian Frank, Jin Suk Bae, Maria Hwang, Heather Lee, Jooyoung Lee, Seiko Mimaki, and Maho Toyoda—to name a few. I thank the Department of American Studies at Brown and the Program in Feminist, Gender, and Sexuality Studies at Stanford for giving me the opportunity to teach a course on transnational reproductive politics, which helped frame my work in a broader context.

This research would not have been possible without the generous backing of a number of organizations, archives, and their staff. I owe special thanks to the grants provided by the Rockefeller Archive Center, the Gordon W. Prange Collection at University of Maryland, the Sophia Smith Collection at Smith College, and matching grants from Brown University. I am particularly indebted to archivists and librarians who facilitated my research and brought my attention to many invaluable materials that I would not have discovered without their suggestions: Mary Ann Quinn at the Rockefeller Archive Center; Eiko Sakaguchi and Amy Wasserstrom at the Prange Collection; and archivists and staff at the Countway Library of Medicine at Harvard University, Harvard-Yenching Library, the Manuscript Division at the Library of Congress, the National Archives at College Park, Maryland, the Sophia Smith Collection, and the National Diet Library of Japan.

The editors of journals and anthologies to which I contributed articles related to this book provided constructive criticism and advice that helped strengthen my overall research. I owe special thanks to Charles Hayford and the late Anthony Cheung of the *Journal of American-East Asian Relations*; Allen Tullos and Frances Abbott of *Southern Spaces*; and Liping Bu, Darwin Stapleton, Ka-che Yip, Gillian Frank, Bethany Moreton, and Heather White, as well as the anonymous reviewers for my articles.

I am extremely grateful to the current and former editors at Stanford University Press, especially Margo Irvin, Nora Spiegel, Gigi Mark, Gretchen Otto, Cynthia Lindlof, Eric Brandt, Friederike Sundaram, and Kate Wahl, for guiding me step by step throughout the publication process.

Finally, I dedicate this book to my family. I thank my parents, Ryusuke and Kyoko Takeuchi, for providing the best place to stay during my research in Japan, and of course, for always being my moral support and guidance; Hasan Demirci, for picking up and returning all those library books for me and promoting my book project on every social occasion, long before its publication; and my angels, Kenji and Emi, who were born during this project and literally grew up with it, for providing me a deeper understanding about life and reproduction.

Abbreviations

EMCO	Eugenic Marriage Consultation Office
EPL	Eugenic Protection Law
FPFJ	Family Planning Federation of Japan
ICPP	International Conference on Planned Parenthood
ICW	International Council of Women
IPH	Institute of Public Health in Tokyo
IPPF	International Planned Parenthood Federation
IPR	Institute of Pacific Relations
IUD	intrauterine device
LDP	Liberal Democratic Party
MHW	Ministry of Health and Welfare (Japan)
OPR	Princeton Office of Population Research
PHW	Public Health and Welfare Section
PPWA	Pan-Pacific Women's Association
PPWC	Pan-Pacific Women's Conference
RF	Rockefeller Foundation
SCAP	Supreme Command for the Allied Powers
WCTU	Woman's Christian Temperance Union
WILPF	Women's International League for Peace and Freedom

Note on Japanese Names and Words

This book uses the Japanese convention of placing surnames first before given names. Macrons are used to describe long-vowel Japanese sounds. Exceptions are made when referring to Japanese words that are commonly used in English vocabulary (such as "Tokyo" and "Osaka") or Japanese authors whose English-language works have been cited. All translations from Japanese-language sources are mine except for publications that provide their own English titles.

Contraceptive Diplomacy

Introduction

> Almost from the time of landing I had been deeply conscious that I was in one of the most thickly populated countries of the world. . . . I could not believe any country could contain so many babies. Fathers carried them in their arms; mothers carried them in a sort of shawl; children carried babies; even babies carried smaller babies. . . . It was even then too late for birth control to offset the inevitability of her overflowing her borders; the population pressure was bound to cause an explosion in spite of the safety valve of Korea. How long this could be delayed was a matter of pure conjecture.
> —Margaret Sanger, *An Autobiography*

Margaret Sanger, the iconic leader of the American birth control movement, visited Japan for the first time in March 1922. By this time, she had already established her reputation as a controversial birth control activist both at home and abroad, and this was her first trip to Asia for the purpose of birth control advocacy outside the United States. She shared the impression that many American visitors had about Japan at the time—that the small island nation was packed with people, especially babies. It was here, even more than in her own country, where she found the dire need for birth control. But the significance of spreading birth control, Sanger believed, went beyond the individual needs of women and families. She was determined that the birth control cause could help resolve international tensions and contribute to world peace.

Contraceptive Diplomacy examines the development of ideas about birth control, contraceptive technology, and reproductive politics in the midst of imperial struggles between the United States and Japan by following the activism of Margaret Sanger and her Japanese counterpart, Ishimoto Shizue (later known as Katō Shizue after her second marriage in 1945).[1] These two feminists undertook a program of transnational activism in the mid-twentieth century, when liberal and radical actors across the Pacific came together to find amicable solutions to domestic and international tensions caused by industrial development and imperialist competition. For labor activists, birth control represented a tool to empower workers worldwide exploited under the global capitalist economy. For social reformers, it was a key to solve the problem of overpopulation, which they asserted was the root cause of many imperialist struggles, including Japan's aggressive expansionism in the Pacific. Intellectuals, philanthropists, and politicians across national borders exchanged social and scientific ideas about fertility control in the hopes of avoiding a fatal—seemingly inevitable—clash in the Pacific.

Sanger's new mission to spread birth control in Japan attracted the support of American reformers and scholars who embraced eugenic ideas. The development of the American birth control movement in the early to mid-twentieth century was deeply tied to white America's struggle for world hegemony. Concern about competition from Japan, coupled with eugenic fears about a declining "white civilization," pushed American leaders to cast aside wariness about the spread of birth control among white women and embrace it as a necessary tool to reduce the size of the teeming masses of Asia. The colonial enterprise of the crowded nation revived Western fears of a "Yellow Peril."[2] Japan's expansionism not only jeopardized American political interests in China but also seemed to threaten the lives of ordinary (white) citizens on the US mainland as the excessive population emigrated overseas and propagated at a higher rate than that of white Americans. Political pundits and intellectuals feared that differential fertility between the white and yellow races would eventually break the balance of power—or the white domination in world politics. In such a political and social context, it seemed justifiable—even humanitarian—to spread the practice of contraception to populations stigmatized as dangerously prolific and aggressive. These elites successfully separated the matter of birth control among nonwhite races across the world from the controversies at home over women's rights and sexuality when practiced among white middle-class women.

Sanger's birth control advocacy also found ardent supporters in Japan, who saw reproductive control as an effective tool to build a Japanese citizenry capable of competing with other imperial powers and leading the Asia-Pacific world. Japanese intellectuals with a penchant for new Western ideas asserted their ability to master—and even surpass the West in—birth control technology, which was seen as part of a neo-Malthusian economic theory.[3] For them, birth control represented modernity, scientific advancement, and a key to eugenic improvement of the Japanese race. The liberal elites strove to teach the idea not only to the Japanese masses but also to other Asian people. Tied deeply to notions of national prosperity and racial fitness, birth control advocacy in Japan survived, with a brief interruption, the pronatalist regime of the wartime government and further expanded during the postwar years, when overpopulation seemed to threaten the racial well-being of a defeated empire.

The transnational politics of reproduction helped gradually break down the social and legal barriers against birth control, enabling the democratization of birth control information and technology even in the domestic context. Had it not been for these extended discussions on birth control in international politics, many women across the world would have had more limited access to knowledge and tools of reproductive control. As Linda Gordon has argued, the primary obstacle to birth control was politics, which in turn often thwarted technological development of contraceptives.[4] I further extend this idea by maintaining that international politics and transnational networks helped advance birth control ideas and technologies when laws and social barriers in the domestic context frustrated the efforts of activists.

Even with the support of some liberal elites and professionals, birth control was still a radical subject that most Americans avoided discussing in public, much less endorsing. When she continued to face countless obstacles and alienation at home, Sanger often felt more welcome abroad. While one might imagine that she would face just as many protests and just as much bigotry—or perhaps more—among the indigenous people for preaching such a controversial topic, instead, as Sanger recalled, she was greeted with "respectful attention," "decency," and "consideration" in Asia.[5] In particular, she came to see Japan almost like her second home, visiting the country seven times throughout her lifetime and forming lasting friendships with a number of Japanese men and women and their families. By earning the respect of the Japanese people and their government, Sanger made her ultimate goal to win the battle against sexual oppression in her own country.

This book situates Margaret Sanger's political trajectory in broader intellectual trends and movements that transcended national borders. The birth control cause attracted the interest of transnational elites from across the political spectrum: first the radical socialists, then liberal reformers, and eventually some conservative nationalists. Sanger and Ishimoto flexibly shifted their sails according to the social tides and political winds of the time, soliciting support from those with political and financial influences. Along the way, the nature of the transnational birth control movement had evolved as well, although political ideologies that gained influence in the movement during certain times (liberalism, nationalism) did not completely replace another (radicalism).

The eugenic philosophy was a key concept that remained central to the birth control movement throughout the decades. Broadly defined as theories of individual or racial betterment, the idea fascinated many intellectuals and professionals—moderate, conservative, as well as radicals—who believed in the evolutionary notion of progress and development. A number of scholars have exposed Sanger's involvement in the eugenics movement in the domestic context. They tend to interpret Sanger's commitment to eugenics as her own political decision to align with elite conservatism, making birth control into a racist campaign benefiting only the white race.[6] While it is true that the stronger backing of eugenicists had transformed the birth control movement in general from a grassroots, antiestablishment campaign to a centralized and professionalized cause, this view tends to overlook how ideologically powerful and widespread the eugenic philosophy was at the time. Eugenics in the early twentieth century represented a cutting-edge science that traveled beyond national and racial borders and attracted the era's most brilliant and progressive intellectuals across the world. The transnational circulation of knowledge about race betterment, in turn, affected domestic politics, economics, laws, scientific research, and social norms about procreation and the future of the nation. The transnational birth control movement, in other words, developed alongside the global spread of the eugenics movement.

A close examination of the individual works of transnational birth control activists illuminates the limits of liberalism in advancing the rights of women and racial minorities. Sanger, Ishimoto, and many other birth control supporters, including eugenicists, were liberal reformers who strove to bring peace and stability to the world by assisting the "needy" peoples. They sincerely believed that the poor and the fertile races needed the guidance of white Americans; otherwise, the nation—and the world—would descend into chaos and even extinction. By presenting this imperialistic logic of humanitarianism, their transnational activism often masked the fundamental and structural inequalities and injustice that US and Japanese imperialism had generated.

As transnational birth control leaders immersed themselves into eugenic or neo-Malthusian debates about racial betterment and national well-being, they tended to neglect the needs and health of individuals whom they claimed to save. By the postwar period, they were working along with demographers, scientists, and policy makers in their efforts to develop modern and effective contraceptives—specifically the oral contraceptive pills and intrauterine devices—in the battle against global population explosion, while failing to improve women's social status or to spread sexual and reproductive education. In other words, advances in reproductive technology and the wider availability of contraceptives to women of all social and economic statuses did not guarantee the expansion of women's health and reproductive rights. A feminist mission to give women across the world the tools and knowledge to decide their reproductive fate had thus, over four decades, evolved into a state endeavor that effectively disempowered racially and economically marginalized women.

The Transpacific Politics of Reproduction

Contraceptive Diplomacy situates the history of reproductive politics at the intersection of transnational feminist activism and US-Japanese relations. It narrates the development of contraceptive knowledge and technology from a transnational standpoint, specifically, a transpacific one, closely examining how international politics affected domestic conversations on race, gender, and sexuality. Women activists, in particular, became key agents and facilitators of transnationalism.[7]

Whereas many studies on Japanese modern history either end with the demise of the "empire" after the Pacific War, or start with the rise of a new "democratic" nation in the postwar era, this book covers the period before, during, and after World War II. It highlights the continuity of transnational exchanges between American and Japanese intellectuals, politicians, and activists across the twentieth century. The military battles in the Pacific in the 1940s were not the sole defining event in the history of US-Japan relations. Reproductive issues, as they were intricately tied to nationalist concerns over population size and racial quality, appeared prominently in political debates regarding some key global struggles that affected US-Japan relations: the Russian Revolution of 1917, the immigration restriction movement in the United States in the early 1920s, the imperialist struggles for Asian territories in the 1930s and 1940s, the postwar Allied Occupation of Japan, and the beginning of the Cold War in the 1950s. All of these major events in world politics involved extended discussions over protecting or building stronger national bodies in face of competition with the Other: the capitalist, another race, or the communist.

The story of a transpacific politics of reproduction serves to decenter the Euro-American viewpoint in cultural and intellectual histories. Based on multinational and multilingual research, this study illuminates the *mutual* interactions and influences between individuals and institutions in Japan and the United States over the matter of reproductive control. It takes into account historical contexts, political ideologies, and social thought in both countries, against the backdrop of Japanese as well as American imperialism. While the legacy of European colonialism and Euro-American connections provided a powerful subtext, transpacific relations played critical roles in the development of political thought and racial theories that affected the birth control movements in both nations.[8]

Despite their rivalry, Japanese and American liberals shared much in common in terms of political ideology and geopolitical interests. Individual politicians and intellectuals had formed cooperative and oftentimes friendly relationships.[9] Indeed, birth control advocates in both countries were able to maintain contact throughout the war years, albeit with limitations in an environment of mounting diplomatic tension. This is by no means to suggest that there was no tension between the liberal actors of the two nations, which often expressed itself in racial terms.[10] Nonetheless, birth control activists represented a sizable group of influential individual actors who searched for ways to build mutually beneficial relations even during difficult times in official foreign relations.

The transnational circulation of knowledge regarding female fertility first took place as a form of what historian Akira Iriye calls "cultural internationalism," an idea and movement that flourished during the interwar period in the context of Wilsonian internationalism.[11] While World War I damaged European nationalism and colonialism, the United States emerged more powerful and expanded its influence abroad, especially in the Asia-Pacific region through the Open Door Policy. American liberals sought to bring Japan into the American-led "community of ideals, interests, and purposes," an initiative to which many Japanese leaders responded positively.[12] The elites often expressed these international endeavors in the form of liberal, humanitarian ideals, even while they were fundamentally driven by economic and geopolitical interests.

American-led internationalism, as William Appleman Williams illustrated, was a form of imperialism without direct territorial governance. The goal of US "imperial anti-colonialism" was to achieve world domination without having to actually go to war. The new international order was based on the balance of power, not the denial of power itself. It was an "essentially conservative" system that privileged America's efforts to achieve both domestic well-being and world hegemony.[13] Sanger and her supporters, many of whom were liberal internationalists, aimed to bring a "slow process of reform" without the need of a radical revolution.[14] While many of them, both American and Japanese, were actually anticolonialists, in that they opposed imperialist aggression and emigration resulting from overpopulation, they cannot be presumed to have been antiracist champions of participatory democracy in weaker, poorer nations. In the end, their version of anticolonialism promoted an orderly world safe for the interests of imperial superpowers. The liberal internationalists' efforts in most part fell short of extending their humanitarian impulse and professed principle of self-determination to non-Western peoples.

From the vantage point of American birth control activists, the support of eugenicists was crucial to the expansion of the birth control cause across national borders, especially to non-Western countries. High-profile political leaders such Woodrow Wilson and Theodore Roosevelt, as well as civilian reformers and eugenicists, shared the same fears that the rise of Japan posed a threat to world stability.[15] US political leaders recognized Japan's military power and accorded it a special position in Asia, but only to protect and expand US interests in China. In the end, Japan was still inferior and unfit for leadership. Eugenicists used science to justify white leadership and colored subordination. Without the "superior" qualities of self-restraint and foresight that white men possessed, they argued, the yellow race would lead the world to chaos and darkness. Japan's desperate search for an outlet for their surplus population as a result of their "reckless" breeding seemed to be a case in point. It was part of the "white man's burden" to educate the Japanese in the civilized practice of birth control.

Even as they struggled to make sense of the inferior status assigned by Westerners, Japanese leaders selectively used Western power and knowledge to advance their own interests. Many Japanese advocates of birth control were transnational figures who actively consumed Western knowledge, interacted with Western intellectuals, and occasionally traveled abroad themselves. They often invoked the concept of Western progress and Eastern backwardness when they advocated the need for fertility control as a token of modernity. Such admissions did not suggest that the Japanese passively accepted their inferiority. Rather, Japanese elites envisioned themselves as leaders of the Pan-Asian regional order—more suited to the task than Americans, since they were, after all, Asians too—and as the only "Oriental" nation that had successfully assimilated "Occidental" modernity. In many cases, Japanese intellectuals sought not just to emulate Americans but to exceed them in their mastery of contraceptive knowledge and technology. Other times, they found the need to reject, adapt, or modify American-imported ideas and practices to adjust to domestic politics and indigenous demands. By mastering Western knowledge and practices, Japanese supporters of birth control claimed to set an example for other Asian countries to emulate.

This book highlights, in particular, the role of private ambassadors and transient visitors in fostering cross-cultural and cross-racial relationships across the Pacific.[16] It features the works of those who lived or traveled abroad for shorter periods of time, ranging from weeks to several years, and who frequently moved back and forth between their "native" and "adopted" countries. Their citizenship and loyalty to their home country remained the same, but they invested a great deal of time and energy in learning about their adopted country and negotiated an identity that bridged nations. Just like permanent and long-term immigrants, these transnational figures played crucial roles in challenging and redefining another country's conceptions about race, citizenship, and national identity through discussions over reproduction. They often faced obstacles in entering the other country, but their relative mobility and flexibility allowed them to communicate and travel across borders even during volatile times for official diplomatic relations.

The cultural diplomacy of birth control activists in fact had impacts on policy formation and lawmaking in both direct and subtle ways. Their transnational ties, for example, brought a crucial change to the birth control law in the United States in 1936, when Sanger and her supporters won a lawsuit against the US government for confiscating a package of pessaries sent to their clinic from Japan for medical use. The court decision of acknowledging contraceptives as a legitimate part of medical practice in effect nullified the Comstock Law, a law that had forbidden the distribution of any birth control information or devices since 1873. Soon after the decision, the American Medical Association formally endorsed contraception.[17] In Japan, a number of influential birth control advocates became members of the National Diet or ministry officials during the US Occupation after the war, including Ishimoto (by then Katō) Shizue. With the help of US officials, these Japanese bureaucrats played crucial roles in drafting and passing the 1948 Eugenic Protection Law (Yūsei hogo hō), which legalized abortion and stipulated programs for birth control instruction. The purpose and actual outcome of these national policies and laws aimed at reproductive control did not necessarily reflect the original spirit of birth control activism, placing national interests over those of women. Nonetheless, these policies and laws helped bring the idea of reproductive control to national attention and advance the knowledge and technologies of contraception.

It would be misleading, however, to assume that the cultural diplomacy of elite citizens always dovetailed with official concerns for racial or national prosperity. The transnational birth control movement differed from most other forms of cultural diplomacy led by missionaries, businessmen, and other liberal elites, in that discussions of female sexuality were potentially subversive to the male-oriented national order.[18] In fact, exchanges of information about birth control between the United States and Japan first took place through a network of radicals and socialists who were dissatisfied with the imperialist and capitalist social order. Birth control, they argued, could liberate women workers across the world subjected to inhumane exploitation by capitalists for both reproductive and wage labor.

Their unrelenting activism made national and international headlines and provoked the interests of both the elites and the masses in the matters of reproduction and sexuality. Although the endorsement of professionals and politicians eventually blunted the potentially more radical nature of the birth control movement, the drive to create and spread more female-oriented contraceptive methods—rather than male-centered ones such as condoms—remained central to the birth control movement throughout the twentieth century.

By looking into an issue that fundamentally affected women themselves, this book sheds light on the role of women activists in international politics. Much of the history of international relations has been narrated from the perspective of male leaders, whether on official or private levels.[19] Yet, as some historians have highlighted, the backdrop of imperial competition provided new opportunities for some women leaders to have their voices heard.[20] Although often marginalized and discriminated against by male scientists and officials, Margaret Sanger and Ishimoto Shizue represented various aspects of the birth control movement, uniting different political constituencies and maintaining transnational connections even during the difficult years of war. Their gender worked both as an advantage and disadvantage in their transnational activism. They suffered from gendered biases and discrimination in the field of politics and science and experienced extra difficulty convincing people to take their work seriously. At the same time, their femininity and exoticism often worked to lower the guards of their foreign audience over such a controversial topic as birth control. Their personal experiences as mothers reinforced their universal appeal to women's rights to control their bodies. In other words, their campaigns resonated more broadly and deeply with people beyond national or racial borders than the policies and propaganda promoted by male intellectuals and politicians.

Sanger and her feminist supporters always had ambiguous and volatile relationships with the intellectuals and elites surrounding them. Even as they depended on their power and money to expand their cause, they remained critical of the hypocritical and misogynistic arguments of their male supporters. During the 1910s and 1920s, many birth control feminists both in Japan and the United States piggybacked on the socialist movement, but their ties to that community quickly unraveled, not only because of persecution against radicals worldwide but also because of many male socialists' ignorance of women's needs and demands. Liberal reformers who aided the birth control cause after the socialist decline continued to distance birth control from the issue of female sexuality and liberation. While they advocated the benefits of birth control to the nonwhite races or lower classes, they stopped short of doing the same to women of their own race or class. Sanger's feminist circle, however, remained strongly critical of such artificial distinction between whites and nonwhites, rich and poor, in regard to women's right to control their own bodies. For that reason, the Sangerist style of birth control activism remained controversial and marginalized even among liberal internationalists. When they could not win the backing of their domestic peers, however, the activists turned abroad for support.

Because of their equivocal relationship with the nation, I refer to the overall activities of birth control activists as a *transnational* movement. I use the word "transnational" to describe the interconnected movements of people, ideas, and practices that extend beyond national borders, not necessarily representing the state, but those that are still based on the framework of the nation-state.[21] Transnational initiatives often challenge and decenter state authority, while at other times reinforce it in unofficial manners. Sanger and her supporters' worldwide activism was truly a transnational endeavor, as they sought to reach out to men and women across the world on individual levels with or without the sponsorship of the government. At times, the state saw their campaigns as a threat to official diplomatic relations because birth control activists often deliberately challenged the state's patriarchal policies on women's sexuality and reproduction. Both the US and Japanese governments' attempts to bar Sanger from entering Japan illustrated the state's suspicion and antagonism against these individuals. At other times, however, state officials took advantage of Sanger's popularity and influence when, especially during the postwar years in Japan, population reduction seemed to dovetail with the nation's goal for economic and social development. Supporters of birth control in turn skillfully used state institutions and policies whenever such collaboration seemed advantageous to them.

Indeed, the transnational birth control movement could also be described either as a form of *international* ambassadorship or even *global* enterprise. International, by definition, refers to the mutually supportive relationships between national governments or agencies. Many nonstate actors who took part in international endeavors during the interwar decades worked dialectically with official diplomacy and voluntarily—and sometimes unknowingly—promoted the interests of the nation-state. In many instances, birth control activism closely aligned with the goals and practices of internationalism, even though they did not represent a central part of these elite activities. Furthermore, the population control programs during the postwar decades are often described as a global phenomenon that encompassed the entire world. Matthew Connelly's historical account of the global population control movement illuminates the postwar population control initiatives led by some of the world's richest and influential nongovernmental organizations (NGOs), such as the Ford and Rockefeller Foundations, the United Nations agencies, and the World Bank.[22] The process of globalization does not negate the boundaries of the nation-state either, even though the lines are less visible. In fact, what we see as global issues are usually based on American-led international networks to facilitate the function of capitalism. For example, the Rockefeller Foundation's public health projects often evoked American capitalism as well as liberalism. With it came both the positive images of American grandiosity and generosity and the negative connotations of American imperialism. The transnational birth control movement, to which these American NGOs provided significant support, shared many of the characteristics of internationalist and global activities.

The transformation of a transnational *birth control* activism to a global *population control* enterprise represented not simply a shift of terms but the changing nature of the cause itself. When Sanger coined the term "birth control," it had a strong association with sexual liberation and women's right to control their own bodies. Transnational radicals and socialists endorsed the idea as a challenge against Western capitalism and colonialism by giving power to female workers. As liberal elites took control over the movement, however, the term "birth control" gradually became interchangeable with—and was eventually replaced by—"population control" or "family planning/planned parenthood." Population control treated fertility control as a matter of global or international interest, and family planning confined the discussion to the context of the nuclear family and the well-being of the national body. Leaders of the global population control movement came to emphasize the benefits of having fewer children for the family, the nation, and the world rather than the liberating aspects of birth control in terms of women's sexuality and independence. They consciously toned down the radical images associated with birth control to attract the broad support and understanding of national leaders, including social and religious conservatives.

The transnational birth control movement thus came to embody many of the ideologies that guided US foreign relations: evolutionism, expansionism, exceptionalism, imperialism, liberal developmentalism, and the Cold War modernization theory—all based on the Enlightenment philosophy of linear progress from a "traditional" society to a "modern" one.[23] According to this line of thought, the United States had the moral obligation to "uplift" less developed, non-Western societies by applying their "advanced" experiences and "superior" knowledge, especially in the field of science and technology. While this evolutionary thought placed the West and non-West at opposite ends of the progression toward modernity, Japan did not neatly fit into this binary; the Japanese considered themselves "honorary whites"—racially Asian but culturally as advanced as Western countries—and therefore in an ideal position to guide other Asian countries.[24] At times, Japanese leaders consciously challenged the Western assumption of white superiority. Despite the rivalry and clashes, American and Japanese leaders worked side by side to bring reproductive modernity to the Third World through the use of the latest contraceptive technology, which, they assumed, would help solve other social, economic, and political issues. This modernizing project was a male-centered endeavor that paid little, if any, respect to cultural variables or the will of individual women. The top-down nature of the global population control movement would define the direction of future birth control initiatives for decades to come.

The Biopolitics of Reproductive Bodies

Contraceptive Diplomacy reveals the multiplicity of power struggles that took place over the female body, not only within a nation but also between nations. The knowledge and discourses regarding female reproduction have been socially constructed to justify hierarchical power relations: between men and women, Westerners and non-Westerners, whites and nonwhites, and the elites and the masses. Under the modern system of biopower, the sexual conduct of a national population was treated as an economic and political problem, regulated by the government yet constantly resisted and negotiated by multiple social actors.[25] Ideas about female bodies traveled beyond national borders, were exchanged through transnational contacts, and then readjusted to indigenous circumstances. In particular, this book analyzes the politics of the female body from three overlapping angles: the sexual body, the racialized body, and the national body. Intersecting ideas about gender, sexuality, and race operated to discipline the individual body to be more docile yet useful to the nation in the contest for world leadership.[26]

The production of modern scientific knowledge and ideas reflected continuous struggles to discipline the female sexual body. Especially since the rise of modern science and medicine in the nineteenth century, the female body has been treated as the other, pitted against the rational male mind. It became a passive object to be controlled, tamed, and conquered by doctors, scientists, and politicians. As anthropologist Emily Martin shows, modern science has fragmented women's bodies, separating her uterus as a machine that produces babies under the supervision of doctors.[27] In modern Japan, similar references to women's "borrowed wombs" (*hara wa karimono*)—an idea that negated women's control or ownership of their own bodies—frequently appeared in medical textbooks and public discourses.[28] At a time when women were expanding their sphere of influence in politics and society, science served as a new rationale to legitimize female inferiority and subordination by attributing them to women's biology.[29]

Access to birth control became problematic to the patriarchal order because it gave women the power to regulate their own bodies, specifically their ability to reproduce offspring. As Silvia Federici demonstrates in her study on medieval witch-hunts, women's nonprocreative sexuality became a threat to the capitalist system, which was based on the devaluation of reproductive labor and the subjugation of women.[30] Over and over, therefore, we see male and elite leaders trying to take control of the discussions and knowledge concerning reproduction through legal restrictions, medical supervision, and the construction of social norms and knowledge. Both in the United States and Japan, the medical profession monopolized the knowledge of reproductive control, while politicians created and enforced laws regulating its dissemination. Abortion became illegal in Japan in 1880, for example, as the country adopted the modern system of reproductive control enforced in other Western imperial nations. In the United States, the Comstock Law of 1873 prohibited the mailing and advertising of any information regarding reproductive control as "obscene" material just as more and more women started to expand and explore beyond the domestic sphere. Furthermore, the Malthusian theory, espoused by intellectuals across the world, pathologized women's reproductive roles as a cause of overpopulation, racial degeneration, and war.

In this misogynist climate, Margaret Sanger and her feminist supporters strove to give women equal access to medical and scientific knowledge, usually monopolized by men of power. They were only partially successful, however, as male leaders with political and financial power continued to dominate and regulate the production of knowledge regarding female reproduction. Even when these female activists initiated the changes, in most cases male politicians and scientists eventually assumed control over the outcome of laws, international meetings, or scientific research on contraceptives.

The imagery of the fertile female body was, moreover, frequently racialized in social and scientific discourses. If women's reproductive role made them closer to nature and to animals, as Donna Haraway, Londa Schiebinger, and other feminist scholars have demonstrated in their investigations of modern science, then women of color were considered more likely than white women to "multiply like rabbits."[31] Asian women, in particular, were highly sexualized in the American imaginary.[32] Combining these two images of Asian women's fecundity and sexuality heightened anxieties about the dangers of the Yellow Peril to the Western world in the campaigns against Japan's overpopulation and expansionism. Meanwhile, the Japanese elites who endorsed birth control utilized the racialized image of the nonwhite female body as a way to exhort their own people to become more civilized—if they could not be white or truly Western—by adopting the modern practice of contraception. In other words, the Japanese struggle for acceptance as an international, imperialist power was a process of deracialization of the (middle-class) Japanese body by simultaneously racializing others: the working-class Japanese, the mentally and physically "unfit," other Asian ethnicities, and other peoples of color.

Finally, this book illustrates how the individual female body became a site of power struggles between two empires across the Pacific. Nationalism and imperialism accorded special meanings to the female body as a machine to reproduce strong and healthy future soldiers and citizens. Male experts needed to place women under their guidance so that they could teach them rational marriage and sex that would lead to racial fitness and national prosperity. The nationalist leaders warned, however, that the selfish use of birth control by individual women would degenerate the race and lead to the demise of a nation. Historians have thoroughly examined the domestic policies of social control over sexuality as part of the nation-building effort, whether in modern Europe, Japan, or the United States.[33] This work goes beyond the framework of a single nation-state and closely examines how international dynamics and transnational relationships directly impacted domestic politics and discussions about the national body.

The foreign influences on the female body, moreover, were not necessarily unidirectional, that is, from the colonizers to the colonized. Rather, discussions over international politics and birth control reflected the struggles for "survival of the fittest" among different races and competing empires.[34] American eugenicists were apprehensive about the differential fertility between white women and women of color, both at home and abroad, which they feared could undermine white hegemony in the world. Japanese politicians and intellectuals used the Western-inspired knowledge about race improvement to build a stronger race that would lead the Pan-Asian empire. During the Cold War, American officials and scholars, self-proclaimed leaders of the "free world," worked side by side with Japanese leaders to bring "reproductive modernity" to Japan, which would serve as a bulwark against the "uncontrolled fertility" of the communist empire in Asia. Japanese elites, on the other hand, used American power and resources to recover from racial devastation resulting from wartime and postwar distress and to reclaim their position as rulers of the Asia-Pacific region.

Despite the apparent racist thinking and imperial politics behind eugenic policies and ideas, many eugenicists considered the study of race improvement a scientific endeavor that required collaboration among scientists and policy makers worldwide, including Asia. While the general interest in and knowledge on eugenics has mostly centered on Nazi Germany's horrific eugenic genocide during World War II, this book demonstrates how eugenics represented one of the most internationally active fields of research, where intellectuals worldwide have exchanged theories and practices regarding women's reproduction and race improvement since the early twentieth century. A number of important studies have brought attention to the transnational exchange of eugenic knowledge, especially

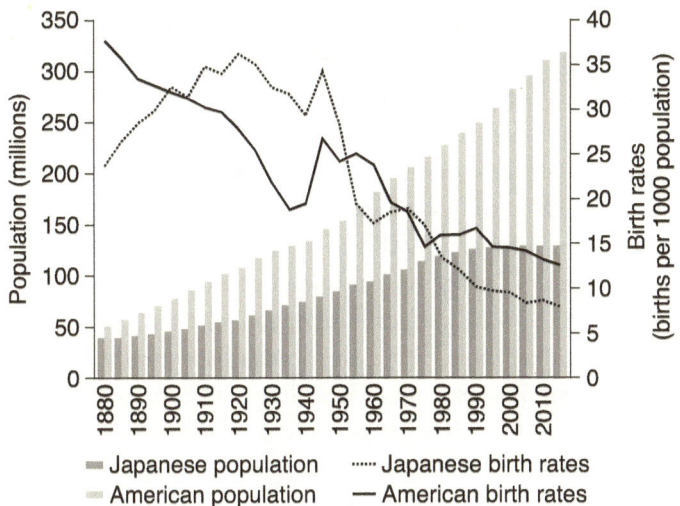

FIGURE O.I. Population and birth rates in Japan and the United States, 1880–2014. From Statistics and Information Department, Minister's Secretariat, Ministry of Health, Labour and Welfare, "Vital Statistics," http://www.mhlw.go.jp/toukei/list/81-1a.html; Statistics Bureau, Ministry of Internal Affairs and Communications, "Population/Family," http://www.stat.go.jp/data/chouki/02.htm; Centers for Disease Control and Prevention, "Vital Statistics of the United States," https://www.cdc.gov/nchs/products/vsus.htm; United States Census Bureau, "Statistical Abstracts of the United States," https://www.census.gov/library/publications/time-series/statistical_abstracts.html.

across the Atlantic between the United States and Europe and transhemispherically between the Americas.[35] However, comparatively little attention has been paid thus far to the transpacific history of eugenics.[36] This book highlights the American attempts to spread eugenic measures in Japan as well as the Japanese desire to learn the most advanced knowledge of race improvement from Americans (and Germans). Through both competition and cooperation, leaders of both nations applied the latest knowledge of eugenics to women's reproductive bodies to articulate their visions of a nation and race that would dominate the Asia-Pacific world.

. . .

Because this work focuses on the thoughts and activities of transnational leaders, it may be replicating the same faults of these elite activists: not fully taking into account the experiences of women affected by these birth control initiatives and acknowledging their perspectives. The lack of sources has often made it difficult to assess how women themselves felt and how they actually responded to these top-down discourses. However, we can still see a glimpse of their views revealed in some of the personal accounts of birth control leaders or in national surveys. Contrary to many elites' stereotypes about the ignorance and lack of awareness of average women, evidence often suggests the agency of women to either acquire birth control information for their own personal use or to reject any semicoercive measure that went against their will or the needs of the family. Of course, the majority of women did not even have a chance to express their opinion or were led to believe that whatever the officials or doctors said must be in their best interest. It is nonetheless meaningful to know that some women actively made efforts to take charge of their own bodies and their lives, however limited their choices might have been.

Indeed, history has revealed that it was the power of women's own will that ultimately gave momentum to birth control movements across the world. Despite eugenicists' warning about the impact of Japan's high fertility on world politics as well as the quality of the race, Japanese birth rates had been on a downward trend, except during the brief wartime and postwar years, since the 1920s (Fig. 0.1). During the postwar years, Japan achieved a remarkable reduction of birth rates by relying primarily on "traditional" methods of contraception—such as condoms, the withdrawal method, and even abortion—instead of the more "advanced" means promoted by global population control leaders—the pill, intrauterine devices, and sterilization. In other words, technology had little to do with the reduction of fertility, even though the spread of birth control ideas and practices might have prompted the development of contraceptive technologies. Broader changes in social structure and industrialization also affected reproductive patterns, but in the end women's own determination played a key part in Japan's fertility trend. Sanger may not have *caused* the decline, but she served as an important catalyst to this lasting trend that permanently affected Japanese women's reproductive practices and the fate of an entire nation.

ONE

The Women Rebels

Transnational Socialism, Feminism, and the Early Birth Control Movement

One snowy afternoon in January 1920, Baroness Ishimoto Shizue was invited to a tea party arranged for her at Margaret Sanger's apartment in Greenwich Village, New York. In her autobiography, Ishimoto described her first impression of her lifelong friend:

> I felt instantly her magnetism and my respect for her deepened as she talked about her difficulties. Listening to her account of the birth control movement, the memory of the overcrowded miners' huts in Western Japan came back so vividly that the idea of my true mission in life flashed over me. "Yes, Mrs. Sanger's fight has to be fought in my country too! I will carry the banner of birth control in Japan!"[1]

The meeting of the two feminists took place during the aftermath of World War I, when leftist intellectuals and socialists across the world searched for order and peace after the chaos caused by imperialism and capitalism. The bohemian community in New York City emerged as a hub of radicalism, including birth control advocacy, attracting activists of various nationalities. It was this multinational network that brought together the former nurse from an Irish American immigrant background and the aristocratic wife of a Japanese samurai family. Meeting Sanger triggered both a political and personal awakening in Ishimoto. Before moving to the United States, Ishimoto had witnessed firsthand the harsh life of working mothers suffering from multiple pregnancies and poverty at a rural coal mine in Japan, where her husband had worked as a deputy engineer. Her husband, the young baron, had turned his back on his aristocratic privileges and embraced socialist idealism. He also encouraged his wife to become an independent and self-supporting "New Woman" of Japan. Having grown up exposed to Western-imported humanist ideals, Ishimoto thereupon decided that it would be her calling to bring "the banner of birth control" to poor families in Japan.

Two years later, Sanger's transnational socialist connections led her to Japan. This chapter examines the Japanese responses to Sanger's arrival and the indigenous birth control campaigns that took place throughout Japan after her visit. The Japanese public compared Sanger's visit to Japan, which opened Japan to new ideas and practices of sexuality, to the arrival of Commodore Matthew C. Perry's "black ship" in 1853, a historic event that opened Japan to foreign interaction after two hundred years of seclusion. Whereas the momentum of radicalism weakened significantly after World War I in the United States, anti-imperialist and anticapitalist thoughts gained ground in Japan during the liberal Taishō period (1912–26) as many intellectuals searched for answers to the social problems that had emerged against the backdrop of rapid industrialization. In particular, birth control seemed to be a helpful tool to solve the pressing issues of overpopulation, poverty, and labor disputes in Japan. Liberal and socialist leaders believed that adopting this practice could strengthen the bodies of the Japanese masses, who had been exhausted and weakened by the rigorous demands of industrial labor. Japan thus became an outpost for a potentially revolutionary birth control movement that Sanger had initiated in the United States.

The introduction of Sanger's birth control movement beyond national borders simultaneously underscored the use of birth control as a eugenic tool to reify national identity. Neo-Malthusian intellectuals treated birth control as part of a Western philosophy and practice for the Japanese to master to compete with other imperial superpowers. Japanese elites expressed a mixed emotion of excitement and intimidation about receiving the famous American woman who preached to the Japanese to limit their fertility. To preserve their nationalist and masculine pride, they feminized Sanger, downplayed her subversive nature, and boosted their ability to rival—or even outdo—Western knowledge and technique that she had brought. By the late 1930s, many liberals who previously showed interest in anticapitalist and anti-imperialist ideas gradually came to emphasize birth control as a eugenic tool to *strengthen* the nation and race *within* the imperialist world system.[2] They thus projected their own visions of race and the nation onto the female body in the context of Japan's emerging presence in the world of Western capitalism and imperialism.

Although feminists initially took an active part in the birth control movement in Japan, they remained secondary participants in the debates regarding reproductive control. Sanger's original emphasis on women's rights to "voluntary motherhood" held a strong appeal to these New Women, including Ishimoto, who were exploring new roles in society and in the workplace during Japan's modernization process. Ultimately, however, male neo-Malthusians and socialists took control of the consumption of its knowledge and the mastery of its technology. Disagreement and conflicts over the purposes and goals of practicing birth control became especially apparent among feminists, as they prioritized the political interests of the class position to which they belonged. As a result, the idea of female rebellion against the patriarchal demands for reproduction—an idea that first drew Japanese feminists to Sanger's birth control cause—failed to materialize in Japan during the prewar decades.

In the end, throughout the prewar years birth control remained an intellectual tool reserved only for the privileged, not a practical tool available to the general public. Despite the surge of public discussions that followed Sanger's visit and the subsequent grassroots activities to spread the practice to the average household, nationalist pressures eventually frustrated these liberating endeavors. As the nationalist state tightened its regulations against contraceptives in the late 1930s, the knowledge and technology of birth control remained inaccessible to the general masses.

Modernization, Industrialization, and Gender Ideologies in Japan

The modern women's movement and socialism in Japan shared roots in the Freedom and People's Rights Movement (Jiyū minken undō) of the 1880s. With the influx of new ideas about sexuality from the West, represented by the work of Sigmund Freud, Havelock Ellis, and Ellen Key, both groups soon developed a special interest in the subject of reproductive control, although they each approached the topic from different angles. Feminist interest in birth control developed as part of their exploration of new roles in society and politics. However, male leftists typically treated birth control and *josei mondai* (the woman question) in general as Western-imported knowledge that should be thoroughly examined in the process of Japan's modernization.

The Meiji Restoration of 1868 and the opening of Japan to Western political thought and systems both challenged and tightened gender ideologies in Japan. Some women started to speak up in public assemblies for equal rights for women during the nascent Freedom and People's Rights Movement.[3] Women, however, were soon excluded from any political activity or participation. The government foreclosed the possibility of women's suffrage by limiting the franchise to male adult citizens (*kōmin*; literally, public person). Furthermore, the Public Peace Police Law (Chian keisatsu hō) of 1900 barred women—along with minors, soldiers, sailors, and police officers—from joining political associations or attending political meetings.[4] At the same time, the government was forced to revise the traditional ideal of *ryōsai-kenbo* (good wife and wise mother) against the backdrop of Japan's rapid modernization and Westernization. Specifically, government officials and Enlightenment thinkers felt pressed to elevate the status of wives along the lines of contemporary Britain and the United States by according them the mission to manage the household and educate the children.[5] In short, the government restricted women's participation in the political world outside while giving them more discretion over their roles within the household.

In particular, as in Western nations, the Japanese government strictly regulated women's sexuality and reproduction within their roles as housewives and as citizens of the nation-state. Based on the national policy of *fukoku kyōhei* (enrich the country, strengthen the military), it became increasingly important to produce healthy and prosperous future national subjects, specifically male soldiers and workers. In 1880, the Meiji government established a penal code that nationally banned abortion and infanticide, a law modeled after the French Criminal Law. The law was also a culmination of Japan's pre-Meiji history of banning and criminalizing abortion for economic as well as moral reasons.[6] Based on the suggestion of foreign consultants and the reports of Japanese officials traveling in European countries, state bureaucrats devised a modern system of licensed prostitution, which had also existed before the Meiji government's Westernization reforms. But the modern version placed women's bodies under direct and strict state surveillance by subjecting prostitutes to mandatory medical examinations for venereal disease and criminalizing unlicensed prostitutes. Many national leaders perceived the modern licensing system as an integral part of Japan's military expansion abroad and colonial ruling.[7]

Even while the modernized Japanese family system confined women's roles and sexuality to the domestic sphere, in reality, more and more women, especially those in rural areas and the young, were driven into the labor force to sustain the nation's rapid industrialization. The government therefore sought to defend the gender division of labor and the *ryōsai-kenbo* ideology by emphasizing the patriarchal idea that women were weak and inferior to men, therefore in need of state protection. The Factory Law (Kōjō hō) of 1911, intended to prevent employers from exploiting pregnant and nursing women, was the first law that clearly presented this idea of "motherhood protection." The aim of the law was not to protect the rights of women as workers, however, as adult male workers were not seen as needing protection. The paternalistic mission to protect women was nonetheless compromised by the demand for profitability of industries, as evidenced by the long delay in enacting many of its provisions. Even after enactment, the law covered workers only in factories of a certain size, and the regulations of working conditions in other industries were achieved on an industry-by-industry basis. Despite its ineffectiveness, the Factory Law symbolically established the role of the state in protecting women exclusively as mothers, not as workers or individuals.[8]

Meanwhile, the Japanese government's efforts to elevate the educational standards of women as good wives and wise mothers led to a formation of a new generation of professional women who came to lead the bourgeoning women's movement in Japan. Because these women were barred from public speaking, journals and newspapers became the primary means for them to express their political and personal thoughts. The influential feminist journal *Seitō* (Bluestocking), established in 1911 by Hiratsuka Raichō, became an important arena where women discussed and challenged the *ryōsai-kenbo* ideology and debated ideas about women's roles and rights. Subjects previously considered taboo frequently appeared on the pages of *Seitō*, including discussions of sexual morality, abortion, and prostitution.[9] Two strands of feminist thought were represented by the two *Seitō* editors: Hiratsuka Raichō's maternalism, which was influenced by Ellen Key, and Itō Noe's anarchism, which was inspired by Emma Goldman. It is noteworthy that the *Seitō* editors idolized two feminists who were also keenly devoted to birth control—one to protect the value of each child (Key) and one from the perspective of women's control over their lives (Goldman). The two different approaches to birth control would later divide Japanese feminists as well. Birth control was still not specifically discussed during the *Seitō* years (1911–16), but the journal helped expand the boundaries of public discussions about female sexuality and women's roles in a changing society.[10]

Male liberals and socialists also started to debate women's new roles in society and politics, inviting some feminists to their discussions. Since the 1900s, left-wing intellectuals had started to explore *josei mondai* through their analysis of the work of world-renowned socialist theorists such as August Bebel, Friedrich Engels, and Thomas Morgan. The Heiminsha (Commoner's Society), one of the first socialist organizations formed in 1903, included the participation of several women. Socialist newspapers such as *Heimin shinbun* (Commoner's news) and *Chokugen* (Plain talk) frequently published articles and pamphlets on women's roles in politics, usually offering socialist revolution as key to women's economic and political independence.[11] Mainstream liberal journals, *Taiyō* (Sun) and *Chūō kōron* (Central review), each featured issues devoted to *josei mondai* in 1913, and *Kaizō* (Reconstruction) in 1920. These magazines also regularly carried articles written by leading feminists such as Hiratsuka Raichō, Yosano Akiko, Yamada Waka, and Yamakawa Kikue.

At the core of many of the debates among feminists and male leftists on *josei mondai* was the perceived conflict between women's economic independence in the workplace and their role as wives and mothers inside the home. The so-called motherhood protection debate (*bosei hogo ronsō*) between a prominent poet Yosano Akiko and Hiratsuka Raichō erupted in 1918 in *Fujin kōron* (Women's review) and resurfaced later in *Taiyō*. In this debate, Yosano insisted that women should be treated as equals to men in the workforce. She opposed Hiratsuka's support for state protection of female workers as a sign of "dependence mentality" (*irai shugi*). Believing that women should be treated as individuals first, rather than solely as mothers, wives, or daughters, Yosano accused Hiratsuka, a devoted follower of Ellen Key, of glorifying motherhood as a central part of women's lives. Socialist Yamakawa Kikue intervened in the debate and presented yet another perspective. She pointed out that neither woman actually challenged the capitalist system, which she insisted was the original source of women's oppression.[12]

Many male intellectuals, while supporting the idea that women were not necessarily inferior to men in mental ability, were ambiguous about women's expanding roles outside the home. In presenting their viewpoint on *josei mondai*, they often revealed their personal support for the *ryōsai-kenbo* system and the gender division of labor. For example, the male contributors to *Kaizō*'s special issue on the "women's liberation issue"—including labor activist Kagawa Toyohiko, medical writer Fujikawa Yū, and noted novelist Arishima Takerō—stressed that women were biologically weaker and more emotional than—although not necessarily inferior to—men. In particular, they warned of the negative effects that labor in the workforce could have on women's chief function: to bear a fit and healthy future generation, especially male progeny.[13] Even the members of major socialist groups with female members, such as Heiminsha and Yūaikai (Friendly Society), often accepted the gender division of labor within the socialist family and treated their female comrades either as wives of male workers or as women workers in need of state protection.[14]

By the late 1910s, the debates on women's reproductive and wage labor in Japan extended to the matter of birth control. The same feminists who initiated the motherhood protection debate led these discussions on birth control. Yosano Akiko, who bore eleven children throughout her lifetime, lamented that the *ryōsai-kenbo* ideology had driven Japanese women to bear too many children at the expense of their own health, personal lives, and the well-being of their children.[15] Hiratsuka Raichō, based on her reading of Ellen Key's works, endorsed birth control from a maternalist perspective, claiming that women should be educated about birth control to maximize the eugenic and sacred functions of reproduction. Continuing her ideological opposition to Yosano, Hiratsuka attacked her for setting a bad example for other Japanese women by publicly admitting her own thoughtless pregnancies.[16] Yamakawa Kikue presented yet another opinion about birth control. As a socialist, she saw birth control as essential to the liberation of working women suffering from the double oppression of patriarchy and capitalism. There were also feminists who opposed birth control, such as Yamada Waka, who insisted that birth control would undermine the "psychological love" between husband and wife and hinder their "psychological development" as parents.[17]

These women were by then familiar with the birth control activism of Margaret Sanger in the United States and Marie Stopes in England.[18] Hiratsuka refused to identify herself with the type of birth control advocacy represented by Sanger, which, she believed, could lead Japanese women to indulge in sexual decadence and to "profane" their reproductive functions.[19] Yamakawa was more sympathetic to Sanger's philosophy, as she identified with Sanger's emphasis on women's fundamental desires to be freed from reproductive and sexual slavery. In particular, she was inspired by Sanger's first book, *Woman and the New Race* (1920). Based on her reading, Yamakawa insisted that women should not reproduce because factories demanded workers, the nation needed soldiers, and the ruling class fed on slaves. Instead, she maintained, the decision to reproduce or not should be theirs to make. At the same time, responding to a criticism by a male socialist that she was "idolizing" Sanger, Yamakawa differentiated herself as a revolutionary socialist from Sanger's social reformism. While liberal neo-Malthusians—the Japanese saw Sanger as part of this group—advocated birth control to *prevent* a radical revolution in society, Yamakawa and other socialists desired one. Nonetheless, Yamakawa supported Sanger not as a neo-Malthusian theorist but as a female rights advocate. She identified with Sanger's disappointment at the responses of socialist leaders, who believed that liberated women would naturally want as many children as possible. She reiterated Sanger's contention that all liberated and independent women would always wish for reproductive freedom and choices, whether in a capitalist or socialist society.[20]

Male intellectuals discussed birth control mainly as part of a Western idea rather than a matter of women's liberation. Neo-Malthusianism, an economic theory that linked overpopulation to various catastrophes such as disease, famine, and war, was first introduced in Japan from Britain at the turn of the twentieth century. The theory began to attract wide attention among liberals and socialists alike after World War I and the Russian Revolution, when riots and protests among laborers and farmers erupted throughout Japan.[21] Concurrently, intellectuals discussed the matter of birth control as a neo-Malthusian solution to overpopulation and all the social evils that it supposedly caused. *Kaizō*, for example, featured discussions and analysis of neo-Malthusianism in its October 1920 issue. One of its contributors was Yamakawa Kikue's husband and leading socialist, Yamakawa Hitoshi. In his article, Yamakawa observed that socialists across the world had different attitudes toward neo-Malthusianism and birth control: British socialists tended to reject it entirely, whereas many socialists in the United States and France at least partially accepted the validity of reproductive control. In the end, he supported the position of American socialists by claiming that birth control was both a moral and logical solution to alleviate the immediate suffering of the working class.[22] In June 1921, *Kaizō* introduced Margaret Sanger as "the authority in neo-Malthusianism," along with her article "Birth Control—Past, Present, and Future," which explained the history and development of Malthusianism and neo-Malthusianism.[23] By this time, some Japanese socialists were in direct contact with Sanger in New York and likely to have obtained the latest information on birth control activism abroad from the socialist community there.

Despite the lively discussions in intellectual magazines, birth control was still little more than a subject of intellectual curiosity among a small group of feminists and male reformers. The dissemination of information about birth control to the general masses was still strictly regulated. Birth rates moved generally downward during World War I and the subsequent influenza epidemic but then shot upward in 1920 to reach the highest levels ever recorded in Japan.[24] These facts and figures suggest that birth control was not part of a normal practice or everyday conversation among the Japanese public in general, who were struggling from the repercussions of imperialist wars and industrial developments.[25] It was not until Sanger's arrival in Japan in 1922 that the topic became much more widespread both within and beyond the intellectual communities.

Transnational Socialism

Meanwhile in the United States, New York City had emerged as a common meeting ground for radicals of different nationalities and different political shades after World War I. The bohemian community in Greenwich Village became one of the central locales of sexual revolution and other socialist activities. The bohemians' critique of sexual repression was, as Linda Gordon describes, "part of a growing attack on hierarchy, authoritarianism, and all forms of social repression."[26] Although most of them were from prosperous, native-born families, the community also attracted those of working-class or immigrant backgrounds, female activists, and foreign socialists in exile. In this context, a small group of Japanese socialists in New York came into contact with American radicals, including Margaret Sanger.

Sanger started her birth control activism when American radicalism was at one of its peaks in strength and breadth.[27] She moved to Greenwich Village in 1910 after her marriage to a young architect and aspiring painter, William Sanger. The Socialist Party and the socialist journals there introduced Sanger to radical feminism, which attacked capitalism as a system that forced women into cheap, industrial labor. Dissatisfied by the conventional socialist organizing, which focused on legislative campaigns for a wage-and-hours bill, Sanger gradually drifted toward the party's left wing, advocating anarchist tactics of direct action and helping workers, especially textile workers, organize strikes against the capitalists.[28]

Birth control was not necessarily her central focus during her early years of activism, but there had been many occasions before she became politically active in which Sanger witnessed women suffer as they gave birth to multiple children. Sanger herself was the sixth of eleven children in an impoverished Irish household. She had seen her mother, a devout Catholic, suffer from multiple pregnancies and eventually die of consumption at the age of fifty. In her autobiography, Sanger described an "awakening" that allegedly occurred while working as a visiting nurse in New York's Lower East Side in 1912. Sadie Sachs, a young Jewish immigrant woman dying from the complications of a self-induced septic abortion, pleaded for Sanger to tell her the "secret" of not having any more babies. Unable to save Sachs and other desperate poor women, Sanger asked doctors and searched in books for answers about contraception. As she struggled to find adequate information on the subject—"like the missing link in the evolution of medical science"—she became strongly convinced of the need to take action to make such knowledge available to the public.[29]

Soon after she became actively involved in socialist activities, Sanger emerged as a leader on the subject of female sexuality and reproduction, and her charisma began to attract the attention of other radicals. Hired as an organizer for the Women's Commission of the Socialist Party, Sanger began making speeches at meetings and gatherings for socialists and laborers. With her background as a nurse, her speeches on women's health and sex education, in particular, were enthusiastically received and made her a popular activist in the community. She was then asked by editors of the socialist daily *Call* to write on sex education and health for the women's page in the Sunday supplement. Her columns in 1912 and 1913 under the heading "What Every Girl Should Know" aroused furor among many *Call* readers. Once Sanger's column started to deal explicitly with the subject of venereal disease, however, the Post Office rejected the article under the Comstock Law, a law that forbade the mailing of "obscene, lewd, or lascivious" matter.[30] Undaunted, in 1914 she started her own magazine, the *Woman Rebel*. The publication was intended to directly challenge the Comstock Law while stimulating working women to fight against oppression. It was from one of the meetings with the supporters of her magazine that the term "birth control" was conceived. After multiple attempts to push the boundaries of speeches on sex, Sanger was finally arrested by federal authorities in August 1914 for violating the Comstock Law. She was released until the trial but then decided to flee to Europe, via Canada, under an assumed name.

During her one-year exile in Europe, Sanger met prominent sexologists and birth control activists such as Havelock Ellis and Marie Stopes, who provided Sanger with important theoretical background and scientific knowledge on birth control. She visited birth control clinics and talked to doctors. She was particularly impressed by the clinics in Holland. Once the charges for her earlier arrest were dropped as a result of the support of her European friends, Sanger traveled throughout the United States to give public speeches. In 1916, she opened America's first birth control clinic in the Brownsville section of Brooklyn, only to be raided by the police for selling contraceptive devices and distributing obscene literature. Undaunted, she founded a new magazine, the *Birth Control Review*, in March 1917.

Sanger's European education, however, would also blunt the radical nature of her activism. In Europe, she was mentored by intellectuals and professionals who were respected reformers of the community, not radical anarchists. By the time Sanger returned from Europe, she had left the Socialist Party and embarked on an independent path from leftist organizations. In fact, the nexus between feminism and socialism in general began to dissolve after 1920 in the bohemian community. When Goldman and other radicals were arrested and deported as patriotic hysteria swept the country during World War I, Sanger's tactic to keep an independent path from other socialists and to narrow down to one specific cause enabled her to survive these extremely difficult years for socialists in the United States.

Meanwhile in Japan, Ishimoto, like Sanger, became exposed to the world of socialism through her husband, Keikichi, and eventually crossed the Pacific with him to New York. During the Taishō period, many liberal intellectuals in Japan dabbled in socialism as a form of new Western thought. The couple were both exposed from an early age to new ideas and customs from the West and were in close contact with prominent scholars of liberalism. What Shizue described as her "mental awakening" came from her uncle Tsurumi Yusuke and his mentor, Nitobe Inazō, an American-educated and renowned Christian humanist. Shizue recalled that she read over and over the books given to her by Nitobe, "like a Christian girl reading her Bible," as she became "baptized by the spirit of humanism."[31] Keikichi was also one of Nitobe's disciples, and it was at one of the meetings of the study society held at the Ishimoto family's house that Shizue came to know Keikichi. As a young woman of high social status, however, it was more difficult for Shizue than for her husband and other men of her generation to completely immerse herself in liberalism. Even though her father, an engineer with Western training, brought Western customs, clothes, and furniture into the Ishimoto household, she recalled that as a girl she was always reminded to become a traditional "obedient wife and wise mother."[32] It therefore fell to her husband to open the way for Shizue to explore beyond the protected world of her class and to become an economically and emotionally independent New Woman of Japan.

A defining moment for both Keikichi and Shizue that brought them in direct contact with the depressing repercussions of rapid industrialization in Japan was their experience of living at a rural mining village. In 1915, Keikichi was sent to the Miike Coal Mines as a deputy mining engineer for the Mitsui Mining Company. An idealist and passionate humanist, Keikichi worked under the same harsh working conditions and for the same long hours as other low-paid manual workers. Ultimately, the Ishimotos were ordered to come back to Tokyo after two years in the field due to Keikichi's deteriorating health. But Keikichi was not satisfied with his career in a chemical laboratory in Tokyo. Japanese society at the time was greatly influenced by the Russian Revolution of 1917, and liberal intellectuals devoured Russian revolutionary literature as social unrest and riots increased in their own country. In 1919, Keikichi decided to go to New York to pursue his studies in socialism. He asked his wife to join him in his revolutionary quest.

Keikichi had connections with Japanese socialists living in New York

City and knew that it was an ideal place to extend socialist networks and meet socialists of various nationalities. Keikichi was one of the many Japanese students of liberalism and socialism who traveled to the United States in search of alternative solutions to Japan's social problems caused by rapid industrialization and modernization. Many influential socialists spent some time in the United States as students, political refugees, or activists. The majority of the original twelve members of the Shakaishugi kenkyūkai (Society for the Study of Socialism), the first socialist group formed in Japan in 1898, were Christian humanists, and some of them (Katayama Sen, Abe Isoo, and Murai Tomoyoshi) studied in US seminaries.[33] The visits of these socialist leaders—Katayama, Abe, and Kōtoku Shūsui—to the United States in the early 1900s inspired the creation of socialist groups in California. The United States was a place where many Japanese socialists found direct applicability of their theories. They developed a keen awareness of racial discrimination and harsh working conditions to which the Japanese farmers and low-wage workers in America were subjected. The socialist leaders brought back their experience and observations to Japan and also helped Japanese immigrant workers develop a deeper understanding of labor issues and radical thoughts in a broader transnational context.[34]

Katayama Sen, an internationally renown Japanese communist who was later designated Asian representative to the Comintern, played a vital role in organizing and developing socialist activities between Japan and the United States. Katayama first sailed from Yokohama to San Francisco in November 1884, inspired by his friend who had also left for the United States for study. Once in America, Katayama converted to Christianity and attended several schools, including the Andover Theological Seminary in Massachusetts and the Yale Divinity School. Only after he returned to Japan and after the Sino-Japanese War of 1894–95 triggered socialist and labor movements there did Katayama become involved in socialist activities. In 1904, after attending the Second International at Amsterdam as the sole Asian representative, Katayama briefly lived in Texas, where he observed firsthand the agricultural enterprise of Japanese immigrants and sought to encourage further migration of Japanese farmers to the United States. Back in Japan, the High Treason Case (*Daigyaku jiken*) of 1910 drove Japanese socialism into hibernation until after World War I, and it became almost impossible for Katayama to continue his activities there.[35] In 1914, he left Japan for good and settled in California for a couple of years, where he launched his own bilingual periodical, *Heimin* (Commoner). However, his socialist activities failed to attract support among Californian Japanese, largely because of the Japanese government's surveillance of subversive activities of radicals abroad, especially in California. Part of his solution was to move to the East Coast, where there were fewer Japanese and no organized movement among Japanese workers.

Katayama moved to New York in 1916 at the invitation of an old socialist acquaintance, S. J. Rutgers, to join a group of radicals of various nationalities.[36] Initially, there were no visible socialist or labor activities among the Japanese in New York despite the growing number of low-paid domestic workers there.[37] The atmosphere of the Japanese community in New York was generally conservative, with a relatively large number of government officials, bankers, and businessmen. This started to change after the Russian Revolution of 1917 and the 1918 rice riot in Japan, as inspired students, workers, and artists started to organize and formed the Japanese Socialist Study Group under the direction of Katayama. The so-called Katayama boys included Taguchi Unzō, who had attended the Third Congress of the Comintern; Minawa Suekichi, an ex-sailor who jumped ship to the United States; Ishigaki Eitarō, a young artist and acquaintance of Katayama since his days in California; and Inomata Tsunao, a young economist trained at Waseda University and the University of Wisconsin. The group maintained contact with socialists and leftists in Japan—among them, Ishimoto Keikichi.[38]

When the Ishimotos moved to New York City in 1919, Margaret Sanger had already gained a high reputation as a radical activist in the transnational socialist community. Although she had gradually drawn apart from radicals and socialists, she did not immediately sever all ties with them. She still lived in Greenwich Village for a while, and many of her former comrades continued to support her cause. Ishimoto first heard about Sanger and her birth control cause from a Japanese acquaintance in New York. At the time, she had not even heard of the term "birth control" despite the growing attention to women's reproductive roles among feminists and liberals at the time. Sanger's story, however, immediately reminded her of the working mothers at the Miike coal mines suffering from multiple pregnancies and poverty.

Ishimoto's wish to meet this inspiring female activist was soon realized by the introduction of another prominent female radical, Agnes Smedley.

Smedley was well acquainted with the Japanese socialists and intellectuals in New York, including the Ishimotos. She was also at that time working for the *Birth Control Review*.[39] Its June 1919 issue carried Smedley's article "Babies and Imperialism in Japan," in which she criticized the Japanese government's propaganda to "increase and multiply" as an example of "imperialistic traits and designs," not just true of Japan alone but "an echo of ourselves, in so far as its national policy is concerned." In such an imperialist state, she contended, "the people, particularly the women upon whom the burdens of empire building fall, are given no voice in determining national policy." The following month, the magazine carried Keikichi's letter in response to Smedley's article. Keikichi felt the need to inform Americans of the "new spirit of the masses of the Japanese people," who could now "understand the true meaning of democracy, hate militarism, and believe in Birth Control." He also emphasized the powerful activism of socialist women, who "walked side by side with their comrades, lecturing, distributing literature, organizing, and going to jail" regardless of the official prohibition on their attending public meetings.[40]

Smedley was apparently so impressed by Keikichi's response that she wrote a follow-up article a few months later, "The Awakening of Japan." She reported that many Japanese men, notably government investigators, had visited the office of the *Birth Control Review* over the past several months, seeking information about the birth control movement. These young Japanese leaders allegedly started to realize that economic and physical exploitation of their women and children could run counter to national interests in the long run. To illustrate the "awakening" of Japanese men and women, Smedley cited an excerpt from one of Yosano Akiko's columns in *Taiyō*:

> We Japanese women have borne too many children. Of course, after we have borne them, we wish to care for and educate them. . . . But we are not in condition to realize this ideal, or even to clothe and feed them properly. . . . I have no intention of recommending the two-child system practiced by European women; but at the same time we Japanese women endure such economic hardships that we are now understanding the wisdom of European women who have adopted the two-child system.[41]

According to Smedley's reading, Yosano's article revealed that "the interest of Japanese women in Birth Control is of economic origin."[42] Yosano was never a socialist, although she strongly advocated women's work outside the home for their individual fulfillment.[43] Yet, for Smedley, the economic burden of fertile women described in the passage served to illustrate the suffering that capitalists had imposed on working women beyond the West. Yosano's piece also illuminated the willingness of Japanese women to stand up against such oppression.

The correspondence between Smedley and Ishimoto Keikichi in the *Birth Control Review* shows that there was a great deal of interaction among socialists and liberals between the United States and Japan on the issues of women and workers in the context of industrialization and imperialism. Not only did Japanese socialists import American literature on socialism, including discussions of birth control, but American socialists regularly obtained the English translation of Japanese articles carried in liberal and socialist magazines.

The transnational network of Japanese and American socialists continued after the Ishimotos had left America later in 1920, a connection that realized the plan to invite Sanger to Japan. Sanger had dreamed up the idea of visiting "the Orient" for the first time during the tea party with Ishimoto Shizue in New York. Although it seemed like "a remote possibility" at the time, an invitation for her visit came from a group of Japanese liberals and socialists by the end of that year. A Japanese artist and socialist, Ishigaki Eitarō—one of the "Katayama boys"—had an art studio in the same building as Sanger's Greenwich Village apartment. After Katayama had left for Russia in 1921, Ishigaki assumed the role of coordinating socialist activities between New York and Japan, forwarding articles and pamphlets to socialists in Japan. One of his contacts included Kaizō Publishing Company, to which he forwarded Sanger's aforementioned article, "Birth Control—Past, Present and Future," for publication in its June 1921 issue. The company had established a program to bring an outstanding world figure each year to lecture to the Japanese public: the first was Albert Einstein; the second, Bertrand Russell. Sanger visited Ishigaki's studio and asked if he could send a request to Kaizō to invite her to Japan. Kaizō accepted, and Sanger became the third guest lecturer—and the first female one.[44] Sanger thus arranged her first trip around the world, starting from Japan, then stopping in Korea, China, Hong Kong, Singapore, Ceylon, and Egypt before arriving in London to attend the Fifth International Neo-Malthusian Conference. Ishimoto Shizue volunteered to be Sanger's hostess during her stay in Tokyo.

"The Black Ship of Taishō"

Sanger's arrival in April 1922, dubbed by the press as the "black ship of Taishō," suddenly made birth control a household topic, beyond the confines of leftist intellectual circles. The "black ship" was indeed an accurate expression describing the Japanese public's response to Sanger's arrival on Japanese shores. Just like the original black ship event half a century before, Sanger's visit precipitated a mix of fear, excitement, and confusion over the American mission to open Japan to new Western practices and ideas regarding reproduction and sexuality.

The Japanese government was indeed confused over how to treat the sudden arrival of a controversial guest—this time a female one. When Sanger went to the Japanese consulate in San Francisco to apply for a visa, much to her surprise she learned that the Japanese government had cabled directions to refuse her admission. Apparently, the Japanese police had classified her speeches as "dangerous thoughts" after learning that the New York police had forbidden Sanger to address a town hall meeting.[45] The head of the government's Police Bureau reportedly attested that they were cautious about Sanger's visit because the Western-imported theory of birth control could "corrupt public morals."[46] The Japanese parliament had just passed a bill that censored "foreign thoughts," particularly radical socialist and communist ideas, which was later enacted as the Public Peace Preservation Law (Chian iji hō) in 1925. Meanwhile, feminists were lobbying to repeal Article 5 of the Public Peace Police Law of 1900, which prohibited women from attending and speaking at public political assemblies. Contrary to the liberal image often accorded to the Taishō period, women and socialists were under strict government scrutiny. Therefore, government bureaucrats believed that they had many reasons to be cautious about the arrival of a female radical from the United States. Sanger nonetheless managed to obtain a ticket to Japan—through her Chinese visa—and got on board the ship.

Sanger and some others believed, in retrospect, that the Japanese government's pronatalism nearly thwarted Sanger's visit. They felt that Sanger's visa application came at a particularly inopportune time—during the Washington Naval Conference of 1921–22. The disarmament conference forced the reduction of the Japanese naval fleet to limits much below those accorded to Britain and the United States but still above the numbers for France and Italy. Sanger and her supporters therefore assumed that Japanese conservative politicians had interpreted Sanger's visit as another attempt by the West to limit Japan's military power, this time through population control.[47] The ship that Sanger boarded, the *Taiyō-maru*, carried Japanese delegates returning from the Washington Conference. During her voyage, Sanger actively talked to the Japanese leaders about her birth control cause to win their respect. One of them, Vice Minister of Foreign Affairs Hanihara Masanao, was allegedly able to help Sanger when she landed in Yokohama. After lengthy negotiations with government officials, she was finally allowed to step onto Japanese soil by signing an agreement not to speak publicly about birth control.

Despite suspicions among some officials about Sanger, many young elites in Japan endorsed birth control as a neo-Malthusian solution to the problems of food shortage and riots resulting from overpopulation, as Agnes Smedley also observed in her aforementioned article. They accepted the idea of birth control as a Western intellectual theory but rejected its subversive and feminist components. The authorities' tolerance for birth control as a reformist, rather than revolutionary, neo-Malthusian doctrine is illustrated by the fact that they allowed Sanger to speak at one of the public lectures sponsored by Kaizō by changing its title to "War and Population," focusing specifically on Germany during World War I. Sanger recalled her conversation with a bureaucrat of the Ministry of Home Affairs: "When I sketched an outline of a possible population lecture we laughed and agreed the Empire of Japan was not, as a result, going to fall."[48] The authorities nonetheless forbade her from referring to any specific terms or practical methods of birth control, which could be associated with female sexual liberation and working-class rebellion. There were, however, no restrictions imposed on private, closed meetings, where male intellectuals and physicians made up the majority of the guests. Although it was the socialist network that enabled Sanger's visit, once she entered Japan, the authorities sought to control the nature of the discussion by taming any radical nature of her presence.

As the news of Sanger's visa controversy traveled back home, Americans did not seem to appreciate the publicity that this female radical had stirred abroad. Not only religious conservatives but also those who normally asserted the need for Japanese to limit their population admitted that the Japanese government's act of barring Sanger was justifiable, even beneficial, for the sake of preserving friendly international relations.⁴⁹ Likewise, the US government refused to facilitate Sanger's trip. When Sanger contacted the US Consulate General in Japan to make a formal request to permit her stay, not as a propagandist but as a private citizen, her government made no response. Eventually, the Japanese government gave her permission without the sponsorship of the US consul.⁵⁰

The Japanese press followed every detail of Sanger's arrival. Regardless of the authorities' attempt to contain the subversive nature of Sanger's visit, the government's confusion over the issuance of her visa certainly helped publicize her presence, and *Sangā-fujin* (Mrs. Sanger) became the best-known American woman in Japan. According to the news reports, however, many Japanese felt disappointed after actually listening to Sanger's lectures. Newspapers carried headlines such as "Sanger's 'Controlled Lecture' Did Not Touch on Birth Control, Ends in Failure; Audience of Five Hundred Men and Three Hundred Women Seemed Very Disappointed"; and "Sanger's Reputed Lecture, All Smoke, No Substance—the Audience Disappointed."⁵¹ While men and women from all walks of life flocked to learn the "magic trick" of birth control, they were said to have felt betrayed that Sanger's actual speech did not touch on its practical aspects.⁵²

The Japanese intellectuals who spoke with Sanger in private meetings, where there was supposedly no restriction on the specific discussions of birth control, similarly expressed mixed feelings and disappointment. One in particular, Yamamoto Senji, a biology professor and labor activist, wrote in detail about his experience of meeting Sanger. Yamamoto, who developed his Christian socialism while he lived in Vancouver as a student, was appointed to serve as a translator for Sanger's Kaizō lectures.⁵³ Although the public lectures in Kyoto were canceled as a result of government pressure, Yamamoto and his cousin Yasuda Tokutarō, a physician, still managed to secure a private meeting with Sanger during her stay in Kyoto. To prepare for the meeting, Yamamoto and Yasuda avidly studied Western medical literature on birth control and sexology in order to discuss them with such an authoritative figure on this topic. At the actual meeting, however, much to their dismay, Sanger did not even take a look at the texts they presented for her opinion; unable to read the German titles, she merely rejected them as outdated. While impressed by Sanger's engaging personality and sophisticated demeanor, they found her attitude and response too "smooth" and "diplomatic." "I was expecting her honest opinion about Japan," Yamamoto confessed, "but with her diplomatic conversation skills, she avoided disclosing her real thoughts."[54]

Sanger's inability, or perhaps unwillingness, to give direct responses to their questions, however, boosted Yamamoto's confidence that they could debate on equal terms with—or even excel—the supposed world authority in neo-Malthusianism and sexology. Sanger's bold attitude and confidence despite her mediocre medical knowledge appeared in Yamamoto's eyes as "typically American" in the way she saw everything American as the best in the world. He proudly recalled that Sanger appeared perplexed by Japan's quick mastery of Western knowledge. Yamamoto thus summarized his experience: "Recalling the hype over the arrival of the black ships forty years ago [and how Japan had advanced since then], I was greatly satisfied with the high level of the Japanese medical world (those not under the control of the authorities) and with the decline of worshiping the West."[55]

By comparing Sanger to the black ship, the Japanese public, especially intellectuals, thus showed complex feelings about the arrival of an American guest with the mission to open Japan to modern sexual practices. Just as Perry's expedition to Japan showcased American technological prowess and missionary certitude, Sanger's arrival also represented American confidence in spreading the gospel of birth control to the backward areas of the world.[56] Yet, since the original black ship incident Japan had undergone drastic modernization; a first imperialist war with China in 1894–95; and a victory over a Western nation, Russia, in 1905. By the time Sanger arrived in Japan, therefore, Japanese leaders and intellectuals had gained significant confidence in relation to Western nations. The disappointment that they expressed over Sanger's actual ability to showcase American superiority in science and technology was a reflection of this newfound confidence and growing sense of nationalism among Japanese leaders of the new era.

The Japanese often used gendered expressions to describe that the "black ship of Taishō" was not as threatening as they had anticipated. The feminization of Sanger was a striking difference from the Japanese impression of Perry, who represented what historian Michael Adas described as a "manly dignity."[57] Because the news of her radical activism in New York created an image of an aggressive and masculine figure in the minds of Japanese, many were pleasantly surprised to find instead what they considered a fragile and feminine lady. Yamamoto's cousin recalled his encounter with Sanger: "I was expecting a masculine and intimidating old woman,

FIGURE 1.1. Portrait of Margaret Sanger and her son Grant. From "Mrs. Sanger and Her Beloved Son Grant Arrive in Japan and Gain Popularity," *Yomiuri shinbun*, March 11, 1922.

but I was surprised to find instead a beautiful young lady, as if she were a wife of a diplomat."[58] Similarly, the Japanese newspapers typically provided positive descriptions of her outward appearance, such as the "gentle smile on her beautiful face" or her sophisticated demeanor in a "simple black dress"—certainly not the "witch" that they had imagined.[59] The media reports also emphasized that Sanger was a devoted mother of two decent sons. They often carried photographs of her with them, especially ones with her younger son, Grant, who accompanied her on the trip (Fig. 1.1).[60] In fact, the chief of imperial police who detained her on the boat before approval of landing seemed to have been favorably impressed by her children. This impression, Grant recalled, worked to their advantage in their negotiations.[61]

Yamamoto satirically characterized Sanger's stay in Japan: "arriving like a shogun, hastily leaving like a virgin." News of Sanger's arrival stirred a sense of curiosity, excitement, and fear across the nation, as she was greeted in Yokohama like a victorious warrior from the West. Yet by the time she moved on to Kyoto, most Japanese had purportedly lost interest, partly because the Kaizō organizers, worried that they might upset the authorities, canceled all of Sanger's public appearances after her first "War and Population" lecture in Tokyo.[62] Yamamoto's impression, however, was that Sanger was so worn out by the intense and advanced scientific discussions with Japanese professionals that she spent the rest of her stay merely enjoying a boat ride along the river and watching the Cherry Dance show—"like a typical American lady."[63]

Despite the initial sense of camaraderie among socialists and feminists beyond national borders that had brought Sanger to Japan, national competitiveness and gender biases characterized many of the impressions that the Japanese intellectuals formed about Sanger. In other words, many of them perceived Sanger as an ineffectual, even pitiable, American guest, not as an influential fighter for women's rights or for the liberation of workers. As Yosano Akiko observed, however, what Sanger actually said or did in Japan mattered less than the attention that the issue of birth control received among the Japanese public as a result of the authorities' attempt to prevent her landing.[64] Sanger's presence in Japan indeed triggered widespread attention throughout Japan on the subject of birth control and prompted activists to launch their own campaigns under indigenous circumstances.

Post-Sanger Transnational Birth Control Exchanges

Sanger's impact lasted far beyond the duration of her visit. Not only did articles on practical birth control discussions proliferate in women's magazines, but Japanese advocates of birth control also started to take actual steps toward public enlightenment by setting up clinics and holding public lectures.[65] Some of them, such as Ishimoto representing the bourgeois birth control movement in Tokyo and Yamamoto leading a proletarian one in Osaka, maintained personal contact with Sanger. Through Sanger, they reinterpreted and adapted American knowledge on birth control for practical and immediate use for Japanese women.

A month after Sanger's visit, a group of male activists and female leaders in Tokyo, including Yamakawa Kikue and her husband, Hitoshi, as well as physicians such as Majima Kan and Kaji Tokijirō, gathered at Ishimoto's house and formed the Japan Birth Control Study Society (Nihon sanji chōsetsu kenkyūkai). The group translated several of Sanger's pamphlets for distribution and also published their own magazine, *Shō-kazoku* (Small family).[66] A member of the Japan Birth Control Study Society and a labor leader, Katō Kanjū (Ishimoto Shizue's future second husband), invited Ishimoto to speak to miners and their wives about birth control at the Ashio Copper Mines, located north of Tokyo. The Japan Birth Control Society dissolved after a year, but the birth control supporters in Tokyo came together again and formed the Birth Control Popularization Society (Sanji seigen fukyūkai) in 1927 under the leadership of Abe Isoo, moderate socialist and professor at Waseda University. Its periodical, *Sanji seigen* (Birth control, renamed *Sanji seigen hyōron*, or Birth control review, from October 1929) carried articles by birth control advocates of various political and class positions, from labor activists to sympathetic doctors.

The leaders of this nascent birth control movement in Japan maintained contact with Sanger and her supporters in the United States. Sanger's *Birth Control Review* carried the writings of the Ishimotos, Abe Isoo, and Nitobe Inazō. Each of these advocates reported the activities and developments of the birth control movement in Japan and described the pressing population problem in the country that made their work so vital. The population in Japan had started to increase rapidly since the Meiji Restoration and was, by the early 1920s, growing by seven hundred thousand to nine hundred thousand every year. Food production could not match the rate of population growth, and, according to the views of these progressives, emigration was not a realistic solution for reasons both practical (e.g., the number of ships needed to transport emigrants, competition with cheaper labor, opposition of receiving countries) and psychological (e.g., the emotional attachment to ancestral homeland, inclination toward isolationism). They thus offered birth control as the most practical solution to the potentially perilous international issue.[67]

The reasons and purposes they raised for practicing birth control in Japan, however, were quite different from those presented in earlier discussions on the subject, before Sanger's arrival. In fact, as Sanger's speech in Tokyo highlighted, the birth control philosophy among liberal intellectuals in Japan had become increasingly closer to the neo-Malthusian doctrine rather than a revolutionary socialist or a radical feminist scheme. Under the spirit of Wilsonian internationalism, the control of a national population became a diplomatic tool to maintain the balance of power. Internationalist liberals both in Japan and the United States proposed birth control, not so much for the physical and economic relief of women and workers suffering under industrialization and patriarchal oppression but for the sake of peaceful international relations. Japan's search for outside territories to feed and support their excessive population, they argued, was posing a menace to world peace. The blame for poverty and overpopulation was no longer on the government's imperialist policies or the exploitation of workers by the capitalist class. Instead, they assumed a distinctly neo-Malthusian position by blaming the fertility and behaviors of workers and farmers, including Japanese immigrants abroad.

Meanwhile, a more grassroots and proletarian-based birth control movement developed in the Kansai (Kyoto-Osaka-Kobe) region under the leadership of Yamamoto Senji. Despite the disappointment he felt about Sanger's apparent lack of professional knowledge, he was nonetheless inspired by her parting words to him: "There are many people across the world suffering from multiple pregnancies. I know that my methods are still very crude and immature, but I have been fighting to spread the practice of birth control even while I repeatedly got arrested. It is my hope that you will join me in this fight for the liberation of the world's working-class people and for world peace."[68] Yamamoto kept his promise to Sanger by organizing and leading a number of activities to spread the knowledge of birth control among working-class communities in the area.

Soon after Sanger's departure, Yamamoto translated Sanger's pamphlet *Family Limitation*, the only practical piece of information on birth control that he was able to obtain from her. In 1914, Sanger had published this sixteen-page booklet containing basic technical instructions on how to prevent pregnancy. A medical self-help guide written specifically for working women, several hundred thousand copies of the pamphlet were distributed personally through Sanger's birth control clinic and by networks of radicals and left-wing women even while the Comstock Law prevented the mailing of such material. Adding his own commentary and critiques, Yamamoto published it in Japan as *Sangā-joshi kazoku seigenhō hihan* (Critique of Mrs. Sanger's family limitation methods) and distributed it to university professors and physicians. To avoid censorship violation, Yamamoto purposefully added the word "critique" to the title, marked the word "top secret" in red on the cover, and placed a special note that indicated that the distribution of the pamphlet was limited to experts, physicians, and pharmacists. Yet several left-wing members of Osaka labor unions soon learned about the pamphlet and, with Yamamoto's approval, distributed it to the members of the labor movement.[69] The activists then invited Yamamoto as consultant and formed the Osaka Birth Control Study Society (Osaka sanji seigen kenkyūkai) in 1923, using Sanger's translated pamphlet as textbook for its members. Concurrently, Yamamoto started to offer lectures in laborers' schools, which included the subject of birth control.

Yamamoto's "critique" of Sanger's methods, however, was not necessarily directed toward Sanger herself but toward the intellectual and bourgeois classes in general, whom he denounced for monopolizing expert knowledge and concealing it from the general masses.[70] Yamamoto pointed out that the high expectation that the medical community had for Sanger—as if she held a "treasure box" (*tamatebako*) of secret knowledge on contraception—reflected how they themselves always stashed away professional knowledge from the general masses. He also criticized the Japanese militarists who painted Sanger as a racist who tried to limit the population growth of the colored races, arguing that such hypocritical language served only to reveal their true intent: to censor any information that would counter their political goals. Yamamoto instead commended Sanger for her bold actions and bravery to stand up against the conservative, misogynistic male professionals in her own country and her attempts to enlighten the general public about sexual knowledge that was otherwise hidden from them. As a "semi-expert" (*han-kurouto*) dedicated to public enlightenment, Yamamoto shared much in common with the goals and tactics of Sanger's early activism.[71]

Since their meeting, Sanger and Yamamoto had exchanged private letters and materials—publications as well as samples of actual birth control devices—reporting their activities to each other. Yamamoto subscribed to Sanger's *Birth Control Review* and sent copies of his own publications on birth control and sex education. Responding to Ishimoto's accusation against Yamamoto, which appeared in the *Birth Control Review*, for "only criticizing others, and doing no positive work himself," Yamamoto updated Sanger with a detailed record of his "secret" activities after Sanger left Japan. He underlined in red some remarks in the letter he advised Sanger not to reproduce, even in the United States, for fear of state interference.[72] Sanger chose not to comment on Yamamoto's activities in her journal because she worried that it might still "give [him] away" to the police. She further explained to Yamamoto:

> It is most encouraging for us to learn that you are working with labour groups, for, after all, this is where the book belongs. If we did not have restrictive laws which must be changed, all of our work would be directed to the working class, but as it is today, we must have our laws changed and only the well educated and well-to-do people have any influence to get such laws changed.[73]

It is clear from these remarks that, while appreciating Yamamoto's working-class-based activism, Sanger herself had gradually shifted her tactics, from rallying with radicals and working-class activists to strengthening her ties with "the well educated and well-to-do people" to achieve her goals. Nonetheless, Sanger invited Yamamoto to the upcoming Sixth International Neo-Malthusian and Birth Control Conference, to be held in New York in 1925, although it was quite obvious that Yamamoto's political position made it impossible for him to attend. She sent him the proceedings after the conference, for which she also enclosed a bill for the cost of the volumes. Bluntly put, maintaining the interest of Yamamoto and other Japanese activists translated into continuing financial support for her cause.[74]

Finances did condition the activists' ability to connect with their colleagues abroad. For that reason, Yamamoto and other proletarian activists were less successful in maintaining transnational connections than their bourgeois counterparts. Yamamoto wrote an essay, "A Fantasy of an International Confederation for Birth Control," for the preface of a sexology book to be published by Kaizō. Using again his wry humor, he fantasized how he would use the money earned by selling his books to mobilize the "leisured" bourgeois class to his activities. His plan was to first build a head office of the "International Confederation for Birth Control" and hire various activists in its publicity department, including Ishimoto Shizue for the "ladies' division" and Abe Isoo for the "elderly men's division." He would also send many publicists abroad and call for support from leaders across the world, such as Margaret Sanger, Marie Stopes, and British neo-Malthusian leader Charles V. Drysdale. Yamamoto's cynicism toward the capitalist class, including the publishing industry, incurred the displeasure of Kaizō's president. As a result, the book project was called off, and so were Yamamoto's tongue-in-cheek plans to earn money and establish an International Confederation for Birth Control.[75]

Despite the limited contact that Yamamoto was able to maintain with Sanger, her birth control instructions and knowledge did penetrate widely among the Japanese masses in the years following her visit. Even while the medical community disregarded the methods introduced in Sanger's pamphlet as rudimentary, working-class activists—and even some government officials—considered it a valuable source of information and actively tried out the methods. Within several years since its publication in 1922, more than fifty thousand copies of *Critique of Mrs. Sanger's Family Limitation* were distributed throughout Japan, and more than five thousand members joined Yamamoto's Birth Control Study Society, the majority of whom were working class, including men and women from Manchuria, Korea, and Taiwan.[76] Yamamoto and other labor activists believed that a "new science" could be developed only through practical application of knowledge in indigenous settings. They recommended and tested out all of the methods introduced in the pamphlet, including pessaries, vaginal suppositories, and vaginal douching. While most methods described in Sanger's pamphlet were already available in Japan, although not widely known beyond the medical community, there were also some new ones, including the so-called contraceptive pin (*hinin pin*), or the "wishbone" pessary. This new device was popularized among working-class people throughout Japan, until it was banned under the Ordinance Regulating Harmful Contraceptive Devices (Yūgai hinin kigu torishimari kisoku) of 1930.[77]

At the same time, Yamamoto and other sympathetic physicians were aware of the limits of contraceptive use among the general masses under different circumstances in Japan at the time compared to the situation in the West. For example, most of the methods introduced in Sanger's pamphlet required vaginal douching after intercourse. In Japan, however, not only were most women ignorant or embarrassed about touching their private parts, but in a typical multigenerational household setting, women normally did not have the privacy to prepare contraceptives in advance and clean their bodies immediately after sex. For these reasons, Yamamoto recommended vaginal suppositories or condoms as relatively easy methods for the average Japanese people. But he also warned that the kinds of contraceptives available in Japan at the time were mostly ineffective or inconvenient and urged further scientific research and technological development.[78]

Yamamoto and the members of the Osaka Birth Control Study Society therefore provided individual consultations to the masses through birth control clinics. In his aforementioned letter to Sanger, Yamamoto asked Sanger for practical advice on birth control consultation as well as for samples of devices that she might recommend for use in his clinics.[79] After Yamamoto's death, his efforts to provide direct guidance to working-class families were undertaken by the Japanese Union for Birth Control (Nihon sanji seigen kyōkai), established in Osaka in 1930. The top priority of the union, the members declared, was to set up a Eugenic Counseling Office. The founders emphasized the eugenic purpose of the clinic in part to avoid police crackdown on birth control as proletarian propaganda against poverty. Sanger and her supporters apparently took notice of the office, as the news of its founding appeared in an English-version newspaper of the Osaka Mainichi Publishing Company.[80]

Meanwhile, in Tokyo, Ishimoto Shizue remained a loyal propagator of the Sanger school of birth control technology. Based on her three-month internship at Margaret Sanger's Clinical Research Bureau in New York City, Ishimoto founded her own "scientifically operated birth control clinic" in 1934.[81] In the first two months of operation, Ishimoto's clinic received 754 inquiries by letter and fifty visitors.[82] She reported to Sanger's secretary, Florence Rose:

> I hope you will imagine me in our new birth control clinic. I wear my white gown over my American suits, when I instruct mothers there. I sit on the silk Japanese cushion on the green mats-room. There are [a] low table in the center and an alcove on the north side of room. Always beautiful rolled picture is hanging on the wall according to the season and the other day, there was a picture of ancient court noble with music instrument and a few bunches of cherry blossoms were arranged in the beautiful vase.[83]

Ishimoto thus created an ideal setting for birth control instruction in her own country: providing poor mothers with the state-of-art birth control technology imported from the United States in a beautifully crafted Japanese traditional setting. In particular, Ishimoto's clinic supported the "Dutch pessary," or a spring-type vaginal diaphragm. This method was developed in Sanger's clinic with the cooperation of medical doctors and the financial backing of business moguls. In response to the spread of medical quackery and the issuance of the Ordinance Regulating Harmful Contraceptive Devices, Ishimoto and the physicians who supported her strongly advocated this "scientific" method in Japan.

Japanese eagerness to capitalize on the reputation of "Margaret Sanger the Invincible" and to master the modern and scientific methods of contraception on their own had an unexpected effect on the American birth control movement.[84] In 1932, a doctor in Osaka, Koyama Sakae, sent Sanger samples of the pessaries he specially made to fit Japanese women in the hope of gaining her endorsement and selling the rights to market them in the United States and elsewhere in the world.[85] The pessaries, however, were confiscated by US customs for violating the Comstock Law. At the urging of her attorney, Sanger used this "opportunity" to challenge the federal legislation. In the case, known as *United States v. One Package of Japanese Pessaries*, the US District Court for the Southern District of New York ultimately ruled in December 1936 that the tariff prohibitions could not be used to prevent the importation of contraceptives intended for legitimate medical use. The decision in effect nullified the Comstock Law, a law that Sanger had long been fighting since the very beginning of her activism. Ishimoto warned Sanger about her suspicions that Dr. Koyama was one of the "many quack dealers making use of [Sanger's] name . . . as a means of promoting their selfish interest."[86] Whatever Koyama's intentions may have been, Sanger exultantly welcomed the court's decision as the "greatest legal victory in the Birth Control Movement."[87]

Despite strenuous efforts by advocates on both sides of the Pacific, however, there was still no reliable, simple, and affordable method of contraception available in Japan or the United States during the prewar decades. The Ordinance Regulating Harmful Contraceptive Devices of 1930 reflected the hostility of the general medical community against birth control propaganda and the growing trend toward pronatalism among bureaucrats in Japan. The contraceptive pin and other devices that had begun to gain wide acceptance were banned under the law. The Dutch pessary was not suitable for the general masses because it required medical guidance, advanced preparation, and the cooperation of commercial manufacturers. It also cost more to use than other basic methods, such as sponges, spermicide, and condoms. For these reasons, many proletarian-based advocates rejected this device and were forced to rely on more rudimentary and ineffective—and often dangerous—methods.[88]

While the concept of birth control gained popular acceptance after Sanger's arrival in Japan, the actual rate of practice remained limited throughout the prewar years, especially among rural, working-class families. Contraceptive practice was making slow but steady progress in both urban and rural areas, but, according to the public opinion survey conducted by the Mainichi Newspapers, the initiation of contraceptive experience was overwhelmingly concentrated in the postwar period. The diffusion rate of birth control was about 10 percent among married couples before the war and 13 percent at the end of war.[89] Despite birth control activists' efforts to disseminate contraceptive practices among laborers and farmers in particular, there was still a wide gap in fertility rates between urban and rural areas, suggesting that women in the latter had little knowledge of or access to reliable methods of reproductive control.[90]

Political Battles

Increasing nationalist pressure eventually frustrated the activists' efforts to bring contraceptive knowledge and technology to the general public. Liberals in the late 1930s emphasized birth control advocacy as a eugenic measure to improve national fitness and a diplomatic tool to consolidate Japan's position among other imperialist powers rather than a matter of individual women's well-being. Proletarian activists, subjected to intense political suppression, began to distance themselves from the bourgeois-led birth control movement. They eventually described birth control primarily as a defense strategy against poverty and capitalist exploitation. Ultimately, they too saw birth control as a political weapon to improve the general strength of Japanese workers as a whole and paid less attention to it as a means to help individual women. Bourgeois and proletarian women each followed the political priorities set by their male colleagues. As a result, the issue of women's rights and reproductive freedom, regardless of class position, faded to the background in the political discourses regarding birth control.

Regardless of political positions, birth control supporters shared some of the main purposes of the cause—especially its eugenic functions. The rivalries between bourgeois and proletarian movements in Japan were mostly ideological, not entirely class based. In fact, many of the proletarian leaders, such as Yamamoto and Yamakawa, were highly educated and economically comfortable.[91] Before the nationalist crackdown on radicals in the 1930s, therefore, representatives of both the bourgeois and proletarian camps worked together to spread the knowledge and technology of contraception to the Japanese masses, although gender biases often prevented female activists from working alongside their male counterparts on equal terms.

Initially, Ishimoto sought to join forces with the birth control campaigns in the Kansai region through Yamamoto Senji. Soon after Sanger's visit, Ishimoto wrote to Yamamoto to exchange information on their birth control activities. Agreeing with Yamamoto's contention that direct importation of foreign birth control methods would not work in Japanese indigenous settings, Ishimoto sought further professional advice from him.[92] Yamamoto failed to follow up on Ishimoto's request; as he explained in the aforementioned letter to Sanger, the state supervision against their proletarian group in Osaka prevented him from "communicating our secret activities even to our comrades in Tokyo." Ishimoto apparently did not take Yamamoto's "unavoidable negligence of our intercommunication" very positively. Yamamoto sarcastically described Ishimoto's response: "Mrs. Ishimoto took my white camouflage for [a] true garment and could not recognize its red contents."[93] Yamamoto's comment revealed his implicit contempt for this bourgeois lady, whom he thought was too naïve to recognize the secret tactics and activities he had been using to shield himself from official scrutiny.

Yamamoto, however, failed to notice that Ishimoto had developed a decidedly negative view of him because of his sarcastic remarks toward her, Sanger, and other bourgeois women. In particular, Ishimoto took umbrage at Yamamoto's critique that there was nothing new in Sanger's *Family Limitation* other than the common knowledge held by anyone in the medical profession.[94] She took Yamamoto's words as an expression of masculine arrogance. From time to time, Yamamoto did in fact reveal his own prejudice about women, especially the "Society Women" in Japan, ridiculing their supposed lack of scientific knowledge and penchant for sensational subjects. In refuting the conservative opposition that the availability of birth control knowledge would promote sexual decadence, Yamamoto asserted that upper-class women typically did not have the "scientific knowledge or attitude" to understand and carry out the specific birth control methods introduced in Sanger's pamphlet.[95] Whether it was because of Ishimoto's naïveté or Yamamoto's contemptuous attitude toward bourgeois women (but not necessarily toward working-class women), the two leaders in the end pursued their activism in separate ways. When in 1925 Yamamoto established his own birth control periodical, *Sanji chōsetsu hyōron* (Birth control review), Ishimoto declined to take part ostensibly because she wanted to "leave the project in the hands of experts."[96]

Meanwhile, Yamamoto worked collaboratively with several male liberals in Tokyo for a legislative reform to recognize the need for birth control as a national policy. For labor activists, the cooperation of moderate and liberal reformers was necessary to turn their visions into political action. In 1929, members of the Osaka Birth Control Study Society and the Japanese Birth Control Study Society in Tokyo together wrote a Proposition for Birth Control (Sanji chōsetsu kengian). The petition asserted that birth control was desirable not only from the perspective of the proletariat but also for new representatives of all parties.[97] Yamamoto, who had just been elected a member of the House of Representatives from the Labor-Farmer Party (Rōnōtō) in 1928, the first election since the passage of legislation in 1925 granting universal male suffrage, was going to present it to the Lower House. The plan never materialized, however, as he was stabbed to death in 1929 by a right-wing extremist after his speech in the Diet against the Peace Preservation Law.[98]

As the proletarian activists suffered from increasing nationalist suppression, the Japan Birth Control Federation (Nihon sanji chōsetsu renmei), led by Abe Isoo in Tokyo, took on the birth control legislation in 1931, placing more emphasis on the eugenic purposes of birth control in forming healthier and stronger Japanese subjects rather than its revolutionary aspect. The Japan Birth Control Federation dissolved after a year as a result of conflict between its male and female members—specifically, between Ishimoto and physician Majima Kan (the quarrel between the two would continue into the postwar decades). Explaining the dissolution as a result of "a systematic failure," the female members reorganized the group as the Japan Women's Birth Control Federation (Nihon sanji chōsetsu fujin renmei). The Women's Federation submitted the birth control proposition to the Diet in 1932. Their campaign still gave physicians and scientists extensive power over birth control knowledge and devices. The Home Department nonetheless rejected the petition, just as the Japanese military became increasingly preoccupied with its imperialist missions in Manchuria.[99]

The scientific and eugenic approach to women's reproductive and sexual issues presented both the potential and limit of bourgeois women's activism. While celebrating that the Japan Women's Birth Control Federation was reestablished exclusively by women—"returning to the original purpose of the birth control movement"—the female leaders set as their priority strengthening the scientific and medical aspect of their efforts.[100] Their emphasis on science was, to be sure, driven by their genuine concern for women. Piggybacking on the surge of public interest in birth control, quack doctors and salesmen emerged across the country, attempting to sell ineffective, and sometimes harmful, contraceptives, to women. It was therefore an urgent mission for feminists to protect women's bodies from these potential dangers associated with sex, pregnancy, and childbearing at the time by establishing birth control as part of a legitimate medical practice. The campaigns for eugenic legislation, although unsuccessful most of the time, provided a platform for women to have their voices heard in national policy discussion that affected women's bodies. But because they accorded the state and the medical authority special power to protect women's bodies, they were ultimately at the mercy of paternalistic control. In other words, women were able to participate only in scientific and legislative efforts to protect women's bodies and sexuality that dovetailed with nationalist interests: to produce fit and healthy Japanese subjects.[101]

Women leaders of different political affiliations, however, had difficulty finding a uniting ground on which to base their advocacy for birth control. The split had already been apparent in the women's movement in general since the 1920s, as many socialist feminists felt disconnected from their bourgeois sisters' suffrage campaigns and instead started to organize their own groups.[102] The rift between women of different social and political backgrounds on the subject of birth control came to the surface when some female members associated with the underground Communist Party in Tokyo formed the Proletarian Birth Control Union (Musansha sanji seigen dōmei) in June 1931 in direct opposition to the Japan Birth Control Federation. In its founding manifesto, the Proletarian Union criticized the "bourgeois reactionary birth control groups" as agents of the capitalists, who simply blamed the prolific working class for causing population problems, food shortages, and poverty. Their goal was therefore to reveal the "hypocrisy" of bourgeois activists, whose aim, they claimed, was to "numb the fighting spirit" of the working-class people.[103] A member of the Proletarian Birth Control Union, Iwasaki Motoko, wrote an article in direct confrontation with Ishimoto's approach to the birth control movement. In response to Ishimoto's criticism that the proletariat activists saw birth control only through the lens of class struggles, Iwasaki argued that Ishimoto could never understand their position because she was too immersed in a social structure that privileged the bourgeois class. While agreeing with Ishimoto about the benefits of birth control in protecting maternal health, she pointed out that in reality working-class women did not have access to even basic medical care and health.[104]

Just as bourgeois women came to reframe their support for birth control primarily as a eugenic strategy for Japan to prevail in imperial competitions, many socialist women had to prioritize other political goals of the proletarian movement over women's personal desire for reproductive control. The Osaka Birth Control Society voted *against* the proposal to include birth control in the political agenda of labor unions. A core female member of the group explained their decision: "Birth control is only a personal means of self-defense, and the union cannot include it in their present agenda when it has millions of other issues to solve."[105] In Tokyo, the Proletarian Birth Control Union started as the Birth Control Women's Association (Sanji chōsetsu fujin renmei) but decided to expand its membership to unite as a proletarian group as a whole. The founders asserted that women's liberation could not be achieved solely by birth control, but they should work in coordination with labor unions, farmers' groups, and proletarian doctors.[106] In other words, solidarity among members of the proletarian class was more important than the unity of women from different social and economic backgrounds.

The gap between women of different social and economic classes over the meanings and purposes of birth control also became evident among the Japanese living in the United States, who learned much of the discussions surrounding the issue from Japan. Some elites expressed its eugenic value for the Japanese American community as an outpost of the Japanese Empire. A doctor based in California, for example, proposed to establish a free clinic that provided genetic counseling and birth control guidance to young Japanese American couples. Such a clinic, he believed, could contribute to the improvement of fitness and health of the Japanese race outside Japan.[107] Apparently, some maternity clinics had already existed, in which doctors provided free birth control instruction for the Japanese in California as a "community service."[108] Meanwhile, early socialist interest in birth control had quickly waned when the socialist group dissolved after Katayama's departure from the United States. Since then, the subject of birth control had rarely appeared in newspaper discussions among Japanese American laborers and socialists. Women who struggled between childbearing/child rearing and wage labor usually proposed a better childcare system—modeled after that in the Soviet Union. On the occasions that they mentioned the subject of birth control, they stressed that working women needed birth control out of sheer necessity, not as "a personal choice" that it seemed to be for some affluent housewives.[109]

By the 1930s, socialist women in Japan, including Yamakawa Kikue, for the most part had abandoned their earlier approval of Sanger's argument that, whether in a capitalist or socialist society, women shared a universal right to control their own bodies. While admitting that birth control was "a necessary and absolute measure to protect the interests of women and their children regardless of class," Yamakawa herself began to assert that the practice was less an urgent matter for bourgeois women who had money, time, and health. It was the working-class men and women who really needed birth control, she stressed, as a "self-defense measure" against capitalist and imperialist exploitation.[110] The momentum of the grassroots birth control movement in Japan, inspired by Sanger's transnational campaigns, thus declined significantly as feminists and other activists became preoccupied with political goals that placed women's concern as a secondary issue.

. . .

In her first article introduced in *Kaizō* in 1921, "Birth Control—Past, Present and Future," Sanger declared that her "'Birth Control' agitation was inaugurated not upon the basis of the Malthusian theory of population, not to check the increase of population, but to . . . answer to the cries of anguish that came to me from thousands of poor and diseased women."[111] She submitted another article, "Woman's Power and Birth Control," which was published in *Kaizō* to coincide with her visit to Japan. In this piece, she further emphasized that women should be the masters of their own fate by using the power of modern science, specifically the knowledge of birth control.[112] In short, Sanger's original goal was to empower all women, especially the most marginalized and exploited ones—not the liberal reformers, capitalists, and socialists—with the tools of knowledge and technology. This message resonated deeply with Japanese feminists who were exploring their voices and positions in a rapidly changing society under industrialization and Westernization. Ultimately, however, nationalist interests blunted this feminist message. Male intellectuals in Japan interpreted Sanger's birth control philosophy primarily as a neo-Malthusian solution to social issues arising as a result of Japan's integration into global capitalism and imperialism. As we see in the next chapters, Sanger herself failed to overcome the imperialist pressure to which her birth control cause was increasingly subjected.

Observing that bourgeois and proletarian feminists were growing increasingly hostile to each other, Ishimoto claimed that she maintained an "independent path."[113] Nonetheless, she apparently worked much more closely with the liberal feminists than with her radical sisters. For a while, Ishimoto aided the bourgeois feminist activities, especially the suffrage campaigns. She would soon relinquish her hopes for these domestic political activities, however, as she despaired that "deep-rooted feudal forces" and "the sudden rise of the fascist power" had forced the budding feminist movement in her country to retreat before it had the chance to bloom.[114] Instead, she would look toward her Western sisters for guidance and support to develop her feminist aspirations and, in particular, the birth control cause.

TWO

Spreading the Gospel of Birth Control
The Limits of International Women's Activism

A couple of months after the United States entered World War I in 1917, Margaret Sanger wrote an article strongly opposing war. In one of the first issues of *Birth Control Review* she wrote:

> Woman hates war. Her instincts are fundamentally creative, not destructive. But her sex-bondage has made her the dumb instrument of the monster she detests. . . . Too long has she been called the gentler and weaker of humankind; too long has she silently borne the brunt of unwilling motherhood; too long has she been the stepping-stone of oligarchies, kingdoms and so-called democracies; too long have they thrived on her enslavement.[1]

On one level, she essentialized women's nurturing role as mothers, claiming that it made them "fundamentally creative, not destructive." At the same time, this passage showed Sanger's belief in women's collective power to stand up against war and patriarchy.[2] Sanger's faith in women's potential for power allowed her to connect her opposition to war to her advocacy for birth control. By using birth control, she argued, women could both physically and spiritually free themselves from "sex-bondage" and "enslavement" and thus make a greater difference in the world.

Sanger's pacifist statement was in line with the international peace movement among elite women that arose in the aftermath of World War I under the spirit of Wilsonian internationalism. Indeed, the 1920s saw a blooming of international movements, especially in the Pacific area, where liberals imagined a more egalitarian and friendly world order as an alternative to the nationalist tensions caused by European colonialism. As Akira

Iriye argues, the interwar period was not simply a narrative of a singular and inevitable "road to war." Instead, many private international initiatives sought to create multiple "roads to peace."[3] Women in particular used their biological capacity of reproduction as the basis of their pacifism, proposing a universal female bond of motherhood. Not just Western women but also non-Western women took active part in the pacifist endeavors during this period. Through their international contacts, women were able to find new opportunities and roles abroad, away from the patriarchal and nationalist pressures at home. This chapter examines how Margaret Sanger and Ishimoto Shizue each incorporated the ideals of maternalist pacifism and liberal internationalism into their birth control activism abroad. For these birth control activists in particular, the transnational networks provided them more freedom and opportunities to present their views to the foreign audiences, when at home multiple political forces often frustrated their activism and silenced their voices.

The topic of birth control was still far more radical than what other internationalist feminists typically discussed, such as suffrage, education, and temperance. Liberal internationalist women tended to avoid touching the issue of birth control, as this was a divisive subject that could harm the friendly and "ladylike" atmosphere of international gatherings. I call the activities of these women "international" because they generally operated on a semiofficial level, and the female delegates had a strong sense of representing their own country. Sanger and Ishimoto worked parallel to, but not within, the mainstream women's movements. The isolation from their domestic peers forced them to forge a path independent of other official international gatherings of women. But it also gave them opportunities to interact with foreign women as individuals, not as delegates representing their own countries with a set of clearly defined political agendas. In fact, both Sanger and Ishimoto were often critical of the elitist and nationalist attitudes of other liberal reformers. By highlighting these rather extraordinary feminists, one can imagine a grassroots and informal form of transnational activism, which at times went beyond the official discourses about women, race, and the nation.

Ultimately, however, birth control failed to serve as a unifying subject for women across national borders because of the same limitations that qualified elite women's internationalism in the interwar period in general: activists' ambiguous relations to the patriarchal state and racialist nationalism. Their liberal discourses did not claim to overturn the family and motherhood within the nation-state system. Neither did their approach aim to form a truly egalitarian relationship beyond racial boundaries. Internationalist women, including Sanger and Ishimoto, both consciously and unconsciously internalized the discourse of "feminist Orientalism," a concept that polarized the "progressive" West and the "backward" East in hierarchal rankings. As birth control became increasingly tied to discussions of overpopulation and imperial competition, Japanese internationalist women often defended their country's military expansionism in Asia, while Western feminists sought to avoid such divisive conversation altogether. Just as other political goals pushed feminists' claim for voluntary motherhood to the background in the domestic birth control movement, birth control also became intricately tied to discussions of imperialism and nationalism in the international arena. Women's presumed love for peace, as mothers of humankind, gradually transformed into their love for the country at a time of war, as mothers and caregivers of soldiers.[4] Once the peace movement fell apart in the late 1930s, so did Sanger's and Ishimoto's stated goals to unite women beyond races and nations for reproductive freedom.

The Rise of International Women's Networks

Sanger and Ishimoto started their transnational activism at a time when international women's networks started to form not just among Western countries but also across the Pacific between the West and the East. Like Sanger and Ishimoto, women who participated in these early internationalist endeavors were mostly Christian bourgeois women, and motherhood was one of the common themes that united women of different nationalities. Sanger and Ishimoto were involved in some of these semiofficial activities among internationalist women, as they shared their spirit of maternalist pacifism. They were by no means central participants, however, because most international gatherings of women avoided the controversial discussion of birth control.

As Leila J. Rupp demonstrates, efforts to organize women across national borders, mainly among European countries and the United States, began in the late nineteenth century. A variety of movements, including abolitionism, socialism, peace, temperance, and moral reform, brought together women from these different nations in mixed-gender meetings. As women on both sides of the Atlantic started to exchange feminist ideologies, a group of women activists planned a conference committed to women's rights rather than some other cause. The First International Congress of Women's Rights convened in Paris in 1878 in connection with the World Exposition. A decade later, the US National Woman Suffrage Association organized the founding meeting of the International Council of Women (ICW), the first lasting international women's organization. The crisis of World War I led to the formation of the International Committee of Women for Permanent Peace in 1915, which adopted the name Women's International League for Peace and Freedom (WILPF), in 1919.[5] Margaret Sanger became a member of WILPF, and Ishimoto Shizue participated in the International Congress of Women held in Chicago in 1933.

While Protestant, elite women of European origin dominated these organizations, from the 1920s they sought to extend their membership to women in Latin America, the Middle East, and the Far East. Their attempt to diversify their memberships reflected what Leila Rupp and other historians have called "feminist Orientalism." According to this ideology, Western women utilized the assumption of Eastern backwardness to accentuate the degraded status of women and to solidify their leadership role toward the united goal of liberation.[6] Nonetheless, it also showed their efforts, however limited, to confront the issues of imperialism at a time when World War I shook the foundation of European world dominance and partially set off the process of decolonization. Moreover, Asian women were not simply observers of Western culture. They often brought to the table their own social, national, and racial agenda to extend their spheres of influence both domestically and internationally.[7]

The internationalist reformers' search for an alternative world order, other than the transatlantic hegemony, became further evident in new developments in the Pacific area. Amid growing imperial tensions in the region, leaders of different nations came together to form a Pacific community, under US leadership but with a strong cooperation of Asian powers—Japan and China. The emerging momentum to establish a Pacific-centered internationalism materialized with the formation of the Pan-Pacific Union in 1917 and the Institute of Pacific Relations (IPR) in 1925.[8] Under the auspices of the Pan-Pacific Union, the first Pan-Pacific Women's Conference

(PPWC) was convened in Honolulu in 1928. The meeting brought together more than two hundred delegates from ten different countries, including twenty women from Japan.[9] During the second conference two years later, the Pan-Pacific Women's Association (PPWA) was formed. The PPWA meetings became one of the rare venues in which women exchanged their views about women's fertility control and population problems in international politics.[10]

Many of these new transpacific movements during the interwar period were based on Christian and missionary networks between the East and the West that had been established since the late nineteenth century. In particular, the Woman's Christian Temperance Union (WCTU) served as a precursor of transpacific women's activism, especially between the United States and Japan.[11] Many women who participated in the international women's organizations were members of Christian organizations such as the WCTU and Young Women's Christian Association. To be sure, these international organizations included members of different denominations with different social views and dealt with both moral and political subjects. Nonetheless, as Fiona Paisley points out, they ultimately shared the values of "liberal Christianity," which emphasized individual fulfillment through social reforms in the areas of education, health, public life, and employment to expand the influence of women.[12]

In addition to religious affiliations, social class and financial background defined the types of women who participated in these international networks. Because women usually had to undertake lengthy and expensive travel, only those with personal or organizational subsidies or with independent means could afford to participate in these activities. Language barriers also made it difficult for women who were not versed in the official languages used in the meetings—usually English, French, and German—to participate. Elite Japanese women educated in Western countries, such as Inoue Hideko (president of the Japanese Women's Peace Association and dean of the Women's University of Japan, studied at Columbia University) and Ide Kikue (professor at Kobe College, studied at Wellesley College), or Christian women educated by missionaries in Japan, such as Gauntlet (Yamada) Tsuneko, typically represented the Japanese delegations.[13]

Motherhood often served as a uniting theme for women of various nationalities. Women's biological capacity for reproduction, internationalist women argued, made them inherently pacifist; no woman would willingly go through the agony of childbirth, they insisted, only to lose that child to war. The politics of what Leila Rupp calls "maternalist pacifism" characterized many of the international women's movements during the interwar period.[14] In preparing for the first PPWC in 1928, Jane Addams, president of WILPF, requested that motherhood be the focus of the meeting, hoping to avoid the division she experienced at previous Euro-American women's conferences. In the opening address of the 1928 conference, Addams evoked an essentialist notion of women as nurturers and therefore closer to nature.[15]

The binary notion of men as belligerent hunters and women as peace-loving nurturers frequently translated to the contrast between the West and East. Addams stated in her speech: "This Pacific area is nearer to this basic culture of women's founding [in nature] than are the Occidental countries where the culture taken over from Europe has become so highly mechanized."[16] In other words, motherhood was one of the few themes that Western women and Eastern women could discuss on equal terms; in fact, white women could even learn from women of color, who were presumed to be closer to nature than women from more "civilized" societies.

Despite the focus on women's reproductive capacity, internationalist women, most of whom were Christian and elite, remained ambivalent about birth control. The ICW, for example, refused to discuss the question of birth control because it fell into the realm of religion. WILPF concluded that "full weight should be given to the judgment and opinion of women" and recommended that national sections individually take up the "problem of population."[17] The US National Board of WILPF, of which Sanger was a member, passed a resolution in 1934 to support the National Committee on Federal Legislation for Birth Control, a lobbying group that Sanger organized with the goal to repeal the Comstock Law. The resolution emphasized the eugenic value of "the proper and intelligent use of scientific, contraceptive methods" to keep "all patriotic Americans . . . vigorous and healthy both physically and mentally."[18] In other words, WILPF described their support in terms of national and racial fitness, not in terms of women's rights and reproductive freedom. Similarly in Japan, many prominent feminists accepted the use of contraception primarily as a means to protect the maternal body against venereal diseases for eugenic purposes. A leading female physician, Yoshioka Yayoi, who delivered multiple papers on maternal health in the 1928 PPWA meeting, was actually an outspoken opponent of birth control.

Consequently, Sanger's and Ishimoto's transnational birth control activism did not represent the international elite women's networks at large. They themselves rarely participated in the official gatherings organized by these international women's groups but instead carried out their transnational activism on their own. They were much more critical than their peers of the racial and national prejudices that they considered were hampering the bonds of international friendship.

Nonetheless, a closer look at their observations of and relationship with women abroad shows that they shared much in common with these internationalist women, specifically the idea of maternalist pacifism, which they believed could be achieved by extending the Western-inspired gospel of birth control to women across the world. Just as some women found suffrage and temperance uniting themes to bring liberation to women across national borders, Sanger and Ishimoto preached birth control as a means to achieve international peace and friendship. And just like many of these internationalist movements, they would fall short of their goals of universal sisterhood, as they failed to directly confront the fundamental causes of women's oppression.

Sanger's Orientalism

When Margaret Sanger traveled to Japan for the first time in 1922, she truly believed that she would bond with Japanese women. She imagined that they would overcome racial and national boundaries and unify under a common goal of reproductive freedom and maternal love. In a prepared speech, she appealed to the "men and women of Japan" for "international emancipation, based upon free, conscious maternity."[19] On her way to Japan on board the *Taiyō-maru*, Sanger observed the xenophobia and racism of her fellow Americans. In her diary, she described "the grim fact of separateness of the two people" and the "spirit of antagonism" of the Americans, including Christian missionaries who held the same unflattering views toward the "Orientals" as those expressed in the "Californian papers [on anti-Japanese immigration]." Separating herself from other Americans, she was determined to go beyond these stereotypes and prejudices and to actively involve herself in a two-way conversation with the Japanese "in order to have a better understanding of each other."[20]

During the course of her trip in Japan, however, Sanger would fall short of her self-proclaimed mission to bring together people, especially women, of different races and nationalities on equal terms. She seemed to enjoy the company of male elites but failed to connect with Japanese women regardless of social classes or background—not because of the lack of intelligence on the part of Japanese women but mostly because of Sanger's unacknowledged prejudice against them. Indeed, her diary entries and memoirs show that her observations of Japanese women became increasingly colored by common Orientalist perceptions as she traveled across the "land of the cherry blossom."[21]

On her first day in Japan, Sanger was received by a female editor of a women's magazine as well as a delegation of six women representing "the New Women's Movement of Japan." Given the growing interest in the topic of birth control among intellectual women, it was quite natural that these women were some of the first to greet Sanger. Yet, instead of going straight into a discussion on women's reproductive issues, Sanger was immediately mesmerized by "these adorably perfect doll women" dressed in traditional costume, whose charm "ushered [her] into a new world of womanhood" and the "perfume of a fairyland." She had to remind herself that "these little New Women in Japan [were] the instruments to carry out the real dreams of an emancipated womanhood in Japan," as they conveyed to Sanger the strong desire of many Japanese women to learn the methods of birth control.[22]

Sanger shared with other contemporary middle-class women the idea of "feminist Orientalism": women in the East represented the most oppressed status of women, whereas Euro-American women were well on their way to emancipation. She contrasted what she saw as the lack of individuality of Japanese women with the versatility of American women, who, she described, were "heterogeneous, changing, plastic." She found it "impossible to discover any such wide variation in type and spirit" in Japanese women—"from the lowest serving maid to the finest and most beautiful production of countless generations of aristocracy." For Sanger, all Japanese women shared a "fluttering and birdlike" voice, a demeanor of modesty, and "the silence and subservience to the male, particularly to the husband."

Unlike American women, she assumed, Japanese women could not express their individuality because they were too deeply steeped in the "feudal psychology" of silence and subservience to the male. While she conceded that there was "nothing essentially Oriental" in the general servile role of women to "her lord, her king, her governor," she compared the "attitude of the typical Japanese woman" of the time to the women in a Shakespeare play—a fictional world and a distant historical memory for Western women.[23]

Interestingly, the only women who were able to "think independently and to do anything with their lives," according to her judgment, were those who had turned Christian. "To be a Christian seemed to imply being a rebel or radical of some kind," Sanger observed. "They told me it with great secret pride."[24] It is true that many progressive and radical intellectuals in Japan studying new ideas from the West in the Meiji era converted to Christianity. For a Japanese woman to convert to Christianity, her action often demanded her to be "strong-willed," especially if she had to rebel against the orders of her parents, husband, and teachers.[25] Ishimoto, too, was deeply influenced by Nitobe Inazō's Christian humanism during her formative years, although in her case it was her family and husband who brought Christianity to her. By the time Sanger visited Japan, however, many of these early sympathizers, including Ishimoto, had abandoned their interest in Christianity. It is rather ironic that Sanger believed that only Christianized spirits could bring true liberation to women in Japan, when earlier she had denounced the racial antagonism of some American Christian missionaries.

Sanger was, however, more contemplative and less superficial in her observation of working-class women in Japan during her 1922 visit, reflecting her earlier interest in the working condition of poor women when she was affiliated with the Socialist Party. During her stay, her Japanese hosts took her to one of the largest cotton mills in the country. Sanger defiantly wrote that she was not deceived by the "type of paternalistic welfare work" the factory provided, which included a day-care facility for female workers, nor by "the extreme courtesy of [her] hosts." She deplored the lack of protection against the terrible working conditions of these women, as she heard about the open violation of factory laws. The experience made her realize that these women were not only subjected to the gendered prejudice of feudalism but were now even more oppressed by the arrival of industrialization and Westernization, a system that required a continuous supply of cheap and unskilled labor. In Sanger's eyes, the advent of industrial machinery had destroyed the "cherry-blossom fairyland of the familiar Japanese print," as young girls no longer walked down the streets in decorative clothes but were instead increasingly drawn to factories to work long hours for minimum wage.[26]

Yoshiwara, an infamous prostitution district, seemed on the surface to represent a colorful and attractive, ancient Japanese culture of geisha girls and decorative ladies. "Small wonder," Sanger wrote, "that the girls preferred to live there rather than to seek a living in dismal factories or to endure the squalor, poverty and hunger of the poorer quarters." After a lavish reception, which gathered some 150 government officials, physicians, and other male professionals, her hosts took Sanger to Yoshiwara. As they walked down the streets, Sanger was horrified to see the prices of girls presented above the doors of the brothels. She felt "almost helpless against the crowd of men swarming almost like insects automatically reacting to the stimulus of instinct" and questioned the "morality" of those who tolerated such sexual behaviors of men while questioning the "morality" of birth control.[27]

By presenting to readers the misery of Japanese women in factories and brothels, Sanger sought to show the real picture of women in modern Japan. She hoped to correct the "romantic fallacies" that most Westerners had about the "decorative ladies of the old feudal regime," as represented in the "gaudy theatricalism" of *Madame Butterfly* and the *Mikado*. In her 1923 article, part of which was later included in her autobiographies, she told her Western readers:

> Too long have we been told and shown how posteresque and how picturesque the women of Japan are, how different they are from our own flappers and feminists, or the plodding workaday women of our drab Western civilization. It is my conviction, strengthened by a limited but intensified visit to the "land of the cherry blossom," that [it] is our first duty to find out, not how mysteriously Oriental the Japanese are, but how fundamentally alike they are to the rest of us. Skim over the surface of the Japanese scene, in the manner of the average American tourist, and only the decorative differences appear. Delve beneath the surface and gradually inevitably you cannot escape the conclusion that contemporary Japan is confronted by the same complex problems generated by modern industrialism.[28]

Sanger genuinely intended to bring about "international understanding and amity" by going beyond racial and gendered stereotypes that most contemporary Americans had about the Japanese. She tried to identify the common cause of women's oppression—feudalism and modern industrialism—and to unite under the shared goal of liberating all women beyond different nationalities through the means of birth control.

Sanger derived much of her understanding about the history and status of working-class women in Japan from an article written by socialist feminist Yamakawa Kikue, "Woman in Modern Japan," which appeared in the English edition of the *Shakai-shugi kenkyū* (A monthly study on international socialism and the Labor movement) from January to September 1922. In a 1923 unpublished article, "The New Women of Japan," Sanger cited Yamakawa as an "authority" on the history of women in Japan. Sanger's article heavily relied on Yamakawa's tract to explain the process through which a feudalistic system of female oppression took place in Japan, from the early matriarchate stage of society to the rise of powerful military lords, which placed women into complete subjugation.

By juxtaposing Sanger's and Yamakawa's articles, however, one can detect Sanger's selective interpretations based on her preconceived ideas about Japanese women. In particular, while Sanger replicated much of the information on the oppressed status and voicelessness of Japanese women from Yamakawa's article, she largely overlooked Yamakawa's description of the indigenous women's movement, especially among working-class and socialist women.[29] In the end, Sanger agreed with Yamakawa's conclusion that middle-class women were "in general passive, home-loving, and self-centered." As a socialist, however, Yamakawa intended to criticize the bourgeois feminist movement, which was completely oblivious to the needs and rights of working-class women. For Sanger, however, this statement simply helped reaffirm her impression of *all* women in Japan. Sanger's interpretation of Yamakawa's research was a striking contrast to the remarks made by Mary Ritter Beard, another American friend of Ishimoto's, regarding the same article. Beard felt that Japanese women had actually made *more* contributions to society than what Yamakawa described.[30]

As a result of her limited contact with Japanese women, as well as her ignorance toward the indigenous women's movement in Japan, Sanger declared that "one hears much of the 'New Woman' [in Japan] but one seldom sees her."[31] There is no record showing that she talked with Yamakawa in person, let alone with women working in the factories and brothels. Sanger herself did not plan the visits to the cotton mill and Yoshiwara. Even as she distinguished herself from the "casual visitor," she had the chance to see these places simply because her social reformist hosts took her there during the gaps in her schedule between professional meetings and dinner parties. She left only a limited record, in her diary and autobiography, of her personal conversation or interaction with Japanese feminists. The only woman, other than Ishimoto, whom Sanger met and mentioned by name in her diary—although she could recall only the first letter of it—was Yoshioka Yayoi. This prominent female doctor, however, was a vocal *opponent* of birth control. Not surprisingly, Sanger noted that Yoshioka's concern about the immorality of birth control was "very reactionary and [a] hundred years behind" some of the male physicians.[32]

Sanger thus accorded the task of liberating women and bringing "radical changes" in New Japan to Japanese men who had "assimilated our Occidental ideals of individualism and personal ambition."[33] She came to believe that Japan was the only place where she found men, rather than women, more enthusiastic about the birth control cause. She wrote in her diary that she was "impressed by the advance the men had made in comparison to that made by women," especially by their "desire for knowledge."[34] As we have seen, male intellectuals were in fact in control of much of the discussion over birth control in the 1920s and 1930s in Japan. However, a number of leading feminists also actively participated in the nascent birth control movement. This skewed impression that Sanger formed about the Japanese was mostly a result of how she chose to interact with them. During her visit, she devoted much more time and attention to her conversations with male "experts" and "competent authorities" in the government, while she observed Japanese women only in superficial ways and ignored their contributions in politics.[35]

Assuming that Japanese women did "not possess in her typical psychology, the strong desire of rebellion or of change," Sanger asserted that their "self-realization" should instead come through "a gradual assertion of [their] power in [their] own sphere rather than in that of men"—in their "womanhood." Just like other Western "romanticists," Sanger found the inner beauty and potential of Japanese women in ancient Japanese culture, represented by the bright and colorful silks they wore underneath the dull brown or black kimono. Even while she stressed that everything old and traditionally Japanese worked to further oppress women, she still believed that a Japanese woman need not—and should not—"discard her beautiful costume or sacrifice her esthetic sense upon the altar of Occidental progress and materialism."[36] Although Sanger ostensibly claimed that Japanese and American women were essentially similar and attempted to build a bridge of understanding between the races, in the end she admitted that it was best for a Japanese woman to stay in the past and that her traditional aesthetic beauty was the only thing that made her unique and valuable.

Like many other internationalist white women of her time, when she went abroad, Sanger found new roles and possibilities outside the domestic context of Victorian womanhood by taking on her country's mission to "enlighten" the rest of the world. Sanger was indeed far more critical than her peers of the xenophobia of Americans and the evil effects of modern industrialism on women's bodies. Nonetheless, once abroad she could not escape the sense of representing the United States—the black ship—whether she desired it or not. While she insisted that she "did not go to the Far East as a self-appointed prophet to reform the habits of the yellow race," her personal writings show that she apparently considered it her mission to spread the gospel of birth control to the backward women in Japan.[37] This unacknowledged imperialist logic ultimately prevented her from truly connecting with the people whom she originally intended to reach: non-Western, and especially working-class, women.

Ishimoto's American Tours

Despite her general low regard of Japanese women, Sanger showed special esteem for her friend Ishimoto Shizue, her loyal disciple of the birth control cause. She praised her as "tall for her race," "speaking a clear and fine English," and "lovely to look at" either in American dresses or native costumes.[38] In other words, Sanger credited Ishimoto with characteristics and accomplishments that met Western standards. Indeed, Ishimoto not only introduced Sanger's birth control philosophy and methods in Japan, but she also embarked on transnational activism by traveling across the United States to present her own birth control work to American audiences. Americans in general, however, typically exoticized this guest from the Far East and failed to accept her message of sexual and social liberation for women across national boundaries.

After her first visit to the United States in 1919–20, during which she met Sanger, Ishimoto followed her husband again in 1924 for a shorter stay. During this second visit, Ishimoto reconnected with some of her old friends, including Mary Beard and Sanger. In addition, she was entertained by leading American feminists, notably Carrie Chapman Catt and Harriot Stanton Blatch. Ishimoto was fascinated by these "happy and healthy American women," who "never seemed afraid of anything." For Ishimoto, American women represented "joy and freedom," while her Japanese sisters were "bound by the chains of tradition and conventions." From them, Ishimoto learned about the long and hard battles for enfranchisement in the United States and England. Catt, who declined to give her name as a sponsor to Sanger's American Birth Control League, inscribed a copy of her book, *Woman Suffrage and Politics*, with her "encouraging words" on the flyleaf: "To Baroness Ishimoto who, I predict, will lead the women of Japan to their emancipation from outworn traditions." American feminists treated Ishimoto as a diligent student of the Euro-American women's movement, not as an equal partner in universal women's liberation. Nonetheless, Ishimoto was "thrilled at the idea of mutual respect and understanding overriding the barriers of distance and race," which she believed she had found in her interaction with these feminists.[39]

In the 1930s, Ishimoto again traveled across the Pacific twice, but this time on her own, to give lectures at local women's clubs, churches, and professional societies across the continent about Japanese culture, society, and women. For Ishimoto, the lecture tours, sponsored by the Feakins Lecture Bureau, signified both financial and emotional independence from her estranged husband. Disillusioned by his earlier socialist aspirations after being denied entry to Russia, the baron had now left the family to pursue another elusive dream in Manchuria.[40] His conversion from humanist and socialist sympathizer to nationalist was by no means an exception. Reformism in the 1920s and totalitarianism in the 1930s were common responses among many contemporary Japanese intellectuals and politicians to the threats and problems that the country faced in relation to other imperialist powers.[41] To make matters worse for Ishimoto, her husband's imprudent investments had depleted the family's fortune, and she needed to search for means to support her children and herself. Her uncle Tsurumi Yūsuke, who himself was on a lecture tour through the Feakins Bureau, suggested that she follow his example to earn money by herself. With Tsurumi's introduction, Feakins quickly arranged for Ishimoto to deliver her lectures in 1932.[42]

Her tour, however, began shortly after the 1931 Manchurian Incident, which represented a new stage of Japan's imperialist expansion into other Asian territories. International tensions were building up against Japan's action. William Feakins was initially concerned that it was not "a very propitious time for a Japanese to be booked in America." He wrote to Sanger that they were "keeping in mind to emphasize the fact that the Baroness is not talking politics, but is speaking about the women of Japan, the children and the artistic life."[43] A month later, however, Feakins reported again to Sanger that they were finding "considerable interest" in booking requests for Ishimoto even though she was announced "late in the season."[44] In October, they issued a press release that Ishimoto would be speaking on "The Manchurian Question and the Birth Control Movement" and that she proposed birth control rather than emigration as "the key to Japan's destiny."[45] Rather than downplay the political implications of her lectures, they now found it advantageous to capitalize on it. Ishimoto's maternalist pacifism, they believed, could appease the American public's fears and anger about Japan's imperialist actions abroad.

Arriving in San Francisco on October 14, 1932, Ishimoto moved east across the continent to New York and Boston as well as south to Dallas. Her public lectures covered three topics: "The Aesthetic Life of Japanese Women," "The Manchurian Question and the Birth Control Movement," and "The Societal Position of Japanese Women." In New York, a lavish tea party was held in her honor, to which were invited distinguished professors, doctors, journalists, artists, "prominent clubwomen," wives of attorneys and other professionals, and representatives of birth control organizations.[46]

Her second lecture tour in 1937, the year in which the Sino-Japanese War broke out, turned out to be as successful as the first. Ishimoto's uncle Tsurumi proudly told his niece after his own lecture tour in the United States: "When 99 percent of Americans have negative feelings about the Japanese, 'Baroness Ishimoto' remained the only popular Japanese."[47] With so many requests for her appearances, even her hosts and organizers were not prepared for her degree of popularity. In fact, Ishimoto was in such great demand that the tour manager decided to reject any "unpaid public appearance" of the baroness.[48] Gladys Delancey Smith, director of the California Birth Control Committee, who arranged Ishimoto's schedule during her stay in California, joked that her new full-time job was as a "booking agent" for the baroness.[49] Ishimoto was so popular that she even attracted those who would normally refuse any association with discussions on birth control. When an influential physician in Los Angeles, John D. Barrow, and his wife hosted a private dinner party in Ishimoto's honor, Mrs. Barrow, a Roman Catholic herself, was able to bring two other influential Catholic women in town, who had previously "laid Mrs. Barrow out for pushing and talking 'BC.'" At the event, Gladys Smith proudly reported, even these conservative women "talked the 'principles' of BC very freely—and all in a most 'friendly' spirit."[50]

Why was Ishimoto so popular despite deteriorating US-Japanese relations and moral opposition to birth control among many of her elite female clients? As the press coverage regarding Ishimoto's tours revealed, Ishimoto's appearance of exotic charm helped counterbalance the threatening image of Japanese military expansion. Indeed, most newspaper coverage and advertisements referring to Ishimoto appealed to her Oriental femininity, evoking a fairy-tale land of the ancient East. Media accounts described her as "charming and attractive," "exotic," and "gentle, soft-voiced and assured, with the poise of generations of Oriental aristocrats of her background."[51] A March 1933 issue of *Vogue* carried a feature article on Ishimoto, "Kimono into Décolleté." When she published an autobiography in English in 1935 with the help of Mary Beard, her American readers were more interested in her description of her early childhood in a traditional samurai family than what she had to say about her birth control activism and the history of women in Japan. "Labor reform, feminism, birth control," one reviewer wrote, "these are strange subjects to come from the pen of one who looks like a lovely print by an old Japanese master of the brush."[52] Ironically, one of the reasons Ishimoto published an autobiography in the United States was to correct misrepresentations of Japanese women and aesthetics in popular culture. Shocked by the improper way of donning a kimono in a Broadway performance of *Madame Butterfly*, Ishimoto hoped to educate the public by presenting the "correct" way of wearing it.[53] The American audience, however, saw little distinction between the real Japan she sought to express and the misrepresented world of *Madame Butterfly*.

At the same time, the American media also stressed that inside the Oriental beauty was a progressive, Westernized spirit. Just as Sanger found the sole potential of female leadership in Christianized Japanese women, Ishimoto's English skills and friendship with some American feminists made her an ideal "Japanese feminist" in the eyes of the American audience. One newspaper cited Ishimoto as describing American objections to birth control as "incredible innocence," thus placing her in a position to preach the benefits of birth control to America's domestic opponents.[54]

In short, Ishimoto was an embodiment of the best of both worlds: the feminine beauty of the East and the progressive spirit of the West. An article featuring Ishimoto, "A Japanese Feminist," described her as "the embodiment of the best of her country": "a slim young figure in quietly smart American clothes" whose "face held the classic beauty of an old Japanese print." Her "careful English speech," the article continued, "held captivating suggestion of an ancient East expressing itself in the more serious phrases of the experimenting young West."[55]

As nationalist tensions across the Pacific intensified, the American media contrasted the peace-loving and progressive nature of Japanese women to the militaristic and violent inclination of Japanese men. At first glance, it seems contradictory that Japanese women, who represented the fairy-tale land of the ancient East, could simultaneously have a progressive and Westernized state of mind. Yet, for the American public, such representations of Japanese women offered the hope—albeit a slim one—for a "road to peace," an alternative to the growing tensions and conflicts between imperialist powers in Asia in the 1930s. The contrast between the actions taken by Ishimoto and the fate of her husband became a prototypical example of this gendered representation of Japanese men and women in the American media. Whereas her husband was described as "one more example of the man of high principles who became corrupted by a willingness to accept ignoble means," Ishimoto herself had "made the jump from what corresponded to Europe's Thirteenth Century to the present in a short generation."[56]

It was then no surprise that Ishimoto was invited to represent "the woman movement in the Far East" at the International Congress of Women held in Chicago in July 1933, called by the National Council of Women. This was an especially challenging time for internationalist women, as the worldwide Depression and the raising of tariff walls had threatened cooperative and friendly relations between nations. "The Disarmament Conference has failed. The London Economic Conference has failed," Marianne

Beth of Austria deplored. "Never was international feeling running lower than now." ⁵⁷ In this context, Ishimoto was introduced as "Tokio's first business woman, opening a little shop in which she sold American yarn and taught girls to knit after the same fashion as American girls."⁵⁸ After returning from her first stay in the United States, Ishimoto had opened a small shop selling imported yarns mostly to wealthy female customers. She closed the store in two years, however, after the 1923 Kantō Earthquake. She was by no means the first businesswoman in Tokyo, although it was rare for a woman of her class to dabble in business. Nonetheless, the image of a Japanese woman selling American products and spreading American practices effectively illustrated the feminine and amiable relationship that women abroad had with American culture.

While introducing her as a progressive Japanese feminist, the conference organizers ignored Ishimoto's main interest in birth control. The chairwomen of the sessions described Ishimoto's interests in "the condition of labor, woman suffrage, the scientific control of population, and the cause of peace" but strangely avoided using the term "birth control."⁵⁹ In her actual speeches, Ishimoto depicted the "overcrowding" in her country in the context of world depression and imperialism and offered "the idea of scientifically planned population" as a solution. There is no record of further discussion in direct response to Ishimoto's speech, other than the facilitator's short comment praising "the courage and reality" in her statement. ⁶⁰

As it was during many other international conferences at the time, cultural diversity as represented by the various native costumes, especially those of non-Western women, was the main attraction for women attending the 1933 conference. As she sat beside Selma Ekrem of Turkey, who was also in her native apparel, Ishimoto felt "utterly at home" in her native dress, unlike the awkwardness she often felt in other public lectures and formal dinners where she was the sole target of the Orientalist gaze. In her speech, Ishimoto emphasized the advances that Japanese women had made, appealing to her Western audience that "your sisters in Japan are no longer the object of romance, wearing long-sleeved kimonos, and standing beside red bridges with gay paper parasols."⁶¹ Nonetheless, she seemed to contradict her own statement by Orientalizing herself as well as her fellow non-Western delegate for their Western friends.

The atmosphere of cultural diversity on this international stage, however, inspired and empowered Ishimoto, regardless of its implicit hierarchal relations. Surrounded by women representing their respective nations, Ishimoto felt "more dignified than exotic" in her native dress. Impressed by Selma Ekrem's "skill in handling the English language, by her directness of expression, and by her knowledge," she felt encouraged to "represent [her] own race too." As she listened to the speeches of "such forceful women as Mrs. Carrie Chapman Catt, Jane Addams, and Margaret Bondfield of England," Ishimoto was determined more than ever to fight for the "Common Cause—Civilization," the conference's theme, along with these women leaders of various nationalities.[62] Fiona Paisley, in her analysis of the roles of non-Western women at the PPWC, corroborates Ishimoto's vision of national pride by arguing that the presence of Asian women and their ability to mobilize a complex dual identity as both traditional and modern figures complicated the Western notion of progress and modernity.[63]

Not all non-Western women at these international gatherings bought into the ideal of cultural pluralism. As Manako Ogawa illustrates in her analysis of WCTU women, some Japanese women suspected that their wearing a kimono would reinforce the licentious images of geisha girls and refused their Western members' requests to do so. Others were wary of its impracticality and restriction of movement and felt more liberated in Western clothes.[64] In fact, Ishimoto also expressed discomfort about donning a kimono. Growing up in a Westernized household, she frequently confessed that she felt more comfortable in Western clothes and rather exotic in her own native dress. She recalled how, during her busy lecture tours, she had to swiftly change into her formal attire after getting off the train before reaching her next lecture stop—"like a kabuki actor changing costumes between scenes." During such hassles, she would sigh over the complexity of traditional costumes, which required a lot of knotting and binding.[65] In addition to the kimono's inconvenience, she was aware of the geisha image that contributed to the fantasized image abroad of Japanese women in kimonos. While stressing that she was not "one of those Confucian Puritans who despised these girls merely as evil women," she denounced the licensed prostitution system itself as "the enemies of domesticity and, as such, enemies of civilization in Japan."[66]

Nonetheless, Ishimoto still chose to wear a kimono at public lectures and formal dinners because she believed it created "the best atmosphere for friendship."[67] Whether the Western notion of cultural diversity actually advanced or hampered the goal of universal sisterhood, most women at these meetings believed that fashion was one area where they could form friendly bonds, when all other discussions on political and economic matters were frustrated by nationalist tensions. By doing so, they intended to extend their mutual understandings and respect to a deeper, spiritual level. Similar to how Sanger felt when she visited Japan, Ishimoto believed that beyond the superficial differences of skin color, facial features, and sartorial customs, women could bond through the common goal of building a peaceful and loving world. The limits of this idealized vision of universal sisterhood, however, soon became apparent as international relations further intensified in the Pacific in the late 1930s.

From Pacifism to Imperialism

Despite all the efforts both by Ishimoto and her hosts to keep her relationship with the American audience on friendly terms, Ishimoto at times could not escape the criticism directed toward her because of the action of the Japanese Army in Manchuria. She tried to distance herself from political debates—only in vain—by stating that she was far more interested in birth control as a sole issue than she was in Japan's strained relationship with the League of Nations.[68] She sometimes received angry questions about Manchuria from the floor during her public lectures. On one occasion, "a sturdy American patriot and national naval hero" sitting at her side burst forth with anti-Japanese sentiments, to which she recalled she responded in a calm manner.[69] From the perspective of her American audience, however, she did not appear as neutral or level-headed as she claimed to have been. Asked about Japanese women's response to Japan's withdrawal from the League of Nations after the Manchurian Incident, she reportedly responded that "in emergencies like that" women of her country would back their own men and their decisions in international politics. She further defended her own government's imperialist actions by claiming: "As long as England has India and the United States has the Philippines and other countries have outside territory, we think Japan has a right to have Manchuria." The reporter noted that Ishimoto presented her argument "with as much conviction *as if she were not a pacifist at all*."[70] As imperial tensions intensified in the 1930s, Ishimoto and other internationalist women found it difficult to maintain their maternalist pacifism and ultimately prioritized the interests of their respective nations.

The records of the International Congress of Women in Chicago show that Ishimoto made similar comments, suggesting her tacit approval of Japan's imperialist invasions abroad. She denounced "excessive nationalism" as a primary source of international conflicts, but she never expressed any outward opposition to her government's war policy in China. On a panel discussion under the theme "Security against War" at the conference, she attempted to justify the actions of the Japanese government as a struggle for survival among other imperial powers:

> Japan today is regarded as threatening world peace with oriental anger. It is said that the Japanese people's intention is to destroy the old gates and historical walls in the cities of China, but that is not true. Japan's action is the expression of [a] desperate effort to relieve the people in the islands of the empire from dire necessity induced by their overpopulated situation. . . . Manchuria is our life or death line, according to the official doctrine. They are right, as things stand.[71]

After a period of rapid industrialization, she argued, the nation faced an unexpected problem of excessive laborers in a small island with limited resources. Ishimoto even blamed other Western nations for their unequal treatment and racism toward this new imperial power:

> In the meantime, the Japanese are working hard. The laborers migrated to the western part of the United States, to the Hawaiian Islands, to Canada, and South America, for they thought the earth belonged equally to all humankind. But the Westerners who had helped to open the doors of Japan to the world, closed their own doors to the Japanese. Australia insisted upon a white Australia. The United States erected barriers against the yellow race. Then Japan patiently tried to support this huge population by developing markets in India, Africa, the Dutch Indies, China, and the United States. Some countries protected their own industries by putting up high tariff walls.[72]

After explaining the desperate position that Japan was forced into, Ishimoto appealed to her Western audience for understanding: "What, then, can Japan do under the present system of free competition? Simply regret that she allowed her country to enter upon a world intercourse, and commit suicide with her starving population?" Her answer was that "the Japanese [were] too energetic and vital for that."[73]

Throughout this emotionally charged argument against national interests and racist exclusion, Ishimoto failed to recognize her own government's imperialist actions or the damage and suffering that they caused in the colonies. Some Japanese Americans took note of Ishimoto's lack of critical insight on Japanese imperialism. New York–based *Nichibei jihō* (Japanese American commercial weekly) reported that Ishimoto did mildly criticize the Japanese government after the Manchurian Incident, but only its increasingly pronatalist stance.[74] Socialist writer Ishigaki Ayako (wife of Ishigaki Eitarō, who arranged Sanger's trip to Japan) showed interest in and even respect toward Ishimoto's cause but also recognized the limitations of her liberal pacifism. While praising Ishimoto's autobiography for showing "a final willingness to face up to the full implications of capitalist exploitation and imperialist aggression," Ishigaki lamented that Ishimoto remained "silent about the Japanese invasion of Manchuria and north China." In particular, Ishigaki was critical of Ishimoto's remarks when she encountered Chinese coolie workers in southern Manchuria: "We were gratefully reminded of the Japanese Mikado; and of the fact that there is no class of human beings in Japan as unprotected as the Chinese coolies." "Does Baroness Ishimoto forget," Ishigaki asked, "that her Emperor's police and armed forces brutally crush strikes and murder workers and peasants?"[75] As a leftist feminist observing Japan's imperialism from outside, Ishigaki was able to see how deeply immersed Ishimoto's views were in the Japanese military government's official discourses on expansionism.

Ishimoto's description in her 1935 autobiography of her first trip to Korea and Manchuria in 1922, to which Ishigaki specifically directed her criticism, indeed reflected her naïve internalization of the Japanese colonizers' paternalistic attitudes toward their "brothers and sisters" in Asia. In the book, Ishimoto reproduced her actual diary entries during her stay in Korea and China. These notes revealed Ishimoto's biases against the Koreans in particular and justified Japan's colonial rule over these people. As she traveled across Korea, she was impressed by "how actively the Japanese directed this annexed people," who, according to her observation, lacked vitality. She did not realize that this perceived "lack of vitality" among Koreans was a result of Japan's colonization. Rather, she found it to be an inherent quality of Koreans and believed that it was the task of Japanese conquerors to uplift them to the standard and quality of the industrious Japanese. As she pondered the future of Korea, she was hopeful that the Japanese colonizers could bring prosperity to "our Korean brothers." Ishimoto was more respectful toward the Chinese, however. She found them to be "a busy people" struggling to make a living after "the ruins of a great empire." She sympathized with the Chinese laborers in southern Manchuria, who were "exploited by foreign capital" and "devoid of a strong government to protect them."[76] At the time of her original notes in 1922, she may not have expected that Japan would yet extend its empire to this area. Nonetheless, the fact that she uncritically reproduced these earlier diary entries in her autobiography suggests that, at least at the time of publication in 1935, she did not fundamentally alter or reject her belief in the Japanese imperial government's paternalistic role in Korea, Manchuria, and other parts of Asia. Because Ishimoto intentionally published her autobiography in English for the American audience, she apparently did not write this for the purpose of pleasing the Japanese authorities by showing her support for Japan's imperial projects abroad.[77]

Ishimoto's ignorance and naïve approval of Japan's paternalistic roles in Asia were perhaps a typical response to Japan's Manchurian invasion among many contemporary Japanese bourgeois women. For example, Hiratsuka Raichō, who was more critical of the military's imperialist actions than her fellow feminists, criticized the Japanese delegates of the 1928 PPWC for neglecting to address the issue of Sino-Japanese relations at the conference. In particular, Hiratsuka described the pacifism espoused by the Women's Peace Association in Japan, headed by WCTU leader Gauntlet Tsuneko, as a "childish abstract theory." She thus demanded practical discussions on the matter, but her own vision of maternalist pacifism also remained vague and confined within the state apparatus. Hiratsuka was, in fact, a leading force behind feminist efforts to enlist state support for motherhood, as best exemplified by the 1920 campaign, under the auspices of the New Women's Association (Shin fujin kyōkai), to prohibit men with venereal disease from marrying.[78] After the Manchurian Incident, Gauntlet did issue a statement of "apology" to the Chinese, which, on the surface, seemed to refute Hiratsuka's previous accusation that women's international pacifism was nothing more than a "festive party."[79] In reality, however, the Euro-American women of WILPF had urged Gauntlet to oppose the Japanese government's policies in Manchuria. Later during a four-week inspection tour of Manchuria, Gauntlet allegedly strengthened her conviction that the Japanese presence was necessary for the development of Manchuria.[80]

Even after the eruption of war with China in 1937, Ishimoto continued to possess an idealized vision of universal sisterhood without questioning the actions of the Japanese military abroad. Ishimoto was, in fact, aware of the atrocities in Nanking by the Japanese Army in December 1937, because her American friends in Japan had shown her some photographs of the incident.[81] Nonetheless, in a letter to Gladys Smith dated February 23, 1938, she simply noted in regard to the war situation in China: "We are sorry for the Chinese people but we too have to suffer much."[82] In a letter to Sanger's secretary, Florence Rose, Ishimoto similarly stressed that soldiers and people in both countries were "suffering alike," although this time she added that "it would be much worse in China which we feel sorry for them."[83] Still at this point, she did not absolutely denounce the Japanese military's actions, even in these private English letters.

The American public, however, did not accept Ishimoto's appeal to share the sorrow and suffering of war beyond national hostilities. In 1939, Ishimoto's English translation of Tamai Katsunori's (pseudonym Hino Ashihei) *Wheat and Soldiers*, a common Japanese soldier's account of serving in China, appeared in American bookstores. Many American readers were critical of the book for glossing over the evils and horror perpetuated by the Japanese against the Chinese. Reviewers saw Ishimoto as an apologist who had converted to a pro-military position to atone for her previous antigovernment activities advocating birth control.[84] In fact, Ishimoto did not believe that the young soldiers were responsible for the brutal acts; only the leaders were. As a mother of two soldiers herself, Ishimoto intended to present the story as a "human cry" of a common soldier and an "indignation against war," to which, she expected, the American and Japanese readers alike would respond with "human hearts."[85]

Ishimoto soon realized that her ambiguous position toward Japan's imperialist invasions could cause a rift with her beloved American friends. Soon after the publication of *Wheat and Soldiers* in the United States, Ishimoto received what she described as a "breakup letter" (*zekkōjō*) from Mary Beard. Beard reproached Ishimoto for taking up such a project that appeared to glorify Japan's military invasion. Ishimoto was so shocked by Beard's response, she recalled, that she shed tears of frustration and lost her appetite for days. She despaired over the fragility of her cosmopolitan ideals and transnational friendships.[86] After that incident, Ishimoto started to express, mainly to her American friends, harsher criticism of the Japanese Army's actions in China and distinguished herself from her former liberal friends who had embraced militaristic ideas.[87]

Similarly, nationalist tensions started to hamper the friendships and networks of other internationalist women in the late 1930s. In fact, the tensions were much more explicit than what Ishimoto had experienced, as many of these bourgeois women became directly co-opted into the state apparatus and actively supported the war effort. Many Japanese women leaders increasingly defended their government's vision of a new regional order in Asia under the Japanese Empire, often at the expense of their friendships with Asian and Western colleagues. Manako Ogawa describes how the Japanese WCTU women, for example, created their own version of the Greater East Asia Co-Prosperity Sphere by reaching out directly—without American and British interference—to the Japanese residents and natives in Manchuria, northern China, and Taiwan, and absorbing the Korean WCTU branch under Japanese auspices.[88]

Like Ishimoto, Japanese internationalist women defended Japan's expansionism when they brought up their overpopulation issue as a matter affecting world peace. While typically "etiquette forbade" internationalist women from discussing the matter of birth control in international meetings, the Japanese delegates requested that the "population problem" be included in the agenda of the 1937 PPWC in Vancouver.[89] The Women's Peace Association in Japan, headed by Inoue Hide, president of Japan Women's University, organized the Sub-Committee for the Study of the Population Problem to prepare a special report for the Population Pressures Round Table at the conference. In the document, the Japanese representatives illustrated the seriousness of Japan's population situation by comparing the population density of Japan with those of other small and populated nations such as Great Britain, Belgium, and Holland, whose degree of density, they claimed, decreased significantly after taking into account their respective colonies. To alleviate the situation, they argued, Japan needed to further industrialize itself by gaining equal access to raw materials and foreign markets. Although emigration itself would not solve the overpopulation problem, the Japanese representatives believed that it could serve as a "psychological outlet for the public mind." They asserted that an "experimental emigration" program to Manchuria since 1931 had shown satisfactory results, even though the severity of the climate limited the possibility of mass-scale migration of the Japanese to this land.[90]

The conflict between nationalism and internationalism among internationalist women immediately came to the surface during the Round Table discussion at the 1937 conference. The Japanese delegates pleaded for "a spirit of friendliness and fairness"—beyond "emotional prejudices" based on racial grounds—on the part of Western nations blessed with land and resources. At one point, one of them posed fundamental questions to the Western women in the room: "Why do you exclude our people? Are we inferior?"[91] A Chinese delegate turned the tables on the Japanese, arguing that Japan had seized an area that the Chinese themselves needed as a population outlet and market. Since the previous conference in 1934 Chinese internationalist women, too, had pleaded for "non-aggression and the friendly attitude of foreign powers"—especially their "immediate neighbors." At the same time, they stopped short of bringing the Manchurian problem "up for discussion" in a direct and confrontational manner. The Sino-Japanese War erupted during the 1937 PPWC, and Gauntlet privately requested that delegates not bring up the subject during the meeting.[92]

Despite the inevitable nationalist tension, delegates from Canada, Australia, and the United States, who directed and facilitated the Round Table, pleaded for a "non-emotional consideration of this question."[93] They attributed the "racial feeling" and "discriminating immigration policies" of their nations to the "economic slump" as well as the lack of "conscious effort to become a citizen of his adopted nation" on the part of immigrants from overpopulated countries. Downplaying the racial and political aspects of exclusion policies specifically targeting Asian immigrants and instead framing the issue primarily in economic terms, the Western women avoided further direct confrontation of racial and national matters that threatened to thwart their internationalist efforts and friendship.[94]

One thing that the women at the PPWC representing different national interests and perspectives seemed to share, however, was their ambiguous position in regard to practicing birth control in their own countries, even for the sake of international peace and economic security. The Japanese report mentioned the impact of Margaret Sanger's 1922 visit to Japan and Ishimoto Shizue's subsequent activities to spread the philosophy of birth control. They denied its effectiveness, nonetheless, due to the opposition of authorities and the supposed lack of interest among both the upper and lower classes of women. While the "desirability of birth control is often mentioned by foreigners," they argued, "it must be remembered that birth control is not a legalized method for reducing population, either in Japan, or in other countries throughout the world."[95] Even though the directors of the Round Table urged delegates from "underpopulated areas" to also consider the state of birth control policies and their usefulness, most Western women were obviously uncomfortable when discussing the birth control situation in their own domestic contexts. The admission by one US delegate of the wide use of birth control among Christian women reportedly caused consternation among other Western delegates.[96] Among the recommended readings in preparation for the Round Table, the Western organizers listed only one work in which Sanger was involved: the first of four volumes for the proceedings of the Sixth International Neo-Malthusian and Birth Control Conference held in New York in 1925, edited and published by Sanger as *International Aspects of Birth Control*. Given this conservative position in regard to birth control as a personal and domestic issue, it is not surprising that both Sanger and Ishimoto, the two women representing the birth control movements across the Pacific, were mentioned only in passing.

Birth control thus failed to serve as a unifying subject for female empowerment or as a pacifist topic for international understanding during the interwar period. Even as these internationalist women emphasized women's roles as mothers in forming bonds and friendships beyond national differences, in the end they could not escape the paternalistic oppression against women's sexuality at home as well as the imperialist pressures for hegemony in international politics.

. . .

If feminists failed to discuss birth control—whether as a women's rights issue or a peace issue—in international meetings in the late 1930s, it became even more difficult for them to bring up the topic in political activities and conversations at home. Even though Ishimoto did not directly confront the nationalist and imperialist discourses of her government, she was nonetheless considered a "black sheep" among her fellow bourgeois women in Japan.[97] In fact, under the wartime pronatalist policy, her reputation as a birth control advocate automatically made her the subject of police surveillance. In December 1937, Ishimoto was arrested as part of a massive police raid against radicals harboring "dangerous thoughts." Although she was quickly released from jail, she was one of the two women—out of nearly five hundred people—arrested in the raid. American newspapers also delivered the news of the arrest of America's favorite Japanese feminist.[98] The reports indicated that the military had finally silenced one of the last pro-American voices in Japan.

Meanwhile, suffrage leader Ichikawa Fusae and many other women leaders actively assisted the nation through government councils and women's organizations such as the Greater Japan Alliance of Women's Organizations (Dai-Nihon fujin dantai renmei) and the Patriot Women's Association (Aikoku fujinkai). The Japanese WCTU severed its affiliation with Anglo-American branches and earnestly supported official campaigns against smoking, drinking, and prostitution.[99] Many of the feminist leaders who had previously shown interest in the birth control cause now focused their maternalist campaigns on securing state assistance through legislative reforms aimed to protect the eugenic fitness of Japanese children. The Mother and Child Protection Law (Boshi hogo hō) was promulgated in 1937 to assist mothers and children in fatherless families.[100] In 1938, the Greater Japan Alliance of Women's Organizations resumed the petition campaign to prohibit marriage by individuals with venereal diseases. The new campaign no longer singled out men as carriers of diseases but asked for strict medical examinations for infected pregnant women and prostitutes.[101] Even though Ishimoto shared with these patriotic women the belief in state protection of motherhood, she did not take part in these wartime activities and chose to retreat from public life for the duration of war.

As I describe in detail in the following chapter, Sanger, too, despite her initial effort to transcend racial and national borders, would be caught in the tension of imperialist conflicts. While she remained a radical in the eyes of many of her contemporary feminists, she increasingly distanced herself from her earlier socialist associations as well as from her feminist aspirations. Perhaps more rigorously and explicitly than Ishimoto, Sanger aligned her birth control activism with the interests of other social reformers in the United States seeking to establish a renewed world order in the Pacific under white leadership.

THREE

Danger Spots in World Population
The Eugenic and Imperial Struggles in the Pacific

In 1939, the *Los Angeles Times* gave a rave review of Ishimoto Shizue's autobiography, *Facing Two Ways*. Calling it "a noble book written in a noble cause by a noble woman," the article praised Ishimoto as the "Margaret Sanger of Japan."[1] The author of the piece was Fred Hogue, an active member of the American Eugenics Society, who wrote a column called "Social Eugenics," which ran in the Sunday edition of the *Times* from 1935 to 1941. Having lived in Japan for a few years, Hogue had developed a special interest in the Japanese government's population and sterilization policies and frequently wrote about them in his columns. Hogue's review of *Facing Two Ways* piqued the interest of his readers, prompting some of them to write to ask for more information about Ishimoto. The following week Hogue obliged, writing another article that described the development of the birth control movement in Japan after Sanger's visit in 1922. "The seed then sown did not all fall on barren soil," he reported, "for the Japanese government has since legalized sterilization of the unfit, and birth control clinics now operate in leading Japanese municipalities."[2]

Hogue and other American eugenicists' interest in spreading birth control in Japan represented an ongoing discussion about differential birth rates between races across the world. Social and scientific ideas about race and fertility reflected the anxiety that many intellectuals and national leaders had felt since the turn of the century as the United States emerged as a world leader, replacing the European powers. Declining birth rates in western European countries, as well as among the "native-stock" population in

83

the United States, triggered discussions on race degeneracy and "race suicide." Those with such concerns directed their fear to what they considered the overly fertile, colored races. The increased nonwhite population, they argued, resulted in the outward thrust for immigration and military expansionism of these peoples across the planet. The demographic Yellow Peril seemed to threaten the stability of white world hegemony. These eugenic fears propelled the anti-Japanese immigration campaigns in California, which emerged following the anti-Chinese movement around the turn of the century and intensified in the early 1920s. Although the passage of the 1924 Immigration Act had codified the national body and its citizens as white, some Americans still worried that the Japanese, now denied the option of international migration to places considered white people's territories as outlets for their excess populations, would increasingly resort to aggressive military expansionism to obtain land abroad, especially in China. As far as the eugenicists could see, the immigration policies could address only the domestic problems of race relations. They therefore believed that international cooperation or agreement was further needed to deal with the differential birth rates of nations and races across the globe for the sake of world peace.

In this context, a new generation of scholars in "population studies" emerged in the 1930s as practitioners in a legitimate academic field to study the problem of differential fertility among races and nations across the world. Nongovernmental and private organizations such as the Rockefeller Foundation played a crucial part in supporting these studies on human fertility across the world, especially in Asia. By this time, a growing number of social scientists had become vocally critical of the pseudoscientific work of their precursors, what historian Daniel Kevles calls "mainline" eugenics. The "reform" eugenicists—most scholars in population studies belonged to this new branch of eugenics—claimed to use more objective and mathematical methods of analysis than the value-ridden and politically charged approaches of mainline eugenicists.[3] In reality, however, they reiterated many of the same political concerns regarding race, class, and fertility. Eugenicists of whatever stripe agreed that it was imperative to spread the practice of birth control to those deemed as undesirable elements of human society, domestically and internationally, to prevent the otherwise inevitable decline of their great civilization. Nonetheless, similar to the liberal internationalist women's networks that flourished during the interwar period, these eugenicists represented a pacifist and anti-imperialist movement to prevent war and clashes of interests in the Pacific believed to be caused by the outward thrust of overpopulated peoples with limited resources.

As their fears of overpopulation in Asia intensified, eugenicists turned their attention to Margaret Sanger's transnational birth control campaigns. Whereas birth control failed to gain wide support at home for fears about its dysgenic effect of reducing the birth rates among upper- and middle-class women, it was touted as a solution to reduce the world's teeming populations. In other words, while eugenicists saw birth control as "racially devastating"—as described by Charles Darwin himself—if practiced too widely by white women, they saw it as noble and humanitarian when advocated to the impoverished and overpopulated colored peoples abroad.[4] For this reason Fred Hogue would approvingly note that "Margaret Sanger, condemned to prison for her birth control activities in the Untied States, [was] regarded in Japan as the greatest woman America has produced."[5] Despite the actual mixed perceptions about Sanger and increasing regulations against birth control activities in the 1930s in Japan, Hogue and many other American eugenicists stressed the importance of spreading reproductive control exclusively in such crowded nations, as desired by the men and women in the East themselves.

Sanger took advantage of this growing interest in birth control among eugenicists concerned about international relations. To gain their endorsement, however, she increasingly distanced herself from her radical, feminist, and antiauthoritarian associations to assume a more respectable, scientific, and international approach. She gradually shifted the nature of her activism to adjust to the interests of male professionals and eugenicists, who sought to obscure their involvement with Sanger and took control of the professional gatherings that she organized. Developments in international politics as well as Sanger's own efforts thus helped expand the birth control movement in the decades leading to World War II, unwittingly at the sacrifice of its original spirit of feminist rebellion and women's liberation worldwide.

The Rising Tide of Color

The "race suicide" debate took place in the United States between the 1890s and the 1930s, just as white and middle-class women started to espouse the idea of voluntary motherhood. Fears that immigrants and the poor were reproducing at a faster rate than the "native" Anglo-Saxon stock had existed since before the Civil War. These concerns, however, became more tangible when in 1891 noted economist Francis Amasa Walker presented the first comprehensive statistics documenting the declining birth rates of native Americans from 1850 to 1890, which, he argued, had been caused by the presence of foreign immigrants.[6] As historian Gail Bederman argues, what was new in the 1890s was the growing fear among American elites that the white civilization was becoming more decadent and effeminate.[7] Such fear among white middle-class men emerged in response to various changes in American society during the turn of the twentieth century, including the rise of the women's movement, economic competition with working-class and immigrant men, and the new challenges that the nation faced as it expanded its influences abroad, especially in Asia.

Sociologist Edward Ross first coined the term "race suicide" in his 1901 speech "The Causes of Race Superiority." After laying out the superior qualities that supposedly characterized the (Anglo-Saxon) Americans—energy, self-reliance, foresight, and self-control—Ross noted that there was one respect in which those very qualities that "marked the higher race [dug] a pit beneath its feet": low fertility. Ross explained that Americans tended to refrain from increasing their families to maintain a high "standard of comfort," a phenomenon that created "a fatal weakness" in them when they attempted to "compete industrially with a capable race that multiplies on a lower plane." To illustrate this point, Ross cited the example of "Asiatics" who "flock[ed] to this country and, enjoying equal opportunities under our laws, learn[ed] our methods and compete[d] actively with Americans." According to Ross, there were three possible outcomes of such competition. First, the Americans would relinquish their high standards and begin to multiply as freely as their Asian competitors. The high value attached to the quality of life, Ross believed, made this theory unlikely. Second, the Asians would adopt the standards and customs of Americans. Ross also ruled out this possibility because he believed that Asian immigrants would not relinquish their cultural pride and heritage. The final scenario was "the silent replacement of Americans by Asiatics . . . until the latter monopolize all industrial occupations, and the American shrink to a superior caste . . . hopelessly beaten and displaced as a race." This, Ross declared, was nothing less than "race suicide."[8]

In his influential book *The Old World in the New* (1904), Ross further warned that the influx of "low-standard immigrants"—Italians, Hungarians, Portuguese, Greeks, Syrians, Hebrews, Slavs, and Russians—was "the root cause of the mysterious 'sterility' of Americans." "The fewer brains they have to contribute," he asserted, "the lower the place immigrants take among us, and the lower the place they take, the faster they multiply."[9] About a decade later, Madison Grant further popularized this apocalyptic message in his best-selling book *The Passing of the Great Race* (1916). Grant lamented that America had been infiltrated by "a large and increasing number of the weak, the broken and the mentally crippled of all races drawn from the lowest stratum of the Mediterranean basin and the Balkans, together with the hordes of the wretched, submerged populations of the Polish Ghetto." In the end, Grant predicted that the resulting decline in birth rates among the Nordic race in America would soon drive the ruling race to extinction. All the while, the new immigrants would "adopt the language of the native Americans; they [would] wear his clothes; they [would] steal his name; and they [were] beginning to take his women."[10]

Scientific knowledge of heredity provided further justification to these exclusionist sentiments. The vogue for eugenics was sweeping the nation during the first few decades of the twentieth century. Local eugenics groups sprouted up across the United States, leading to the formation of the American Eugenics Society in 1923. The Eugenics Record Office established in Cold Spring Harbor, New York, in 1910 became the bastion of eugenics pedigree studies, collecting the genetic backgrounds of both "gifted" and "burdened" American families.[11] In 1908, psychologist Henry H. Goddard brought the Binet-Simon intelligence tests from Europe to the United States to quantitatively measure the degree of intelligence and, in particular, to prove the heritability of feeblemindedness. The results of these tests suggested that the Alpine and Mediterranean races were intellectually inferior to the Nordic race and that the average intelligence of immigrants was declining.[12]

While anti-immigration sentiments against Asians developed in tandem with eugenic efforts to exclude the inferior races from southern and eastern Europe, racial fears about Asian immigrants were quite different from the concerns about their European counterparts, who were ultimately expected to Americanize. The problem of Asian immigrants on the West Coast was not the degenerative effects of assimilation. Instead, the unassimilability of these alien immigrants, both for social and biological reasons, was the prime reason for their exclusion. Because there would be no or few intermarriages, eugenicists declared that the result would be a "race war" between the "Asiatics" and the white Americans, the former outnumbering and outliving the latter.

International politics further complicated domestic policies about Japanese immigration, and the US president soon weighed in on the issue. Theodore Roosevelt, who espoused Edward Ross's race suicide theory, believed that the importation of Japanese immigrant labor would cause permanent damage to the American racial body. Roosevelt used social Darwinist and evolutionary theories of race to explain the US roles and position in the world.[13] He had no problem defending the exclusion of Chinese immigrants, who he claimed had fallen into "racial decadence," as well as America's imperialist domination over the Filipinos and Latin Americans, "backward peoples" who needed white men's tutelage and protection.[14] Roosevelt, however, struggled to justify the exclusion of Japanese immigrants, whom he praised as "a great civilized power of a formidable type." As the rise of a Japanese Empire became a more realistic threat after its victory over Russia in 1905, his pro-Japanese perceptions were increasingly tempered by racial fear. Japanese immigrants could not only emasculate white men as breadwinners but, with their presumably virile sexual behavior, could even steal their women. He therefore rejected mass Japanese immigration not because "either nation is inferior to the other" but because the two races were fundamentally different and any intermixture could end "disastrously." The resulting measure was the Gentlemen's Agreement of 1907, in which Japan agreed not to issue passports to laborers while the United States in turn continued to admit the arrival of "gentlemen," students, and the families of immigrants.[15]

Soon intellectuals across the nation heatedly debated the impact of Japanese immigration on the eugenic future of the United States. In September 1909, the *Annals of the American Academy of Political and Social Science* featured an issue on "Chinese and Japanese in America."[16] Supporters of anti-Japanese measures expressed the same racial images of the Japanese as articulated by Ross, Roosevelt, and other adherents of the race suicide theory to justify their exclusion from the United States. Not only did they draw a distinct line between the assimilable European immigrants on the East Coast and the unassimilable Asians on the West, but some also tried to sort out the differences between the Japanese and the Chinese, the latter already barred by the Chinese Exclusion Act of 1882. The situation was more pressing than it was before, they argued, because unlike the "patient, "docile," and "submissive" Chinese immigrants, the Japanese were "virile," "energetic," and "versatile." These qualities could be especially threatening to the poor whites competing in the same farm industries, who could consequently be rendered into a "menial caste." Moreover, America's foreign relations were at stake. They considered the "Japanese problem" an especially "thorny" subject because there was "no prouder or more sensitive race than the Japanese"; if they used the same "methods pursued in the exclusion of the Chinese," they could provoke a "race war" with this Oriental power, which would likely end in "mutual destruction."[17]

Another influential book, *The Rising Tide of Color against White World-Supremacy* (1920) by Harvard-educated historian and eugenicist Lothrop Stoddard, further helped popularize the idea of an impending Yellow Peril. Stoddard based his theory on earlier works of eugenicists such as Edward Ross and Madison Grant, who blamed the cause of race suicide and race degeneracy primarily on southern and eastern European immigrants.[18] America, however, was now facing an even greater threat, as Stoddard wrote:

> This extended discussion of the evil effects of even white immigration has, in my opinion, been necessary in order to get a proper perspective for viewing the problem of colored immigration. For it is perfectly obvious that if the influx of inferior kindred stocks is bad, the influx of wholly alien stocks is infinitely worse. When we see the damage wrought in America, for example, by the coming of persons who, after all, nearly all possess the basic ideas of white civilization, we can grasp the incalculably greater damage which would be wrought by the coming of persons wholly alien in blood and possessed of idealistic and cultural backgrounds absolutely different from ours.[19]

Stoddard thus stressed that the threat posed by immigrants on the East Coast, who were after all "kindred stocks" of "white civilization," was trivial compared to the gravity of the effects of Asian immigration—the "wholly alien stocks"—on the future of their white nation.

To fully understand the threat of growing Asian immigration to the white land, Stoddard explained, one needed to study world politics and international race relations after 1905. The Russo-Japanese War was a watershed moment, as it proved that "the yellow and brown races . . . stirred by the very impact of Western ideas, measured the white man with a more critical eye and commenced to wonder whether his superiority was due to anything more than a fortuitous combination of circumstances which might be altered by efforts of their own." Subsequently, World War I—the "White Civil War"—showed a "frightful weakening of the white world," opening up revolutionary possibilities for the colored races. In fact, Japan presented itself as the champion of the colored races at the Versailles Conference by urging a formal promulgation of racial equality as part of the peace settlement, especially in regard to immigration. The Russian Bolshevik Revolution of 1917, what Stoddard called "a war of the hand against the brain," was a final blow to white solidarity. The revolution represented an atavistic tendency that was crippling the white race, he argued, as the Russians sought to form a revolutionary block with the Orient.[20]

Stoddard's work represented a new trend among American intellectuals, in which authors emphasized the unity of the white race in opposition to the colored races. Stoddard accepted the hierarchal relation of the three main "subspecies" of the white race—the Nordic, the Alpine, and the Mediterranean—but still considered all these European groups "ranking in genetic worth well above the various colored races."[21] As historian Matthew Jacobson analyzes, since around the 1920s, the perceived differences within the white race lost salience in public concern, replaced by a preoccupation with the "major divisions": the Caucasian, the Mongolian, and the Negroid. Jacobson identifies some factors that led to this transition, including the passage of the 1924 Immigration Act, which effectively ended the debates over European immigration; the massive migrations of African Americans from the rural South to the cities in the North and West between the 1910s and 1940s; and, later, the racial policies in Nazi Germany in the 1930s.[22] Stoddard's work and the race suicide debates preceding it show another important factor that affected the American perceptions about race *before* the 1920s: the rise of Japanese power.

The "Picture Bride Evil"

The scholarly discussions about race suicide, differential fertility, and the eugenic impact of immigrants on the American national body in the early twentieth century developed in tandem with the ongoing anti-Japanese campaigns in California. They provided scientific credibility and political urgency to provincial labor disputes, connecting the matter to the well-being and future survival of the entire nation, specifically the white race. By the 1920s, Japanese female immigrants were often singled out for perpetuating the evils of invasion into white lands, not only as laborers but also as fertile producers of nonwhite offspring. This was not the first time Asian women were the target of anti-immigration sentiments. The Page Act of 1875 barred the importation of women from "China, Japan, or any Oriental country" for the purpose of prostitution.[23] This legislation in effect excluded most Chinese women from the United States, regardless of whether they actually engaged in prostitution or not. The law successfully prevented most Chinese immigrants from forming families in the new land. Decades later, Japanese women were starting to enter the country as wives of immigrants, most of them newlyweds. The arrival of these young women posed a renewed threat to nativists, as their entry meant that the Japanese immigrants would settle and propagate in the white land. The anti-immigration debates led to many political and legal measures, ultimately leading to the exclusion of all Asian immigration through the 1924 Johnson-Reed Immigration Act.

Even though hostility against Japanese Americans subsided temporarily during World War I, anti-Japanese sentiments resurged after the war, and eugenic ideas appeared prominently in policy discussions on both local and federal levels. Although the California legislature passed the Alien Land Law in 1913, which banned land ownership by "aliens ineligible of citizenship," legal ambiguity left the law virtually ineffective in excluding Japanese farmers.[24] The state legislature therefore proposed in the spring of 1919 further legislation against the Japanese. Upon hearing the news, however, Secretary of State Robert Lansing cabled from Versailles and advised the legislature to defer any action. Lansing was allegedly concerned that anti-Japanese legislation might negatively affect the negotiations at the peace conference, in which the Japanese delegates accused the United States of racist immigration laws.[25] Despite this setback, exclusionists who were dissatisfied with the anti-Japanese land laws at the state level started to appeal directly to Congress to take remedial measures at the federal level. In June 1919, the House of Representatives convened hearings before the Committee on Immigration and Naturalization, chaired by Congressman Albert Johnson (Republican, Washington), in Washington, D.C. Vocal anti-immigrationists, such as California newspaperman V. S. McClatchy and US senator James D. Phelan, testified and made lengthy statements on the undesirability of Japanese immigrants.[26]

These anti-Japanese agitators put forth three main reasons for excluding the Japanese: (1) the nonassimilability of the Japanese race, (2) economic competition with white laborers, and (3) the unusually high birth rate of Japanese women. They used these claims to argue that the attitude of Californians was not a matter of racial prejudice, even praising the Japanese as industrious and respectful. Rather, they attributed their exclusionist reaction to the scientific facts of biological differences and emphasized that it was simply a defensive act for self-preservation.[27]

The issue of birth rates, in particular, was a new focal point that emerged in the anti-Japanese immigration debates after World War I. Exclusionists frequently pointed out the violation of the Gentlemen's Agreement and singled out one group in particular as the primary source of such evil: the "picture brides."[28] These Japanese women who immigrated through arranged marriages based solely on prior exchanges of pictures posed a new threat to Californians not only as laborers but also as mothers of Japanese subjects. McClatchy claimed that the picture brides would usually give birth once a year after they arrived.[29] Citing the vital statistics obtained from the California State Board of Health from 1906—before the Gentlemen's Agreement—to 1917, Phelan similarly asserted that, while white births decreased by 8 percent, there was a marked increase in Japanese birth registrations: from 134 to 4,108—a 3,000 percent increase.[30] If this trend continued, he warned, it would mean "the end of the white race in California, subdivision of American institutions and the end of our Western civilization."[31] Lothrop Stoddard also described in *The Rising Tide of Color* that the agricultural lands in California "teem[ed] with babies" of Japanese immigrants. The resulting fate of whites in America, he claimed, would be "social sterilization and ultimate racial extinction."[32] These alarmist arguments popularized the idea that the Yellow Peril came not just from the virile Japanese men but now even from their women and children.

To give substance to these perceived dangers, Governor William Stephens of California requested that the State Board of Control compile necessary information to urge further action both by the state and the federal government. In his letter to Secretary of the State Bainbridge Colby dated June 19, 1920, the governor laid out all the familiar arguments for excluding the Japanese: "the ethnological impossibility" to assimilate Ori-

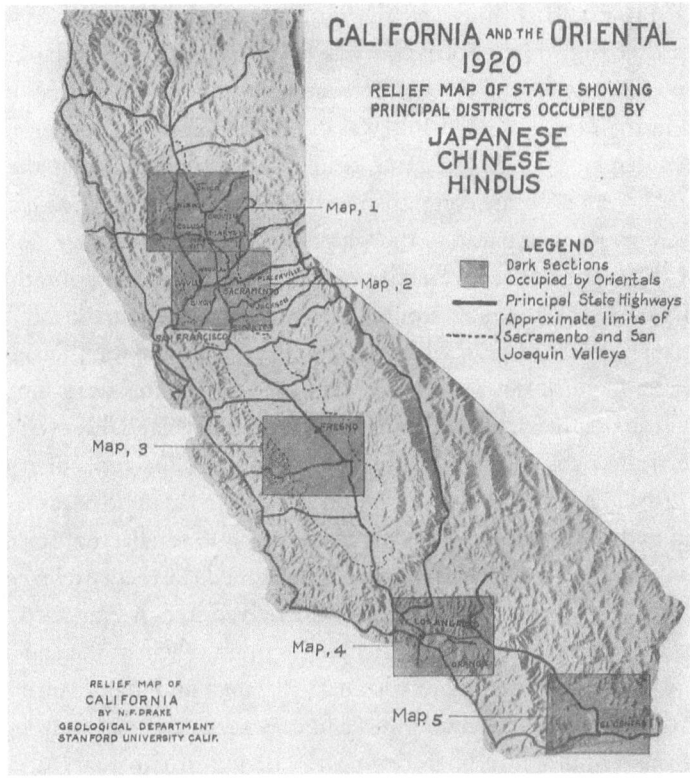

FIGURE 3.1. Map of California showing the "dark sections occupied by Orientals." From California State Board of Control, *California and the Oriental*, 54.

ental blood; the racial qualities of the Japanese as "virile, progressive and agressive [sic]"; "the principle of race self-preservation" with no "pretensions of race superiority"; the "skillful evasions" of the Gentlemen's Agreement; and the fecundity of Japanese women that "far exceeds that of any other people." Stephens thus declared: "Unless the race ideals and standards are preserved here at the national gateway the conditions that will follow must soon affect the rest of the continent."[33]

Accompanying his letter, Stephens sent to Washington the report made by the State Board of Control, which "graphically" told their story in "its cold, statistical way."[34] The report carried statistics that focused on the increasing Japanese population in California and the high birth rate of Japanese women compared to that of native white women (Fig. 3.1). Contrary to the tone of Stephens's letter and the alarming statistics presented by other exclusionists, however, the numbers did not necessarily support the idea that the white population was being replaced by the Japanese. It did show that the fecundity rate (percentage of births to mothers) of white women in their fertile ages in 1910 was 9.9 percent and 28.8 percent for Japanese women in 1919. At the same time, the report noted that the numbers were not an accurate comparison, since the Japanese, being new to the land, were young compared to the whites, who had resided there for a longer period of time. If these variables were considered, the authors admitted, "the disparity in birth rates would undoubtedly be less marked." The report further conceded that, while the Japanese birth rate was "far in excess of other nationalities in this state," such high birth rates were "not infrequently true of a new people immigrating into a new land." It even carried a quote from a statement made by the Japanese Association of America, which insisted that the birth rate would fall as the Japanese became Americanized and obtained better social, economic, and intellectual status. The report's data on picture brides further undermined the theory of excessively fertile Japanese women: of 524 brides who arrived in San Francisco during the year 1918, there were 182 recorded births among them at the end of 1919. As Sidney L. Gulick, a former missionary in Japan and major voice in support of the Japanese, contended, these figures suggested that only 34.8 percent of these brides gave birth during the period of two years, a number not in any way high for a group of newlyweds.[35]

The report nonetheless served to confirm the widely popularized perception of the Japanese invasion in California. The authors in the end found the potential gravity of the Japanese situation in the gap in ratio between Japanese men and women in California: 3 to 1. "What would it be," they asked, "were there Japanese women in California sufficient for each Japanese man to establish a household?"[36] In other words, even if the figures did not yet suggest any overwhelming evidence of differential fertility, there could still be an impending threat assuming that Japanese women would continue to immigrate until they reached the same proportion as the number of men. The *Los Angeles Times*, in covering the synopsis of the report, further distorted the situation with a sensational headline: "The Jap Menace in California: State Board of Control's Report Gives to Federal Government Startling Proof of the Coming Domination of State by Yellow Hordes from Far East."[37]

With growing attention to the topic, in January 1921 the *Annals of the*

American Academy again ran a special issue devoted to the topic: "Present-Day Immigration with Special Reference to the Japanese." Contributors to this issue included state officials such as chairman of the State Board of Control Marshall de Motte and State Controller John S. Chambers, as well as other prominent anti-Japanese advocates such as James Phelan, V. S. McClatchy, and Lothrop Stoddard. To give a fair treatment to the matter, the journal also carried the views of those defending Japanese immigrants or criticizing the "anti-American" attitude of their opponents, including former missionary in Japan and secretary of the National Committee for Constructive Immigration Legislation Sidney L. Gulick, prominent Seattle businessman Reginald H. Parsons, and general secretary of the Japanese Association of America Kiichi Kanzaki.

Indeed, the articles in the *Annals* revealed that there was a small, but vocal, group of Americans—clergymen, businessmen, university professors, and Japanese Americans—who spoke against the anti-Japanese sentiments sweeping across the nation.[38] But much like that of the anti-immigrationists, their contention was not so much about the individual rights of immigrants and women but instead reflected their concerns for the US image in the world. While some defended Japanese immigration based on the principles of democracy and equality, others worried that local racial agitation could hurt US diplomatic and trade relations with Japan. These critics used the same numbers presented by the State Board and other census reports to argue that the difference between the birth rates of white and Japanese populations was not as striking as it was often portrayed.[39] As secretary of the American League of Justice Earl S. Parker put it, the real Yellow Peril in California was not Japanese immigration but "yellow journalism and yellow politics."[40]

As the heat of anti-immigration debates intensified, the House Committee on Immigration and Naturalization traveled to California in July 1920 to hold hearings specifically on the Japanese immigration question, beginning in San Francisco, continuing in other California cities, and concluding in the state of Washington.[41] Just as in the articles in the *Annals*, the testimony represented both strong anti-Japanese and more favorable opinions. As Sidney Gulick observed, however, none of the witnesses actually called for unlimited Japanese immigration; the pro-Japanese spokesmen focused their attention on providing equal treatment to those who were already in the United States.[42] The hearings, together with State Board's report, played a crucial role in the passage of a referendum in California in November, which aimed to tighten up the 1913 Land Law to prevent further acquisition of land by the Japanese.[43]

Meanwhile, a US Supreme Court decision that denied Japanese immigrants' eligibility to citizenship further aided the ongoing anti-Japanese campaigns. Before 1922, there was no specific reference to the eligibility of the Japanese in the naturalization act, which restricted the right of naturalization to "free whites" and "persons of African descent." The Chinese Exclusion Act classified the Chinese as inadmissible into citizenship, but it did not mention the Japanese. Finally, in its l922 landmark case, *Takao Ozawa v. United States*, the Supreme Court cleared the ambiguity surrounding the racial status of the Japanese by declaring that the Japanese, classified as members of the Mongolian race, were ineligible for citizenship.[44] The court ruling thus confirmed one of the core arguments of anti-Japanese debates: the nonassimilability of Asian immigrants.

Soon after the court decision, the House Committee on Immigration and Naturalization submitted a bill to Congress to ban Japanese immigration. Since there was not enough time to pass the bill in the Sixty-Seventh Congress, a clause barring the immigration of "aliens ineligible to citizenship" was inserted into an immigration bill proposed in the next congressional session in December 1923, which targeted immigrants from mainly southern and eastern Europe. Although the bill did not specifically single out the Japanese, it was clear that they were the main targets because other "aliens ineligible to citizenship," such as the Chinese and Asian Indians, were already banned by previous immigration laws.

The immigration bill was a crystallization of eugenic fears about differential fertility and racial degeneration in the United States. While eugenic ideas were already present in previous immigration laws, in the 1920s their impact was much more tangible.[45] Nationally prominent eugenicists such as Harry Laughlin, Lothrop Stoddard, and Madison Grant provided critical testimony before Congress and helped frame the actual bill with the bill's cosponsor, Albert Johnson, who was also an ardent adherent of eugenics. With the concerted support from powerful eugenicists, the Johnson-Reed Immigration Act was passed in 1924.

At this point, the anti-immigrationists/eugenicists did not necessarily advocate birth control to Japanese American women as a solution to their supposed high fecundity; closing the doors for immigration was the top priority. Many eugenicists were still ambivalent about endorsing the idea of birth control, at least until the mid-1920s. However, immigration restriction could protect the eugenic future of American citizens only within the borders. As the people of overpopulated nations seemed to resort to even more aggressive means—military invasion—in search of outlets abroad, many eugenicists eventually came to advocate the practice of birth control to women whose fertility was deemed to endanger world peace.

World Eugenics and the Rockefeller Foundation

While a series of discussions about the eugenic fate of the nation led to the passage of the 1924 Immigration Act, some American eugenicists made further efforts to extend their research abroad. To improve the racial fitness of the white race, international cooperation, specifically among Euro-American nations, was vital. In addition, Western eugenicists found the need to educate and enlighten non-Western nations about the principles of eugenics and population to prevent the seemingly inevitable clash between races that they believed were fundamentally different in nature.

Global networking among eugenicists, chiefly under Anglo-American leadership, officially began in 1912 at the First International Congress of Eugenics in London.[46] The International Eugenics Committee, which came out of the congress, held its first meeting the following year, gathering prominent leaders from the United States, England, Belgium, Denmark, France, Germany, Italy, and Norway. Many of the transatlantic eugenics projects were supported by American philanthropic sponsors, such as the Rockefeller Foundation and the Carnegie Institution.[47]

These international initiatives rarely included eugenicists from non-European countries. Interactions took place between North American and Latin American eugenicists, as their geographic proximity made it more urgent to study the issue of immigration and racial hybridization. As a result, in 1927 the First Pan-American Conference was convened under the direction of Charles Davenport.[48] The International Commission stopped short of extending membership to Japan and India, however, as some members doubted the "desirability of inviting other races" into their organizations.[49]

This does not mean that American and European eugenicists were not interested in the eugenics movements in non-Western countries. In fact,

American eugenics journals frequently carried articles and reports on new developments of eugenics research in these areas.[50] In addition, some American eugenicists individually supported non-European eugenicists. Charles Davenport and Harry Laughlin, for example, each accepted Japanese eugenicists' requests for advice and assistance regarding the launching of a new eugenics journal in Japan.[51]

In the 1920s, Japanese eugenicists debated how to interpret Western attempts to check the population increase of fertile nonwhite races based on eugenic reasons. Some considered Margaret Sanger's preaching birth control to the Japanese as an insult, treating them at the same level as black and poor white people in the United States.[52] Japanese scientists also heatedly discussed the eugenic reasoning behind the passage of the 1924 law. Biologist Tanaka Yoshimaro, for example, admitted that the Japanese in general were physically inferior to whites, but at the same time insisted that there were many Japanese with qualities that made them unique and genetically superior. He therefore proposed an immigration policy that selected immigrants according to their individual qualities, not their race.[53] Another prominent biologist, Matsumura Shōnen, expressed a more critical view toward the exclusionist law. Matsumura devoted a chapter on this subject in his book *Shinka to shisō* (Evolution and thoughts, 1925), in which he condemned the act as a "grave insult" to the Japanese and urged his fellow Japanese to "racially awaken" in the struggle for survival among races. If the entire world wished to keep all races eugenically fit, Matsumura maintained, there should be a universal agreement on a uniform birth rate among nations, just as there was an international agreement on limiting the number of naval ships in 1922.[54] The fact that this biologist drew an analogy between national fertility and military strength indicates how intricately linked these two were in the minds of many elites.

While most Japanese intellectuals rejected a general birth control and population reduction policy, they nonetheless agreed that top-down measures were needed to reduce the birth rate of those who were mentally or physically handicapped or doomed to be a burden to the nation. To achieve that end, they earnestly studied the negative eugenics measures practiced in the United States and Europe, such as sterilization and marriage restrictions. As they keenly felt the need of more research and public enlightenment on eugenics to compete with Western imperialists, Japanese eugenicists proposed the founding of a eugenics institution in Japan, something equivalent to the Eugenics Record Office in the United States.[55]

In this context of heightening interest on both sides of the Pacific, the Rockefeller Foundation (RF) played a pioneering role in extending the eugenics studies of race to Asia. The Rockefeller families have a long history of developing international projects, particularly in the fields of medicine and public health. One of their first public health projects was the eradication of hookworm in US southern states, initiated in 1909 by the Sanitary Commission. In 1913, the commission extended this campaign to some tropical areas around the world, renaming itself first the International Health Board and, in 1927, the International Health Division.[56] By the 1920s, the focus had shifted from the control and eradication of specific contagious diseases to the promotion of health and general well-being. The mission to establish public health and nursing schools across the world started in major cities in North America and Europe but later extended to some parts of Asia as well, including Tokyo and Calcutta. The RF's funding for international projects soon expanded to include eugenics. As a field that concerned the well-being of human beings, eugenics was a logical extension of the RF's earlier efforts in public health issues.[57]

The so-called Human Biology Commission (1924–27), led by RF secretary Edwin R. Embree, undertook the first major international project in "race biology," focusing on the Asia-Pacific region. In 1924, Embree was appointed director of the Division of Studies, which was formed to develop projects not immediately relating to public health and medicine. Embree used this new division to explore topics in human biology, especially issues related to race betterment and race mixture.[58] While some of his projects involved providing assistance to these fields in American universities, the main focus of this new division was on the fieldwork and projects in the Asia-Pacific region: Australia, Hawaii, Japan, and China.[59]

Embree's investigatory trip to Japan took place from January to March 1926. He invited Edwin Conklin, Princeton professor of biology, to accompany him.[60] In accepting Embree's invitation, Conklin suggested a list of subjects in human biology that they might explore:

1. Racial stocks
2. Interracial breeding

3. Population growth
4. Relief for overpopulation (extension of territory, emigration, birth control)
5. Defectives and dependents (institutional segregation and other measures)
6. Records of superior inheritance
7. Effects of environment and food (on alcoholics, addicts, or leprosy)
8. Eugenics and social education
9. Influence of this education on militarism, democracy, and feminism[61]

While Embree agreed that Japan—"composed of many racial elements"—offered "a promising field" in anthropological studies and human heredity, the main issue of interest for American scholars was population.[62] Raymond Pearl, professor of biometry at Johns Hopkins University, whose research focused on the problem of differential fertility in the United States, also advised Embree before the trip to pursue his investigation with the population issues in mind. Pearl also informed him that there were many Japanese scientists interested in the topic.[63]

During the trip, Embree and Conklin were further convinced of the pressing need to deal with the population problem in Japan. Just as Pearl had predicted, the Japanese intellectuals they met were eager to learn the Americans' views about Japan's population issue. Embree noted in his diary that after Conklin delivered a lecture at Tohoku Imperial University in Sendai (northern Japan), an active discussion ensued not just on the subject of human biology but also on US immigration policies and birth control.[64] "More conspicuous in Japan even than ancient art or modern industry are babies," Embree reflected in his journal. "They are everywhere." The Japanese, according to Embree, were beginning to realize the acute crisis facing the nation in the near future. He observed that neither colonization/emigration nor industrial development could offer a permanent solution for the constantly increasing population. "During the next three to five decades some solution must be found," he warned, "else this brilliant nation will, by the results of the very sciences she has so efficiently adopted, be plunged into the lowest of living standards, into misery and woe with a debacle as dramatic as has been everything else in her history."[65] In other words, the matter of overpopulation was of great interest to students of human biology because it could cause the quality of a race or a nation to deteriorate.

Although Embree and Conklin held more optimistic and democratic views about race relations than earlier eugenicists such as Lothrop Stoddard and Madison Grant, their understanding of the Japanese population problem was heavily influenced by the eugenic thinking prevalent in earlier anti-immigration debates. As a biologist, Conklin agreed with many of his contemporaries about the perceived dangers of differential birth rates at home and overpopulation in certain sections of the world. He promoted reproductive control as a rational solution to overpopulation in these areas, even while he spoke strongly against the spread of the practice among the "educated-class" of women at home. He urged for "intelligent and ethical control of reproduction, and not mere selfishness" for the white race; otherwise, he warned, "Orientals would within a few generations overflow all barriers and boundaries and ultimately replace the white race."[66]

The assumed naturalness of white superiority was evident in the field notes and reports that Embree and Conklin wrote regarding their survey in Japan. In their report to the RF, they noted that Japanese scientists were "by nature jealous and suspicious and lacking in ability to cooperate" and that their research was "often perfunctory and imitative." They made sure that such observation about the Japanese character was not based only on their personal prejudice, as they added that "these criticisms [were] often made, occasionally by Japanese as well as foreigners."[67] Even though Conklin admitted that, from a biological point of view, all races had both good and bad qualities, he was convinced that there was "no doubt that the white, yellow, and brown races lead [over the red and black races], and probably in the order named."[68] Embree's diary was even more explicit about his fundamental belief in the hierarchy of races. "The real offense to the white man," Embree stated, "lies at heart in the fact that the Japanese of all the Orientals, of all the yellows and blacks and reds and browns of the earth, refuses to recognize the inherent and inalienable superiority of the white." Embree suggested the difficulty that the white man might have in dealing with the Japanese, because the "Oriental" from other countries was "indulgently fondled and praised by his tutors" as long as he "bow[ed] before the great white brother and [kept] his place.'"[69]

After their Japan trip, Embree and Conklin made two concrete suggestions to the RF in regard to the development of human biology in Japan: send American biologists to Japanese universities as visiting professors and provide fellowships for young Japanese biologists to study in the United States. Both of these RF projects had a strong emphasis on population studies. The selection and invitation of Japanese fellows to American universities proceeded rather smoothly, as they had already formed personal connections with many Japanese scientists during their stay in Japan. Conklin wrote to Embree commending the selection of Japanese scientists, particularly Dr. Terao Arata, noting that his "eugenical and mathematical background would make him an especially good man for work on population problems and race betterment."[70] Yamamoto Senji was also considered a candidate in connection to a plan to establish a eugenics institute in Kyoto, although the plan was never realized because of Yamamoto's expulsion from professorship at Dōshisha University for political radicalism.[71]

As for the plan to send American biologists to Japan, Raymond Pearl strongly recommended that sending "a well-trained man [in statistics and human biology] might get important information bearing upon the population problem by work in Japan."[72] With Pearl's suggestion, Thomas J. LeBlanc of the University of Cincinnati was selected in 1928 as a visiting scholar for Tohoku Imperial University in Sendai.[73] Data and observations that LeBlanc obtained during his duty in Japan appeared in the newly launched journal *Human Biology*, which Pearl edited. The articles examined the vital indices of Japan, and of Sendai in particular, with special reference to the issue of differential fertility according to class, geographic area, age, and nationality. The articles highlighted Japan's rapid transition from an agricultural society to an industrialized one, represented by booming cities such as Sendai. Because birth rates tended to decrease along with urbanization, the implication was that Japan's population increase would stabilize sometime in the future, following the pattern of other Western countries.[74] The September 1932 issue carried LeBlanc's essay "Sidelights on the Population Problem in Japan." Unlike many scholars of international relations studying the demographic Yellow Peril, the tone of LeBlanc's analysis was decidedly dispassionate and impartial. He attributed the source of population pressure in Japan not necessarily to the lack of food but to the need of markets and resources to sustain its rapid industrialization. LeBlanc thus concluded that "Japan's action in Manchuria and China [was] not unexpected but rather an inevitable result flowing out of certain trends that have been part of the national picture for many years."[75]

In fact, Edwin Conklin, Raymond Pearl, and Thomas LeBlanc together represented a new generation of biologists who distanced themselves from the earlier works of so-called mainline eugenicists.[76] They sought to detach themselves from political assumptions and instead emphasized scientific objectivity through experimentalism and statistical analysis. Conklin and Pearl each warned Embree and the RF about the rising criticism toward "the tendency to propaganda at Cold Spring Harbor," to which the organization was providing financial support for genetic research.[77] Both of them, nonetheless, strongly urged the RF to continue its support in the field of human genetics and heredity—only "slowly and with [a] critical attitude."[78]

Many core officials of the RF, however, were growing uncomfortable with the RF's involvement in mainline eugenics projects. Their new commitment to pure science was represented by the appointment of former physics professor Max Mason as director of the new Division of Natural Sciences, and in 1929 as president of the RF, the first scientist to be appointed to the position. Mason unequivocally rejected any project related to eugenics or any type of work associated with political propaganda.[79] Embree's projects in race biology with their explicitly eugenic motives proved too risky and controversial to be carried out under the formal auspices of the RF, although the foundation continued to assist similar research under the banner of genetics, psychiatry, brain research, anthropology, or sociology.[80] Embree tried to rescue his projects by explaining to the trustees that they were part of the foundation's overall concern for individual health.[81] Despite his efforts, the Division of Studies and the Human Biology Commission were both terminated in 1927.

"Danger Spots" in World Population

As mainline eugenics came under attack, "population studies" emerged in the 1930s as a legitimate field that claimed to objectively examine the issue of differential fertility in world politics. American scholars, with the help of private NGOs, outlined the danger that overpopulated countries posed to international peace and stability. Despite their anti-imperialist argument and their commitment to objective science, however, they essentially reiterated the same racist warnings about differential fertility that earlier eugenicists had presented since the turn of the twentieth century.

Warren Thompson, sociologist at Miami University in Ohio, was one of the leading figures in this new area of research. Earlier in his career, he wrote on the topic "Race Suicide in the United States," which was published in the *American Journal of Physical Anthropology* in 1920 and was also carried in Sanger's *Birth Control Review* with an added emphasis on the benefits of birth control for certain classes of people. While underscoring the high birth rates of rural populations, most of which were of "old (Nordic) stock," Thompson supported the idea that the Anglo-Saxon stocks in the cities were being supplanted by the newer immigrants. Even though he admitted that there was "no convincing proof" that poorer immigrants were "essentially inferior to the older stocks," he nonetheless argued that most of the "biological degenerates" belonged to this group. If immigrants were allowed to enter without restriction, he warned, "the situation [might] soon be beyond control."[82] At the same time, however, Thompson accused other eugenicists, especially biologists, for inciting the pseudoscientific and jingoistic tones that had come to characterize public discussion over differential fertility. Instead, he proposed a "rational eugenic program," free of deterministic assumptions and biases, in which they would better detect and eliminate the "defective" while creating a social environment where "non-defective" families could comfortably raise more children.[83]

A breakthrough in Thompson's career came in 1929 with the publication of two major works: the article "Population" in the *American Journal of Sociology* and the book *Danger Spots in World Population*. In "Population," Thompson presented the relationship between socioeconomic change and demographic transition, which became a prototype of a widely influential demographic model later known as the "demographic transition theory." Thompson was not the first to assert the idea of demographic transition, although his work was the most comprehensive formulation published in the United States at the time. Precursors included the work of Edward Ross, who also warned about the disequilibrium of birth and death rates that could bring about rapid population growth. Ross wrote in 1912 in *Changing America*: "Where a backward folk is brought under efficient modern administration, the proportion of deaths may be rapidly reduced even though the people continue to breed in the old reckless way. . . . If ever pacific

China flames out into a Yellow Peril it will be in that momentous interval between her laying down drains and her quitting ancestor worship."[84] The problem of overpopulation, in other words, came from countries that reduced the death rates with the aid of Western medicine and hygiene but had not yet adopted the practice of conception control.

Thompson classified nations into three groups according to demographic patterns. Group A represented countries with stationary or declining population due to rapidly declining birth rates and low death rates: Western Europe and countries largely settled by peoples emigrating from this area. Group B included countries with death rates declining more rapidly than birth rates, thus causing a natural increase of population: central and southern Europe. Group C consisted of countries whose birth and death rates were not yet under voluntary control and where positive checks, such as famine and disease, determined population growth: most of Asia, Africa, and South America. Thompson adopted the evolutionary thinking of many of his contemporaries by placing the countries in hierarchal order according to the degree of industrialization (i.e., Westernization) in correlation with declining death and birth rates. In other words, Group A represented the ultimate, final stage of progress in the demographic transition model. Some countries in Group C that had started to adopt Western customs and technologies, such as Japan and Russia, were entering a stage of expansion and thus moving closer to Group B. One of the urgent problems facing the world was, Thompson thus argued, the readjustment of resources and land to meet the demands of these expanding peoples from Group B.[85]

In *Danger Spots in World Population*, Thompson further described the political and economic situations of the "danger spots in population," areas where the rate of population increase was greater than the availability of land and resources: the western Pacific, Indian Ocean region, and central Europe (including Italy).[86] Among the specific cases he studied, Thompson accorded special attention to Japan. What made Japan particularly dangerous, as he and many scholars before him had argued, was not simply the sheer lack of food to feed its rapidly increasing population. In fact, in regard to starvation and malnutrition, countries such as China and India faced more calamitous situations. In the case of Japan, rapid Westernization not only reduced death rates but also brought about the rise of military power, nationalism, and industrialization. This placed Japan in a position to demand equal access to resources and lands from other Western nations to satisfy its national ambitions. The rejection of these demands through naval restriction treaties and immigration laws, however, left Japan increasingly frustrated. In short, it was this *felt* population pressure rather than the *actual* rate of population increase that made Japan a special danger to world order.

Thompson nonetheless avoided any overt racial prejudice or hostility in his analysis of world events. He refuted the "fantastic" fear of an alliance between the colored races against the white race, what Lothrop Stoddard had alarmingly described a decade earlier, by arguing that antagonistic economic interests could develop *between* the colored races as they could against the white races. He rejected the Anglo-Saxon exclusionist vision as the "chosen people" and criticized in particular the "white Australia" policy that kept colored labor from making use of unused lands and resources. Thompson therefore asserted that imperialist nations—Britain, France, Holland, and Australia—should be willing to consider "the voluntary cession of some of their unused lands" to the "swarming" peoples, if they wish to avoid an otherwise inevitable war. At the same time, he insisted that the United States, where agricultural settlement had started much earlier, had little further room on the mainland or in external possessions for use by needy people.[87]

Thompson's work in world population issues, especially in Asia, came to attract strong institutional support. One of the first organizations to recognize the importance of this emerging field of population studies was the Scripps Foundation. Concerned about the population of the Far East, Edward Scripps, head of the newspaper chain, searched the library at Columbia University and found Thompson's dissertation dealing with the Malthusian theory. He then invited Thompson to accompany him on his trip to the Far East and the South Sea Islands. In 1922, he set up the Scripps Foundation for Research in Population Problems, located at Miami University in Oxford, Ohio. Pascal K. Whelpton, an agricultural economist from Cornell University, joined Thompson in 1924 for a program to rotate two scholars between the United States and a year's residence abroad.[88]

Thompson's early investigation into population problems in Asia was supported by another institution, the IPR, which originated from a conference held in Honolulu in 1925 in response to the Asian exclusion movements and the subsequent 1924 Immigration Law. The conference concluded that the population pressure in Pacific countries was fundamental to the broader issues concerning racial and national conflicts. Consequently, a research committee was formed to gather adequate data on the subject, the results of which were presented at the second conference in Honolulu in July 1927. The IPR, unlike most of the other population associations dominated by white American professionals, brought a fairly large number of scholars from Asia. Since Japan seemed to face the most urgent problem pertaining to population increase, a Japanese economist, Nasu Shiroshi, took the lead in the discussion. The conference's research committee then set up plans to initiate international projects investigating the issues of food supply and population pressure. China was chosen as the principal site of study because of the lack of accurate knowledge and data on the topic, whereas a relatively large number of official and private studies already existed in most of the other Pacific countries. The IPR accordingly sent field workers and experts from the United States to the University of Nanking; Warren Thompson was one of them.[89]

The RF, despite its avoidance of mainline eugenics projects, soon joined these institutional endeavors to aid the development of population studies. In 1942, Thompson submitted a grant request to the RF to aid further research for a book project on world population issues. He initially envisioned the project to be a revision of *Danger Spots* but soon realized the need to rewrite it to concentrate specifically on the Pacific region. In the research proposal to the RF, Thompson anticipated some pressing population problems that were likely to arise after the end of war, including the question, "What is likely to happen to the Japanese if Formosa and Manchuria are returned to China and Korea is given complete independence?" His aim was thus to provide a better understanding of the issue to "increase the probability of a workable settlement."[90] Although his original proposal, which urged Western powers to distribute some land and resources to "needy" nations, seemed unrealistic to most Western leaders, his work provided the necessary groundwork for tackling the global population problem in the following decades.

The broad institutional backing that Thompson's population work attracted was by no means exceptional. The RF, along with the Milbank Memorial Fund, assisted other projects with similar goals through its funding of the Princeton Office of Population Research (OPR). The OPR was established in 1936 as a result of Frederick Osborn's promotional work at

Princeton University and the Milbank Memorial Fund. Osborn was one of the founding members of the American Eugenics Society and later elected president after the war (1946–52). Under the directorship of Frank Notestein, the OPR became the hub for policy-oriented population studies. During the war years, the US Department of State arranged for the OPR to conduct studies on Asian populations, which were later published as *The Population of India and Pakistan* by Kingsley Davis and *The Population of Japan* by Irene B. Taeuber.[91] The demographers at the OPR and their wartime studies played crucial roles in population control projects throughout the world, especially Japan, after the war.

The Co-optation of the Birth Control Movement

Ultimately, the threat of overpopulation in Asia outweighed many eugenicists' ambivalence about birth control advocacy. Proponents of race suicide blamed white American women for declining birth rates—and eventually the decline of their race and civilization. As the demographic Yellow Peril seemed an ever-pressing reality in the 1930s, many of them loosened their general hesitation about the practice—even though they still expressed pronatalism toward white women—and began to partner up with Margaret Sanger in her mission to spread birth control to women whose reckless breeding was deemed a threat to world peace. Even though Sanger was initially critical of many male eugenicists' pronatalist contention, she learned to downplay her disagreement to maintain their support. The eugenicists, however, marginalized her involvement in the supposedly joint effort to conquer the demographic Yellow Peril.

Many eugenicists who warned about differential fertility among races at home and abroad remained extremely cautious about how and to whom they promoted reproductive control. As Raymond Pearl stated, "The wrong kind of people have too many children, and the right kind too few."[92] If left without control, they insisted, the selfish and decadent practice of birth control would usually spread disproportionately among the upper-class women. They condemned the higher education and suffrage of women as encouraging women to yearn for careers and to neglect their reproductive duties. Edwin Conklin asserted in his lectures at Northwestern University and later at Princeton that the feminist movement, as far as it meant freedom from reproduction among intellectual women, would be suicidal to the survival of the white race.[93] Lothrop Stoddard similarly contended that white families should recognize the "supreme importance of heredity," in particular the "science of race betterment," to prevent further racial degeneration and to stand up together against the "yellow tide."[94] In short, eugenicists' pronatalism for the fit (white women in general) and the restriction of birth for the unfit (those who were mentally challenged, the poor, immigrants, and the "colored" races in general) were two sides of the same coin. Both mainline and reform eugenicists alike openly expressed anti-feminist and racist arguments against the uneven spread of reproductive control.

Margaret Sanger initially rejected the advocacy of positive eugenics—reproductive control that *encouraged* more childbirth to certain women—describing it as the "demand of masculine 'race suicide' fanatics." In her earlier writings, she criticized the "distinct middle-class bias" or "peculiarly Victorian conservatism" of eugenicists trying to divide the population into the fit and the unfit, which, she insisted, could lead only to a "cradle competition" between the two groups.[95] She pointed out the futility of setting a quota restriction for immigrants while the government made no attempt to "discourage the rapid multiplication of undesirable aliens, *and natives*, within our own borders."[96] In defending the "foreign stock," Sanger usually referred solely to European immigrants. Coming from an Irish immigrant family, she believed that America, the "melting pot," could express the "best of all racial elements" by providing the wisdom of reproductive control to all women, native and foreign alike. She remained silent about the anti-immigration movements in California, however, and apparently did not count Asian immigrants as part of the American melting pot.[97]

Sanger did wholeheartedly endorse "one branch of this philosophy": negative eugenics for the poor, the diseased, and the "undeniably feeble-minded" parents.[98] Because Sanger had been educated by British neo-Malthusians, many of whom were also ardent eugenicists, this negative eugenic philosophy defined Sanger's birth control movement from the beginning. Since its inception, her *Birth Control Review* had carried numerous articles by eugenicists and biologists, including Raymond Pearl, Paul Popenoe, and Lothrop Stoddard.[99] By the mid-1920s, the slogan printed on the cover of each issue shifted from a radical feminist tone ("Dedicated to the Principle of Intelligence and Voluntary Motherhood") to more decidedly eugenic phrases such as "Fewer Babies Better Born," "For Those Who Believe in the Great Future of Our Race," "In the Creation of New Life There Should Be Full Scientific Knowledge and Deliberate Planning," and "Non Quantitas, sed Qualitas."

Since the early 1920s, Sanger had actively sought the cooperation and endorsement of leading eugenicists and population scientists, many of whom were respected members of society, to bring scientific credibility and societal recognition to her birth control advocacy. She vigorously networked with professionals in her capacity as the organizer of the First American Birth Control Conference in 1921, a meeting that led to the inauguration of the American Birth Control League . She was able to convince famous eugenicists to lend their names to the Conference Committee and later to the National Council of the league, including Irving Fisher (Yale economics professor and first president of the American Eugenics Society), Lothrop Stoddard, Clarence C. Little (president of the University of Michigan and fourth president of the American Eugenics Society), and Raymond Pearl. Her recruiting efforts were not always successful, as some conservative eugenicists, such as Charles Davenport, firmly refused to be associated with the "propaganda" efforts of birth control activists.[100]

Ultimately, the perceived impact of overpopulated Asia on world politics and the future of the human race brought more and more eugenicists closer to the birth control cause. At the 1921 American Birth Control Conference, Lothrop Stoddard presented a paper, "The Population Problem in Asia," in which he declared: "Asia cannot expect any Western nation to jeopardize its whole social and racial future by becoming a dumping ground for Asia's boundless spawning."[101] The Fifth International Neo-Malthusian and Birth Control Conference in London in 1922—the conference Sanger attended after her first trip to Asia—consolidated the union between Malthusians, many of whom promoted eugenics theories, and birth control advocates. It also, for the first time, invited representatives from Asian countries, Japan and India, suggesting the interest of Western eugenicists in spreading the birth control philosophy to the "Oriental" world.[102] A number of eugenicists presented the alarming story of differential fertility in world politics at the next International Neo-Malthusian and Birth Control Conference in New York in 1925, another major conference Sanger organized. Under the auspices of the American Birth Control League, the meeting became the largest and most significant event to date that brought together scholars of population studies and eugenics to discuss birth control openly and seriously.[103] Sanger was able to gather more than a thousand delegates and solicit supportive messages from prominent figures, including W. E. B. Du Bois, Bertrand Russell, and Havelock Ellis.[104] At the conference, even conservative eugenicists such as Harry Laughlin admitted that "the efforts of eugenics and of Birth Control [were] tending, more and more, to work for the common end."[105] Raymond Pearl also declared that "the Birth Control movement after a long and bitter struggle ha[d] attained a certain academic sort of respectability." As Pearl put it, "Rhetoric about race suicide, the decline of the empire, and so on, will never be accepted by the potential parent as a substitute for an economic guarantee. But if it is not possible to make desirable people have more babies, why not try teaching other people how to have fewer?"[106]

Japan, in particular, became the main target of eugenics campaigns for birth control. The session on "War and Population" was, according to Sanger, the highlight of the Sixth Neo-Malthusian Conference.[107] Presenters in these sessions described the Japanese as an "energetic and warlike people, rapidly increasing in numbers," and blamed them for the "chief though not the only reason" that peace had not arrived in the world after World War I.[108] Warren Thompson became an important supporter of the birth control cause with his influential theory demonstrating the danger spots in world population. His essays frequently appeared in Sanger's *Birth Control Review*. In "Overpopulation and Migration as Causes of War," for example, Thompson warned that "in less than three-quarters of a century Japan has come out of her seclusion and is strong enough to resent, with force if need be, the way in which Europeans are ordering the world for their own benefit and are excluding other peoples from their preserves."[109] The Japanese invasion of Manchuria in 1931 served to corroborate Thompson's theory. At the American Conference on Birth Control and National Recovery, held in Washington, D.C., in January 1934, Thompson presented a paper, "Population Growth and International Relations," which primarily dealt with Japan and the Manchurian issue and proposed birth control as the ultimate solution. At the same conference, Henry Pratt Fairchild gave an opening speech stressing that "Japan needs the fullest resources of scientific control [of reproduction] that the western nations are capable of giving."[110]

Eugenicists, nonetheless, remained ambivalent about their relationship with the birth control cause throughout the prewar years. Although Thompson considered birth control to be a long-term solution to population pressure in "needy" countries, he was well aware of the persisting moral oppositions to the practice both in the West and in Asia. He therefore stressed that he was "not advocating it as a personal practice (that would indeed be carrying coals to Newcastle) but as an essential part of a larger international program." Admitting that birth control by itself would not be able to yield immediate results for several generations, he also proposed other (temporary) solutions: the abolition of barriers to resources, to markets, and, to some extent, to migration.[111] It should be noted that Thompson would reverse his position in the postwar period, offering birth control as the primary and immediate solution to overpopulation in Asia over other alternatives, once the perceived urgency of global overpopulation outweighed moral reservations against contraceptive control at home. During the prewar decades, however, he withheld any full support for birth control.

Despite Sanger's behind-the-scenes efforts to bring together high-profile professionals from across the world, male scholars sought to hide or downplay their relationship with Sanger by highlighting the scientific aspect of their work. Biologists, sociologists, and economists using mathematical formulas and statistical data dominated the 1927 World Population Conference in Geneva.[112] The issues of overpopulation, war, and eugenics were the common topics of papers and discussions, while the matter of women's rights and the personal aspects of birth control were given minimal, if any, attention. Although Sanger was the organizer, the conference was in effect hijacked by population scientists, particularly by Raymond Pearl, who insisted that the topics should be "strictly scientific."[113] After the conference, Pearl created the International Union for the Scientific Investigation of Population Problems, with an organizing committee dominated by British and American scientists. The American members of the committee considered themselves "the crème de la crème" of the demographic establishment and would reconstitute the group as the College of Fellows of the new Population Association of America. During its founding process in 1931, a crucial milestone in population studies, the male members actively sought to keep free of any attachment to the birth control movement. Initially, Sanger raised the necessary money from the Milbank Memorial Fund and urged Henry Pratt Fairchild, sociologist and anti-immigration activist, to call an organizing meeting among interested scientists for a new organization on population studies in the United States. Despite her efforts, the male scientists who gathered for the meeting feared that the inclusion of Sanger's name in a prominent position in the association would tarnish its scientific image. However, the election of Henry Pratt Fairchild as president for its first four years illustrates the centrality of eugenics in the new field of population studies. Despite the growing criticism against mainline eugenics, the presence of extremists such as Charles Davenport and Harry Laughlin among its core members was not as troublesome as the inclusion of birth control advocates. In short, male eugenicists of all degrees were still considered legitimate scientists, while birth control activists, especially women, were little more than lay propagandists. The first official meeting held in May 1931 invited important actors, both liberal and conservative, involved in the debates regarding race suicide, immigration restriction, and differential fertility, including Edward Ross, Harry Laughlin, Albert Johnson, Frederick Osborn, Charles Davenport, Paul Popenoe, Edward East, Clarence Little, Roswell Johnson, and Raymond Pearl. A core figure in this new group of professional demographers, Frank Notestein, later recalled: "It really took us an incredible time to realize that the birth controllers and other action groups were probably less eager to capture the academics than the academics were to avoid capture."[114]

While some eugenicists eventually expressed lukewarm support—at most—for birth control advocacy, Sanger needed to adjust her views more radically to win their support, even if that meant she had to condone their elitism and pronatalist position toward white women. During the 1921 American Birth Control Conference, for example, Sanger allowed a pronatalist resolution to be passed, which demanded "a recognition of the necessity of reproduction by those of unusual racial value."[115] Similarly, at the final session of the Sixth Neo-Malthusian Conference, a so-called eugenics resolution was adopted, encouraging more offspring to "persons whose progeny give promise of being of decided value to the community." As the resolution provoked criticism and confusion among some birth control activists, Sanger was compelled to clarify the American Birth Control League's position on positive eugenics. Before publishing her editorial in *Birth Control Review*, however, Sanger sought advice from her eugenicist allies, Raymond Pearl, Clarence Little, and Edward East, asking them if the statement was "too strong for the eugenic group" for fear it might "offend or antagonize any of our friends whose backing we desire."[116]

Sanger apparently was more concerned about pleasing the eugenicists than the more radical supporters of her cause. The presence of conservative eugenicists at the conferences created friction with some of the progressive and socialist participants. A Boston physician and socialist, Antoinette Konikow, for example, questioned the eugenicists' definition of the unfit and argued that "the question of success in our capitalistic world . . . does not prove that he or she is particularly fit from the sense of the ideal." Sanger, however, paid little, if any, attention to such an antielitist view that she herself had expressed during her early years of activism.[117] Under the banner of Wilsonian internationalism and pacifism, Sanger had unknowingly yielded to the authority of male professionals at the expense of women's individual sexual freedom.

. . .

Imperial struggles in the Pacific in the 1920s and 1930s brought the discussions of reproductive control in Japan to global attention. Many American intellectuals believed that differential fertility between nations and races was the main culprit for international disturbances, as the overpopulated nations represented by Japan aggressively sought outlets abroad. Sanger's transnational birth control movement thus became a relevant and useful cause for many internationally minded eugenicists who saw female fertility as a cause of war and chaos.

The closer Sanger moved toward the eugenics professionals, the more she came to adopt their language. Instead of criticizing the elitist bias of eugenicists, the government's discriminatory immigration policy, or its imperialist aggression abroad, she gradually began to devote her efforts to supporting nationalistic campaigns to enforce negative eugenics programs both at home and abroad. By the 1930s, Sanger frequently juxtaposed her argument for peace and international order with distinctly nationalistic goals and racialist conservatism. To safeguard future citizens from "hereditary taints," for example, she urged Congress to appoint a Parliament of Population that would "direct and control the population through birth rates and immigration." Only then, she argued, would Americans be able to turn their attention to "the basic needs for international peace," as outlined in Woodrow Wilson's Fourteen Points.[118] Sanger also praised Warren Thompson for warning the world, as far back as 1925, that population pressure and the lack of birth control created danger spots in the world. She released a statement to the press condemning these pronatalist and militarist countries, particularly Japan, as "the destroyers of our civilization through their ruthless method of waging arrogant warfare against innocent, peaceful peoples."[119] She did not, however, go as far as to denounce the imperialism of her own country or the pronatalism of many American eugenicists, who encouraged white women to have more babies in competition with the colored races. Instead, she now advocated birth control to aid the country's war efforts, specifically as a tool for "race conservation" and the prevention of venereal disease.[120]

As the issue of female fertility became nationalized and internationalized during the interwar period, the term "birth control" had become synonymous with "population control." The female body was no longer an individual concern but a matter of state policy. This top-down discourse of fertility control cultivated during the interwar and wartime periods would lay the ideological foundation of global population control projects in the postwar decades.

FOUR

Between Democracy and Genocide

US Involvement in Population Control in Occupied Japan

In a letter dated May 19, 1949, Katō Shizue—former Baroness Ishimoto, now officially divorced and remarried to a labor activist, Katō Kanjū—enthusiastically wrote to her old friend Margaret Sanger: "It has been my long cherished dream to invite you and Dorothy [Brush] to a lecture tour in Japan, on birth control and population problems. The Japanese Government and people now begin to take a keen interest in this question. . . . You will surely be warmly welcomed by the people and Government here." The government that had once attempted to reject Sanger in 1922 was now treating her as a savior of a nation plagued with postwar crises, overpopulation being one of them. Sanger was excited about the prospect of going back to her favorite country. She was also realistic about her own government's responses to the plan, as she cautioned Katō that she would need an "official invitation, as our State Department is fearful of Catholic opposition." Katō agreed but reassured Sanger that "if the plan [was] initiated by the Japanese, then the American authorities [would] not object."[1] Sanger eventually received an official invitation from the Yomiuri Newspaper Company, and all seemed to be set.

Despite the precautionary arrangements, the US-led Occupation government, often referred to as SCAP (Supreme Command for the Allied Powers), repeatedly denied Sanger's requests for a visa to enter Japan. The decision prompted strong reactions from people both in Japan and the United States. In response, General Douglas MacArthur, head of the General Headquarters (GHQ), explained SCAP's position on population issues in Japan:

> I have yielded to pressure from neither the group in advocacy nor that in opposition to birth control, but have consistently and publicly taken the position that the subject matter is a social problem for solution by the Japanese people themselves without interference, directly or indirectly, by the Allied Powers.... The entrance of Mrs. Sanger for the purpose indicated could not fail to invite propaganda attributing responsibility to the Allied Powers that which had already been done by the Japanese themselves toward birth control and with it the charge that the Allied Powers in the exercise of their supreme authority through coercion had imposed measures upon the conquered Japanese People leading to genocide.[2]

Even while they maintained a neutral position—often described as "benevolent neutrality"—on the birth control controversy in Japan, SCAP officials firmly denied any role in facilitating Sanger's trip.[3] Margaret Sanger was a controversial figure both in the United States and Japan, and SCAP feared that admitting her to Japan—even if the invitation came from the Japanese themselves—might bring unwanted attention and criticism to American roles in Japan's reproductive matters.

SCAP officials were especially concerned about the Soviet Union's responses to the US Occupation of Japan. With the fresh memories of the Nazi atrocity against the Jews, American leaders feared that any attempt to control the fertility of a conquered race could be associated with genocide and used against them by the Soviets. As the United States solidified itself as a world leader, it became increasingly important to distinguish itself from other hegemons—the Axis dictators, European colonialists, and Soviet communists. American Catholics, who represented a major dissenting voice against the eugenics movement, repeatedly pressured the Occupation government to stay clear of Japan's population issues.[4] The opinion of Catholics, as the vanguard of anticommunism, had a strong influence on US foreign policy decisions during the Cold War era, and SCAP ultimately gave in to most of their demands.

At the same time, the threat of a population "explosion" in Asia, many Americans believed, represented "a serious breach in western defense," as the Soviets were expanding "communism's share of the world" in impoverished and politically unstable parts of Asia.[5] Alarmists warned that unless Japan halted the "cancerous population growth," "the teeming millions of people in the East would embrace Communism" and that they could "face a menace in the Pacific far graver than the menace we fought the long, bloody, heroic, cruel Pacific war to overcome."[6] It was then the moral obligation of the United States, as self-professed defenders of democracy and leaders of the "free world," to stabilize the soaring population in Asia and bring peace and harmony to the world.

This chapter analyzes the tactics and rhetoric that American population control advocates used during the immediate aftermath of war to promote birth control programs in Occupied Japan. SCAP officials welcomed the intellectual input of American demographers, public health officials, and eugenicists, as well as the financial contributions from the RF and other individuals of wealth. Although private initiatives began assisting projects on world population issues in the 1930s, in the postwar period they often worked in coordination with state officials. Once these private consultants started to provoke the censuring attention of some American Catholics, SCAP officials increasingly depended on Japanese leadership concerning the population problem. They actively guided Japanese bureaucrats to implement population policies, laws, and programs under the semblance of indigenous initiatives. They also sent Japanese health officials to the United States, where, free from public scrutiny, the Japanese were mentored by American eugenicists and observed public health programs targeting racially and economically marginalized communities.

The Occupation of Japan provided a rare opportunity for Americans, however covertly, to discuss and implement state-sponsored birth control programs, something that was almost impossible at home. The immediate decline of birth rates in Japan, along with the transformation of a former enemy into a democratic ally, eventually helped legitimize American-led efforts to promote population control in Asia. The success of this "respectable" and democratic cause against global population explosion rested on the further exclusion of feminist activists and women's experiences.

SCAP's "Benevolent Neutrality"

As the result of an unprecedented baby boom and the influx of repatriates and soldiers from its former empire, postwar Japan experienced a sudden increase in population of eleven million people in only five years. American intellectuals frequently pointed out that Japan's expansionism and war in the Pacific were at least partly driven by overpopulation on its mainland. US officials therefore believed that their interference in the Japanese population problem was a matter of "an historical significance of the first magnitude" to develop "a sound economy for a free, noncolonial, democratic Japan" that would "neither need nor want to wage war again." Based on the neo-Malthusian concept linking population pressure to war, they contended that the Occupation had provided them "the opportunity to direct all of their wisdom and good will toward mitigating the tragedies" and to "justify the efforts and sacrifices of millions of people in fighting this part of WWII."[7]

The issue of female fertility, however, was just as controversial as it was before the war—or even more so in the aftermath of the Nazis' eugenics genocide. When the Far Eastern Commission visited Japan in January 1946, the representatives urged Crawford F. Sams, chief of the Public Health and Welfare Section (PHW) of SCAP, to deal with this "big question" of population growth in Japan.[8] In response, Sams gave a statement to the press that population policy in Japan required three measures: industrialization, urbanization, and birth control. He stressed that the last method in particular would have immediate effects and could be carried out by the Japanese themselves. Sams's public endorsement of birth control, however, provoked strong criticism from American Catholics in Japan. As a result, SCAP became defensive and maintained a hands-off policy—what they called "benevolent neutrality"—regarding the population issue in Japan, at least on the surface.[9]

The birth control cause had gained some degree of respectability as it became part of the liberal internationalist and pacifist movements during the interwar decades. While many elites still frowned on the spread of birth control among white middle-class women at home, most American leaders and the public agreed that there were certain classes, races, and nations that needed to be educated about reproductive control for the sake of the well-being of all humankind. As the prominent sociologist and longtime birth control supporter Henry Pratt Fairchild declared, even though it was "debatable" whether the postwar baby boom in the United States was good or bad, there was "no doubt that for the rest of the world, especially countries like China, India and Japan, a drastic check on the birth rate would benefit the whole world."[10]

There were some Americans back home who even proposed such extreme measures as sterilizing the Japanese to keep the nation from further aggression. Two months after the end of World War II, the *Los Angeles Times* carried an article with the headline "Former Prisoner Favors Jap

Birth Rate Curb." The article reported the comments of a former prisoner of war, Ellis Gordon, who contended that two-thirds of the Japanese population should be sterilized in order for the country to remain peaceful.[11] Similarly, Senator Theodore G. Bilbo of Mississippi wrote a letter to MacArthur in September 1945 suggesting the sterilization of all Japanese.[12] Proposals for sterilization even extended to the Japanese Americans on the West Coast. Senator Jed Johnson of Oklahoma, who was critical of the "pampering" of "Japanese war prisoners," allegedly urged Congress to include "an appropriation to sterilize the whole outfit" in the legislation for relocating Japanese Americans from wartime internment camps. Critics quickly denounced Johnson's plan, however, by comparing it to the "psychotic emotionalism" that Hitler displayed.[13]

Indeed, the Nazis' wartime eugenics programs had made any apparent, foreign-imposed policies on another population or race an extremely delicate matter. A number of leading Anglo-American scientists had publicly denounced the racialist programs conducted under the Nazi regime. Their efforts to distance themselves from the extreme type of eugenics based on strict hereditarianism were famously expressed in the "Geneticists' Manifesto," written primarily by H. J. Muller and issued at the Seventh International Congress of Genetics at Edinburgh in 1939.[14] In their 1946 book, *Hereditary, Race and Society*, L. C. Dunn and Theodosius Dobzhansky deplored that "eugenics [had] often been perverted to a pseudoscientific justification of social inequalities and oppression."[15] Therefore, an official in SCAP's Civil Information and Education Section felt extremely alarmed when he learned in 1946 about a discussion in the Japanese government "calling for the replacement of 'the present eugenic policy . . . by a compulsory policy." He strongly urged SCAP to forbid the Japanese government from "undertaking or even entertaining . . . this innocent appearing eugenic program," for "no democratic nation would deliberately adopt a 'race' policy." The memorandum asserted that "without question the entire weight of opinion in the sciences of physical anthropology and genetics in the United States and Great Britain would oppose what is essentially a revival of Nazi race theories and practices."[16]

In the end, Crawford Sams did not try to prevent the Japanese efforts to create the Eugenic Protection Bill in 1948 because he felt that the dangers of overpopulation outweighed these negative concerns over eugenics. He did, however, object to one component of the bill: the provision concerning compulsory sterilization. He found the extensive list of hereditary diseases that targeted people for sterilization "ridiculous" and advised the Japanese lawmakers to "specify only disorders generally accepted by scientists as capable of being transmitted to offspring." Besides this point, SCAP approved the bill with "no objection," as they considered such "radical remedies" admissible given the "mushrooming condition of the population."[17]

Meanwhile, SCAP also facilitated the Japanese efforts to disseminate birth control knowledge through the print media. The Civil Censorship Detachment Division approved all publication of Japanese books on practical methods of contraception. Sams informed the division that the PHW "would always readily advise on the scientific and technical adequacy of the submitted publications."[18] Given the persistent legal and social obstacles against the dissemination of birth control information in the United States, the easy clearance of censorship by US officials in Japan was in itself striking. In fact, although the Comstock Law was rendered ineffective by the *One Package of Japanese Pessaries* decision in 1936, local prohibitions on contraception at the state level persisted—or were even strengthened—in Massachusetts and Connecticut. Clearly, US officials applied different moral standards to birth control policies in the United States and US Occupied Japan.

SCAP's role was not just passive and permissive. By mid-1948, the PHW started to assume a more active role in helping Japanese leaders spread birth control practices among the public through public health centers. When some conservative bureaucrats in the Japanese Ministry of Health and Welfare (MHW) tried to limit public access to contraceptives through the Law on Control of Contraceptive Appliances, SCAP's Narcotic Control Division instructed the MHW to abolish the ordinance. Instead, SCAP told the Japanese leaders to add a list of approved contraceptives to the new Pharmaceutical Law (passed in March 1947 and promulgated in July 1948). As a result of this law, contraceptives were now treated like any other drug that could be advertised and sold openly once approved by the MHW.[19] To advertise the availability of these contraceptives, Sams helped organize a "traveling exhibition" on accepted methods of birth control. The exhibition started in Tokyo in June 1948 and moved throughout Japan during the following year.[20] In addition, the PHW used various media to promote "public health and welfare programs" through daily fifteen-minute radio programs and articles in women's magazines.[21] Sams also worked actively to assure the production and supply of contraceptive materials, in particular, rubber.[22] These efforts led Sams to conclude in mid-1948 that "all measures which [were] practical and sound ha[d] already been undertaken by SCAP to provide incentive and means" of fertility control for the Japanese.[23]

From the perspective of American advocates of population control, however, Sams's attitude toward birth control policies still seemed "less than half hearted or negative." They were particularly critical of what they termed SCAP's "*militant* neutrality" on population issues, as military government officials seemed to be *forbidden* to act or to advise on the subject on their own.[24] In fact, this turned out to be just the beginning of American-devised birth control initiatives in Japan, as American consultants representing the RF served as a "front" to lead these projects on SCAP's behalf.[25]

The Rockefeller Mission

Regardless of its outward position of neutrality, SCAP hired a number of leading American scholars in public health, demography, and natural resources as advisers on Japan's population problem. In June 1948, Oliver McCoy was sent by the RF as consultant to the Institute of Public Health (IPH) in Tokyo and the PHW Section of SCAP. Then in September, SCAP welcomed a group of RF demographers and public health officials, who visited Japan and other Asian countries with a goal to report to the foundation about specific plans to deal with population problems in Asia. The RF, furthermore, sent two prominent demographers, Warren Thompson and Pascal K. Whelpton, as consultants to the Natural Resources Section of SCAP for three months in 1949. These American intellectuals aggressively pushed SCAP officials and Japanese leaders to implement top-down population policies that would have lasting effects on the country's fertility patterns.

As detailed previously, members of the RF had been interested in population growth in Asia since the 1920s. Roger F. Evans, through his service in the Social Sciences Division, had been in contact with Warren Thompson since 1943 about supporting Thompson's studies on the population problems in the Pacific, which prominently featured Japan. Evans and Thompson resumed their conversation on overpopulation in Asia in 1946, but they decided to postpone any concrete proposals until the situation in China had been settled. As the political situation made China less likely to be a site of investigation, the RF staff started to center their attention on Japan.²⁶ A number of foundation officers who visited Japan soon after the war became convinced of the need to act on the problem immediately.²⁷ Their reports heightened John D. Rockefeller III's interest in overpopulation in Asia. Before the war, he served in the Bureau of Social Hygiene, an organization created by his father that supported a number of projects related to birth control and population issues. After the bureau stopped making new appropriations in 1934, he wrote to his father that he "would be more than glad to supplement [his father's] gifts or make independent ones of [his] own" to birth control projects and organizations.²⁸ Rockefeller III's visit to Japan with philanthropic adviser Arthur Packard in August 1947 reaffirmed his conviction to take immediate action on the matter.²⁹ After his trip to Japan, he decided to "go public" on his support for fertility control issues, a significant departure from the "anonymous" contributions made by his father during the earlier efforts.³⁰

As the International Health Division repositioned RF officers in each Asian country after the war—Marshall Balfour in Shanghai, Oliver McCoy in Tokyo, and Richmond K. Anderson in India—time seemed ripe to start working on the population problem in Asia.³¹ Despite the strong interest expressed by a number of individual members, however, the RF as a whole, much like SCAP, was still reluctant to openly enter this field because of the controversial nature of birth control at home.³² With the urging of Rockefeller III, the foundation's scientific directors finally assigned Balfour, a public health graduate from Johns Hopkins and the RF's representative of the International Health Division in the Far East since 1939, to make "a thoroughly critical study of population as it might interest the International Health Division." Euphemistically calling it the "Reconnaissance in Public Health and Demography in the Far East"—more commonly called the Far East Mission—they agreed to set up a survey trip to Asia to serve as "some sort of blueprint" that would help them "chart possible future projects in this field."³³ They appointed four representatives: Frank Notestein (founding director of the OPR at Princeton University), Irene Taeuber (a member of the OPR and author of *The Population of Japan*), Roger Evans (RF officer in the Social Sciences Division), and Marshall Balfour (RF officer in the International Health Division). The group traveled to Japan, China, Taiwan, Korea, Indonesia, and the Philippines from September to December 1948.

During the mission's stay in Japan, Sams and other SCAP members arranged numerous meetings with them, sometimes inviting Japanese leaders in the field, to discuss the population problem in Japan. While SCAP officials repeatedly reminded the RF group about SCAP's official position of neutrality on population matters, they also stressed that the Japanese themselves were not restricted in any way. At a meeting arranged by the Civil Information and Education Section, the group was introduced to major Japanese birth control leaders, including Katō Shizue, Yamakawa Kikue, Majima Kan, and Kitaoka Juitsu. The Japanese representatives used this opportunity to appeal to the American leaders for US support to move their own government.[34]

In particular, the RF members showed a strong interest in the Eugenic Protection Law (EPL) and questioned Japanese leaders extensively about it. The RF representatives believed that one of the most reliable and lasting ways to disseminate contraceptive control was through legal reforms. They found it convenient that the Japanese had been introducing bills, making SCAP's input less visible. These laws could be a firm basis for perpetuating US-induced changes after the end of the Occupation. As mentioned previously, the PHW Section had ensured the legality of contraceptives through the Pharmaceutical Law. It also approved the passage of EPL, despite some hesitation about its provisions for negative eugenic measures. Even with the passage of these laws, however, no action was taken to actually make contraceptive material available to the Japanese people, due mainly to the resistance of Japanese conservative bureaucrats. In fact, the RF group learned from the Japanese that any specific reference to birth control had been deleted from the Eugenic Protection Bill during the revision process.[35]

After the Far East Mission, the RF members focused their efforts on securing the legal basis for disseminating contraceptives across Japan. During the revision process of the EPL in 1949, at McCoy's suggestion, Sams ordered the Japanese officials to add a clause that authorized birth control in health centers—or, as the Japanese called them, "eugenic marriage consultation offices."[36] To further ensure the implementation of contraceptive guidance as specified in the EPL, Sams ordered the IPH to carry out training programs for doctors and medical officers in "model health centers." He asked an American health official to prepare a simple booklet about contraception for distribution to lay people by these health clinics.[37] Sams even defended his decision to distribute contraceptive information and devices in health centers in face of occasional backlash from US Catholics in Japan. After a conference in January 1949, in which Sams gave the military government health officers in southern Japan "a green light in promoting birth control activities in health centers," a Catholic officer gave a local order to cancel Sams's approval. While making sure that the situation was "handled verbally" instead of making any official statement, Sams took immediate steps to revoke this local order.[38] Japanese American officers stationed in local military governments often worked as interpreters for birth control instructions presented to Japanese women's groups.[39]

The RF mission thus seemed to have changed SCAP's hesitance to become involved in population polices in Japan and instead guided SCAP to take active steps. As Pascal Whelpton, consultant to the Natural Resources Section, noted in June 1949, Sams now "seemed fully aware of the importance of publicity of the right kind to speed up the process" of population decline, whereas just several months ago he had "expressed a strong negative attitude with regard to publicity about contraception."[40] The momentum would not last long, however, as the influence of private consultants did not go unnoticed by the Catholic opponents of birth control and communist countries who were the enemies of the United States, forcing SCAP to repeatedly defend its position of benevolent neutrality.

Cold War Politics

As Cold War tensions intensified, SCAP found itself increasingly caught in controversies over whether Americans should intervene into Japan's population problem. As military conquerors, SCAP leaders were "ultrasensitive"—as some RF members described—about the diplomatic repercussions of their work in Japan.[41] American military leaders increasingly saw Japan as a strategically important "workshop" in Asia to help maintain the "balance of power" in the region to defend against communism.[42] The last thing they, as self-professed leaders of the free world, wanted was to invite international criticism, especially from communists, that their role was no different from the Nazis' eugenics genocide program. The conservative turn of Occupation policies in the late 1940s against the backdrop of the

Cold War—what historians call the "reverse course"—significantly impacted SCAP's response to the birth control issue in Japan.

SCAP had first brought American consultants to Japan in 1947 to study the population problem, but they did not attract any public attention. A couple of years later, however, their suggestions of birth control to the Japanese provoked controversy, triggering protests, especially from American Catholics. One of the first major controversies over SCAP's role in Japan's population problem erupted when Warren Thompson, then SCAP consultant to the Natural Resources Section, made a statement encouraging government-initiated birth control programs in Japan in early 1949.[43] Thompson's comment made national and international headlines. MacArthur hastily responded to the publicity, stressing that Thompson's statement was his personal opinion, not a view representing SCAP. Privately, however, SCAP officials agreed that they would still continue to furnish the Japanese with "technical advice and information about birth control" and that they would not censor Thompson's statement. [44] Approximately a year later, another public controversy erupted after the publication of a report, *Japanese Natural Resources*, prepared by Harvard professor Edward Ackerman. The report recommended that Japan stabilize its population through "control of the birth rate" rather than overseas emigration.[45] Ackerman was hired as SCAP consultant to prepare a report intended to be used as an inventory of Japan's food and raw materials for the peace conference. The Catholic Women's Club of Tokyo immediately wrote a letter of protest to MacArthur and then decided to issue the letter to the press. Protests ensued from Catholics worldwide against the US government. As a result, MacArthur agreed to expurgate the objectionable parts and publish the report "privately." RF consultant Oliver McCoy found SCAP's action "unnecessary and unjustified" since the report did not even use the term "birth control," much less advocate it.[46] SCAP nonetheless allowed the Japanese press to publish the Japanese translation of the report later that year.[47]

While SCAP officials ultimately did not censor the "personal" opinions of these male consultants, they were far less supportive of female experts in the field. For example, SCAP turned down the opportunity for a Hawaiian-born Japanese American doctor, Teru Togasaki, to serve as consultant presumably because of her gender and race. In fall 1948, on the recommendation of Francis S. Smyth, dean of the University of California Medical School, SCAP and RF officers considered sending Togasaki as SCAP consultant to institute training programs in contraceptive methods and clinics for maternal and child hygiene in model health centers.[48] In the end, however, they questioned her "qualifications," specifically her "apparent unfamiliarity with population literature" and her "acceptability as a Japanese being American-born."[49] American officials often blamed the Japanese for their reluctance to bring in female scholars. They believed that Japanese men were "not disposed to 'take it'" from female experts.[50] As a result, SCAP never assigned even highly qualified demographers such as Dorothy Swaine Thomas (who headed the Japanese American Evacuation and Resettlement Study) and Irene B. Taeuber as official consultants while they allowed their male colleagues, despite their controversial statements on population in Japan, to assume and continue their roles. Some Japanese male professionals indeed expressed mixed feelings about having female foreigners mentor the Japanese on their own population issue.[51] In the end, however, the exclusion of female consultants seemed to reflect the Americans' own gender bias and sensitivity to the birth control problem rather than just the reaction of the Japanese.

No one else brought as much unwanted publicity to SCAP as Margaret Sanger. Immediately after the war, as early as October 1945, Sanger wrote directly to MacArthur, urging the Occupation government to set up a "population commission" and to appoint Katō Shizue its chief.[52] Ethel B. Weed of the Civil Information and Education Section in charge of the Women's Affairs Branch wrote back, asking Sanger to send "all the information possible about the birth control movement in the United States and other countries."[53] SCAP's attitude toward the issue of birth control, however, had changed dramatically since the start of the Occupation. The PHW Section, not the Women's Affair Branch, soon took charge of the issues of contraception. The demographer-consultants in the Natural Resources Section dealt with the statistical aspect of Japan's population issue. As the United States entered the Cold War, even these SCAP sections had difficulty handling the birth control issue.

Thus, when Katō wrote to Sanger on May 19, 1949, inviting her to make a lecture tour on birth control and population problems, the arrangement did not proceed as they expected.[54] The Occupation government repeatedly rejected Sanger's request for a visa to enter Japan despite a formal invitation from the Yomiuri Newspaper Company. Even those in SCAP who supported population control failed to take any action to help someone whom they considered a "propagandist." In response to Sanger's plea for "suggestions which would facilitate" her trip to Japan, Oliver McCoy flatly told her that no "official SCAP approval . . . [would] be forthcoming."[55] Sanger even attempted to lobby Washington to change the decision. Katō and other Japanese supporters approached SCAP officials and gained support from some Japanese high officials.[56] In the end, all of the efforts made by Sanger, Katō, and their supporters did nothing to change SCAP's decision.[57]

SCAP's official decision to reject Sanger's visit to Japan, however, provoked vehement responses from Americans. The news made national headlines in the United States, including front-page coverage by the *New York Times* and a cover story in *Newsweek*.[58] Letters of both approval and dissent flooded into MacArthur's office, some of which were reproduced in the English-language newspaper *Nippon Times* (later known as the *Japan Times*). So "ill-tempered and extreme" had the debate become, according to MacArthur's own description, that the editor decided to close the column regarding this topic.[59]

The protest letters from Americans directed to MacArthur reflected the growing tensions and gap in views regarding the use of contraceptives both at home and abroad. By the postwar years, most Protestant and Jewish leaders in the United States accepted the practice of contraceptives among its laity as part of "responsible parenthood." Moreover, many Americans considered the spread of contraceptive knowledge and technology to poor, overpopulated countries their "moral obligation," as Christians as well as Americans, since they considered the United States the moral leader of the free world.[60] Protestant ministers and supporters of Planned Parenthood alike questioned MacArthur's "undemocratic" decision to yield to an opinion that denied birth control to the Japanese people—"practiced by many American mothers," including many Roman Catholics—when the world was "rapidly being over-populated," bringing "all the future hazards."[61] Many American liberals were frustrated by growing Catholic influence on politics, as evidenced by the defeat of a proposal to legalize birth control clinics in Massachusetts in 1948 as a result of the pressure of Catholic bishops and the press.[62] They were concerned, quite rightly, that Catholic leaders now had the power to influence US policy decisions abroad.

American Catholics did exert significant political influence in the 1950s as they grew in numbers and economic power. Sanger's supporters were upset that a minority religious group in the United States, a group "virtually non-existent in Japan," could block Sanger's invitation.[63] In reality, however, the American Catholic population doubled between 1940 and 1960, representing more than 20 percent of the population by the 1950s.[64] The postwar economic boom and GI Bill opened wide the doors of higher education and higher-paying jobs for hundreds of thousands of Catholic youth. Many had left their seclusion in urban immigrant enclaves and flocked to new suburban homes to embrace a solid middle-class lifestyle.[65] MacArthur had ambitions to run for the Republican presidential nomination after his duty in Japan and therefore did not want to alienate his Catholic constituency.[66]

Cold War politics further bolstered the Catholic Church's political power. The Catholics represented "the vanguard of the anti-red zeitgeist," as historian Seth Jacobs describes in his work on US diplomatic relations with Vietnam's Ngo Dinh Diem regime, and had a strong influence on foreign policy.[67] A few prominent Catholics, such as Bishop Fulton Sheen, became popular media personalities and helped spread their anticommunist views widely to the American public. American Catholics, along with Protestant and Jewish leaders, emphasized the religious character of the United States—a country of democracy and individual human rights—in contrast to the "bolshevistic and atheistic Communism."[68] The backing of American Catholics, therefore, was vital in the ideological battle between the United States and the Soviets.

At the same time, it was not simply "the attitude of U.S. Catholicism," as Crawford Sams confessed, but "the issues of genocides and communists" that made SCAP leaders especially nervous about any association with reproductive policies in Japan.[69] In a private letter to a Northwestern University professor regarding SCAP's position on Japan's population problem, Sams mentioned that the United Nations had "made an agreement indicating their abhorrence for genocide." He therefore stressed that "it would be most unwise for the occupying powers to come into a conquered country and attempt to force on these people limitation of families.[70] In fact, after the UN's adoption of the so-called Genocide Convention in December 1948, the US Department of State had ordered all American diplomatic and consular offices to alert the department of any communist charges of American "genocide" against domestic or foreign racial groups.[71] It would then be a breach of federal order and a danger to national security to openly advocate fertility reduction in an occupied nation.

The American representatives of the RF mission shared SCAP's concern that even the private acts of "foreign aid" could be misinterpreted as a manifestation of American imperialism and harm their nation's image as the leader of the free world. Roger Evans warned: "America's determination to stop Communism . . . [could] connote imperialism and tyranny more than democracy [to Asian countries]. . . . However good our intentions, America has too often launched her aid programs with a philosophy that 'What's good for us is good for you; what works with us will work with you. Dollars will do it.'"[72] Even Warren Thompson, whose statement endorsing birth control for the Japanese caused controversy, stressed that MacArthur should not *force* the Japanese government to initiate a birth control program because the communists could "make capital of [an] alleged 'American Scheme to Destroy the Japanese Race.'"[73]

It was imperative for American advocates of population control to distinguish their roles in Asia from those of European colonists and Soviet communists. European colonialism, they argued, brought only "superimposed and one-sided development" and destroyed the local infrastructure, which led to the relative reduction of death rates but not necessarily of birth rates. The goal of US leadership was to "stimulate" and "encourage" indigenous initiatives rather than to "dominate."[74] To distinguish themselves from the Soviet rulers, furthermore, they explained that their birth control advocacy was to teach the "principles of democracy"—the value of life and individual rights—in Asian culture, where human life, they believed, was "so cheap."[75]

The goal of Americans then was to aid and stimulate Japanese initiatives in this direction. American population control advocates emphasized that they were simply responding to local demands for leadership in birth control programs in Japan. Some Americans attributed the Asian apprenticeship position to the "Oriental mentality"—the Japanese were "by nature obedient and submissive when orders come from the top."[76] Even if they did not rely on such Orientalist stereotypes, they frequently emphasized that the Japanese themselves asked help from Americans. In fact, many Japanese leaders did seek the tutelage of Americans, or at least American money, in regard to population matters.[77] In face of criticism from American Catholics and the Soviets, Japanese cooperation indeed proved crucial for American leaders to carry out birth control projects in Japan under the semblance of indigenous initiatives.

Importing Birth Control Programs from the US South

As SCAP officials learned that even the views of private consultants were not immune to accusations of US imperialism, they found that the most effective and less controversial way to implement population policies in Japan was by nurturing indigenous efforts. Many Japanese political leaders had been invested in the population problem since the early aftermath of war. Nonetheless, American officials lamented that they could not find any "spirited leadership" in this field—until they discovered Koya Yoshio. Koya was a veteran bureaucrat in the MHW and also director of the IPH in Tokyo. He was not even interested in birth control until after the war; in fact, during the war he was a major proponent of pronatalism. Nonetheless, SCAP consultant Oliver McCoy found a singular potential in Koya, who, he described, had "developed keen interest in the subject of population control" and was "fired with enthusiasm on this subject."[78] Koya was an ideal surrogate to carry out American-devised birth control programs, as he shared the same eugenic and racialist thinking behind population control programs as many white elites.

Koya was a leading medical scientist in Japan who had worked closely with the government on racial hygiene and population policies since the prewar years. After graduating from the prestigious Medical School of the Tokyo Imperial University, Koya spent a year studying at the Kaiser Wilhelm Institute in Berlin-Darlem, Germany, in 1926. During his professorship at the Kanazawa Medical University in Japan, he focused on biostatistics and anthropometry: specifically, research on tuberculosis among the rural Japanese and the racial composition of the Ainu people in northern Japan. Together with his colleagues, he started the periodical *Minzoku eiseigaku kenkyū* (Racial hygiene research) in 1936. He was also vice president of the Japanese Association of Racial Hygiene (Nihon minzoku eisei kyōkai), established in 1930. Koya's reputation for his work on tuberculosis earned him a position in the MHW in 1939. While maintaining this position, he also began working in the IPH in 1941 and was appointed head of the Division of Welfare Science the following year. Investigating population statistics and the health and hygiene of Japanese subjects was the major task of the IPH, which was taken over by the military government during the war. The military government demanded research into the practical matters of colonial ruling, such as the matter of race relations between the Japanese and the colonial subjects.[79]

Despite his wartime research supporting the government's pronatalist policies, Koya made a smooth transition to a new advocacy for population restriction after the war. His fundamental philosophy had not changed over the years: he aimed to protect the *quality* of the Japanese population, and the issue of *quantity* was only a secondary concern. Koya's wartime endorsement of pronatalism stemmed from his concern about declining birth rates and the fragile body strength of urban and educated people, as his own research demonstrated (Fig. 4.1). After the war, Koya merely changed the emphasis from encouraging educated people to have more children to discouraging the rural poor from having as many.[80] He quickly established his leadership role in population reduction, as he headed the MHW Round-Table Conference on Population Problems in January 1946.

Koya was appointed as new director of the IPH after SCAP expelled its wartime leader, Nobechi Keizō, whom they suspected of engaging in unnamed "subversive propaganda."[81] The IPH, established with the assistance of the RF in 1939, worked alongside the PHW Section of SCAP to carry out health reforms in postwar Japan. As consultant to the IPH, McCoy had been in close contact with Koya since the beginning of his duty in SCAP. McCoy furnished Koya with "a batch of literature about family planning and contraception" obtained from the Planned Parenthood Federation of America. Koya, in turn, kept McCoy informed about the decisions and actions of the Japanese government regarding population issues. It was mainly through Koya that Sams and McCoy ensured that a concrete provision on birth control instruction was included in the revision of the EPL. Following the amendment, McCoy worked with Koya to draft a statement of policy to submit to the Cabinet's Council for Population Problems (Jinkō mondai shingikai), which specifically recommended that the government promote birth control. McCoy also had long discussions with Koya each time he gave public speeches and delivered papers on the population problem, making sure that Koya emphasized the duty of public health organizations and medical officials to promote birth control.[82]

SCAP made a major step toward implementing an American-designed population policy in Japan by sending Koya to a reconnaissance mission to the US South from February to April 1950. The trip was supported by

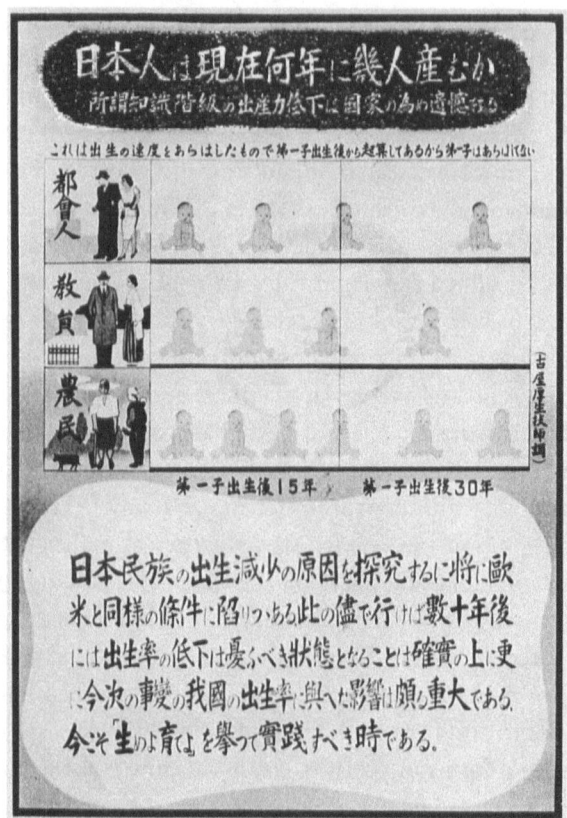

FIGURE 4.1. The poster, created by Koya Yoshio, compares the average numbers and rate of childbirths among city dwellers, teachers, and farmers. The text reads: "As we investigate the reasons for declining births among the Japanese race, we realize that we are following the same fate as Western nations. If this trend continues, Japanese births will decline at an alarming rate, and the recent [Manchurian] Incident has already had a pernicious effect on our birth rates. It is now more important than ever to carry out the slogan: 'Multiply and Prosper.'" From Kōseishō yobōkyoku, *Kokumin yūsei zukai*, 15.

funds from the US Government Appropriations for Relief in Occupied Areas. Among the eleven Japanese officials representing the MHW, Koya and Ishibashi Ukichi, who worked on infectious diseases, were the only ones visiting southern states: Mississippi, Georgia, and North Carolina. The fact that Koya was sent to the southern states suggests that US officials were quite clear about what they wanted him to learn: how to incorporate birth control into state-supported public health programs.[83] The US South had a unique history in regard to birth control and public health. North Carolina was the first state to launch a state-supported birth control program in 1937, an initiative led by George M. Cooper, an assistant director of the state's board of health, and Clarence J. Gamble, heir to the industrial giant Proctor & Gamble and trained medical doctor. South Carolina, Virginia, Georgia, Mississippi, and Alabama followed suit.[84]

Race played a key factor in the development of public health programs in the South. Along with the discovery of germ theory and other scientific knowledge, medical experts and eugenicists pathologized the African American body by linking race to the susceptibility to certain diseases. Under the name of public health, ordinances and programs backed by these new "scientific" theories helped further justify Jim Crow segregation and racial discrimination in the southern states. In particular, campaigns against tuberculosis, syphilis, and hookworm established a powerful model for eugenically informed public health initiatives in the South during the 1920s and 1930s. These prewar public health programs served to solidify the image of the black body as a carrier of disease and agent of contamination, thereby instigating social fears about differential fertility and racial mixture between blacks and whites.[85]

The development of public health programs in the South, however, was rudimentary during the early decades of the twentieth century.[86] Linda Gordon argues that the absence of large Catholic constituencies combined with racism accounted for the pioneering roles of southern states in birth control services despite the general lag in other social-service programs.[87] Economic and eugenic factors attracted many white birth control advocates and health officials to promote birth control among southern blacks. Birth control, many believed, would reduce the number of those on relief or those deemed inferior and undesirable. Advocates of state-supported birth control programs successfully persuaded reluctant county health officials to establish birth control clinics after showing them vital statistics that indicated the higher percentage of black births than white births.[88] Yet most of these programs remained of unequal quality, underfunded, and inconsistent. White professionals who sponsored birth control services for blacks repeatedly changed their minds and terminated financial support without any continuous follow-up programs.[89] What Koya observed in the South was presumably some of these sporadic birth control programs targeting African Americans.

Having studied race relations between the Japanese race and other Asians in a multiethnic Japanese Empire during the war, Koya was keen to learn how a multiracial country such as the United States handled race relations, in particular, the issue of differential fertility. His wartime research included studies on differential fertility between the Japanese and the Koreans, maintaining the common eugenics argument that the "lower" races typically outnumbered the "advanced" ones, who adopted modern practices of birth control.[90] He therefore believed that white Americans would naturally want to limit the uncontrolled population growth of African Americans as a "biological reaction" against the threat of interracial mixture.[91] When he came across data in Mississippi showing an "unusually large budget" allocated to "housing and public health projects," he was convinced that this unexplained budget must have been used to support birth control programs among the black population. This was fallacious reasoning; in reality, the US government provided relatively very little money to public health and welfare services for African Americans before the nationwide War on Poverty campaign of the 1960s.[92] Koya nonetheless confirmed the presumed link between state birth control initiatives and black population control through his field experience in Hattiesburg, Mississippi, a booming small town near Jackson. He spent a week there following white public health nurses to black communities for "health and sanitation services," which, according to Koya's impression, centered on birth control instruction. Koya was impressed by the subtle way in which these white nurses offered guidance to family planning to black mothers without evoking the larger population problem.[93]

While it was Koya's own request to visit these black communities, US officials carefully arranged most of his trip schedule, especially his meetings with important scholars and officials in population problems and public health. At the University of North Carolina at Chapel Hill, Koya was scheduled to meet Harold J. Magnuson, a scientist famous for his syphilis experiments, and Rupert B. Vance, an authority in population problems and migration, particularly in relation to the "black problem." He was unable to see Vance, but the highlight of his stay in North Carolina was his meeting with George Cooper, the state official who famously played a pioneering role in marrying birth control with state-sponsored public health programs. Over the age of seventy at the time of Koya's visit, he was still working at the state's public health department. Already familiar with Cooper's pioneering role, Koya was excited to have an in-depth conversation about how to launch successful birth control programs in Japan. The two doctors first talked about the training courses for medical professionals on contraception offered at the IPH in Tokyo. Cooper assumed that most poor women in remote areas were ignorant about the need and methods of birth control unless they were directly guided by medical professionals. He therefore advised that the IPH initiatives should be followed by even more active measures such as deploying public health nurses as social case workers, a method he used in North Carolina. Cooper also suggested that Koya should, at least in the beginning, offer free contraceptive devices and drugs. Koya was in complete agreement. Despite the inclusion of birth control instruction in the EPL, only a few people—usually urban and educated—visited health clinics for birth control consultation in Japan; the most needy people in rural, working-class areas seemed to show little interest. Koya thus juxtaposed the southern blacks he encountered with these rural people in Japan.[94]

Koya's brief conversation with Cooper had a crucial impact on population policies in postwar Japan. Koya would incorporate many of Cooper's suggestions into legal reforms and birth control programs, such as the strategies of directly sending visiting nurses and of providing easy and simple free contraceptive devices to poor families. Cooper urged Koya to make these birth control reforms in Japan on a national level through official venues. He lamented that the birth control programs in the United States lacked uniformity and remained underfunded due to various political pressures and opposition but believed that the Japanese could bypass such barriers.

Koya's meetings with American mentors ended with the two most important demographers in global population studies: Warren Thompson and Pascal K. Whelpton. If the southern trip could be described as the "main course," Koya later wrote, then this meeting at Miami University in Oxford, Ohio, was the "dessert course of a lavish meal." Thompson and Whelpton had respectively finished their duties as consultant to SCAP's Natural Resources Section in 1949. When the two professors asked Koya whether the Japanese government was taking concrete measures to control population growth, Koya felt embarrassed that he could not give a positive response to the question. "But that does not mean that the government does not care," he hastily explained to the professors. "There is a heightening interest among the public on birth control, and even those in the rural areas are now worried about having too many children. Therefore, I believe that the government would soon prepare an adequate budget and take concrete measures to solve the problem." At the end of their meeting, Thompson implored: "Japan is facing a serious population problem now. I hope you will make every effort to solve the issue." Deeply impressed by their "sincere concern for Japan's future," Koya was, more than ever, determined to carry out what he learned during his reconnaissance trip to the United States in his birth control projects in Japan.[95]

As historian Yukiko Koshiro shows, many postwar Japanese leaders maintained an idea of the Japanese as "honorary whites": racially Asian but culturally closer to white Westerners.[96] They shared with white American leaders the same ideas of modernity, progress, and civilization. They saw their relationship with white Americans based on mutual respect, although not necessarily on equal terms. In other words, they accepted their apprenticeship position toward American leaders. This vision is apparent in Koya's description of his meeting with Thompson and Whelpton, whom he revered as "the world authorities in population problems." He was embarrassed when he could not answer some of the questions they asked about the state of population policies in Japan, but he appreciated their patience for responding to the "very elementary" questions that Koya asked them in return for their opinion. Koya was deeply moved, not only by their tutelage on population policies but also by the warmth and care that these white hosts exhibited to their special guest from Japan. Thompson appeared in Koya's eyes "like a fatherly master" (*shifu*), literally. He recalled the kind, parental manner in which the elderly scholar woke him up after Koya fell asleep on the drive back to his hotel in Thompson's car.[97] Koya was indeed an ideal apprentice for American population control leaders. Not only did he share with white Americans the racist and eugenic logic behind birth control programs, but he also appreciated the help and guidance of US leaders and gratefully accepted all the advice they had given him.[98]

Koya was not the only public health official with a special interest in birth control to be sent to the United States during the Occupation. Other leading experts in public health or in population studies followed. Tachi Minoru, head of the Institute of Population Problems in the MHW, stayed in the United States from December 1950 for several months to study population statistics, including his visit to the Princeton OPR.[99] Muramatsu Minoru, head of the population section of the National Institute of Health in Japan, went to the United States in 1951 to study public health. He chose to study at Johns Hopkins University instead of Harvard because birth control was illegal in Massachusetts.[100] Kitaoka Juitsu, former director of the Institute of Population Problems and managing director of the Birth Control Association of Japan, headed to the United States in early 1950 with travel expenses paid by a private American organization. SCAP consultants helped Kitaoka arrange meetings to discuss the Japanese population problem with American leaders in Washington, D.C., and New York.[101] Whether their travels were government supported or privately sponsored, SCAP not only approved their travels but also helped arrange and monitored their personal meetings with American individuals. As Sanger commented, "Though MacArthur won't let us go to Japan, I am gradually seeing some of the Japanese notables whom he is sending to this country."[102] The transpacific connections made between American and Japanese birth control advocates in the United States apparently did not violate SCAP's neutrality position because they were not publicized and were made "voluntarily" by the Japanese—even though in many cases the Americans arranged the meetings with the Japanese visitors. American activists further provided both financial and technical support to birth control programs in Japan through private and anonymous correspondence—with the knowledge and even approval of SCAP officials.

The "Silent Partner"

After he returned to Japan, Koya wasted no time carrying out what he learned in the United States. The key figure who realized Koya's birth control programs was the American millionaire Clarence Gamble.[103] SCAP obviously could not provide direct financial support. SCAP's official position of neutrality also limited the Japanese government's willingness to allocate any significant budget for birth control programs. Under these circumstances, private donations from Clarence Gamble first bankrolled Koya's and other birth control projects in Japan.[104] With Gamble's assistance, in September 1950 Koya launched the famous "Three Village Studies" in the outskirts of the Kantō district (eastern-central Japan), representing the mountains (Minamoto-mura in Yamanashi prefecture), plain (Kamifunaka-mura in Kanagawa prefecture), and seacoast (Fukuura-mura in Kanagawa prefecture).[105] Through Koya, Gamble was able to covertly monitor the birth control programs in Japan and experiment with certain methods and strategies that could effectively lower the fertility rate of the rural Japanese.

Clarence Gamble began his career as a biologist and medical doctor just as Margaret Sanger was making headlines for her birth control activism and eugenics philosophy was sweeping the intellectual world in the 1910s and 1920s. In graduate school at Princeton University, Gamble worked under Edwin Grant Conklin, the biologist sent by the RF to Japan in 1922. After graduating from Harvard Medical School in 1920, he continued medical research at the University of Pennsylvania. In 1924, he met gynecologist Robert Dickenson, founder of the National Committee on Maternal Health, who urged Gamble to "take up the work" of establishing birth control as a legitimate medical practice. As a result, Gamble contributed money, knowledge, and advice on birth control to maternal health clinics in Philadelphia and Cincinnati.[106] (Koya visited the latter during his 1950 trip, although at the time he was not aware of Gamble's earlier involvement in the clinic.)

Race and eugenics were important elements that motivated Gamble's birth control work. It was Gamble who helped George Cooper set up state-supported birth control programs in North Carolina. Cooper was "a perfect lamb" to realize Gamble's idea to integrate birth control into public health services aimed at poor, rural people.[107] Gamble also worked with Margaret Sanger on the so-called Negro Project, launched by the Birth Control Federation of America in 1939. Even though black communities themselves actively took part in grassroots birth control activities with their own agenda and concerns in mind, the project resembled a kind of "social science laboratory," as historian Johanna Schoen has described it, when the federation accepted Gamble's advice to focus on establishing "demonstration clinics" after Sanger's suggestion for a grassroots educational campaign.[108] To avoid being "misunderstood by Negroes" as a white conspiracy to trigger black "race suicide," Gamble assured that the program should "appear to be of, by and especially for the colored race."[109]

Venturing into population control in Japan was a continuation of Gamble's prewar activities in the South to test simple and effective methods of contraception, but it also represented his first project abroad beyond the forty-eight states and Puerto Rico. Gamble learned about the population situation in Japan during his 1949 Princeton reunion from Frank

Notestein, director of the Princeton University OPR and leader of the RF Far East Mission. He then asked SCAP consultants Warren Thompson and Oliver McCoy about any "possible means of aiding the propagation of information about birth control in Japan." Both agreed that "such knowledge is badly needed" and suggested he send his money for use by Katō Shizue and Kitaoka Juitsu in their work on birth control.[110] Daniel B. Luten Jr., technical adviser to the Natural Resources Section, assisted Thompson in the process of transferring Gamble's money to Katō and Kitaoka.[111] Through McCoy, Gamble soon got in touch with Koya as well.

In accordance with their position of neutrality, however, SCAP officials were worried about the publicity attached to this millionaire, who had worked with Sanger on birth control projects.[112] They denied Gamble's request to visit Japan, which arrived soon after the controversy over Sanger's visa, despite his attempt to emphasize the scientific aspect of his work.[113] At the same time, McCoy and other RF consultants did not discourage Gamble's involvement in Japan's population programs as long as it was not exposed to the public eye. Even though McCoy explained that the arrangement was made "during [his] absence," he was fully aware that Gamble made donations to Koya to support his village studies. Despite their suspicion that "when Dr. C. J. Gamble put [his] hand to something, it [brought] trouble just as often as benefit," in most cases SCAP and RF officers believed it would be "a legitimate gamble" to accept his money.[114] Gamble himself was well aware that it was wiser to keep his involvement invisible from the public. As in the prewar "Negro Project," he insisted that it was important to "make the work seem to be entirely Japanese." He requested that Katō keep his contribution anonymous to obviate "the possibility that the public [would] think that Americans [were] trying to decrease the Japanese race."[115]

Gamble's influence was not limited to finances. As McCoy reported to his RF colleague, Gamble was apparently "trying to guide the project through correspondence."[116] Gamble was known for having a "one-track mind and ego," being very particular about how his money would be used in the project.[117] For example, he demanded that his money be used for propaganda and educational campaigns at governmental clinics rather than for traveling clinics, which Katō had initially requested. He also pointed out that Katō had "misunderstood [his] suggestion" to pay nurses or mothers to advertise the clinic, not to pay directly to mothers themselves to use birth control.[118] While working with Koya on the village experiments, he insisted on testing one contraceptive at a time. Koya, however, feared that such an approach might draw criticism that they forced the use of a particular method. In the end, Gamble accepted Koya's plan to give free choices from a variety of simple methods—"cafeteria style."[119] Nonetheless, he persisted in his eagerness to test the effectiveness of certain methods. For example, he urged Koya to test the jelly-and-syringe method rather than the sponge-and-powder technique, which Koya favored.[120] At Gamble's insistence, Koya also included the sponge-and-salt-solution method, a method later criticized for its ineffectiveness and health risks.[121] Gamble insisted on testing these methods despite Koya's reports that the women in the experiments stopped using them because of their ineffectiveness, inconvenience, or discomfort.[122] However, Gamble rejected Koya's suggestion to promote other methods such as the rubber cap, a type of proto-condom, as he personally could not find any advantage in them. Only occasionally did Gamble and Koya agree on the potential and effectiveness of certain contraceptives, such as the Sampoon foam tablet.[123]

In addition to his suggestions of specific contraceptive methods, another major strategy in Gamble's birth control experiments took root in Japan: the use of case workers to directly visit the houses of needy women in rural areas to disseminate birth control information and techniques. Gamble had already suggested this idea to Katō in their early correspondence, but Koya actually realized the plan in his capacity as a public health official.[124] Koya first learned about using case workers in birth control programs during his US trip from George Cooper, who had originally adopted this strategy from Gamble. After the meeting of the MHW's Committee on Birth Control in December 1951, Koya officially assigned public health nurses and midwives as case workers in rural areas. Based on the model he saw in the United States, Koya had initially planned to use only nurses trained under the modern public health system. However, nurses were "handicapped by the fact that many are young and unmarried," a factor government officials believed would be disadvantageous when instructing reluctant wives about birth control. Accordingly, the leaders agreed to employ both nurses and midwives, although they found the latter rather difficult to use due to their age, experience, and professional pride.[125]

Koya's training in birth control work by his American mentors had tangible policy effects. He successfully persuaded Health and Welfare Minister Hashimoto Ryūgo to take action against the soaring number of abortions since their legalization in 1948.[126] Accordingly, based on a cabinet resolution in October 1951, the MHW announced a specific "plan to promote birth control" and sent it to all prefectural governments in June 1952.[127] Members of the National Diet, the Japanese legislature, made further revisions to the EPL to implement these governmental announcements. The 1952 revision changed the name "Eugenic Marriage Consultation Offices" (Yūsei kekkon sōdanjo) to "Eugenic Protection Consultation Offices" (Yūsei hogo sōdanjo), thereby making advice about birth control more explicitly part of their mandate. They also added a provision that officially assigned the role of case workers for contraceptive guidance to midwives and nurses.[128] While SCAP consultants approved these changes, at this point—approaching the end of the Occupation in 1952—they no longer found the need to actively "interfere with Japanese legislation unless it upsets the balance of the budget."[129] By guiding Japanese leaders to undertake the work of population reduction and tacitly using American private consultants to contribute money and expertise, SCAP had successfully defended their position of benevolent neutrality.

Legitimizing Global Population Control

The information and experience American demographers and health workers gained during the US Occupation of Japan provided an important blueprint for birth control projects in the rest of Asia in the coming decades. The Japanese experience of rapid reduction in fertility in the postwar years—with birth rates starting to decline as early as 1947—soon became the focus of discussion among American leaders interested in population control abroad, especially in Asia. In fact, American demographer-consultants during the Occupation already had in mind the significance of a successful population policy in Japan to the rest of Asia, especially China and India. Ever since the RF mission in 1948, Princeton demographer Frank Notestein was convinced that the Japanese case "might well set the precedent for the whole of East Asia."[130] P. K. Whelpton, during his duty as SCAP consultant, similarly contended that "if Japan [could] develop this program [to encourage fewer children] successfully she can set a splendid example for other over-populated areas of the World."[131] The

RF mission members and Rockefeller III were therefore seeking an opportunity to turn their recommendations on the population problem in Asia into broader action. In the end, they successfully used the Japanese story to convince philanthropists, government officials, economists, scientists, doctors, and other prominent professionals to actively engage in the matter of global population explosion—beginning with a private meeting in Colonial Williamsburg, Virginia, which led to the establishment of the Population Council in 1952.

To start with, however, the RF population control advocates often faced difficulty convincing their own RF trustees to venture into population control abroad. Approximately a year after the Far East Mission, Marshall Balfour, along with RF biologist Marston Bates, presented a report to the scientific directors of the International Health Division euphemistically termed "Human Ecology." Balfour, however, was skeptical about the idea of expanding the theme to "human ecology," which emphasized a broad study into "human environmental problems" through the synthesis of diverse fields. He felt that the RF trustees may or may not get to the basic issue, which was essentially "population as the real interest and crying need."[132] Although the directors accepted Balfour's proposal, the slow progress left Balfour confused and disappointed. He was informed that some senior members were still wary about entering this field—"whether it is called a population problem or human ecology."[133] While Warren Weaver, head of the Natural Sciences and Agriculture Division, believed that studies on population would be of interest to the RF as a whole, he was in favor of conducting basic research rather than setting up "an operating program"; the latter, he feared, could result in the "crystallization of immature dogma."[134] Meanwhile, Rockefeller III had also been making strenuous efforts to push the RF to become involved in global population issues, resulting in a series of frustrations and disappointments. An opportunity finally arrived after a series of dinner meetings beginning in December 1951 with Detlev Bronk (head of the National Academy of Sciences and soon-to-be president of Rockefeller University), Warren Weaver, and Lewis Strauss (chairman of the US Atomic Energy Commission and consultant to the Rockefeller brothers), in which they developed concrete plans to organize a conference specifically devoted to the global population problem. Although Balfour's human ecology proposal failed to materialize into concrete programs, Weaver incorporated much of its concept into this new plan.[135]

The resulting event was the Conference on Population Problems, which took place at Colonial Williamsburg, Virginia, on June 20–22, 1952. The private, invitation-only meeting was sponsored by the National Academy of Sciences. The list of invitees included nationally prominent demographers such as Frank Notestein, Warren Thompson, Pascal K. Whelpton, and Kingsley Davis, as well as leading eugenicists such as Frederick Osborn, Fairfield Osborn, William Vogt (director of Planned Parenthood Federation of America), and even Nobel laureate Hermann J. Muller. A number of participants were involved in the population policies in Occupied Japan. All were white and male, except for two female demographers, Irene Taeuber and Dorothy Swaine Thomas. Margaret Sanger was not invited.[136]

Demographers and public health experts at the conference emphasized that postwar Japan set an important precedent in demographic history, where changes in fertility patterns occurred outside Europe in an astonishingly short period of time.[137] According to the classic demographic transition theory based on the demographic patterns of eighteenth- and nineteenth-century European countries, changes in fertility patterns were a slow and tedious process—centuries of changes from agrarian to industrialized economies and consequent shifts in people's attitudes about family size and lifestyles. As the RF Far East Mission's official report had stated, however, "The East, unlike the West, [could not] afford to await the automatic processes of social change, incident to urbanization and industrialization, in order to complete its transition to an efficient system of population replacement."[138]

The scholars at the Williamsburg conference repeatedly stressed that in agrarian societies such as India, the prospects of fertility decline accompanying urbanization and industrial development was "not encouraging." Neither did migration, another classic approach to population problems, offer any hope, since, as Thompson noted, "after all, we don't have another North America, and we don't have very many Javas left in the world." Using Japan as a case in point, Thompson further claimed that the crowded nation would need to move five thousand people per day just to keep even. Thompson had previously proposed immigration to "unused" lands in the world as a primary solution to the world's population pressure. After the war, based on the Japanese experience, Thompson and other leading demographers admitted that circumstances had changed and that propaganda campaigns for birth control—rather than immigration, increased production, or foreign trade—were the only hopes for solving the matter in a timely manner.[139]

The revised demographic transition theory thus argued for an immediate reduction of birth rates through the dissemination of birth control *without* waiting for the long and tedious process of social and economic development.[140] Many population controllers doubted that a transition to an industrial economy was desirable for these Asian countries, as it would shift a large portion of the labor force away from agriculture and therefore damage the resource base. Under the international division of labor, Western intellectuals believed that these countries would fare better if their economies remained specialized in the agricultural sector.[141] Besides, industrialization and urbanization in Asia did not guarantee a reduction in fertility, as Irene Taeuber demonstrated in the case of Chinese-based populations in Manchuria and Taiwan.[142]

While American scholars sought to differentiate the Japanese experience from the classic Western demographic patterns, they found little need to consider the specificities of each Asian society that defied generalization. As Michael Adas has contended, under the rubric of modernization, social scientists of the postwar period treated these "underdeveloped" societies as "a single, undifferentiated entity" and "obscured elements of diversity through essentialized analyses of a timeless and unified tradition."[143] To be sure, Western demographers recognized that Japanese society, unlike the vast majority of rural Asia, had already gone through a rigorous modernization process since the late nineteenth century and that birth rates had started to decline—except during the war years—since the 1920s. Yet the members of the RF mission had expressed their impression during the trip that the material standard of living in Japan was markedly less than what they had anticipated. Despite the relatively poor living conditions, they contended, the Japanese started to follow a more advanced fertility pattern because of governmental education on birth control.[144] Koya's case studies in rural villages in Japan—also a subject of attention at Williamsburg—seemed to confirm that top-down birth control programs could successfully convert those previously considered resistant to the idea of family planning: rural farmers, coal miners, public relief recipients, and other "marginal" people. Consequently, policy-oriented demographers generalized the Japanese experience and contended that fertility decline could be directly induced through top-down programs in agrarian societies in the rest of Asia even "*before* achieving Japan's degree of literacy, economic development, urbanization, and modernization."[145]

The participants at Williamsburg thus agreed that active, state-imposed fertility control programs were the key to the rapid reduction of fertility in Japan and elsewhere in Asia. Those familiar with the Japanese situation—Rockefeller III, Whelpton, and Thompson—commented on the sudden proliferation of information and discussion on birth control in Japan as a direct result of the government's propaganda campaigns. The demographic transition and fertility reduction in Europe were a "natural" process of evolution resulting from industrialization and urbanization, but they stressed that "exceptions" should be made in postwar developing countries in which "imposed progress" through "outside assistance" was necessary.[146]

Many American leaders in global population control strongly believed that they had the moral responsibility to help Asia solve its population problem. In addition to the tradition of the "white man's burden," the population problem had a special bearing on those involved in public health, as they believed that the Western efforts in eradicating diseases and lowering death rates in Asia had actually "contribut[ed] to the creation of this population problem."[147] As historian Laura Briggs has illustrated in her analysis on the Cold War imagery of transnational and transracial adoption, US opinion leaders and the media repeatedly evoked images of women and children in need of "rescue" by white men. Similarly, American leaders in global population control frequently used images of poor mothers with multiple children, often juxtaposing it with paternal American figures visiting the country to help them solve the problem (Fig. 4.2). Such gendered representations of American benevolence helped mask the structural inequalities and misery caused by US imperialism and led the American public—and the world—to believe that "only US intervention could solve the problems that US intervention had wrought."[148]

The frequent reference to maternal and child health among population controllers, however, did not stem from their concern for women's reproductive health and rights.[149] Instead, it was a "strategic" matter of using "acceptable words" in the face of moral and political opposition.[150] As Isador Lubin, economist and government official, stated during one of the sessions at Williamsburg, "The United States ha[d] a responsibility to make discussions on populations and their control a respectable subject."[151] Only once during the three-day meeting was the issue of women raised, when

FIGURE 4.2. Crawford F. Sams, head of the Public Health and Welfare Section of SCAP, making visits to check if Japanese children were healthy and well nourished. His autobiography notes that it was "then contrary to Japanese norms for an army officer to show interest in children other than his own" (*Medic*, 46). Photo from Crawford Sams papers, 79066 m*B (map case), Hoover Institution Archives.

Lubin inquired whether factors such as "the emancipation of women" and "the revolt of the women" played a part in Japan's rapid reduction of birth rate. Irene Taeuber, who had studied the relationship between women's changing role in society and fertility trends in the US domestic context, did not have the chance to respond to this question. She was allegedly discouraged by her male coworkers from extending her expertise on women's social status to global family planning projects.[152]

Instead, Marshall Balfour responded to Lubin's question by pointing out the role of abortion as an unstated factor leading to a marked reduction of fertility in Japan.¹⁵³ Apparently, however, Balfour did not mention abortion as a matter of women's reproductive choice and improved social status. Instead, he and most population controllers saw it as an effective—albeit extreme—means of population control. Even though they did not actively advocate the practice, American health officials claimed that abortion in Japan, unlike in the United States, was medically safe and morally acceptable. In reality, however, there were many medical complications and moral conflicts over the practice in Japan.¹⁵⁴ Yet the rather casual reference to abortion among Americans, at a time when even birth control advocates were "steadfastly opposed to abortion," indicates that Japanese women's physical and mental well-being was not their concern.¹⁵⁵

At the end of the conference a resolution was passed to establish an international organization devoted to global population control. The plan soon materialized with the formation of the Population Council, an organization independent of the RF, on November 7, 1952.¹⁵⁶ Participants at Williamsburg agreed that an "international" action on a nongovernmental level was desirable to avoid the impression of "American attempts to interfere in their affairs." At the same time, some worried that if the proposed international council recruited representatives "on too wide a basis" from all countries, it would be "hamstrung in its activities." They found it "preferable if the council were started on a small scale and then grew."¹⁵⁷ With the council's board heavily represented by American leaders, it was clear that the United States would play a central part in this international endeavor.

The successful population programs in postwar Occupied Japan—under the covert guidance of Americans—laid an important theoretical and ideological foundation for subsequent population programs to be extended to other developing countries. American scholars who were sent to postwar Japan by the RF—Warren Thompson, Frank Notestein, Pascal Whelpton, and Marshall Balfour—figured prominently in the discussion at Williamsburg and continued to play pivotal roles in the global population control movement. Notestein, in particular, would succeed Frederick Osborn in 1959 as vice president of the Population Council. American advocates of population control thus used the Japanese example to establish their work as respectable, humanitarian, and democratic endeavors in the face of imminent threats of communism and population explosion.

. . .

In the early postwar years, US leaders sought to salvage Asian nations, starting with Japan, from communism by helping them fight overpopulation while establishing themselves as moral leaders of the world. To accomplish this end, they had to actively disassociate reproductive control from controversial subjects such as eugenics, imperialism, and feminism. Accordingly, Sanger was excluded from most of the professional events on global population control, including the Population Conference at Williamsburg. While the first annual report of the Population Council acknowledged prewar initiatives in population studies by the Milbank Memorial Fund, the Scripps Foundation, the National Committee on Maternal Health, and the United Nations, it made no reference to Sanger or Planned Parenthood. Despite John D. Rockefeller Jr.'s anonymous donations to Sanger and her organizations during the prewar period, the RF staff did not believe that Sanger's international work on population was worthy of support.[158]

Even while her compatriots frequently marginalized and discriminated against her, Sanger's supporters abroad still revered her as the most prominent and influential leader in the field. The transnational bond that Sanger formed with Katō Shizue and other activists in Japan, in fact, strengthened after the war, as the tide of birth control finally turned in their favor. The Mainichi Newspaper Company again invited Sanger to Japan soon after the end of US Occupation of Japan in 1952. Because she was no longer sabotaged by the US authorities and the Catholics, this became a much anticipated visit for both Sanger herself and the Japanese public. From Japan, Sanger traveled to attend the Third International Conference on Planned Parenthood held in Bombay, India, as honorary chairman. The conference, which launched the International Planned Parenthood Federation (IPPF), realized Sanger's longtime dream of an international body for birth control work. This 1952 trip to Asia, she triumphantly stated, represented the "culmination" of her work.[159] Japanese birth control advocates as well as Sanger herself would use her celebrity to advance their own goals to spread the knowledge and advance the technology of birth control in the postwar decades.

FIVE

Re-producing National Bodies
Promoting Eugenic Marriages in Postwar Japan

Despite the Occupation authorities' attempt to downplay her influence, Margaret Sanger appeared everywhere in the Japanese media. Even "Sazae-san" talked about her. *Sazae-san*—rather like *Blondie* in the United States, as the heroine was also a housewife—was a popular newspaper comic strip that picked up some of the most popular topics of the time and presented them in humorous and pithy ways. This particular piece on Sanger appeared in *Asahi shinbun* on November 3, 1952, during Sanger's first postwar visit to Japan. The fact that Sanger appeared in the comic strip indicated how widespread the news of her arrival was in Japan—just as it was during her first visit as the "black ship of Taishō" in 1922.

In the first frame of the four-panel cartoon, Sazae-san and another housewife discuss whether they are for or against *Sangā-fujin* (Mrs. Sanger). A profile image of Sanger appears in the balloon, indicating that the Japanese people could recognize this American woman with her signature hat. Then another woman passes by with a baby on her back and carrying a big bag full of groceries. Unlike the other two women, who are clearly middle class, this woman is marked as working class by her dress. The two women ask this passing woman about her opinion on the subject, but the working-class mother bluntly answers that she has no time for such a discussion. Later, Sazae-san, passing by the woman's house, discovers chaos, as the woman was trying to feed eight other unruly children around the dining table.

The comic strip skillfully illustrates the impression that many Japanese pundits and elites held about the distressed situation of postwar Japan in relation to birth rates, economic plight, and racial quality. They feared that, despite Sanger's arrival and national attention on birth control, only middle-class people cared about the issue. Working-class families—those whom national leaders thought really needed birth control—had no interest in the practice and continued to reproduce at an alarmingly high rate. The result was that the poor-quality Japanese citizens would replace those with superior genes, creating a phenomenon called *gyaku tōta* (reverse selection).[1] Spreading birth control to the working-class masses therefore became a matter of national and racial survival.

National leaders frequently used the idea of "eugenic marriages" (*yūsei kekkon*), the state and popular regulation of marriages based on scientific theories of race improvement, when they advocated the need to spread contraceptive practices. Unlike the United States and other Western countries, where eugenics became stigmatized—at least on the surface—by the Nazis' genocide program, the Japanese in general continued to use the word *yūsei* with positive connotations. The word literally means "to live well" and can refer to all aspects of life improvement, both hereditary and environmental. Eugenic marriage was a familiar concept that Japanese leaders had employed since the prewar decades, combining traditional Japanese concepts of family and Western science. In their efforts to convince pronatalists and moral conservatives, postwar birth control advocates described population programs in terms of *yūsei* with the goal to protect marriages and ultimately the national family (*kokka*). The goal of the birth control policies was not to reduce the population per se, they emphasized, but to protect the quality of the Japanese race. Because the Japanese were confronted by a crisis in racial survival and national integrity, the rhetoric of eugenic marriages gave them a sense of control over their racial future after the demise of the Japanese Empire.

What was particularly unique in the postwar period was that women of all social and economic backgrounds became active participants in the conversations about eugenics, marriage life, and reproductive control. Women's magazines were filled with both practical information and theoretical discussions about birth control. Scientific publications and eugenic marriage consultation centers actively reached out to women to educate them about the theories of eugenics.[2] Midwives played a crucial role in disseminating contraceptive knowledge and tools directly to rural women, seeing it as a new calling when their profession of attending home births seemed to face extinction after Occupation reforms. While some families perceived the aggressive birth control campaigns as state intrusion into private lives, many others welcomed the new nationwide openness about reproductive control—not necessarily for eugenic reasons but mostly for their personal benefit.

Even though the government saw the official promotion of birth control as a temporary measure, its effect on the Japanese people was permanent. Laws, public health programs, and media discussions certainly helped bring people's attention to the issue and made knowledge and technology available to them. But in the end, the power and decisions of average women brought down birth rates in postwar Japan. It may have been true that working-class women did not care about the elite debates over "Sangerism"—whether it promoted or prevented the *gyaku tōta* phenomenon or the corruption of sexual morals among the youth. What they cared about was that Sanger's arrival had again opened the gates for discussion and information on sex and reproduction that many women so desperately wanted.

The postwar reduction of birth rates in Japan, however, did not necessarily indicate women's reproductive freedom; it was instead based on the personal "sacrifice" of many women. Midwives who worked as birth control case workers, in particular, suffered from the lack of compensation for their work, the lack of respect from government officials and physicians, and the hostility of local families who saw them as agents of state policies. Despite the aggressive state initiatives and the media hype, many average Japanese suffered from the dearth of accurate information and safe and reliable methods of contraception, often resulting in mental and physical pain. The official discourses of eugenic marriages and national prosperity through the successful adoption of birth control had effectively obscured these grassroots experiences and individual voices.

The Eugenic Protection Law

As historian Sheldon Garon illustrates, postwar social and political campaigns in Japan usually did not show a clear polarization between conservatives and progressives but instead represented elite leaders' efforts to find common ground and consensus beyond different political goals.³ This was certainly the case in reproductive politics in postwar Japan. The compromise between political parties—the conservative Liberal Democratic Party (LDP, or Jiyū minshu tō) and the progressive Socialist Party (Shakai tō)—on the subject of birth control and population was evident in the lawmaking process of the 1948 Eugenic Protection Law (Yūsei hogo hō), which legalized abortion, sterilization, and birth control for eugenic purposes.⁴ In most cases, male physicians were the most powerful ones among the actors involved and took control over the legislation of reproductive policies and the discussions about eugenics in postwar Japan. Although liberal politicians—Katō Shizue and two other Socialist Party members—first took the initiative in drafting the bill, the language and intent of the resulting law showed a great deal of compromise with conservative forces. The drafters avoided any specific reference to the population problem or to women's rights in the legislation and instead described the function of the law as a measure to prevent *gyaku tōta*—as a way to legally restrict the fertility of the poor and those who were mentally or physically handicapped.

The prospect of overpopulation in a devastated economy and society began to concern Japanese bureaucrats soon after the end of war. As early as October 1945, the government set up the New Population Measures Committee (Shin jinkō taisaku iinkai) under the leadership of Koya Yoshio. Following this, the MHW held a Round-Table Conference on Population Problems (Jinkō mondai kondankai) in January 1946. The meeting led to the reestablishment of the Association of Population Problems (Jinkō mondai kenkyūkai), a semigovernmental research institution first created in the 1930s. In addition, the MHW established the Institute of Population Problems (Jinkō mondai kenkyūjo) in April that same year.⁵ The US Occupation government closely monitored these early developments in population policies in Japan, but these preliminary initiatives came primarily from the Japanese themselves.

In November 1946, the Association of Population Problems offered concrete proposals to cope with the prospects of overpopulation in the "New Guidelines for Population Policies" (Shin-jinkō seisaku kihon hōshin), including a call for strict enforcement of compulsory sterilization. The association gathered wartime proponents of eugenic policies, such as Nagai Tōru, Nagai Hisomu, Koya Yoshio, Tachi Minoru, and Kitaoka Juitsu, as well as feminists, including Katō Shizue and Ichikawa Fusae. The members noted that, while birth control might not have any immediate effect on the overpopulation problem, "under current living conditions in the nation, it seems crucial that birth control be disseminated, *whether one likes it or not.*" At the same time, the guidelines listed several precautions in implementing a birth control policy. For instance, they warned that uncontrolled dissemination of birth control could cause a decline of sexual morality and offset the process of *gyaku tōta*. In addition, the report noted the views of some committee members who were firmly against birth control. These opponents proposed "more constructive" ways of dealing with the population problem; such as advancing agricultural and industrial technologies; streamlining the distribution of clothing, food, and housing; and negotiating with other countries for overseas emigration. This ambiguous position in regard to birth control reflected in the guidelines continued to characterize governmental actions on population matters.[6]

Some members of the Socialist Party took the first step toward introducing a birth control bill to the first postwar Diet session in 1947, but their proposal was met with equal measures of resistance and indifference. Katō Shizue, who was newly elected to the Lower House of the Diet as a Socialist Party member in the first postwar election open to female candidates, called out to her colleagues Ōta Tenrei (physician and inventor of the Ōta contraceptive ring) and Fukuda Masako (physician and later president of Junshin Women's Junior College). Together they drafted a bill that aimed to replace the wartime National Eugenic Law (Kokumin yūsei hō) and to remove obstructive restrictions on fertility control, specifically eugenic sterilization, abortion, and birth control. The Eugenic Protection Bill was first introduced into the Lower House of the Diet on August 28 as a "private member bill" and was brought before the Health and Welfare Committee for discussion. Katō appealed to committee members to consider the bill's primary purpose—the protection of maternal health and the eugenic wellbeing of the child—rather than perceive it as a population policy. Despite the drafters' attempt to remove the bill's controversial aspects—its connection to birth control and population reduction—their proposal received no response and was put aside indefinitely for future discussion.[7]

Meanwhile, the socialist legislators also struggled to obtain the Occupation government's approval. American leaders were concerned about international repercussions, especially the responses of Catholics and the communists, of promoting eugenic birth control programs in Japan. Even though SCAP in the end approved the bill, the first Diet session ended before it could be voted on.[8] Katō believed that SCAP's "hands-off" policy on population matters had discouraged Japanese legislatures from expressing any concrete opinion in regard to the population problem.[9]

Nonetheless, socialist supporters of a population control policy were eventually able to compromise with some conservative physicians in the LDP, who had also shown an interest in a eugenics law. Beginning with the July meeting of the Japan Medical Association, physician leaders discussed the idea of revising the National Eugenic Law to safeguard their practices against accusations of criminal abortion. On August 2, before the socialists proposed their bill, an obstetrician-gynecologist and Upper House representative, Taniguchi Yasaburō, presented questions to the cabinet concerning the government's position on the population problem and fertility control. The prime minister responded positively to the questions, agreeing that the government would work on these matters—not necessarily for the sake of population restriction but for medical and eugenic purposes. Having heard about the failed Eugenic Protection Bill, Taniguchi approached the socialist legislators and proposed that they join forces to pass the bill in the next Diet session. Although the socialists hesitated about having the conservative members "take over" the bill, they agreed to delegate the primary sponsorship to Taniguchi in hope of increasing the chances of a speedy passage through the Diet. With Taniguchi's support, the Eugenic Protection Bill was reintroduced as a "government-sponsored bill" and successfully passed both the Upper and Lower Houses. The EPL was promulgated in July 1948.[10]

The EPL, as revised by Taniguchi, was not necessarily what the socialists had envisioned, since it was designed to give power to medical professionals. Even while it legalized abortion and sterilization, it strictly limited the procedures to those necessary for eugenic purposes and mandated that they take place under a doctor's surveillance. Taniguchi eliminated a provision that would have allowed abortion in case of "financial hardship," as he gave in to the pressure from conservative colleagues who were concerned about "the lack of precedent" among advanced countries.[11] The law stipulated that only designated doctors certified by the local medical association could perform abortion and sterilization operations and that they could only do so for what they determined to be hereditary reasons or life-threatening pregnancies. To perform an abortion for non-life-threatening, general health reasons, designated physicians were further required to apply for and obtain special accreditation from their local Eugenic Protection Committee (Yūsei hogo shinsakai). The latter procedure was intended to discourage otherwise fit and healthy women from easy access to abortion. The new law thus not only provided legal protection for physicians against charges that they had performed criminal abortions, but it also gave them the power to control reproductive outcomes for eugenic reasons, instead of leaving the decisions to individual women.

A major disappointment for the socialist sponsors was that the EPL eliminated the provision on birth control, a central aspect of the original bill. The Pharmaceutical Law, which SCAP had helped pass in March 1947, had already established the legal guidelines on prescriptive contraceptive medicine and devices. Both Japanese bureaucrats and SCAP officials therefore found the provisions in the original draft legislation on birth control unnecessary.[12] Moreover, conservative physicians and eugenicists worried that the general promotion of birth control could in effect encourage educated people to decrease their numbers, while those truly in need of fertility control remained indifferent. In other words, the law could actually *accelerate* the process of *gyaku tōta* rather than prevent it. Reflecting such conservatism, the EPL specifically *forbade* the use of sterilization among the "fit and healthy" for the purpose of general birth control.[13]

Despite concessions made on the matter of birth control, both the LDP physicians and the socialist legislators shared the core philosophy declared at the beginning of the bill: "to prevent the birth of unfit offspring while protecting the health of the maternal body." None of the progressive drafters had any objection to the provisions on eugenic sterilization in the EPL. In fact, the socialists' draft of the original bill placed utmost importance on eugenic operations, forced sterilization in particular. When Katō introduced the bill before the Health and Welfare Committee, she criticized the wartime eugenic measures for having been ineffectual in preventing the spread of "poor heredity" because they were overly difficult to implement.[14] In fact, even though the imperial government modeled the National Eugenic Law after the German sterilization law of 1933, it did not actually enforce compulsory sterilization due to its overall pronatalist and family-state ideology. There were also objections from scientists who argued that the study of heredity was not scientifically established enough to provide validity for a sterilization policy. The postwar EPL, however, expanded the target of eugenic sterilization and simplified the procedures for voluntary sterilization.[15] The list of hereditary diseases subjected to sterilization was so extensive that even SCAP officials were concerned about its discriminatory implications.[16] The Japanese supporters of the law, however, emphasized the right of the country to protect its common interests even if it went against the will of the individual.[17]

In the end, most of the main components initially eliminated from the original bill were later recovered through revisions in 1949 and 1952—in particular, the "economic reason" provision for abortion and the provision on contraceptive guidance. None of the socialist members, however, co-sponsored these later revisions, and instead the LDP physicians took full control of the process.[18] The seeming liberalization of reproductive choices was coupled with further expansion of medical and state control over women's reproductive outcomes. Abortion operations continued to be strictly limited to designated physicians, and after the 1952 revision, these doctors were able to perform abortions for any reason, including economic reasons, without the approval of the Eugenic Protection Committee.[19] The role of birth control instruction was assigned only to government-approved Eugenic Protection Consultation Offices. The 1952 revisions to the law allowed midwives and nurses who took government-certified courses to work as birth control field instructors but strictly prohibited others "who lack[ed] the appropriate knowledge and skills for birth control instruction" from assuming this role.[20]

The simultaneous expansion and limitation of women's reproductive choices reflected national leaders' conflicting attempts to prevent the process of *gyaku tōta*. As the actual number of sterilizations performed for hereditary diseases remained very limited after the enactment of the EPL, legislators soon found the need to loosen legal restrictions against abortion and birth control to broaden the category of people unfit for pregnancy: the poor and the working class in general. Government officials hoped that, with the 1949 liberalization of abortion restriction, more "women of the night" (*yami no onna*) and mistresses (*mekake*) would undergo the procedure.[21] Some, including Koya Yoshio, were still concerned that war widows, single women, and prostitutes might not make full use of the EPL, especially because the majority of them were not eligible for social welfare and therefore had to pay the fee themselves.[22] Others feared that the increasingly simplified procedures to receive an abortion could further exacerbate the *gyaku tōta* phenomenon by allowing more fit women to easily abort their fetuses without having to seek approval from the Eugenic Protection Committees.[23]

Legislators recognized that the EPL by itself could not prevent the process of *gyaku tōta* because birth control was, after all, an individual act. Under the banner of a democratic New Japan, an overtly coercive sterilization policy was impossible. Moreover, many average doctors remained indifferent to educating the masses about birth control, not only because it was something that they had less control over but also because it was less profitable for them. Although physician-politicians monopolized the legislation of reproductive control, to achieve the EPL's chief purpose—to prevent the birth of unfit offspring—the bureaucrats needed broader cooperation from other professionals and intellectuals. The media thus became an important venue for the initial stage of public engagement on this issue.

Promoting Eugenic Marriages

By the time the EPL was enacted in mid-1948, the topic of birth control appeared everywhere in the media—from women's magazines, intellectual magazines, national and local newspapers, to medical and scientific journals. Media coverage on the issue skyrocketed after SCAP consultant Warren Thompson's public endorsement of birth control hit the press in March 1949. Popular women's magazines included articles by birth control advocates, doctors, and population experts on both the practical methods and ideological aspects of birth control.[24] At the same time, the elite leaders were extremely careful about how they framed the discussions. The fact that birth control was treated as a trendy topic in some popular magazines alarmed eugenicists, who worried that the "careless" use of contraception among middle-class women could only accelerate the process of *gyaku tōta*.[25] Bureaucrats and experts in support of birth control therefore used the media to educate the public about its *proper* knowledge and philosophies as stipulated in the EPL. Like the lawmakers associated with the EPL, these intellectuals and professionals constantly emphasized birth control's fundamental purpose: the well-being of the Japanese race and the recovery of the nation. The term *yūsei kekkon* thus became a catchphrase used along with the discussions of birth control.

The concept of eugenic marriage had already been popularized during the 1930s and 1940s. Ikeda Shigenori, leader of the Japan Eugenics Movement Association (Nihon yūsei undō kyōkai), proposed in 1927 the establishment of national eugenic consultation centers, where officials would promote birth control while at the same time safeguard against its "abuse."[26] In 1930, grassroots birth control groups started to open clinics for the masses, calling them "eugenic consultation centers," partly to evade police crackdowns. The Japan Racial Hygiene Association (Nihon minzoku eisei kyōkai), established in 1930 by Nagai Hisomu, professor of medicine at Tokyo Imperial University, also created its own eugenic marriage consultation center. In 1935, the association launched a sister organization, the Japan Eugenic Marriage Popularization Society (Nihon yūsei kekkon fukyū kyōkai), whose members consisted of prominent women leaders, including Takeuchi Shigeyo (vice president), Yoshioka Yayoi (adviser), Ishimoto (Katō) Shizue, and Ichikawa Fusae.[27]

The idea of eugenic marriage was an amalgamation of Japanese indigenous demands and Western knowledge and practices. Nationalistic conservatives and Westernized progressives alike, whether they were for or against birth control, took part in the efforts to promote eugenic marriages throughout Japan as early as the 1920s. The first legislative movement to spread eugenic marriages throughout Japan took place in the early 1920s, when the New Women's Association proposed marriage restrictions for persons with venereal disease after consulting eugenic marital restriction laws abroad such as in Norway and the United States. Eugenics magazines frequently carried articles introducing the marriage restriction and sterilization laws in these Western nations. Ikeda Shigenori described these Western measures as a modern, democratic, and humane practice based on the principle of self-improvement and voluntary collective efforts to build a better society.[28] After the Nazi government enacted its sterilization law in 1933, conservative eugenicists such as Nagai Hisomu called for more coercive—and effective—measures to prevent the propagation of those considered detrimental to "racial hygiene."[29]

Once the war broke out, eugenic consultation centers quickly transformed into agents of the Japanese military government's pronatalist policies that encouraged the birth of healthy and fit babies (Fig. 5.1). After the passage of the National Eugenic Law, the MHW opened a Eugenic

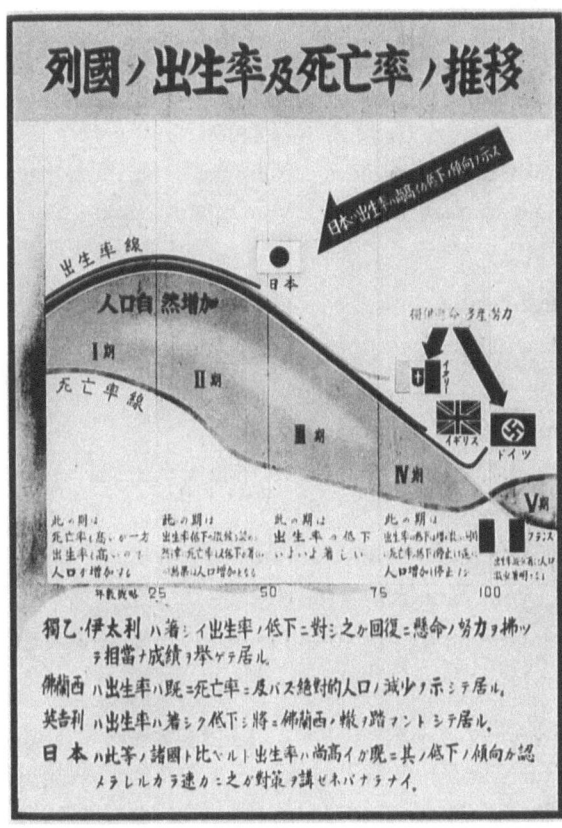

FIGURE 5.1. The chart shows the declining birth rates and population of each imperial power. The text admits that Japan had a relatively high birth rate compared to those of other powers but warns that birth rates were on the decline and that measures should be taken against it. It also notes that Germany and Italy had successfully implemented pronatalist policies to increase their birth rates. From Kōseishō yobōkyoku, *Kokumin yūsei zukai*, 7.

Marriage Consultation Office (EMCO) in 1939 inside a major department store in Tokyo (the Mitsukoshi Department Store at Nihonbashi). Department stores were common locations for EMCOs in Japan, whereas "heredity clinics" in the United States were established in university hospitals around the same time. Although genetic counseling was one of their major functions, the Japanese EMCOs acted more as go-betweens for traditional arranged marriages, providing matchmaking services based on the data on hereditary and ancestry of its members filed at the centers.[30] Women of the Japan Eugenic Marriage Popularization Society, especially female physician Takeuchi Shigeyo, became actively involved in these wartime EMCOs and the population policy-making process.[31]

The government, furthermore, established the "Ten Instructions for Marriage" to be implemented in EMCOs and health centers across the nation:

1. Choose a person you trust as a life partner.
2. Choose a mentally and physically healthy person.
3. Exchange health certificates.
4. Choose a person with good heredity.
5. Try to avoid consanguineous marriages.
6. Try to marry early.
7. Do not be blinded by superstitions.
8. Respect your parents and the elders.
9. Keep the ceremony simple and report your marriage the same day.
10. Bear and rear your children for the nation.[32]

The commandments showed a mix of Japan's modernization (i.e., Westernization) efforts and nationalistic directives. Most prominently, five of the commandments (2, 3, 4, 5, 6) emphasized heredity and fitness, based largely on the scientific knowledge imported from the West over the past several decades. The admonition against superstitions (7) also indicated the government's mistrust toward the premodern and backward masses. The other four commandments (1, 8, 9, 10) aimed to strengthen the Japanese subjects' loyalty to the family and the nation.

After the war, these same leaders upheld basically the same philosophy to promote eugenic marriages among the Japanese. In fact, it seemed even more imperative that the elites should emphasize the concept of eugenic marriage now that legal restrictions on abortion and contraception had been removed and the prospect of racial degeneration seemed ever so real. It is no coincidence therefore that the EPL assigned the roles of birth control instruction to the EMCOs. Takeuchi Shigeyo, who actively supported wartime efforts through the EMCOs, published a book in 1949, *Eugenic Marriage*, as a reference text for the members of the Eugenic Protection Committee in charge of determining who qualified for abortion and eugenic sterilization, as well as for women in general seeking abortion and birth control. She hoped that the book would help the Japanese people take "responsible action" for the nation.[33] Wartime eugenics leader Nagai Hisomu also wrote widely about the concept of eugenic marriage. In particular, he warned of the dangers of "Sangerism," which, he erroneously argued, advocated for the control of quantity over quality of a population.[34] Public and private EMCOs reopened their services soon after the war.[35] The director of the government-operated EMCO in Tokyo and MHW employee Yamagiwa Yoshiko frequently appeared in the media to introduce the office's role in eradicating malignant hereditary and infectious diseases, promoting marriage hygiene, and advising couples to exchange health certificates.[36]

Other societal changes in postwar Japanese society, especially those associated with Western influences, made the promotion of eugenic marriages seem even more vital and pressing. The democratization of marriage under the new Japanese Constitution—the spread of "marriage based on free love" (*renai kekkon*) rather than traditional arranged marriages (*miai kekkon*)—brought a new sense of crisis about the racial fitness of the Japanese. Conservative thinkers worried that young men and women, influenced by the romantic love depicted in Hollywood movies, would marry blindly without looking into the necessary information typically covered in arranged marriages: the pedigree of the partner, especially his or her genetic history.[37] In this context, EMCOs' role as go-betweens of arranged marriages became all the more important.[38] EMCOs would provide the basic genetic knowledge and encourage couples to exchange health certificates before marriage. Still, outright control or prohibition of marriage by the government was no longer acceptable in a new democratic Japan, especially after the worldwide denouncement of Nazi wartime eugenics policies.[39] Health officials determined that if the couple still decided to marry despite "bad heredity" on either or both sides, they would provide the couple with necessary information on birth control so they could voluntarily refrain from passing down the "unfavorable" qualities to their offspring.[40]

The issue of venereal disease (VD) appeared frequently in the discussions of eugenic marriages. The eradication of VD had always been a top health concern for the government.[41] National leaders treated VD as one of the "diseases that affect the entire race" (*minzoku byō*), along with other nonhereditary diseases such as tuberculosis and alcoholism. They found these diseases particularly damaging to the national body because, they insisted, they could be spread to otherwise fit and healthy Japanese men.[42] The sensationalized images of *yami no onna* (women of the night), *pan-pan* (women serving especially American GIs), and other sexually promiscuous women, exacerbated fears of widespread infection.[43] Even though VD was not strictly hereditary, medical and health officials warned that, if not treated properly, it could pass through the wombs of pregnant women, causing miscarriage, stillbirth, or various health issues to the children even if they survived. The spread of VD from prostitutes to "well-bred families" (*ryōke*) was especially damaging to future national fitness because, as Koya Yoshio argued, it could lower their birth rates and decrease the chances of passing down their superior qualities to future generations.[44] In short, the spread of VD was seen as another factor that could contribute to the phenomenon of *gyaku tōta*.

While the availability of contraceptives, condoms in particular, would be useful in preventing the spread of sexual diseases, it also provoked concern that the removal of fear of pregnancy could encourage further licentious attitudes.[45] The idea that the Western practice of birth control could induce sexual corruption and moral decadence had troubled Japanese elites since the prewar decades. The presence of the Occupation army and its broad effects on education, entertainment, and the media exacerbated these fears. The Japanese supporters of birth control therefore needed to emphasize the positive aspects of Western impact by tying the practice to modernity, civilization, and scientific enlightenment.

Modernizing Marriage

Everywhere in the media in the late 1940s, national leaders in support of birth control called for the "scientification" (*kagakuka*) or "rationalization" (*gōrika*) of marriage in "New Japan" (*Shin-Nippon*). One of the common arguments that birth control advocates made was that the use of birth control—within the sanctity of marriage—was an indication of the advanced status of society. A major concern that critics raised about introducing Western sexual practices associated with birth control was the corruption of sexual morality (*tessō*). Proponents of birth control insisted that the problem occurred only when young Japanese misinterpreted the true meaning of democracy and consumed Western culture and practices in superficial ways. To illustrate this point, they referred to the precedents of other "civilized" countries, in which many upper-class families had successfully shaped their youths' sexual morality through strict discipline.[46] Birth control therefore was meant to protect the family and motherhood rather than destroy them. Supporters of birth control portrayed Margaret Sanger as the "mother of the world" rather than a leader of sexual liberation and potential destroyer of the idealized family.[47] The job of national leaders then was to train young Japanese, especially women, to understand the true meaning of democracy and scientific knowledge regarding marriage, heredity, and sexuality.[48]

Scientists actively participated in this mission to establish a "new marriage system" (*shin kekkon taisei*) by joining the discussions about the EPL, eugenic marriages, and birth control. MHW official and EMCO consultant since wartime Kawakami Riichi frequently appeared in the media, explaining the basic mechanism of genetics and heredity.[49] A popular magazine on genetics, *Iden* (Genetics), ran a couple of issues that featured "Marriage and Genetics," including articles written by the nation's leading geneticists, such as Komai Taku, Tanaka Yoshimaro, and Kida Fumio.[50] Beginning in March 1949, the magazine started a special section called "Eugenic Marriage Consultation Room" (*Yūsei kekkon sōdan shitsu*), in which "authorities in genetics" answered questions from readers about genetics and heredity.

Just as they did in prewar eugenics magazines, Japanese biologists frequently referred to the sterilization policies and marriage restriction laws implemented in other civilized countries—such as Sweden, Norway, Denmark, Finland, Switzerland, Germany, Canada, and the United States—when they spoke of the need for eugenic marriages for their compatriots. New knowledge on genetics and heredity from the West available after wartime seclusion further strengthened scientists' conviction to educate and enlighten the Japanese public, the majority of whom they believed were still guided by superstitions and outdated scientific knowledge.[51]

In addition, a combination of postwar Japan's economic, social, and political circumstances reinforced scientists' anxieties about racial degeneration. Having lost the possibility or even hope for emigration abroad, geneticists worried that overpopulation within this small insular country, especially among people with "inferior" genetic quality, could be detrimental to the overall quality of the Japanese gene pool.[52] Economic hardship in rural villages, moreover, increased the frequency of marriages between cousins to maintain properties and fortunes within the family.[53] Since wartime, scientists and government officials had actively disseminated negative images of inbreeding in the nation-building process. Such effort gained new importance in the postwar context.[54] Finally, geneticists worried about the possible effects of radiation after the bombings at Hiroshima and Nagasaki—that it could cause unpredictable mutations in future generations and eventually multiply those deleterious genes widely within the Japanese gene pool.[55] Eugenic marriage, they therefore insisted, was the key to save the Japanese from racial extinction.

Echoing and reinforcing the wartime advocacy of eugenic marriages, scientists and medical professionals emphasized the mother's genetic and social contributions to the nation through childbearing.[56] Scientists who espoused the "epigenetic theory of heredity" (*iden kōsei setsu*), which took into account environmental influences on gene expression, emphasized the importance of pregnant women's prenatal care for the health and fitness of future Japanese children.[57] They argued that postwar social and economic problems—such as malnutrition, infectious diseases (including VD), and environmental hazards (such as radiation)—were just as culpable, if not more so, as genetics for causing mental and physical problems in unborn children. Such scholars pointed out the limits of the EPL in actually improving the overall health of the Japanese, given that only an extremely small number of people with congenital heredity diseases actually applied for eugenic operations. Birth control as practiced by individual women, they thus argued, was vital in improving the general fitness of the Japanese national body.[58]

At a time when the media widely discussed women's newly "liberated" status, young women themselves were frequently brought into these discussions on genetics and the scientification of marriage. An article in *Iden* titled "Women and Genetics" featured a dialogue between a "daughter of a CEO" and a male biologist, in which the latter preached to the former about the importance of basic knowledge about genetics for women as wives and mothers. At one moment during the discussion, the moderator commented, "Observing the two of you talking excitedly about science, I am keenly reminded of the advancement of women."[59] *Iden*'s inclusion of Katō Shizue's article on Margaret Sanger's lifelong battle for birth control also reflected the journal's attempt to recruit more female readers.[60] In another issue, the magazine brought together a biologist at the University of Tokyo, EMCO consultant Yamagiwa Yoshiko, a medical scientist, a female office worker, and a female college student to discuss the question, "How scientific should marriage be?"[61] The EMCOs in department stores had targeted women since the prewar period, combining modern scientific knowledge with "women's consumer citizenship."[62] But it was only after the war, as Yamagiwa proudly reported, that the majority of clients visiting EMCOs were women.[63] An editor of *Iden*, in his interview with Yamagiwa, noted the "beautiful and bright face" of this female director and her friendly smile, which, he observed, would dispel any anxiety that clients might have in visiting a marriage consultation office.[64]

The "average" women who participated in these discussions and the readers of these academic magazines were, of course, predominantly urban and middle class. So were the clients of EMCOs. Marriage consultants frequently complained that those who consulted doctors about birth control were mostly educated men and women influenced by the discussions in the media and concerned about their immediate family finances.[65] However, they claimed, those with hereditary diseases, prostitutes (including widows whose reduced status forced them to do sex work), and the rural poor remained indifferent to the matter of birth control and eugenics. Reports of marriage frauds in some private EMCOs drove many offices out of business.[66] National leaders therefore had to find other means to directly reach those deemed unfit, lest the spread of birth control, as many predicted, accelerated the process of *gyaku tōta*. Midwives played a crucial role in this next step of public enlightenment.

Midwives as Birth Control Instructors

The dramatic shift of national policies and elite opinion from pronatalism to population control directly impacted the profession of midwifery. Since most childbirths, especially in rural areas, took place at home at the time, advocating birth control and fewer childbirths to women nationwide essentially meant taking away the jobs of midwives. Personal letters intercepted by SCAP censors, for example, revealed the "gloomy future" that midwives foresaw if birth control was "the coming thing."[67] The situation that midwives faced after the war was strikingly different from that of doctors, whose source of income was already protected through the EPL by monopolizing the operations of abortion and sterilization. In face of such adversity, some midwife leaders and physicians advocated for midwives' new calling in birth control instruction.

Midwives had been fighting for their profession even before birth control became a national policy in 1952. Americans in the Occupation government sought to eliminate midwifery in Japan altogether in 1946, or at least incorporate it into the general nursing profession. In the United States, midwives existed mainly in immigrant communities or in southern black neighborhoods. As a result of the Americanization of European immigrants as well as the medicalization of child birth in general, midwives by the 1930s were associated exclusively with black "granny midwives," whom the medical establishment stereotyped as ignorant, superstitious, and filthy.[68] Many also believed that midwives regularly performed backdoor abortion. Based on these perceptions about midwifery, US officials found it imperative to "raise the standard of the profession" in Japan and replace "outdated" customs with modern and scientific procedures as practiced elsewhere in the United States.[69] Despite the strong opposition from some midwives, SCAP merged midwifery into the general nursing profession by establishing the Japanese Midwives, Clinical Nurses, and Public Health Nurses Association (Nihon sanba kangofu hokenhfu kyōkai) in November 1946. A group of midwives later dropped out of the new association, however, forming their own independent organization exclusively for midwives.[70]

Contrary to the negative impression by US Occupation officials, midwifery in Japan was one of the few female professions with relatively high social status and professional credentials. The entire community respected and depended on these typically elderly and wise women. Midwives had also played key roles in carrying out the state's top-down regulations over female reproduction since the late eighteenth century. Especially since the issuance of the Midwifery Ordinance (Sanba kisoku) in 1899, which heightened the educational standards and licensing regulations for professional midwives, childbirth became increasingly subjected to physicians' control and state surveillance. In short, midwives served as a vital link between the state and individual reproductive women.[71]

One of the main missions assigned to the licensed "new midwives" (*shin-sanba*) since the late eighteenth century was to prevent and police abortions and birth control in local communities. The Meiji government strictly prohibited abortion performed by midwives. Midwifery textbooks did not include instructions on contraception. Doctors and bureaucrats regulated the market for contraceptive devices under the banner of "protecting women's health."[72] Still, there were some midwives who actively instructed local women about methods of birth control and even secretly performed abortions. As the government's pronatalist position intensified in the 1930s, these midwives were often subjected to police persecution.[73]

The relationship between midwifery and birth control, as the Japanese state and doctors defined it, changed dramatically after the war. In response to the postwar crisis that midwives faced, government leaders and physicians now encouraged midwives to assume a new role in birth control instruction. Based on a trip to southern Japan in 1948, Katō Shizue reported to the IPH about the idea of using midwives to promote birth control to rural people, whom she believed were "apathetic toward birth control" and were unwilling to visit clinics voluntarily by themselves.[74] Soon after the EPL came into effect, Taniguchi Yasaburō wrote an article in a midwifery magazine, *Hoken to josan* (Health and midwifery), explaining the functions of the law in alleviating the population problem and preventing the *gyaku tōta* phenomenon. He noted that he felt "rather sorry" for midwives because the new national policy would decrease their jobs in assisting childbirth but then proposed that they could use their new "spare time" to teach birth control methods to certain people.[75] Similar advice by male physicians frequently appeared in midwifery magazines, urging midwives to "stand up" and discover their new "calling" in birth control instruction.[76]

Japanese medical professionals often referred to the racialized structure of midwifery in the United States but modified the metaphor to boost a feeling of pride among Japanese midwives about their profession and their nation. To explain the Occupation government's general disregard for midwifery, these doctors described the different styles of childbirth in the United States, where midwifery was largely limited to the rural South. While they usually described the black midwives as rustic and warm-hearted women, they emphasized that they were no equivalent to Japanese midwives, who were, they asserted, well trained, well educated, and highly professional.[77] In reality, black midwives, much like their Japanese counterparts, were highly respected as repositories of knowledge and wisdom by their rural community members.[78] What is important here, however, is that Japanese doctors sought to convince Japanese midwives of the need to continue their profession, which now included birth control instruction, by distancing them from African American midwives whose supposed ignorance and backwardness led to the presumed low status of their work.

Meanwhile, Taniguchi started to draft a second revision to the EPL, which included provisions on the role of midwives in disseminating contraceptive knowledge and tools. Based on Taniguchi's suggestion, the MHW set up the Committee on Contraception in the fall of 1951, which consisted of MHW officials (e.g., Koya Yoshio), physicians (including Taniguchi Yasaburō and Takeuchi Shigeyo), and a midwife leader (Yokoyama Fuku). In one of its meetings, the participants discussed who should be best suited to assume the role of birth control field instructors. Taniguchi's bill assigned the role solely to midwives who had completed the government-approved courses on contraceptive guidance. Public health nurses and general nurses strongly insisted that they should also be added. Koya Yoshio wanted to assign those responsibilities exclusively to public health nurses based on the birth control program he observed in the US South. Midwife leader Yokoyama Fuku vehemently opposed Koya's idea, claiming that midwives were much more qualified for the role.[79] In the end, the committee agreed to use all three professions: midwives had the experience, public health nurses were well connected to local health networks, and general nurses were numerous. These changes were incorporated into the 1952 revision of the EPL.[80]

As specified in the revised EPL, all birth control field instructors had to complete government-certified special courses. These courses offered lectures by public health officials about the functions of the EPL and by physicians about the physiology of reproduction. The lectures were followed by demonstrations of how to insert actual contraceptive devices, using "volunteer" women—usually prostitutes, widows, and female recipients of welfare—as "body models" to practice on. At the end of the course, the students were expected to take a written examination. They had to take a week off to attend the entire course, plus pay the enrollment fee.[81] Some elderly midwives, who had ample experience but limited writing skills, felt rather miserable about having to go through such an intensive reeducation process.[82]

The main issue that emerged once the midwives started the job of birth control instruction in the early 1950s was the matter of charging fees for their services. In most cases, it was essentially volunteer work with almost no financial reward. It was often difficult to charge their clients, especially when serving community members whom they knew personally. Largely because of this ambiguity surrounding the salaries of birth control instructors, their number remained limited and their efforts halfhearted. As a solution, many requested that the government pay them so that they did not have to charge individual families in person.[83]

In connection to the issue of compensation, midwife activist Yokoyama Fuku, who was elected to the Upper House of the Diet in 1953, proposed a solution to the Diet. Yokoyama and other midwives insisted that birth control field instructors should be able to earn some revenue by selling contraceptives. Midwives were able to sell contraceptive *devices* (such as condoms, diaphragms, and sponges), but under the restriction of the Pharmaceutical Law, they were prohibited from selling contraceptive *drugs* (such as contraceptive jelly, cream, oral pills, and suppositories). In many cases, instructors advised women to use contraceptive devices and drugs in combination. After consultation, therefore, individual women would have to go to the pharmacist by themselves to buy the appropriate drug. Bureaucrats were at first reluctant to allow midwives to dispense certain contraceptive drugs, which meant adding "exceptions" to the provisions of the Pharmaceutical Law. They insisted that there were already pharmacists with "ample knowledge and experience" working as "household distributors" (*haichi hanbai-in*). Midwives quickly refuted this view, which seemed to imply that midwives did not have the knowledge that pharmacists did. Instead, they stressed that all field workers had completed the qualifying courses for birth control instruction. One even accused the pharmacists of being "narrow-minded" and trying to monopolize contraceptive sales.[84]

As a result of Yokoyama and other midwives' persistent efforts and with the support of Taniguchi Yasaburō, the EPL was revised in 1955 to make it legal for certified case workers to sell contraceptive drugs as part of their job. The reason for the revision, as described by government officials and physicians, was to simplify the process of dissemination—not to expand the expertise of midwives or to give them extra revenue. Under the old system, they explained, rural and working-class women were less likely to take the trouble to go to the pharmacist to buy contraceptives or were too ashamed to do so; therefore, it would be much easier for them to buy directly and privately from (female) case workers in the comfort of their homes. To emphasize that this was not a permanent population reduction policy or a liberalization of restrictions on contraceptive sales in general, the Diet decided to "temporarily" allow the sales of contraceptives by field instructors for five years, after which the policy would be reviewed and renewed for another five years, if necessary. The government also created a budget for the Project to Promote Contraception to the Poor and Needy (Seikatsu konkyūsha jutai chōsetsu fukyū jigyō), in which they allotted some money to be used as instruction fees for field counselors. By targeting specifically "the poor and needy," this was also described as another measure against the *gyaku tōta* phenomenon, not necessarily a budget to help struggling midwives.[85]

Even while the government turned a cold shoulder to them, midwife leaders often used the same elitist language of modernity and civilization as many other national leaders when they spoke in support of state-supported birth control programs. Many midwives who wrote in midwifery magazines and promoted their new role as birth control field instructors seemed to identify with male politicians and doctors despite occasional conflicts and disrespect they experienced. They sought to convince their colleagues that their activities played a vital part in nurturing a "superior race" and founding a "truly civilized country." Yokoyama Fuku asserted that midwives, more than any other women, should be well aware of the larger political and social issues, refuting an opinion expressed by a local health official that midwives need not be educated about the population problem. On one level, Yokoyama's statement shows midwives' resistance against male contempt toward female professionals. At the same time, it reveals that she chose to approach women's reproduction issues as a matter of national interest, not for the sake of individual health and rights.[86]

Midwives' identification with the notion of national prosperity and progress was further evident in the disdain they expressed toward working-class couples whom they encountered in the field. Many midwife case workers complained that it seemed almost hopeless to convince these couples of the need for family planning given the excuses they offered not to use contraceptives: some hoped to have one "gifted" child out of many; some expected to receive childbirth-related financial assistance from the workplace; others stated that they were unable to resist the "animal-like" sexual drive of their husbands.⁸⁷ Such field experience, one midwife wrote, reminded her of a lecture by a scholar of eugenics given at a midwives' training course organized by the IPH. The lecturer contrasted the backwardness of the Japanese during war, who trained their soldiers with "bucket brigades" (*baketsu rirē*) and bamboo spears, with Americans, who invented a "tremendously amazing" device: the atomic bomb. The Japanese would be full of "idiots," the eugenicist warned, if birth control continued to be practiced only among the educated few.⁸⁸ Another midwife described her strenuous effort to bring the attention of the Eugenic Protection Committee to a "mentally retarded" and "sexually perverted" girl, who had just given birth, as a candidate for forced sterilization. While it was not her role to identify such persons, she explained, she went beyond her usual job of assisting childbirth because she felt it would be "irresponsible" of her to overlook such a "danger" that could undermine the future fitness of the nation.⁸⁹

Most midwives, however, were caught between the obligation to serve the country and the resistance of poor families to birth control. At times, the families they visited would hurl water at them, spit on their face, or throw the contraceptive material back at them, in their attempts to drive the field workers away.⁹⁰ One midwife leader warned her fellow field instructors of the antagonism that many poor people felt against society and their refusal to accept other people's advice. Because they could not force family planning on these people, she emphasized the need to talk of "the personal happiness of the family" in their consultations, even if the larger goal was to control population growth or to produce eugenically fit citizens for the nation.⁹¹

Moreover, midwives who promoted birth control often felt ostracized by other midwives, the majority of whom continued to see their assistance in childbirth as their primary role. They described their decision to assume the birth control instruction job as "self-sacrificing," or even "self-deprecating." Even though the government agreed to provide instruction fees for field workers, this was limited to consultation with indigent families and only for a nominal amount. Unable to charge fees in most cases, therefore, most midwives continued to serve as volunteer agents.⁹²

Despite all the trouble and efforts on the part of midwives, most medical professionals never gave midwives the credit they deserved. There were some physicians, writing in midwifery magazines, who seemed genuinely concerned about the future of midwives and proposed birth control instruction as a last resort for their survival. They nonetheless treated these professional women as if they were incapable of standing up or making adjustments on their own.[93] Discussions among obstetrician-gynecologists themselves, moreover, revealed that they saw midwives only as cheap and available labor.[94] Individual birth control consultation, after all, was a time-consuming job, which often entailed listening to women's "complaints" for hours; doctors did not have time for that.[95] Most doctors in general did not even care about birth control instruction at all, as it did not provide the financial incentive that abortion did.

In the end, Japanese midwives shared much in common with the fate of black midwives in the US South. Despite their disdain toward black midwives, public health officials in the United States continued to use them as vital links between poor African American neighborhoods and public health departments. Black midwives, in turn, used the resources made available to them to assist their communities in health education and childbirth work. Once the systems of modern public health were established in remote areas and the majority of childbirth moved to the centralized, sanitized hospital environment, however, midwives lost their value in the eyes of the state and were essentially eliminated through a "retirement policy" after World War II.[96] Likewise, the Japanese government found midwives as useful conduits to spread the practice of birth control in rural areas. The midwives both resisted and complied with state initiatives. Yet, as birth rates started to decline and family planning leaders relied on advanced contraceptive technologies that obviated the need to educate rural women, midwives' role in birth control instruction was no longer of national interest. Eventually, the majority of them by the 1960s had given up their role as birth control instructors—and their profession itself.[97]

Gauging the Effects

In the end, how effective were government-led policies to disseminate birth control, especially among the rural poor? Birth and fertility rates in Japan both started to decline after 1947. The Mainichi Newspaper Company established the Population Problems Research Council (Jinkō mondai chōsa

TABLE 5.1. Rate of Contraception Use in Japan (1950–2000)

Year	Current user (%)	Once user (%)	Nonuser (%)
1950	19.5	9.6	63.6
1952	26.3	13.9	54.9
1955	33.6	18.9	41.5
1957	39.2	17.3	38.3
1959	42.5	20.2	33.0
1961	42.3	26.1	28.5
1963	44.6	19.1	29.8
1965	55.5	16.5	26.8
1967	53.0	19.2	23.1
1969	52.1	19.1	19.3
1971	52.6	20.2	16.8
1973	59.3	22.0	15.1
1975	60.5	21.0	13.3
1977	60.4	19.4	13.3
1979	62.2	21.5	11.7
1981	55.5	24.2	16.0
1984	57.3	23.4	16.5
1986	62.8	21.1	13.6
1988	56.3	19.6	20.5
1990	57.9	20.4	16.5
1992	64.0	17.0	15.1
1994	58.6	19.8	15.4
1998	54.1	23.1	16.7
2000	55.9	20.3	19.3

SOURCE: PPRC, *The Population and Society of Postwar Japan*.
NOTE: The surveys targeted married women under fifty years of age.

kai) in 1949 and conducted extensive public opinion surveys that focused on birth control. The so-called KAP (knowledge, attitude, practice) surveys sought to gauge and analyze the actual situation of fertility trends and the spread of family planning in Japan for further policy considerations.[98] In the first survey in 1950, the percentage of married couples of all social classes who never practiced contraception was 63.6 percent, whereas only 19.5 percent answered that they were regularly using contraception. But the trend shifted rapidly in the 1950s. By 1957, users (39.2 percent) exceeded the number of nonusers (38.3 percent).[99] These numbers seem to suggest that nationwide birth control campaigns in the 1950s were indeed working (Table 5.1).

What was significant, according to the experts, was that the results further showed that since the first survey the gap between social classes in rates of contraceptive use had gradually narrowed. This, they argued, indicated that birth control had diffused into every class of society, especially among the laboring and the lower educational strata. In the first survey in 1950, there was still considerable difference in the rates of practice according to occupation and education, but over the subsequent surveys the gap continued to close.[100] Population experts thus concluded that rural people, who were previously believed to have been resistant to or ignorant of family planning, actually wanted to have smaller families and would try to do so as long as they had the appropriate knowledge and tools.[101]

Does this mean that the family planning leaders' attempts to disseminate birth control exclusively to the rural poor, first through EMCOs and then midwives, were successful? The same Mainichi surveys show that EMCOs/health centers and field workers were somewhat helpful. According to the first 1950 survey, before the government officially commenced the program to use field workers, 74.0 percent of respondents did *not* seek any advice on contraception. Only 0.2 percent received advice from EMCO counselors, 1.1 percent from public health officials, 1.5 percent from midwives, and 3.0 percent from doctors. The percentage of people receiving personal consultation increased over the next few surveys, with 10 to 20 percent of respondents receiving advice at health centers or from midwives.[102] According to MHW official Okazaki Yōichi's analysis of the surveys, in agricultural villages, where people were presumably still hesitant to talk freely about sex, public health nurses and midwives provided vital sources of information on birth control through home visits. Yet he found that city people were more likely to seek advice from doctors, heath centers, and pharmacists.[103]

It was also the case that in cities *and* in rural areas, mass communication media, particularly magazines, were by far the main source of information about contraception, especially among younger wives.[104] In other words, magazines, more than midwives and nurses, were most likely the key factor in the rapid reduction of fertility rates among the Japanese of all classes. National leaders worried that average women did not care enough to follow the discussions on birth control in magazines and newspapers, and such concern led the leaders to use midwives to directly reach out to the population. These findings, however, suggest that people of all classes did in fact take interest in the topic and actively consumed the knowledge provided in the media.

The survey results also show that families practiced birth control for reasons quite different from the goals that state actors had in mind. The Mainichi surveys asked people why they practiced contraception. The results reveal that throughout the 1950s economic necessity was by far the main motivation (40 to 60 percent), especially among the less educated and working-class strata. To a lesser extent, respondents identified maternal health (30 to 40 percent) as a factor. Very few respondents—only around 1 percent—cited eugenic (heredity) concerns. People were in fact aware of the gap between their personal uses of contraception and the interests of the government. In response to questions about whether the spread of birth control was beneficial, more than half (56.2 percent) replied that it was advantageous to the individual, while respondents were less certain about whether it was advantageous (36.0 percent) or disadvantageous (30.7 percent) to the nation. Nonetheless, many were willing to receive whatever assistance they could from the government, as long as it was not coercive. Asked about governmental measures on population matters, the majority answered that the government should provide facilities and education to aid the public on fertility control (41.2 percent). A smaller percentage of them considered that everything should be left completely to the individual (31.1 percent). Only a fraction supported more drastic measures, such as implementing policies to limit births (10.4 percent) or making it disadvantageous for people to be prolific (1.8 percent).[105] These results altogether suggest that average people practiced contraception for reasons quite different from the purpose of birth control that national leaders highlighted—the creation of a strong Japanese race for the revival of the country. Instead, many Japanese simply took advantage of government-supported initiatives and the discussions in magazines on practical birth control methods to overcome the economic hardship they experienced after the war.

Personal interviews and reminiscences further reveal that many average women were skeptical of government officials' birth control campaigns in local communities. Looking back to their postwar roles in family planning, government officials and medical professionals admitted that most women wished to learn methods of fertility control for personal, economic reasons or simply out of curiosity based on the knowledge they obtained in mass magazines and newspapers. A former government public health official recalled that at a meeting with housewives, one of them challenged him directly: "You folks are like double-tongued spies. Who would believe you when you use such rhetoric as 'the happiness of the family'?"[106] These accounts show that the Japanese public were not simply duped into using contraceptives and often refused to follow the hypocritical orders from above. They present a strikingly different picture from what domestic and foreign leaders often described—that the Japanese people, especially those in rural areas, needed and *desired* orders from above and that they otherwise would not take any action.[107]

The social and political circumstances in which Japanese women lived nonetheless conditioned and limited the reproductive choices that they seemed to make as a result of the nationwide birth control initiatives after the war. In particular, poor and rural women continued to suffer from the lack of accurate knowledge and safe methods of contraception. Just as the act of birth control spread rapidly across Japan, so did abortion.[108] Because the EPL enabled relatively easy access to abortion, this method often served as a backup solution to contraceptive failure. Only in the mid-1960s, when more reliable means and knowledge of contraception became widely available, did contraception replace abortion as the primary method of fertility control (Fig. 5.2).[109] The inclination toward abortion therefore was stronger among less educated, working, older women, who were pressured by the economic need to limit the size of their families by any means available.[110] Even as the use of abortion became prevalent, the majority of women worried about its health risks and were afflicted by the moral guilt attached to it. In fact, early postwar studies on population policies had already confirmed the possible harmful effects of (multiple) abortions on women's health.[111] Contrary to the view among many birth control promoters that women of the lower classes sought abortion out of ignorance, indifference, or selfish choice, these results show that economically and socially disadvantaged women were often placed in situations where they felt they had no other choice but to resort to this extreme measure of fertility control. The prevalence of abortion in postwar Japan, in other words, was not a reflection of reproductive choice but rather a lack of it.

Regardless of the actual circumstances of women, the data and statistics showing the rapid decline in fertility rates and the gradual spread of birth control among all classes of Japanese were enough to satisfy Japanese leaders in family planning. In the face of national adversity, they were convinced that they had successfully saved the nation from racial extinction. What they considered as postwar racial and economic recovery, however,

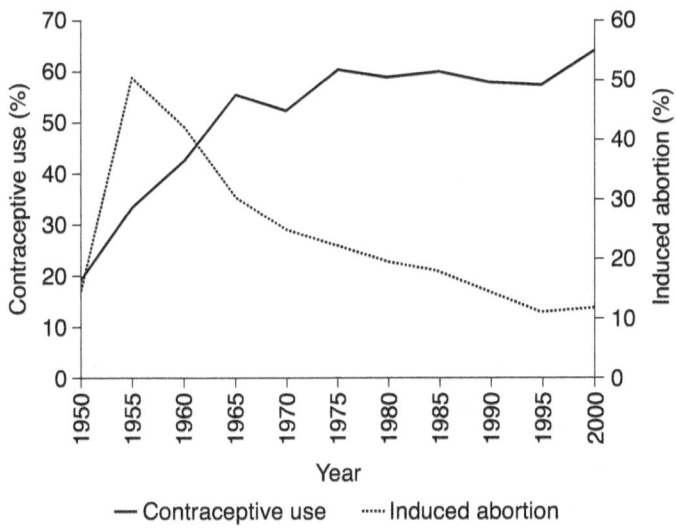

FIGURE 5.2. Rates of contraception and induced abortion in Japan, 1950–2000. Contraceptive use is based on survey results of married women under fifty years of age who are currently practicing contraception. Induced abortion rates are the percentage of abortion cases per 1,000 women ages fifteen to forty-nine. From PPRC, *The Population and Society of Postwar Japan*; Kokuritsu shakaihoshō jinkō mondai kenkyūjo [National Institute of Population and Social Security Research], "Jinkō tōkei shiryōshū" [Population statistics], http://www.ipss.go.jp/syoushika/tohkei /Popular/Popular2016.asp?chap=0.

came from the struggles of individual women to regain control over their bodies and lives.

. . .

Throughout the postwar years, Japanese politicians, medical professionals, and scientists in support of birth control—both male and female, conservative and liberal—used eugenically inspired rhetoric and top-down approaches to spread birth control to rural women across Japan. At the same time, there were also activists who made efforts to return the power of control over reproduction to women themselves. And some turned directly to the iconic pioneer in women's reproductive rights for help. During Sanger's seventh and last trip to Japan in 1959, a group of Japanese wives of wealthy businessmen, many of whom were also public health nurses and midwives, wrote to Sanger. The women deplored the lack of women's own control over reproductive issues in Japan, where women were treated as a "mere instrument for the family production" and men usually led the birth control campaigns. They sought Sanger's suggestions to develop their own women-led campaigns "in the midst of frequent discouragements and difficulties."[112]

Sanger's assessment of the work of these female activists in Japan, however, was not so positive. In a letter to one of the wealthy contributors of the birth control cause, Dorothy Brush, Sanger mentioned this group and their work of sending midwives to the field for birth control instruction. She told Brush, "While [their work] sounds wonderful, when you analyze it, what are the midwives telling the mothers and families? They are not being instructed in methods of contraception by doctors, and often are just telling the mothers about abortion!" She emphasized the importance of having doctors teach contraceptive techniques and therefore urged Brush to support Koya's work of training physicians for birth control instruction.[113] Rather than share with these midwives the passion to help other women, Sanger, like many other elite leaders in Japan, disregarded midwives' commitment and sincerity in spreading birth control information. The negative stereotypes of midwives in America might have affected Sanger's perceptions of their Japanese counterparts. Yet, given her frequent communication with government officials and other family planning leaders in Japan, it is rather surprising that she was either unaware of the governmental training programs for midwives on birth control guidance in postwar Japan or chose to disregard that information.

Her dismissal of midwives' efforts indicates that Sanger by this time appeared more like a business-minded entrepreneur who cherished the connection of those with money and power to carry out her goals rather than a grassroots activist and idealist who remained committed to her philosophy and the people she intended to serve. Sanger devoted considerable time and energy utilizing government resources in Japan and other overpopulated countries to realize her ultimate mission to develop an easy and effective contraceptive for women: the oral contraceptive pill.

SIX

Birth Control for the Masses
Technological Imperatives for Global Population Control

Three years after the founding conference for the IPPF in Bombay in 1952, Tokyo became the host of the Fifth International Conference on Planned Parenthood (ICPP). This turned out to be an especially important meeting for Margaret Sanger, for during the conference she and her collaborators reported something that would revolutionize the history of birth control: the "discovery" of an oral contraceptive pill. It is no coincidence that she chose Tokyo as the venue to make this announcement. Japan was home to a number of loyal disciples of Sanger's transnational birth control mission. She had high hopes for full cooperation on the pill project there, where the government had already taken steps to implement birth control programs in rural areas. Through her extended connections and networks, she organized a group of competent scientists to conduct experiments on hormonal compounds in Japan. She then brought together Japanese birth control activists—despite deep conflicts and divisions among them—to realize her plan for a successful international conference, where scientists from across the world would share their latest discoveries on the biology of contraception.

Indeed, when laws and religious pressure made it difficult to conduct research and field experiments on contraceptives in the United States, Asia and Latin America served as global laboratories for their development.[1] In an effort to disassociate birth control activism from sexual rebellion and radicalism, Sanger and other leaders in contraceptive research capitalized on the idea of global population control as a Cold War weapon against poverty, chaos, and population explosion in Third World countries. Japan served as an important location for contraceptive research intended to serve larger population control projects in areas considered vulnerable to communism, such as India. Japan's rapid reduction of birth rates during the postwar Occupation period validated American involvement—with the cooperation of local officials—in these programs. While semiofficial efforts during the Occupation focused on education and propaganda through local health clinics in Japan, after the Occupation global population control advocates embarked on practical experiments of various simple, yet modern, contraceptive devices in broader Asia.

The American-led global population control movement represented a quintessential modernization project to apply American technological power to solve social and economic problems in less developed areas of the world. Based on the Enlightenment thought of linear progress, population controllers believed that the United States was at an "advanced" state of development, especially in the field of science and technology, and therefore had the ability and duty to help other less developed countries.[2] Focusing on technical assistance and scientific research, they hoped to yield immediate results, bypassing complex socioeconomic factors, moral debates over contraception, or the political implications of their actions, especially their association with imperialism.

Japan, having just been defeated in the Pacific war, served as an important Asian ally in this modernizing mission. Japanese birth control advocates and scientists saw this as an opportunity to redeem themselves as leaders of Asia. They provided technological assistance to birth control workers in other Asian countries while furnishing Western advocates of global population control with model case studies of birth control experiments in rural Japan that could be exported to other Asian areas. At the same time, Japanese leaders, especially those working for the government, made sure that Western population controllers would not use the Japanese merely as guinea pigs for scientific experiments. They were adamant about being in control of these scientific research and experiments, even as they received financial backing and training from the United States.

Gender bias and racial prejudice became increasingly prominent as the birth control movement invested deeply in the field of biological science and technology in the postwar years. Population experts and politicians—both Japanese and American—treated women in the rural Third World as silent, passive test subjects for contraceptive technology. Without their guidance and control, they assumed, these women with their excessive fertility would bring the family and the entire nation into poverty and chaos, a perfect condition for communist infiltration. Although Sanger played crucial roles in coordinating projects and connecting interested scientists and activists across national borders, she chose to allow male colleagues to take the lead and convinced herself to stay in the background. Consequently, leaders of population control consciously downplayed the feminist implications of developing and disseminating female contraceptives. The sexist, racist, and classist nature of many population control projects ultimately led to programs that harmed rather than saved many vulnerable women.

Forming the Family Planning Federation of Japan

Margaret Sanger headed to Japan for the fifth time in the spring of 1954 with a special mission: to help the Japanese prepare for the proposed ICPP to be held in Tokyo the following year. The idea of convening an international conference on the topic in Japan was not simply a random idea of Sanger's; it had been floated around between her and her Japanese friends since before the war. As early as 1931, Katō (then Ishimoto) Shizue shared with Sanger her vision of bringing out "the work of Birth Control in Japan not as a solitary independent movement but in co-operation with other countries as an international movement for the common cause." She informed Sanger that, together with birth control sympathizer Dr. Majima Kan, she was hoping to bring the next international meeting on birth control to Tokyo.[3] As the Japanese government entered a period of aggressive militarism, however, the dream of inviting activists across the world for a co-operative, international cause in Japan was put on hold. Nonetheless, the Japanese activists never forgot the plan. At the Bombay conference, Majima proposed that a meeting be held in Tokyo in the near future, to which Sanger expressed her full support.

The conversation mainly between Sanger and Majima about holding an international conference in Tokyo at first did not sit well with another leader in the postwar Japanese birth control movement, Koya Yoshio. It was not that he was opposed to the idea itself of having an international conference in Japan. The problem was that it did not come from the "right" person and through the "right" route. He confessed to Sanger that he was "greatly surprised" to hear that Majima and those few close to him had decided on a plan "so suddenly without such necessary preparations." In his opinion, he explained to Sanger, "in order to have such a big event in Japan, the proposal should have been made after obtaining the understanding of the Government and consulting with other political leaders and businessmen who are interested in this matter and also who have high esteem of the Japanese society." As a public health official who had successfully used government resources to launch nationwide birth control campaigns in Japan, it is no wonder that he took umbrage at the fact that such an important event was initiated not by him but by those whom he considered old-time radicals of the birth control movement.[4]

Indeed, as the postwar birth control movement gained momentum in Japan, it was simultaneously fraught with friction and conflict among the core leaders. A reporter who covered the Bombay meeting gave an accurate portrayal of the four Japanese delegates, Majima Kan, Yoshio Koya, Katō Shizue, and Ōta Tenrei: "They are all undoubtedly very passionate about birth control, but they never get along well with each other and each have different exterior motives" (Fig. 6.1).[5] Their anger and frustration against one another frequently appeared in their private letters to Sanger. For example, Koya saw veteran activists such as Majima and Katō as socialist demagogues who dismissed the importance of authority and the government. Majima, who was in fact left leaning, criticized bureaucrats such as Koya and Katō as merely using the birth control cause for their political ambitions and not doing any "practical activities" of developing and disseminating contraceptives to the people.[6] Katō felt that male leftists like Majima were holding an unreasonable and unnecessary grudge against her simply because of her gender and class (as she had felt toward Yamamoto Senji in the 1920s). She therefore refused to work with these political foes by declining their invitations to organize birth control groups and meetings together.

The friction among Japanese advocates not only placed Sanger in an awkward position, as she tried to communicate with each of them separately, but it also posed extra difficulty in carrying out the plan of bringing the next international conference to Tokyo. To officially host the conference, the Japanese leaders needed to unite—"at least on paper"—and be

FIGURE 6.1. A drawing satirizing the distinct personalities and rivalry among the four Japanese delegates attending the "Bombay Circus, 1952," or the Third International Conference on Planned Parenthood. From the left: Ōta Tenrei (riding his famous Ōta contraceptive ring), Majima Kan (preparing a dish with an aborted fetus), Koya Yoshio (juggling his "Three Birth-Control Model Villages"), and Katō Shizue (wearing a sash reading "Margaret Sanger of Japan" and Sanger's signature hat). From XYZ, "Sekai kazoku keikaku kaigi ni shussekishita shitennō," 24.

formally recognized as an affiliate group of the IPPF.[7] In the end, the Japanese activists managed to pull together a group, the Family Planning Federation of Japan (FPFJ), appointing former minister of education Shimojō Yasumaro as president on the recommendation of Koya Yoshio. Koya, Katō, and Majima all assumed the role of vice presidents.[8] Wealthy American eugenicist Clarence Gamble also played a part in bringing the Japanese group together. At Koya's request, Gamble, during his visit in Tokyo in March 1953, gathered a dozen Japanese birth control leaders to discuss "the best plan for Japanese sponsorship" of the conference. He reported the conversations to Sanger, emphasizing that the Japanese group strongly believed that the presence of the world-famous Margaret Sanger in Japan would have the most powerful effect in bringing national interest to the issue of birth control.[9] In other words, the Japanese activists also used these American leaders to mend—at least temporarily—their internal chasm and to advance their own campaigns.

Once Sanger successfully convinced divisive actors to unite under the common goal for an international conference, she wasted no time in moving on to the specific planning process. Even as she stepped in as the role of mentor, Sanger was also mindful to preserve the Japanese leaders' self-esteem, especially that of male bureaucrats. In deciding to come to Japan in 1954 to help the FPFJ work out the agenda of the conference, Sanger privately consulted Katō about whether she was not appearing too obtrusive in the eyes of Japanese men. Especially referring to Koya, she wrote: "I can see all at once that being a man and of the type that men lead and women follow, he probably took a somersault at the very thought of my coming to advise him or his Committee as to the details of a Conference." Sanger then wrote directly to Koya, offering to make a stop in Japan, adding that she "did not intend [Koya] to think it necessary for [him] to consult [Sanger] on [their] agenda for the 1955 Conference" if he believed that it could be done without her help. At the same time, she assured both Katō and Koya about her "experience over long years" of putting together national and international conferences that brought together leading scientists across the world on the population issue, including the 1927 World Population Conference in Geneva.[10] At the 1927 conference Sanger had been pushed to the background by leading scientists in the field such as Raymond Pearl. She learned the lesson then to allow male experts to steer the wheel to leave a positive reputation of the international conference as a success among scientists, health officials, and funders, on whose support she depended.

Fortunately for Sanger, Koya and the members of the conference organizing committee welcomed her offer to help them formulate the program. The Japanese population controllers sought to make the most of the opportunity of having this world-famous figure in Japan. Despite Sanger's intent to minimize publicity for this consultation visit in 1954, Koya made sure that she met with some important people in the government. He specifically instructed Sanger to acknowledge to the press that the Japanese MHW was "contributing a great deal to the well-being of mankind and the protection of mothers' health by establishing the first-ranking position in the world regarding family planning." He assured her that by praising the achievements of the Japanese government, including the village studies that Koya initiated, "chances are very likely for us to be able to direct Japanese leading politicians along the line which is most favorable to you as well as our [conference] program being projected now."¹¹ Sanger appreciated Koya's "frank remarks," making sure that they would "watch [their] steps" to successfully carry out the plans for the conference.¹² In the end, both Sanger and Koya agreed on the strategic use of those with power, especially those in the government, to realize their mission to spread birth control to as many people as possible.

Sanger kept her word to show respect to the Japanese authorities in her address "The Population Policy and Family Planning" at a Public Welfare Committee meeting in the House of Councilors of the Japanese Diet. Katō orchestrated the invitation as a Diet member herself, although not a member of the Welfare Committee. Sanger was the first foreigner to receive the honor to speak before the Japanese Diet. This public endorsement by the Japanese government was in sharp contrast to the treatment she received when the Japanese authorities attempted to block her entry to Japan in 1922. While the Japanese brought Sanger to the Diet to provide them with advice on population control programs as a "world authority" in the field, her speech simply reiterated the superiority of Japanese birth control policies, especially those under government initiative, compared to the situation in the United States, where advocates still faced major religious obstacles. Mindful of Koya's suggestions, she praised the EPL and Koya's birth control experiments in rural villages for reaching out to fertile, low-income families with the goal to improve racial fitness.

Sanger even broadcast the Japanese official birth control programs to her American audiences. The American media, however, were more interested in hearing about her visits to the field and the responses of Japanese families on the grassroots level. In preparing for her previous trip to Japan in 1952, Sanger told Katō that she "would like to go down and talk with the mothers in different parts of your country" rather than "to do the travel tourist joy-ride."¹³ Although she did travel to the countryside as well to the slums in the city, just as during her prewar visits, in the end there seemed to be little, if any, interaction or conversation with the people. After seeing the houses of the farmers, for example, she was "weary enough to postpone the acceptance of other invitations" in the countryside but still continued on "a glorious mountain drive up to Hakone Lake [near Mount Fuji]." Everywhere she went, she drew a big crowd, and women were holding meetings on the streets "awaiting a message" from Sanger. Although she rather reluctantly showed up in front of the crowd at the urging of

Katō, she stopped short of explaining to her American audiences what she actually talked about or the women's responses. Instead, her interviews typically ended by her emphasizing the "heroic effort" of the Japanese government and the projects they had launched to respond to the people's demand for fertility control.[14]

Of course, Sanger was no mere puppet of the Japanese government; she was clearly determined to carry out her own agenda as well. In the speech at the Diet, she used the opportunity to emphasize the rapid progress in contraceptive research conducted in the United States. Although she did not reveal any further details, she could barely contain her excitement that a potential breakthrough might just be around the corner. She asserted that the "united efforts of people from Japan, Great Britain, the United States, India, Puerto Rico and other countries" were attempting to realize this dream.[15] In fact, another purpose of her 1954 trip to Japan was to consult with Japanese scientists on the project.

The Launching of the Pill Project

When Sanger got in touch with Japanese birth control leaders in preparation for the Tokyo conference, she had just embarked on a groundbreaking project: the development of an oral contraceptive. Sanger had conceived the idea of a birth control pill in 1912. That vision became a reality when she partnered with Katherine Dexter McCormick, a wealthy woman from a prominent Chicago family. McCormick was not only a woman of wealth but also a lifelong women's rights activist and biologist, the second woman to graduate from the Massachusetts Institute of Technology. In 1950, McCormick contacted Sanger to ask how she could provide financial support for research on hormonal contraception. At the time, birth control advocates still struggled to raise funds to conduct contraceptive research, which was considered a disreputable business. Although the Planned Parenthood Federation of America contributed small amounts of funding to early research, it was McCormick's financial backing that ultimately bankrolled the pill project.

Once Sanger and McCormick teamed up, they contacted Gregory Goodwin Pincus, a researcher at the Worcester Foundation for Experimental Biology in Massachusetts. Pincus had been experimenting with hormonal compounds originally to be used for infertility treatment. McCormick liked what she saw in the Worcester laboratory and by mid-1953 moved the project into high gear. After completing a series of animal experiments with progesterone, Pincus then approached John Rock, an obstetrician-gynecologist at Harvard Medical School, for clinical trials on a small group of women volunteers at Rock's infertility clinic. But they still needed a much larger sample of women who would participate in clinical trials. The laws against contraception in Massachusetts ruled out the state as a site for a large study. They therefore turned their attention abroad.[16]

The context of overpopulation gave the group a perfect opportunity and grounds to take their experiments abroad. Both Pincus and Rock mentioned their concerns about the threat of global overpopulation when they decided to enter this controversial field of research.[17] As Sanger prepared for her consultation trip to Tokyo in April 1954, she wrote to Pincus to ask if there was any information to take to Japan in case there should be a scientific group willing to carry on experimentation with progesterone. Pincus had already made a trip to Puerto Rico to sound out the possibility of conducting an experiment and clinical trial there, returning with some positive responses from local health officials.[18] This provided a sense of reassurance for Sanger and her idea of proposing a similar project to her Japanese colleagues. She told Pincus, "While most of the people in Asia hesitate to be what they call guinea pigs, the fact that Puerto Rican health authorities are willing to initiate an experiment with a substance that you have found harmless, would I believe be most welcome to Dr. Koya and other members of the Institute of Public Health in Tokyo, of which he is Director." While she believed that the Japanese trial might take longer to begin and cost them more money, she was confident that, through Koya, they would be able to obtain several hundred cases within a year in Japan. She also proposed using midwives and nurses to reach out and bring in women to participate in the trial—just as Koya had done to have women participate in his birth control experiments in his "Three Village Studies." Sanger therefore asked Pincus to prepare a letter that she could present "rather privately without publicity" to Koya during her brief stay in Tokyo.[19]

After receiving a positive response from Pincus, Sanger wrote directly to Koya in March 1954, just before her visit to Tokyo the following month. She gave a brief outline of the research and experiments done thus far by Pincus and Rock, adding that there was also "a great deal of enthusiasm" among the medical group in Puerto Rico to start the project on progesterone. She noted that she would bring further material to her next visit in the hope that Koya might corral a group of scientists in the IPH with whom she could consult about the possibility of carrying out this project in Japan. At the end of the letter, Sanger emphasized that the information there was "strictly confidential to you for your consideration."[20] By the time Sanger arrived in Tokyo, the MHW officials had been informed about the experiment of progesterone, and Sanger was able to have a private meeting with its chief, Kusaba Ryūen.

The "confidentiality" of the experiment was almost jeopardized when someone leaked the information about a birth control experiment to the press. As Sanger described, the news caused "considerable excitement," and telephone calls and newspaper reporters flooded into the ministry with inquiries. To this unexpected—but not necessarily unwelcome—attention, Sanger responded that the pill would not be given to the public until "a thorough study and experiment" had been made and that the experiment would be conducted under the auspices of the scientific committee set up by the government.[21]

Once she confirmed a positive response among Japanese leaders during her preliminary visit, Sanger wasted no time moving on to the next step, first by organizing the scientific committee to conduct the progesterone experiment. For that, Koya suggested that Sanger write to the chief of the Bureau of Public Health in the MHW. And thus she did, to promote this "very unusual and splendid project," which they would provide "free of charge" through American private donors. Again, Sanger made sure to butter up the Japanese officials by expressing her "sincere interest in the population problem of Japan" and her "sincere belief in their scientific competency." At the same time, in order not to appear too overbearing, she stressed that "if this research can not be done in Japan there are other groups in other places in Honolulu, Puerto Rico awaiting the opportunity to test out this project."[22] By emphasizing the priority she had given to the Japanese group over others, she sought to boost the pride of Japanese family planning leaders.

Furthermore, she precluded any possible accusation of exploitation of Japanese subjects by giving the Japanese a semblance of control. The Progesterone Committee, selected by Koya and the public health minister, consisted of distinguished medical professors and directors of hospitals. In addition to these members, Sanger requested that they add another Japanese scientist, Matsuba Michio, who happened to have been working in Pincus's Worcester laboratory for over a year on an unrelated project. Matsuba had accepted Sanger's suggestion to return to Pincus's lab for several weeks to study the techniques and procedures in testing with progesterone. Sanger and McCormick believed that it was vital to have someone on the committee receive direct training in the United States. At the same time, they emphasized that Matsuba was willing to go through Pincus's training "on his own initiative," even though they were willing to pay for his travel expenses. McCormick confessed to Pincus that they were "most anxious to do everything to prevent such [a] misunderstanding" that they were merely using the Japanese scientist for American interests.[23]

The Japanese group was receptive to the project, but they made sure that they would also gain something out of this collaboration and that it would be conducted under their own initiative. Koya wrote to Sanger to clarify a couple of points raised in a meeting with the MHW officials. First, he and other government officials demanded that the Japanese group should take the initiative, even while receiving financial assistance from the Americans, so that the project would not cause "a serious misunderstanding" among the Japanese public. In addition, they insisted on starting with animal experiments before human trials "in order to suppress the possible oppositions against such a project." In particular, they were worried—quite reasonably—about the possible side effects of the new drug.[24] Finally, they stressed that the whole project must be under strict government control so it could not be utilized by private groups for commercial interests.[25] Sanger was in complete agreement on the first point. But she considered replicating animal studies in Japan, which Pincus had already done in his lab, simply "a waste of both time and money." If the Japanese still decided to proceed with the animal experiments, she noted, they would assist them with information but not with money. Writing back to Sanger that they would indeed conduct the animal experiments, Koya further requested that they be provided with enough progesterone so that the Japanese could benefit from the medicine when "good results were obtained." In other words, he emphasized, "the Japanese [did] not like to be used only for experiment."[26] Finally, while Sanger agreed that they should keep the project "away from press correspondents and commercial interests," she insisted that the government should have no more than "moral supervision and sponsorship" over the project. She felt that whenever the government took control, there was "always much red tape and usually lack of personal responsibility." Instead, she believed that university laboratories could undertake the actual scientific experiments under government auspices. Koya, a veteran bureaucrat, simply brushed off Sanger's suggestions, and the project continued to be conducted exclusively under governmental control. In the end, Sanger's opinion mattered little to the Japanese decisions on the actual logistics of the experiment—as long as they received financial and technological assistance from the American side.[27]

Despite some disagreements over the details, Sanger and her colleagues were satisfied that they would be able to bring together scientific teams abroad, especially in Japan and Puerto Rico, to carry out the progesterone experiments and clinical trials. As data on scientific research on hormones for contraceptive use accumulated, the time seemed ripe for the group to announce to the world this exciting scientific discovery that, Sanger was convinced, would revolutionize the field of birth control. The upcoming ICPP in Tokyo seemed to be a perfect place to make the announcement.

The Fifth International Conference on Planned Parenthood

The Fifth ICPP held in Tokyo from October 24 to 29, 1955, turned out to be a success for all parties involved. With 101 participants from abroad and 471 from Japan, the meeting became one of the largest international gatherings on population problems ever to be held at the time. Delegates from seventeen countries and territories, including Britain, the United States, Sweden, Puerto Rico, India, and Singapore, gathered in Tokyo to discuss the theories and practices of family planning.[28] For the Japanese leaders, this was a perfect opportunity to publicize to the world that Japan was committed to taking actions to solve the problem of overpopulation. While using prominent Western leaders in population control to enhance the publicity of the Tokyo conference, the Japanese delegates refused to be "dominated" by them. For Sanger and her scientific team, it became the first international arena where they presented the international, collaborative experiments involving a "magic bullet" that would mark a breakthrough in contraceptive technology.

As Sanger communicated with the FPFJ members over the conference agenda, she got the impression that the Japanese organizers did not want Western demographers overrepresented among the presenters. "They want to have it more an Asiatic agenda than the western," she told Vera Houghton, a British member of the IPPF. She reasoned that this was partly due to the "anti-American pressure" that was going on in Japan and India. Trying not to appear too aggressive, Sanger suggested that her Japanese colleagues include Western scientists to discuss research and laboratory techniques on chemical contraceptives.[29] Sanger and other Western members were convinced that scientific research was a safe area where they could contribute to the cause without enticing antagonism and where, they believed, nobody doubted the superiority of the West.

The Japanese, however, wished to focus on the issue of overpopulation and showcase their achievements in front of the international community, especially the Western leaders in the field. The first two days were therefore devoted to speeches and reports on population problems across the world. Despite their hesitance to have the conference dominated by Western speakers, the Japanese committee agreed with Sanger on the importance of inviting Warren Thompson and Edward Ackerman, two of the most prominent figures in demography. Both of these scholars served as consultants to the Occupation government and left a large impact on population policies and public opinion about birth control in Japan. The organizers therefore believed that having them at the conference would enhance the publicity and credibility for family planning.[30]

Not only did the Japanese invite them as honorary guests, but they were also willing to stand up against these Western experts. At the end of the conference, some Japanese representatives objected to some parts of the proposed resolution, which they believed did not fully address other issues that contributed to the world's population problem, such as the unequal distribution of resources between the "white" and "colored" races. Furthermore, some objected to the phrase "overpopulation threatens world peace" in the resolution, which, they claimed, seemed to indicate that countries that did not adopt family planning were not concerned about world peace. Specifically referring to Thompson's work, the language reminded some Japanese intellectuals of the Western attacks against Japan's overpopulation during the war.[31]

Regardless of the underlying tension between Western and non-Western delegates, Sanger emphasized the cooperative nature of this international gathering, especially in terms of science and research. The last two days of the conference centered around scientific discussions on fertility and reproductive issues, as desired by Sanger and her Western colleagues. "The most remarkable feature of the conference," she reported to her American supporters and sponsors, "was the presence of more than a dozen top scientists from Great Britain, India, Israel, Sweden, U.S.A. and Japan," who had reported on the latest findings on the mechanism of human reproductive process and contraceptive research.[32]

The highlight of the scientific sections, for Sanger and Pincus at least, was the panel on "Research into Reproductive Processes and into Biological Methods of Controlling Fertility." In this session, Pincus presented his progesterone experiments on mammals. Based on his animal experiments on rabbits and rats as well as some limited clinical experiments on humans, Pincus concluded that "certain substances having ovulation-inhibiting effects in experimental animals exhibit entirely comparable effects in the human female." He thus declared that through "careful scientific investigation" the prevention of fertility in humans with "no physical cost" was clearly within reach. The Japanese progesterone researchers gave a preliminary report on their initial animal experiment and a small clinical trial of administrating progesterone to thirty women. Compared to Pincus's report, the tone of the Japanese one was much more modest. They stated that they could not confirm the "ovulation inhibitory effect of progesterone," while noting that the medication seemed to alter the nature of cervical mucus during ovulation, making it difficult for the sperm to penetrate. The team thanked Sanger, McCormick, and Pincus for supplying them with sufficient amounts of progesterone for their experiments. Drs. Abraham Stone and Herbert Kupperman from the Margaret Sanger Research Bureau also reported their clinical findings, which demonstrated that out of sixteen cycles studied, in six cycles there was "definite indication of inhibition of ovulation." The doctors also noted that three out of twelve patients with infertility issues became pregnant within two to four months after cessation of the progesterone therapy, suggesting that the studies of fertility inhibition were indeed part of a broader treatment for infertility issues.[33]

Despite Sanger's enthusiasm, however, the supposedly bombshell presentations about the contraceptive pill by Pincus and his collaborators at the conference did not receive the response that they had expected. Hormonal research and clinical trials on ovulation had been conducted since the early 1940s; therefore, many scientists felt there was nothing actually new in Pincus's findings. What was potentially groundbreaking about Pincus's work was that he started to embark on clinical trials with the hope of expanding them on a much larger scale. However, the chairman of the session in which Pincus and others presented, Solly Zuckerman of England, was skeptical whether their findings at that time suggested that oral administration of progesterone to women did indeed show signs of ovulation inhibition. The criteria that Pincus and others used to gauge suppression of ovulation—such as basal body temperature, the character of endometrium and cervical mucus, and the nature of a vaginal smear—were only "indirect signs" and by no means reliable indices for ovulation inhibition. Zuckerman thus concluded that it was still premature to draw conclusions about the effectiveness of the oral administration of progesterone or other hormonal compounds until "very many more fertility records of the kind" became available.[34] Even John Rock, Pincus's collaborator, was cautious about the results. In fact, he had refused to present their preliminary work with Pincus at the Tokyo conference, a meeting that he considered to be a nonscientific gathering mainly for activists. He believed that the scientific credibility of their project had not yet been established and chose to present his results at a later meeting exclusively for scientists specializing in hormonal research.[35]

Even the Japanese collaborators, it turned out, devoted only halfhearted efforts to the hormonal experiments requested by the American team. Sanger, Pincus, and other American sponsors for the pill project were repeatedly disappointed and frustrated over the slow progress and the lack of communication from the Japanese scientific team. After the conference, Pincus wrote to Koya and other members of the Progesterone Committee but received no reply from any of them. Frustrated, Pincus told Sanger, who then gave Koya a prod about the matter. She sympathetically told Pincus, "What great patience one must have in dealing with individuals or groups outside of [the] U.S.A." Koya immediately wrote back to Sanger, explaining that the scientists were busy with the Gynecology Conference and handling issues with the revenue office, who wanted to investigate whether the tablets had been used for commercial interests beyond experimental purposes. Sanger interpreted the incident as evidence that the Japanese government was becoming "proudly national" and seeking to break its dependence on the United States.[36] A year later, Pincus again lost touch with the Japanese scientists, necessitating that Sanger mediate once again. Sanger told Koya in a much stronger admonishing tone: "This is not the way to produce a good feeling in the minds of the American scientists, who are interested in hearing what is being done and would like to see reports of the results. Certainly, they should have an acknowledgement of money and materials received." She further contrasted the Japanese negligence to the progress in Puerto Rico: "Excellent results are reported from Puerto Rico. There is no reason why Japan cannot give us good results as a Roman Catholic country like Puerto Rico." Koya hastily got in touch with the Progesterone Committee and wrote back to Sanger. He explained that there were "many reasons inevitable" for the delay, although he refused to state those exact reasons, and offered to send a report very soon. At the end of the letter, he added, "But, Mrs. Sanger, please [remember] that these people are the best scientists in gynecology in this country, who were selected by the Ministry of Welfare by your desire. I still believe that they will give a very good and reliable report from the scientific point of view."[37] While Koya sought to defend the reputation of the Japanese scientific team, he was actually skeptical about the efficiency of the pill. He confessed to Clarence Gamble after he visited Pincus's lab in Worcester that he was "not nearly as confident of this being a satisfactory birth control method as [Sanger was]."[38]

The Japanese report that Pincus eventually received a couple of months later apparently indicated that there were a number of unpleasant side effects associated with norethynodrel, the drug used for clinical trials and commonly referred to at G.D. Searle and Company as SC-4642 (later marketed as Enovid). Developed by Frank Colton at Searle, SC-4642 served as a substitute steroid for progesterone that could be produced at a lower cost than natural progesterone.[39] Responding to the Japanese preliminary report, Pincus admitted to Koya that "with SC-4642 the incidence of nausea, dizziness, and vomiting appear[ed] to be troublesome." In fact, physician Edris Rice-Way, the main coordinator of the Puerto Rican program, also gave an initial report that the drug caused "too many side reactions to be accepted generally." Nonetheless, Pincus assured Koya that in Puerto Rico, "where such symptoms occurred with less severity and less frequency," they were able to control the side effects by administering antacid tablets to the patients as soon as any sign of reactions appeared.[40] Pincus also ran a placebo trial, which appeared to confirm his suspicion that the suggestion of side effects, rather than the drug itself, was causing the reactions. Pincus revealed his implicit racial and gender prejudice when he blamed the reactions to "the emotional super-activity of Puerto Rican women." Given these results, the subjects were thereafter not warned about the specific adverse reactions. In the end, however, many women dropped out of the trials because of the uncomfortable side effects, whether they were "real" or not. The pill did not necessarily lower the birth rate among participants either, possibly because of the pills missed under doctor's direction or women's own negligence. Moreover, the "rebound effect" seemed to heighten the fertility of women during the months after they stopped using the pill.[41]

Sanger may not have been too off the mark in pointing out the mounting nationalism, if not blatant anti-Americanism, among Japanese national leaders, especially after the 1951 Security Treaty between the United States and Japan, which allowed the continued presence of US military bases in Japan in exchange for security protection. But what affected the progress of contraceptive research in Japan more directly was the renewed concern over the "low birth rate crisis" that gradually came to replace the fear of overpopulation. After reaching a peak in 1947 (34.3 percent), birth rates started to drop steadily and rapidly; by 1955, the rate had already plummeted below 20.0 percent.[42] Population control had also become a lower priority for many Japanese activists. Katō was increasingly consumed by her Diet duties and her newfound cause in the American-led Moral Re-armament (MRA) movement. Koya had retired as director of the IPH. Majima had left for China and Russia to pursue his birth control work there.

In many instances, the American birth control activists seemed more concerned than the Japanese leaders themselves about keeping up the momentum of birth control work in Japan. Sanger continued to be perplexed by the discord among Japanese birth control leaders as she tried to keep the FPFJ alive after the Tokyo conference. She repeatedly reminded Koya and Katō that money from her, Clarence Gamble, and G. J. Watumull (an Indian businessman based in Los Angeles and Honolulu) was already placed aside to assist the organization for the following six months of activity. She begged Katō to "pinch, push, or shove your Committee into national action" and to "try to get dead wood out of first positions, and replace with people who have energy and vision." In the end, the Japanese actors managed to bring the organization back together, electing Koya as the new president. Sanger had originally nominated Katō as president, but apparently her political position caused too many conflicts with some other members of the group. In fact, Sanger received a long letter from Majima, strongly opposing the nomination of Katō to FPFJ's presidency. Majima described Katō as a mere propagandist, lacking commitment and leadership, and complained about her arrogance from his previous experience working with her.[43]

Why, then, were American birth controllers so anxious that Japanese activists continue their birth control work, when the Japanese themselves seemed no longer concerned about the threat of overpopulation in their own country? Access to fieldwork abroad was vital to their mission to develop and spread birth control technology. As the political climate of the Cold War intensified, Western leaders feared that they could lose the overseas "laboratories" to communism. In her opening address at the Tokyo conference, Sanger emphasized the significance of "two great nations in the East"—Japan and India—being the first countries in the world to place population control within the functions of the state.[44] As many Western internationalists sensed a threat of red invasion in the East, these were two major "bulwarks against communism" that they felt they could count on.[45] At the same time, they worried that some of the birth control activists in Asia might already have left-leaning thoughts. Several months prior to the conference in Tokyo, Clarence Gamble advised IPPF executive secretary Vera Houghton that they should keep "the political aspect of the Conference neutral." He cited a letter he received from one of the Japanese birth control leaders, Dr. Amano Kageyasu, who mentioned that one of the Japanese activists (Majima Kan) was assisting Soviet and Chinese communists with birth control work and forming "friendly relations" with them. The letter warned that there were many "left socialists or red sympathizers among us" and that they might use the Tokyo conference as a "political weapon."[46]

The correspondence reveals the ideological and political shift that transnational birth control activism had undergone over the decades: from a radical, socialist challenge to existing social orders to a reformist mission concerned for the well-being of the nation. Whereas in its early days in the 1910s and 1920s, the birth control cause itself represented a "political weapon" against the establishment, in the 1950s leaders paid extra attention to avoid such a label at any cost. Amano's letter might have simply been another expression of internal discord among Japanese birth control leaders.

As mentioned earlier, the Japanese activists expressed hostility and frustration with each other due to clashes of personality or different political views. The Western birth controllers, however, took this suggestion of leftist influence among Japanese colleagues seriously. Against the backdrop of growing fear of communism in the United States, it became especially vital that they assure that their Asian partners remained loyal and committed to the Western ideology of population control.

Most Japanese birth control leaders welcomed their role as mentors and protectors of other Asian nations in the global fight against population explosion (and communism). After receiving the funds from Sanger and other American sponsors for the activities of FPFJ, Koya pledged that he would use the contribution to develop "a bigger and comprehensive system for training family planning people not only in Japan, but also in Asia as a whole."[47] Since his work with SCAP officials during the Occupation, Koya well understood the geopolitical and strategic importance of Japan to Western leaders. He proudly wrote to Rufus Day, the IPPF's American treasurer, that his report on his field experiments with birth control tablets, which he delivered at the IPPF regional conference in Berlin, had prompted the Indian health minister to invite him to India to examine the failed cases of similar experiments there.[48] Koya also recommended Dr. Furusawa Yoshio to the IPPF headquarters as a Japanese delegate to the 1959 ICPP in New Delhi based on his skills in sterilization operations, which, he emphasized, had a great impact on Indian doctors.[49] Koya and other Japanese activists thus used the American interest in spreading birth control in communism-prone Asia to reestablish Japan's reputation as the leader of the Asia-Pacific world.

Technological Imperatives

A central aspect of global population control programs was their emphasis on the power of science and technology. The demographic transition theory reformulated in the postwar period highlighted swift demographic changes induced by top-down birth control programs. The pill project led by Sanger and her collaborators was indeed part of this political and intellectual trend to apply Western technology to "modernize" the Third World in the Cold War climate. Numerous other projects aimed to develop "advanced" contraceptives, in particular the intrauterine device (IUD), to combat the population explosion that took place in the 1950s and 1960s. Few of these endeavors, if any, sought to expand women's reproductive choices or to promote women's health. Rather, their main goal was to reduce the fertility of the masses in overpopulated, developing countries in the most effective—and least costly—way possible through the power of Western science and technology.

Under the paradigm of the modernization theory, efficiency and replicability became the most important criteria for large-scale population control projects in Asia. Changes in social institutions and cultural patterns would require too much time and effort and could still induce local or international opposition. Pilot programs in India showed disappointing results because villagers who initially showed strong interest in birth control stopped using contraceptives as soon as the case workers retreated from the fields.[50] While it was certainly ideal to have all projects in Asia sustained by "concentrated, trained, and competent efforts over a long period of time" to continuously remind people of the benefits of birth control, as Koya did in his experiments, population control workers admitted that such investment was practically impossible when experiments were "all being prepared on populations of a few hundred families."[51]

Population control leaders believed that Americans could legitimately and immediately intervene in Asia's population problem through technological assistance to develop cheap and effective contraceptives.[52] There was no doubt in their minds that the United States possessed the most advanced knowledge, facilities, personnel, and money for scientific research. Since the early twentieth century, they argued, Western science had caused "a revolution in mortality control" in less developed countries through increased food production and effective disease control, which had ironically created the source of the overpopulation problem. It was therefore their responsibility to now use their scientific prowess to solve this problem that they, indirectly and unwittingly, had created. It seemed to them that the rapid decline of fertility in postwar Japan under Occupation signaled "the emergence of revolutionary changes in fertility elsewhere" in Asia, especially in rural areas, through the application of advanced contraceptive technology aided by the West.[53]

The focus of these experiments centered on developing contraceptives for women, not for feminist reasons but for strategic purposes based on sexist, racist, and classist assumptions.[54] Workers in population programs considered poor and rural women more available and more easily convinced than their husbands to use contraceptives when offered. In one of his experiments, Koya showed that the less educated people were, the less likely it would be for husbands to take responsibility for procurement of contraceptive devices, and hence there would be a low rate of successful contraceptive users. Therefore, he contended, the task of birth control workers was to reach these "socio-economically less privileged wives" and to educate them to use contraceptives.[55] In his report to the RF, Frank Notestein presented his idea for a new type of contraceptive in the following way:

> Women are reported to be more easily interested in family limitation than men. Hence it seems likely that a contraceptive requiring female responsibility will be more acceptable than one requiring male responsibility. Unfortunately, of the methods now known, those for which the female is responsible are also those which require complicated instruction by highly trained personnel which is neither available nor likely to become so in the near future.[56]

Notestein's comments revealed his assumption that women in rural Asia could not master "complicated" contraceptives without the help of "highly trained personnel."

In fact, population controllers uniformly blamed women for their supposed inability to sustain motivation, ignoring other social and economic reasons that might have made it difficult for them to continue using birth control. Various factors hindered rural women's use of birth control, such as economic hardship, the lack of understanding from husbands and relatives, moral and religious restrictions, and fewer opportunities to share or learn information about contraceptive use through doctors, friends, or the media. Although Notestein admitted that the development and dissemination of contraceptives would not solve "the problem of motive" needed for consistent uses of contraceptives, he nonetheless insisted that "it would be greatly simplified."[57] In other words, he and other population controllers believed that contraceptive technology by itself would not change people's attitudes toward reproduction, but it could at least bring immediate reduction in birth rates needed to combat the population explosion in the current political climate. The use of simple contraceptives on a mass scale provided a quick technological fix to complex social issues in hopes of yielding immediate results.

Eventually, the breakthrough in global population control arrived when American advocates' vision for a modern, scientific, and simple kind of contraceptive for the female masses became a reality with the development of the IUD. IUDs had been available since the prewar decades through private prescriptions, but the device gained renewed attention for improvement and wider applicability in the context of postwar overpopulation in Asia. One of the earliest advocates and developers of IUDs was a prominent birth control leader in Japan, Ōta Tenrei, who invented a gold-plated IUD design in the 1930s. The development of modern and improved versions of IUDs led by Ōta and other researchers resumed in Japan in the 1950s. These studies in Japan, however, mostly targeted Asian women beyond Japan, as plastic IUDs were officially banned in Japan until 1974 (and copper IUDs until 1999).[58] In particular, the IUD research led by Ishihama Atsumi in 1957 attracted the attention of Western researchers and stimulated the Population Council to sponsor experimental efforts to develop new types of IUDs.[59] The council soon became the primary driving force of research and funding for the application of IUDs in developing countries, especially after Frank Notestein assumed the role of vice president in 1959.[60] Ōta and his supporters claimed that this contraceptive method benefited "the masses of lower intelligence for it [could] be left without danger or care for long periods of time."[61] Similarly, investigators at the Population Council stated, "The intra-uterine device seems particularly appropriate for the spread of family planning in the developing countries in view of its high effectiveness and its single application for long-term effect, *obviating any need for sustained motivation, repeated action, and continued provision of supplies.*"[62] From these statements, we can see that population control leaders' own prejudice regarding Asian women's intelligence and agency underlay the development and dissemination of female contraceptives.

Feminist leaders such as Margaret Sanger were mostly marginalized in these efforts to development cheap and mass-produced contraceptives such as the IUD for overpopulated countries. In the 1920s, the medical profession had criticized Sanger for endorsing an early form of IUD, the so-called wishbone or stem pessary, which they condemned as an unsafe and controversial procedure. She then was pressured to reject the Grafenberg ring, an intrauterine coil made of silver or gold. In the late 1950s, however, members of the American obstetrics community changed their minds and started to support the research for newer IUDs. Meanwhile, Sanger's feminist partner in the pill enterprise, Katherine McCormick, disappointedly admitted to her that the global population control community no longer believed that the pill, another new female contraceptive that they worked so hard to develop, could be used for women in the developing world suffering from the burden of frequent childbearing and child rearing.[63]

In fact, even as the pill research developed in the context of global population control, the pill in the end did not benefit Third World and/or nonwhite women. Oral contraceptives were simply too expensive to be used widely among women in poor, populated areas. Moreover, rural or minority women lacked access to medical clinics that could provide them with prescriptions and follow-up exams. Population controllers preferred to use the IUD over the pill because women did not have to take them regularly like the pill—something many health officials assumed that poor women were incapable of doing.[64] John Rock himself, although he initially saw the pill's potential in solving the global threat of overpopulation, soon realized that this particular contraceptive would not be suitable to poor women in rural areas. He considered that the Puerto Rican trials were successful only because the women who took part in them possessed "a moderately high degree of culture" and a better sense of goals and purposes for attaining smaller families. He was far more skeptical of the pill's effectiveness in places such as rural India, where women had limited access to education, rights, or privacy.[65] Nonetheless, Rock stopped short of proposing that women in such impoverished and remote areas obtain better education and rights that could provide them better access to contraceptives. These facts again demonstrate the prejudice of leaders in contraceptive research that determined the availability and options—or the lack of them—for poor women.

Meanwhile, women in the United States benefited from this newest, most reliable form of contraceptive. Given the lasting hostility against contraceptive research in the medical community and the persisting laws in some states prohibiting the sales and distribution of contraceptives, it is quite remarkable that the US Food and Drug Administration (FDA) approved the marketing of oral contraceptives in the United States in 1960— eight years after Sanger and McCormick conceived the idea and four years after the initiation of mass clinical trials in Puerto Rico. In 1957, the FDA had approved G. D. Searle and Company's application to market Enovid for menstrual disorders. Although many were already aware that this new drug would also work as a birth control pill, few believed that the FDA would approve the drug for contraceptive purposes. As the sales of Enovid climbed, however, Searle decided to file an application to license Enovid as a contraceptive. In December 1959, John Rock and Searle's medical research director set off to Washington for an FDA hearing. Asked by an FDA reviewer about the expected moral and religious objections to the pill, Rock, a professed devout Catholic, allegedly declared that he would never "sell [his] church short." Rock was a highly respected figure in the obstetrics world, and his words of assurance were enough to convince this young reviewer. In most cases, however, government officials tried to stay clear of the moral issues by focusing exclusively on cost and safety concerns. The field studies obtained in Puerto Rico, San Juan, Humacao, and Haiti proved that Enovid did not adversely affect the reproductive system or the menstrual cycle and that fertility returned within several months after discontinuing the treatment. There were still no data on the effect of the pill's longtime use. In May 1960, the FDA granted approval for the prescription of Enovid for contraceptive purposes for no more than two years at a time, thus evading the problem of long-term safety.[66]

Overpopulated, developing countries provided American pill advocates not only with data for pill safety but also with moral justification for preliminary research and clinical use. They were able to convince local health officials and scientists in these countries—including Japan, Puerto Rico, Haiti, Mexico, Ceylon, and Hong Kong—to take part in the scientific experiments and clinical trials.[67] They framed the pursuit for a new, effective contraceptive as a scientific project requiring international collaboration under the united goal to conquer global poverty and overpopulation, not a Western exploitation of former colonial subjects. Japanese officials were willing to take part in this project, at least while the population problem was at the top of the nation's urgent agenda for postwar recovery. Although, in the end, they did not take part in large clinical trials such as the ones conducted in Puerto Rico, the Japanese scientific team continued to present their research findings at international conferences side by side with their American collaborators. At the Sixth ICPP meeting in New Delhi in 1959, the Japanese scientific team again presented a paper on their oral contraceptive studies, along with papers on clinical studies and field trials by John Rock, Gregory Pincus, and other pioneers in the field.[68]

Despite the semblance of an "international" project, national pride and resistance to American invasion among local leaders often affected the availability of contraceptives among non-Western women. Regardless of American population controllers' commitment to frame contraceptive projects as a collaborative endeavor among scientists worldwide, many non-Westerners continued to see this as a form of American imperialism. To the frustration of the American pill developers, the Indian government forbade experimental studies on the hormonal compounds for reasons similar to the hesitations expressed by Koya when the Japanese team initially took part in the progesterone experiment. Like the Japanese scientific team, the Indian regulators were hesitant about accepting American data on the drug without first testing it according to their own criteria. In addition, there was the persisting idea that the pill represented another attempt by Western imperialists to keep the number of Third World people under control.[69] Similar hostility and suspicions against Americans existed in Puerto Rico, where researchers actually embarked on large-scale pill trials. Local newspapers started to run stories that a "woman dressed as a nurse" was distributing "sterilizers" or that "Nordic whites" were using "the coloured races as 'guinea pigs.'" Some local priests and disapproving husbands also persuaded women to drop out of the pill studies. Soon after Edice Rice-Wray, the American doctor in charge of the Puerto Rican trials, filed her report, which contained her apprehension about the problem of side effects, she chose to resign due to growing hostility toward her work.[70]

Many feminists—in Japan, the United States, and elsewhere in the world—also strongly opposed the use of oral contraceptives during the early years of its appearance. They were especially concerned about the health risks of the pill, for good reason. A year after the FDA approval of the pill, tragic news in Europe of birth defects of babies born of women who took Thalidomide to treat nausea during pregnancy frightened women across the world over the use of new drugs. In the United States, Barbara Seaman's 1969 book, *The Doctor's Case against the Pill*, led to Senate hearings on the pill's safety. The Senate hearings, feminist criticism, and the negative press surrounding the pill pressured manufacturers to introduce safer, low-dosage pills and to include explanatory inserts about health risks in all pill packages. Meanwhile, US pharmaceutical companies allegedly "dumped" the old, high-dose pills in Third World countries, further perpetuating the global system of inequality in contraceptive access and reproductive health.⁷¹ Until very recently, the predominant view of the pill among Japanese feminists was decidedly negative because of such concern for its safety. In 1961, female Diet members Katō Shizue and Yokoyama Fuku voiced strong opposition to oral contraceptives during an Upper House Committee meeting. They feared that the government might favor the pharmaceutical industry's economic interests over the health of women, the same way they favored obstetricians' monopoly over abortion. Only in the 1990s did Japanese feminists, including Katō, abandon their earlier rejection of oral contraceptives and advocate for the speedy approval of the low-dose pill.⁷²

The marketing of oral contraceptives was banned until 1999 in Japan, although the law did not prevent doctors from prescribing them to treat "menstrual disorders." The four-decade delay of the pill's approval in Japan, however, does not necessarily indicate that the Japanese government took these concerns of women seriously and was more cautious about the possible health risks of the new drug than other countries were. Rather, an intricate combination of social, political, and economic forces affected contraceptive policies in Japan, as in other countries.⁷³ As the economy developed and birth rates started to drop, many conservative bureaucrats and opinion leaders now worried about depopulation and were increasingly reluctant to deal with contraceptive policies. Unlike in the United States, pharmaceutical companies in Japan were far less powerful politically and therefore unable to push for the marketing of oral contraceptives. However, obstetrician-gynecologists had a powerful influence over reproductive issues in Japan, many of them favoring the lucrative business of abortion rather than providing contraceptive guidance. Where they did support contraceptives, physician members of the Japan Association for Maternal Welfare (Nihon bosei hogo i kyōkai) advocated the IUD over the pill because the IUD supposedly lent itself more readily to physician control.⁷⁴ The government often yielded to their pressure, which partly explains the halfhearted commitment in the early experiments on contraceptive hormones that so frustrated Sanger and Pincus.

In Koya's correspondence with Sanger over the progesterone experiments, one can see that he, as well as many other bureaucrats, prioritized the interests of the government over women's own health. Whereas Sanger hoped that the introduction of oral contraceptives could "relieve [Japanese] women of the necessity for abortion," Koya noted that "induced abortion [might] be considered" as a safeguard against government responsibility "in case any woman should become pregnant in spite of the use of this chemical."[75] Koya's casual reference to abortion is rather surprising, given that publicly and internationally he repeatedly pointed out the health risks of abortion and showcased his efforts in guiding Japanese women away from abortion to successful uses of contraceptives.[76] Moreover, Koya told the Japanese audience that there was no need to rush to legalize such "unnatural" methods as oral contraceptives when abortion was legal and other simple kinds of birth control were available.[77] In a publication intended for the international family planning community, another public health official attributed the main reason for opposing the approval of oral contraceptives to the "customary loose practice" in drug regulation and medical supervision in Japan. He claimed that oral contraceptives therefore could be "seriously misused once they [were] left entirely to the hands of lay people."[78] His statement suggested a deep mistrust of the ability of women to manage their own bodies, thereby justifying the need of unusually strict medical supervision over the administration of the drug. The gender bias in bureaucratic decision making over issues regarding reproduction and sexuality became especially explicit when the anti-impotence drug Viagra was approved by the MHW in 1999 before the pill—after merely six months of deliberations on its safety and effectiveness based on foreign clinical data. The differing treatment of two oral drugs defined by gender indicated once again that social ideas and political forces, rather than technological development itself, affected the availability of contraceptives.

In the end, American population control/birth control leaders failed to apply the most important lesson learned from the birth control field experiments in Japan: education and women's own determination were the key factors leading to lower birth rates. The new model of demographic transition that placed technological solutions over social improvements proved ineffective in bringing actual, lasting effects on the reproductive patterns of women. Birth control workers were perplexed and frustrated by the failure of birth control experiments in India. In fact, none of the "advanced" methods that American population control leaders proposed—the pill, the IUD, or sterilization—played a major part in the reduction of fertility among Japanese women during the postwar decades. Instead, Japanese couples used traditional methods, such as the rhythm method and condoms, and abortion as a backup if they became pregnant (Table 6.1). It is true that government regulation did limit the methods of birth con-

TABLE 6.1. Percentage of use of contraceptive methods in Japan, 1950–2000

Year	Condoms	Rhythm method	Temperature method[a]	Simple methods[b]	Sterilization	IUD, pill[c]	Other methods
1950	35.6	27.4	—	55.0	—	—	15.0
1952	55.8	29.6	9.3	46.9	—	—	10.2
1955	56.8	34.6	9.5	39.6	3.6	—	7.6
1957	56.6	38.4	8.1	38.3	7.1	—	7.0
1959	58.3	40.4	6.1	43.0	6.3	—	5.3
1961	60.5	42.5	—	37.7	8.0	—	5.3
1963	65.9	38.0	—	31.7	6.1	4.4	—
1965	65.5	38.7	—	32.4	5.8	4.3	—
1967	65.2	37.4	—	26.4	3.6	6.1	4.2
1969	68.1	33.9	—	26.7	5.4	8.9	3.8
1971	72.7	32.9	—	21.0	3.9	9.6	4.3
1973	75.0	29.7	—	19.3	3.6	11.4	5.2
1975	77.8	29.9	—	17.3	4.7	12.6	3.7
1977	78.9	27.0	—	15.2	5.3	12.4	3.2
1979	81.1	23.1	—	12.1	4.0	11.5	2.4
1984	80.4	11.8	8.4	6.0	10.5	8.5	5.4
1986	82.1	11.3	10.2	8.9	9.9	8.4	4.3
1988	76.8	6.6	9.7	6.0	7.4	7.0	2.7
1990	73.9	7.3	8.0	9.0	9.8	5.7	2.5
1992	75.3	9.2	7.3	9.8	6.2	6.2	2.2
1994	77.7	7.1	6.8	8.6	7.0	4.3	3.1
1998	77.8	8.4	8.2	9.3	5.9	4.2	2.6
2000	75.3	6.5	9.8	27.5	6.4	4.2	2.4

SOURCE: PPRC, *The Population and Society of Postwar Japan*.
NOTES: The 1950 through 1979 surveys included both current and past contraceptive users; the 1984 through 1998 surveys included only current contraceptive users. All surveys targeted married women under fifty years of age. The total percentage exceeds 100 because of multiple answers given by respondents.
[a]In the 1950 and 1961 surveys, the rhythm method and "other periodical abstinence (including the basal body temperature method)" were combined. From the 1963 through 1979 surveys, only the rhythm method was included.
[b]Simple methods include withdrawal, douche, foam, jelly, sponge, and diaphragms.
[c]IUDs were officially approved in 1974, and the pill, in 1999.

trol available to the people. Regardless of the actual method used, however, what the postwar changes in fertility patterns across the world suggested was that the precise method of contraception mattered less in fertility reduction than the changes in socioeconomic structure that enabled women to have fewer children if they desired.

. . .

As Sanger devoted considerable energy and resources helping government officials, scientists, and other activists in overpopulated countries develop and disseminate new contraceptives, her ultimate goal was to urge her own government to also take the initiative in the same direction. In 1957, she pushed for the sixth ICPP to be held in Washington, D.C., in the hope of arousing the interest of Congress in the population issue, only to be discouraged by her eugenicist colleague Frederick Osborn, who feared that such an attempt might backfire. Consequently, most of the international meetings on birth control/population control were held in Asia during the postwar decades.[79]

Undaunted, Sanger wrote a letter to the *New York Times* on January 3, 1960, publicly denouncing President Dwight Eisenhower's refusal to take part in population programs abroad. By the late 1950s, American NGOs, such as the Rockefeller and Ford Foundations, had openly declared their commitment to fight global population problems. In 1958, a presidential committee on foreign aid, chaired by William Draper, recommended that the US government assist foreign governments in family planning programs as a matter of foreign aid. Pressured by Catholic authorities, however, Eisenhower ignored the recommendation and declared that birth control was "not a proper political or governmental activity or function or responsibility."[80] Sanger insisted that, by refusing to take any actions on the matter, the US government was "increasing the population pressures against peace and bringing ever close the population 'explosion' and World War III." In contrast, she argued, leaders of Asian nations, such as Prime Ministers Jawaharlal Nehru of India and Kishi Nobusuke of Japan, were taking serious steps toward peace through birth control. Even as her own government had let her down, the people of these Asian nations had diligently taken her advice. She proudly presented their growth and achievement: "Government officials, as well as voluntary agencies, scientists, teachers and preachers are responding to the message about birth control which I took to them twenty-five years ago."[81]

It would not be long, however, before the US government finally changed its official position on birth control. In April 1963, President John F. Kennedy endorsed aid for family planning. That summer, Senator William Fulbright added an amendment to the foreign aid bill of 1963 to fund "research into the problems of population growth." By this time, former president Eisenhower had also reversed his earlier dismissal of population control. In 1965, as a result of considerable lobbying by John D. Rockefeller III and William Draper, President Lyndon Johnson stated the need to deal with "the explosion in world population" in his State of the Union speech. That same year, the executive branch became directly involved when the War on Poverty provided federal funds to community groups to initiate welfare programs, including birth control guidance.[82]

It had taken forty years for Sanger's birth control cause to be finally accepted officially at home and abroad. Yet, considering the persistent resistance to the topic until well in the 1950s, the rapid developments in the history of birth control are quite remarkable. The FDA approval of the pill in 1960, followed by the US government's endorsement of birth control as part of foreign aid programs, gave women across the world medical and technological access to reproductive control. Sanger's lifelong advocacy for birth control worldwide seemed to be gaining legitimacy, not necessarily because she was finally able to overcome the social repression of female sexuality but because international politics had further transformed birth control into a tool for patriarchal control and world domination. These developments in the history of birth control nonetheless laid the groundwork for the women's rights movement that would soon take place in the United States and other countries.

Epilogue

Japan remained a special place for Margaret Sanger's birth control activism throughout her lifetime. Such sentiment is revealed in the "will" she handwrote on a scrap of paper with instructions for the disposal of her body upon her death. The will, which was presumably written sometime after her first postwar visit to Japan in 1952, reads:

> In case of my death—I want to be cremated not before 2 weeks later—the heart to go to Japan to be buried in Tokyo—any place the govt. or Health and Welfare Minister together with Senator Shizue Kato wish to have it buried, as it is or in ashes. This is gratitude to the Japanese people & govt.—the only country in the world which has officially recognized me & the BC work also presented to the Emperor.[1]

Her beloved country, in turn, recognized Sanger's achievement and influences in Japan by conferring the Third Class Order of the Sacred Treasure from the Emperor in 1965. Unfortunately, Sanger was too ill to travel by that time to receive the award in person. She died in 1966, just a few days short of her eighty-eighth birthday.

Today, the legacy of transnational activism that Sanger and Ishimoto (Katō) Shizue initiated in the 1920s lives on, most visibly through the activities of the IPPF. Sanger served as its first president for seven years, then as honorary president after her retirement. Katō presided over the Japanese affiliate of IPPF, the FPFJ, for more than four decades. The IPPF has become one of the longest-lasting and most influential organizations serving women across the world. Currently it consists of 152 Member Associations, working in 172 countries. Because of the model of humanitarianism in global family planning established by Katō, who remained engaged in political and social activities until her death in 2001 at the age of 104, Japan has become one of the top contributors to IPPF and other international organizations promoting women's rights and health. From 1986 to 1999, Japan was the leading donor nation contributing funds to IPPF. Although funding has decreased since then, it still remains one of the main countries to provide grants to the organization.[2]

Yet numerous challenges persist for women across the world to gain access to reproductive health care and make autonomous decisions about birth control. Despite their international status, NGOs such as the IPPF are still susceptible to national politics and interests because they operate primarily through governmental grants. In particular, the IPPF and other organizations promoting reproductive services suffered serious setbacks due to decreasing funding from the United States. In 1984, the Ronald Reagan administration established what came to be known the "Mexico City policy," a global gag rule that refused US government support to any agency, American or foreign, that used its own funds for abortion services, counseling, or referral. In addition to a conservative turn in domestic sexual politics, Reagan allegedly needed the support of Pope John Paul II in maintaining sanctions against the communist regime and combating revolution in Central America.[3] The impact of international politics on US reproductive and sexual policies is reminiscent of how US officials in the postwar Occupation government in Japan bowed to Catholic demands to stay clear of Japan's population policies in the context of the Cold War. As a result of the Mexico City policy, many NGOs, including the IPPF, lost a significant portion of their funding, leading to a major layoff of staff, office closures, and program cancellations.[4] Although subsequent Democratic administrations rescinded the policy, only to be reinstated when Republicans were again in power, over the years US funding to these NGOs diminished significantly as a result of increasing backlash against women's reproductive autonomy in domestic politics.

Organizations and activists today strive to offer reproductive knowledge and services for the sake of women's rights and health, not as population control or eugenic programs. Economists and other intellectuals have abandoned the neo-Malthusian narrative of apocalypse resulting from uncontrolled fertility and have realized that population control in and of itself could not solve the problem of poverty, poor health, and social and political instability in overpopulated, developing countries. The idea that governments, international organizations, or individual activists could interfere in personal reproductive decisions and produce changes in fertility patterns for the sake of national well-being or international peace had become obsolete, at least on the surface.

Nonetheless, one cannot simply ignore the fact that many of today's leading NGOs in reproductive health—including the IPPF, United Nations Population Fund, and the Pathfinder Fund (founded by Clarence Gamble)—started out and developed against the backdrop of US imperialism and were immersed in the theories of eugenics. These organizations provided American money and technology through colonial channels to support family planning programs in countries such as India and China, which included coercive measures and abuses.[5] However, they have failed to truthfully acknowledge and address some of the racist thinking of their precursors, their collusion with eugenics, and some of the fundamental flaws in organizations and programs aimed at global population control. Their ambiguity has inadvertently led to backlash from pro-life activists.

Today, opponents of birth control and abortion point to the negative history of population control and label its leader Margaret Sanger as racist to discredit the activities of family planning organizations both in the United States and worldwide.[6] Not just religious conservatives but leaders of racial minority groups have publicly expressed suspicion over the purpose and goals of these programs led by white, middle-class professionals as an act of "genocide" against the colored races.[7] Governments and women's organizations in non-Western countries such as India often refuse Western-devised new contraceptive drugs because of the mistrust toward US-led initiatives that resemble previous global population control campaigns.[8] Without fully understanding the intricate nexus between imperialism and contraceptive history, we would fail to build constructive relationships between nations and communities that could help advance the cause of women's reproductive health. While different political dynamics, economic theories, and social customs affect women's reproduction in the present, a similar set of problems hinders women's control over their bodies today as it did a century ago. Childbearing continues to be tied to ideas about the past, present, and future of the race or nation. National leaders still blame women for their sexual and reproductive behaviors and decisions rather than improve larger social and economic structures. In the United States, the government, the judge, the company, or the school decides the insurance coverage for contraceptives, assuming that women cannot—and should not—make sexual decisions on their own. In Japan, male politicians ridicule childless or infertile women in public discussions, blaming their presumed selfishness or sterility for Japan's decreasing population.[9] As both the United States and Japan face the reality of declining birth rates and changing status in the world order, restrictions and pressure on women's reproductive choices seem to have strengthened in subtle—and oftentimes not so subtle—ways.

. . .

Over the past few decades, a sense of crisis about plunging birth rates (*shōshika*) has permeated public discourse and policy in Japan. The birth control advocacy that started with Margaret Sanger and Ishimoto Shizue's collaboration in the 1920s seemed to have left a lasting impact on the country's reproductive pattern; the birth rate has been declining consistently since 1947, peaking at 34.3 percent, and falling to 7.8 percent in 2016. The total fertility rate—the average number of children that would be born to a woman over her lifetime—reached its all-time low in 2005 at 1.26 and remained at 1.44 in 2016 despite various government initiatives to increase the birth rate.[10] In this context, alarmists have blamed the EPL of 1948, which at the time was one of the most "progressive" policies in the world regarding abortion and birth control, as the main culprit for Japan's decreasing fertility rates. By the 1960s, there had been periodic attempts to restrict women's access to abortion by revising the EPL by eliminating the clause that gave women easy access to abortion under the pretense of economic necessity. Meanwhile, alternative birth control policies lagged behind as soon as overpopulation dropped out of the national agenda, resulting in the delay of approving the contraceptive pill for nearly four decades.

Apprehensions about Japan's international reputation as an "abortion paradise" stirred up antiabortion sentiments and drove the first movement to revise the EPL among conservatives in the 1960s and 1970s. A major newspaper, *Asahi shinbun*, carried an article in 1967 about a Korean-Japanese doctor in Tokyo sending letters to American hospitals and doctors soliciting them to send patients interested in receiving an abortion. The news sparked fury among many doctors in Japan, and the president of the Japan Association for Maternal Welfare accused the doctor in question of bringing "disgrace on the country." Conservative pundits alarmingly wrote that many "blue-eyed" American women envied Japan's lax abortion law and that some even traveled all the way to Japan for the procedure. The image of Japan as an "abortion paradise," one argued, was having negative impacts on foreign relations by undermining the "national dignity" of the "moral leader of the East" (*tōyō kunshi*)—a nation that had already lost its armaments.[11]

At times, feminists and other left-wing activists also used international pressure to push the government to revise the EPL so that it would better serve the interests of women. Two major international meetings, the 1994 International Conference on Population and Development in Cairo and the 1995 UN Women's Conference in Beijing, were the first to officially establish women's reproductive control and health as a top priority of global human rights rather than discuss these issues mainly in the context of population control or international relations. Japanese feminists used such international venues as opportunities to mobilize domestic campaigns to revise the EPL. They partnered with advocacy groups for people with disabilities and capitalized on the renewed focus on individual rights rather than national interests as a way to draw attention to the EPL's lack of concern for women and people with disabilities. They called out the "anachronistic, discriminatory, and coercive" aspects of the law and argued for more individual-centered approaches to reproductive policies.[12] As the world became increasingly critical of discriminatory policies associated with Nazi eugenics, Japanese bureaucrats agreed to remove the eugenic wording in the law and renamed it the Maternal Protection Law (Botai hogo hō) in 1996. Feminist leaders similarly used international pressure to push for legalization of the contraceptive pill. They used international conferences to attract attention to the Japanese government's embarrassing policy of quickly approving Viagra, the male pill to treat erectile dysfunction, while leaving the female pill issue on the shelf for years.[13]

Even as the government seemed to slowly take action to ensure women's reproductive rights, however, it often excluded women's groups and feminists from the decision processes. Many activists were disappointed by the actual outcome of legislative reforms, which still left much to be desired in terms of protecting women's reproductive rights. Even though the Maternal Protection Law seemed to place women at its center, in reality Japanese bureaucrats refused to consider feminists' advocacy for "abortion on demand." The government finally approved the low-dose pill in June 1999, but only under a stringent prescription guideline that clearly discouraged popular use among Japanese women. Even though feminist groups sought to persuade the government to enact more moderate guidelines, the obstetric-gynecological and other professional associations had far more influence on governmental decision making.[14]

While the EPL's name change symbolized a shift of emphasis from nationalist to individual interests, calls for revision for the sake of national survival have persisted in face of an ever-pressing *shōshika* issue. Changes in Japan's international stature—as China replaced Japan as the second economic superpower in the world following the United States—further intensified the sense of national crisis. One science professor, for example, declared that a "proud Japanese race" would not be conquered by another race but would face natural extinction with its declining population. He blamed the GHQ for imposing a law that would "emasculate the Japanese race," while in the United States and many Catholic countries, religion had served as a bulwark against abortion and declining birth rates. The conservative professor criticized existing efforts and discussions on *shōshika* that focused more on social provisions and economic measures such as child-care allowances, parental leave system, and child-care facilities.[15] There is a striking similarity between such contemporary discussion that ties Japan's fate to women's fertility patterns and the racial theories presented by Koya Yoshio and other national leaders in the 1930s and 1940s, when Japan aggressively sought to conquer the Pacific world as the practice of birth control started to spread among urban women at home. Past precedents in Japan and elsewhere have repeatedly shown, however, that an improved social welfare system that supports women's choices and rights, rather than outright regulations on abortion and contraceptive use, has been more successful in both reducing and raising birth rates.[16] Many national elites and politicians nonetheless continue to blame women's reproductive behaviors for causing social problems that jeopardize national and racial well-being.

. . .

Recent policies and debates on reproduction in the United States similarly reflect the nation's preoccupation with world domination, specifically the dominance of its white population. The gradual decline of the national population as a whole, the shrinking white population in particular, and the (perceived) high fertility of nonwhite immigrants and foreigners within its borders continue to occupy the discussions about the present and future of the nation. Eugenic ideologies and ideas of differential fertility between races saturate political debates about the nation's population and its future rather than the actual facts and numbers of population trends. Recent data suggest that immigrants and native-born Latinas have had steeper birth-rate declines than any other groups since the 2007 economic recession. Nonetheless, social debates focus on the declining birth rates of non-Hispanic whites—based on the outdated census category of race—and alarmingly note that "minority births" would become the "new majority" within a generation. Conservative politicians and anti-immigration activists still resort to sensational language and images of foreign and/or nonwhite women outpacing non-Hispanic white women in fertility and thus changing the demographic profile of the United States.[17]

More than half a century after Nazi eugenics, race-based eugenic programs persist today in the United States, although in less overt ways. While few today openly support any program to reduce the fertility of colored races, the coerced control of reproduction—mostly in the form of sterilization—of women considered undesirable to the nation as a whole still occurs. Racial minorities, immigrants, women on public relief, drug addicts, and women in prison are frequently semicoerced to undergo sterilization or to use certain contraceptives, including those now known to have serious health risks, such as Norplant and Depo-Provera.[18] Growing attention to state-supported sterilization programs in the South in the 1960s and 1970s led some southern states, such as North Carolina and Virginia, to issue official apologies to the victims and even discuss individual compensation plans for the injustice. While the apologies seemed to treat these race-based eugenics programs as an unfortunate incident of the past, similar injustice continues in the United States in more subtle ways. The *San Francisco Chronicle* and other media sources revealed that from 2006 to 2010, the state of California paid doctors to perform tubal ligations, in violation of prison rules, on nearly 150 female inmates—and perhaps 100 more dating back to the late 1990s. According to former inmates and prisoner advocates, prison medical staff coerced pregnant inmates deemed likely to return to prison in the future to receive sterilization.[19] These recent allegations suggest that eugenically inspired schemes to reduce the number of the "unfit" population—often defined by the color of their skin and their socioeconomic status—for the sake of the nation's overall well-being persist in our current society.

Eugenic bigotry is even more evident toward foreign-born, nonwhite women. Anti-immigrationists today—like the anti-Japanese eugenicists in the 1920s—still rely on the idea of prolific women of color from abroad when they refer to "anchor babies" in political debates over birthright citizenship and undocumented immigrants. They conjure up an image that hordes of pregnant women are streaming across the border to have babies and to claim various social benefits through their American children. According to a study by the Pew Hispanic Center, however, the vast majority of children of undocumented parents—91 percent—were born at least a year after their parents arrived; 61 percent of parents had children more than five years after their arrival.[20] In other words, they came to the United States for jobs, not necessarily to have babies. Although some undocumented immigrants may come to the United States believing that their children would forge a path toward easy, legal citizenship, in reality, this is an extremely complicated and prolonged immigration strategy.[21] While the "anchor baby" idea may largely be a myth, the language of reproduction and fecundity remains a powerful rhetorical strategy to galvanize support of the dominant race/class/group for its survival against the invasion of the Other.

There is, to be sure, a growing trend of foreign women coming to the United States with the specific purpose of giving birth. Birth tourists, as critics called them, typically refer to wealthy women from Asia—Japan, China, Taiwan, and Hong Kong—who stay in the United States for a couple of months before and after birth for the purpose of adding a US passport holder to their family.[22] The process is technically legal as long as they claim the purpose of their visits as "sightseeing" or "leisure." Nonetheless, local residents have filed public nuisance lawsuits and zoning violations against "maternity hotels" that cater specifically to these tourists. Some critics of birthright citizenship in the immigration debate have highlighted this issue in their political campaigns, applying the derogatory term "anchor babies" to the babies born to Asian tourists.[23] According to the data collected by National Center for Health Statistics in 2015, there were 10,236 babies born to mothers who reported they lived overseas, more than twice the number of those in 2000.[24] Anti-immigrationists argue that the number is too low an estimate because the information is based on self-reporting during hospital stays and many mothers use temporary US addresses for the child's birth certificate. It is nonetheless a tiny fraction of the approximately four million infants born in the United States. Having dual citizenship, moreover, does not necessarily mean that these children would return to the United States for education or jobs, much less bring their entire family to immigrate in the future. It seems more likely that nativists are again dramatizing the impending threat by resorting to the rhetoric of reproduction.

Meanwhile, advances in medical technology have increased the reproductive capacities of those women encouraged to have more children: white and middle-class Americans. Assisted reproductive technology (ART), such as in vitro fertilization and surrogacy, has spread rapidly over the decades to Americans who can afford the expensive procedure. Whereas most developed nations impose extensive regulations on the use of ART, the US federal government has exercised little control over this growing industry, leaving regulation to the states. The lack of regulation has resulted in further commercialization of the procedures and exploitation of women.[25] Varying laws across states and nations have intensified the phenomenon of "stratified reproduction," a term coined by anthropologist Shellee Colen referring to a global system that creates hierarchal structures of women's physical and social reproductive labor.[26] An international division of reproductive labor has become more prominent than ever, with poor women from Third World countries such as India offering their bodies in exchange for money to serve the well-to-do in the First World. Women with the means can travel to receive treatment to bear their own children, whereas marginalized women take on the reproductive labor of others often at the expense of their own reproductive agency. Nowadays, surrogacy is rapidly replacing adoption, as the latter has become increasingly affected by various discords between countries and criminal abuses such as child abduction. Whereas adoptions, the majority of which are interracial and/or international, challenge the notion of family and kinship, women with the means—typically white and educated—can now have their own biological child through ART. As a result, a pro-motherhood ideology has come to portray infertile women or those who choose to remain childless as not serving their reproductive duties.[27] ART offers, to some, the hope for survival of the white race in the United States. Such an idea is based on the persistent stereotype of colored women as fertile breeding machines, but it is less menacing and more beneficial to the (white-dominating) world than previous incarnations of reproductive racism. Most women who rely on ART feel that they have done so as a result of the lack of choices and certainly not to exploit other women or to propagate their own race. Nonetheless, the market-driven nature of ART services prevents its equal availability to women across socioeconomic borders.

. . .

As the history of birth control reveals, many women have actively endorsed or followed top-down reproductive policies that made certain contraceptives available to them. There were many female leaders who were just as preoccupied as their male colleagues with the well-being of the nation as a whole and considered women's reproduction to be a vital part of it. Even feminist activists such as Margaret Sanger and Ishimoto Shizue often ended up assuming women of lower classes would share their particular idea of reproductive choice, which was based on the heteronormative model of family and maternal love for children. Many average women nonetheless utilized the resources that were available to them, even if they were aware of the hypocritical goals of the nation's elites. They followed the nation's reproductive policy, not necessarily because they identified with its eugenic goals but usually to relieve the economic strains in their life, to enjoy sexual freedom, or to conform to societal norms.

How much agency do women have, after all, in making their own reproductive choices? As this study on the history of reproductive politics has shown, it is difficult to isolate women's decisions from the society in which they live. Women's reproductive choices are likely to be shaped by both local and global politics. They may be conditioned by external factors such as their economic conditions, legal restrictions, insurance coverage, and pressures from a medical authority, society, or families. At the same time, however, women's own needs and desires have had crucial effects on government policy and societal norms around sexuality and reproduction—even across national borders. Women chose to bear—or not to bear—children regardless of national policies or propaganda, often forcing elite leaders to adjust their strategies. Both in Japan and in the United States, it was these grassroots initiatives that ultimately helped democratize the practice of birth control.

Sanger and Ishimoto were first motivated by the pressing cry of poor mothers for birth control. When their belief in reproductive freedom went against those of some nationalist elites, the feminist leaders used transnational networks to gain supporters overseas and to extend their birth control campaigns to as many women as possible. Their activism has taught us the potential—and attendant limits and challenges—of transnational feminism to initiate changes and empower women worldwide, regardless of race, class status, or nationality.

Notes

INTRODUCTION

1. Ishimoto's first name was typically spelled "Shidzue" during the prewar period. In this book, I refer to her as "Shizue," following the standard romanization rule.

2. Historian John Dower traces the imaginary of apes, lesser men, children, and madmen that characterizes the Yellow Peril to Aristotle as well as earliest encounters of Europeans with African peoples and Native Americans. Gina Marchetti finds the psychocultural perception of a menace from Asians rooted in medieval fears of Genghis Khan and the Mongolian invasions of Europe. The term "Yellow Peril" itself was coined by Kaiser Wilhelm II of Germany in 1895 to express the perils the European colonists faced in their invasions of China and later to evoke racial fear among Western nations in response to the Japanese military victory over Russia in 1905. For the definitions and applications of the Yellow Peril in American political discourses and popular culture, see Dower, *Embracing Defeat*, 10; Marchetti, *Romance and the "Yellow Peril,"* 2.

3. In 1798, British economist Thomas Malthus presented his famous theory that population increases at a geometric rate ($1 \rightarrow 2 \rightarrow 4 \rightarrow 8$), while the resources for subsistence increase at only an arithmetic rate ($1 \rightarrow 2 \rightarrow 3 \rightarrow 4$). Sooner or later, he argued, population will be checked by famine, epidemics, or war. Given the brutality of these "natural" checks to overpopulation, Malthus advocated for more humane, socially imposed checks by regulating reproduction. As a devout Christian, Malthus emphasized the postponement of marriage and abstinence as means to control birth rates. Later exponents of Malthus's theory, the neo-Malthusians, enthusiastically endorsed artificial birth control as the solution to population growth. This idea did not have an immediate effect in the United States, where

there seemed to be unlimited resources and land to sustain a growing population. But by the turn of the century, as foreign immigrants started to crowd and occupy its major cities, new calls for population control started to emerge in the United States as well.

4. L. Gordon, *A Social History*, xii.

5. Sanger, *My Fight for Birth Control*, 254.

6. One of Sanger's biographers, Ellen Chesler, asserts that Sanger had little choice but to engage with eugenic discourse in the 1920s, since eugenics then enjoyed a degree of respectability that birth control did not. Historians Linda Gordon and David Kennedy also admit that Sanger's alliance with eugenicists was a strategy on her part to give legitimacy to her movement, although they are far more critical than Chesler of this alliance at the expense of her earlier radical approach. For critical investigators of the eugenics movement, such as Angela Franks and Edwin Black, it mattered little whether Sanger herself held discriminatory ideas, as long as her activism induced racist outcomes. See Chesler, *Woman of Valor*, 484; L. Gordon, *A Social History*, 249–50, 274–90; Kennedy, *Birth Control in America*, 111–21; Black, *War against the Weak*, 127; Franks, *Margaret Sanger's Eugenic Legacy*, 40–44.

7. For the intellectual genealogy of the "transnational turn" in American history/American studies, which started around the 1990s and became prominent in the 2000s, see Iriye, "The Internationalization of History," 1–10; Fishkin, "Crossroads of Cultures," 17–57; Tyrrell, "Reflections on the Transnational Turn," 453–74; Pease, "Introduction: Re-mapping the Transnational Turn," 1–48.

8. Since the 2000s, an increasing number of recent studies have paid special attention to transpacific relations in the study of US imperialism. See Shu and Pease, *American Studies as Transnational Practice*; Hoskins and Nguyen, *Transpacific Studies*.

9. Akira Iriye's groundbreaking work *Power and Culture* analyzes the shared political ideology between American and Japanese political leaders during the war period, which derived from the Wilsonian principles of "economic development, political liberalism, and intellectual openness." Iriye, *Power and Culture*, 266.

10. This work is based on John Dower's *War without Mercy*, which systematically examined World War II as a "race war" that caused "a revolution in racial consciousness throughout the world that continues to the present day." Dower, *War without Mercy*, 4.

11. Akira Iriye provides a comprehensive picture of "cultural internationalism" throughout the twentieth century in *Cultural Internationalism and World Order*.

12. W. Williams, *The Tragedy of American Diplomacy*, 140.

13. Ibid., 47, 49, 86.

14. Ibid., 63. Historians and biographers of Sanger and Ishimoto have similarly pointed out the reformist nature of their birth control activism. See L. Gordon, *A Social History*, 257–59; Kennedy, *Birth Control in America*, 111–13; Gray, *Margaret Sanger*, 289–90; Tipton, "Ishimoto Shizue," 351–52; Tipton, "Birth Control and the Population Problem," 56–60.

15. Woodrow Wilson avoided getting involved in what he considered "emotional" debates over racial politics, both domestically and internationally. His desire to eschew the race issue, however, also meant that he silently approved many discriminatory policies against African Americans. During World War I, Wilson worried that "the yellow races" would take advantage of "the depletion of man power" among the "white races" and would attempt to subjugate them. Cooper, "American Sphinx," 156–57.

16. My work builds on a growing scholarship in Asian American history that examines the role of migrants and immigrants as agents and facilitators of transnationalism, including Azuma, *Between Two Empires*; Choy, *Empire of Care*; Yuh, *Beyond the Shadow of Camptown*; Ong, *Flexible Citizenship*.

17. For details about the lawsuit and its impact, see Chesler, *Woman of Valor*, 372–76; Kennedy, *Birth Control in America*, 242–58; Johnson, "Margaret Sanger and the Birth Control Movement in Japan," 88–91, 129–30.

18. For studies on cultural diplomacy among nonstate actors between the United States and Japan before World War II, see Akami, *Internationalizing the Pacific*; Davidann, *Cultural Diplomacy in U.S.-Japanese Relations*; Hirobe, *Japanese Pride, American Prejudice*; Auslin, *Pacific Cosmopolitans*, 84–129.

19. In one of his books, Akira Iriye mentions the rise of women's international organizations and women's activism in the 1920s, including the eugenics and birth control movements, but concludes that such movement was bound with failure and disagreement among women. See Iriye, *Global Community*, 29–30. For studies that showcase women's transnational/international networks, see Rupp, *Worlds of Women*; Paisley, *Glamour in the Pacific*.

20. Other studies that highlight the active role of women, as missionaries, artists, or activists, in the context of imperialism include Wexler, *Tender Violence*; Yoshihara, *Embracing the East*; Bederman, *Manliness & Civilization*, 121–69; Newman, *White Women's Rights*; J. Hunter, *The Gospel of Gentility*.

21. I derive the definitions of "transnational," "international," and "global" from Lee and Shibusawa, "What Is Transnational Asian American History?," viii–ix; Pease, "Introduction: Re-mapping the Transnational Turn," 5–6.

22. Connelly, *Fatal Misconception*, 10–15.

23. For the definition of "liberal developmentalism," see Rosenberg, *Spreading the American Dream*, 7. For more on the modernization theory, see Latham, *Modernization as Ideology*, 4–17; Adas, *Dominance by Design*, 242–46.

24. Koshiro, *Trans-Pacific Racisms*.
25. Foucault, *The History of Sexuality*, 1:25–26, 95, 139–45.
26. Foucault, *Discipline and Punish*, 136–37.
27. Martin, *The Woman in the Body*, 63.

28. Japanese historian Emiko Ochiai shows that anatomical illustrations of wombs in women's bodies, influenced by Western science, started to appear in medical texts in the late eighteenth century. These new medical images dovetailed with the common saying in feudalistic Japanese society that women were mere carriers of "borrowed wombs": the child belonged to the paternal family once she or he was born, and the mother had no further role in it. For the historical context surrounding the concept of "borrowed wombs," see Ochiai, "The Reproductive Revolution," 197–208; Lock, *Encounters with Aging*, 83–84. Japanese American feminist and socialist Ishigaki Ayako criticized the Japanese military government's pronatalism during the war by referring to the idea of "borrowed wombs." Tanaka Mei, "Josei shokan," *Rafu shimpo*, September 13, 1937, 2.

29. Since the 1970s, feminist science scholars have revealed the misogynist process of knowledge production regarding women's bodies. See, for example, Fausto-Sterling, *Myths of Gender*; Harding, *Whose Science?*; Longino, *Science as Social Knowledge*; Haraway, *ModestWitness@SecondMillennium*.

30. Federici links the "population crisis" in sixteenth- and seventeenth-century Europe to the rise of witch-hunts. Federici, *Caliban and the Witch*, 86–91. The subordination of women's bodies also took place during the premodern era and in preindustrial societies, although it was less systematic and rigid. For the premodern or pre-Meiji (before 1868) regulation of reproduction in Japan, see Ochiai, "The Reproductive Revolution," 187–215; Sawayama, "The 'Birthing Body,'" 10–34.

31. Schiebinger, *Nature's Body*, 55–56; Haraway, *Primate Visions*, 149–56; Russett, *Sexual Science*, 49–77. An explicit example of the hypersexualized image of "primitive" women of color is the representation of the "Hottentot" African women in eighteenth- and nineteenth-century Europe. See Fausto-Sterling, "Gender, Race, and Nation," 19–48.; Schiebinger, *Nature's Body*, 160–72.

32. For a historical analysis of sexualized images of Asian women in American popular culture, see, for example, Marchetti, *Romance and the "Yellow Peril"*; Yoshihara, *Embracing the East*.

33. For studies on the regulation of sexuality in modern Japan, see Frühstück, *Colonizing Sex*; Pflugfelder, *Cartographies of Desire*; Fujime, *Sei no rekishigaku*; Mihalopoulos, *Sex in Japan's Globalization*. Other works that have helped shaped my understandings about the body, sexuality, and nationalism include Mosse, *Nationalism and Sexuality*; Poovey, *Making a Social Body*; Stewart-Steinberg, *The Pinocchio Effect*; Surkis, *Sexing the Citizen*.

34. For studies on the influence of the Spencerian notion of the "survival of

the fittest" (social Darwinism) on American and Japanese imperial discourses, respectively, see, for example, Bannister, *Social Darwinism*; Chung, *Struggle for National Survival*.

35. See, for example, Kevles, *In the Name of Eugenics*; Barkan, *The Retreat of Scientific Racism*; Kühl, *The Nazi Connection*; Connelly, *Fatal Misconception*, 61–62; Black, *War against the Weak*, 207–318. For the history of eugenics in Latin America, see Stepan, *"The Hour of Eugenics"*; Briggs, *Reproducing Empire*.

36. For the history of eugenics in Asia, see Dikötter, *Imperfect Conceptions*; Sitcawich, "Eugenics in Imperial Japan"; Suzuki, *Nihon no yūseigaku*. While these studies highlight alternative histories and models of eugenics to the Euro-American ones, they do not fully explore the relationships and interactions between Eastern and Western eugenics.

CHAPTER ONE

1. Ishimoto, *Facing Two Ways*, 183.
2. As Sumiko Otsubo Sitcawich has shown, Western-inspired eugenics was a powerful ideology for Japanese intellectuals, including feminists, to elevate their status as racially marginal Japanese—vis-à-vis Westerners—or as socially marginal women. Sitcawich, "Eugenics in Imperial Japan," iii.
3. One such influential woman was Kishida Toshiko, whose working experience at the Meiji Court brought her face-to-face with women's vulnerable and degraded status. She resigned this job, made connections with the popular-rights leadership, and soon became one of the Liberal Party's most celebrated speakers. After two years of political activities, organizing associations, lectures, and study groups, Kishida was arrested in 1883. For details of her activities, see Sievers, *Flowers in Salt*, 33–42.
4. These state restrictions did not mean that women stopped engaging in political activities entirely. For example, Elizabeth Dorn Lublin illuminates how some women, through the activities of the Woman's Christian Temperance Union, found ways to assert themselves politically, advance their rights, and negotiate with the state. See Lublin, *Reforming Japan*.
5. Garon, *Molding Japanese Minds*, 118–23; Mackie, *Feminism in Modern Japan*, 21–29.
6. Although the effectiveness of these earlier attempts at punishing abortion and infanticide was minimal, the negative discourse on abortion had become widespread before the Meiji period, preparing the ground for this modern system that posited abortion and infanticide as criminal acts. For social, medical, and political discourses surrounding reproduction in eighteenth- to nineteenth-century Japan, see Ochiai, "The Reproductive Revolution," 187–215.
7. Garon, *Molding Japanese Minds*, 88–94; Fujime, *Sei no rekishigaku*, 88–99.

8. A draft of the Factory Bill was first prepared in 1902 but was postponed by the Russo-Japanese War of 1904–5. The bill was then presented to the Diet in 1909, but it took another two years for it to be promulgated due to opposition by industrialists. See Mackie, *Creating Socialist Women in Japan*, 74–76.

9. For example, Harada Satsuki's powerful story of a woman who was imprisoned for procuring an abortion appeared in *Seitō* in June 1915 and triggered the so-called abortion debate.

10. Mackie, *Feminism in Modern Japan*, 46–51; Fujime, *Sei no rekishigaku*, 134–36.

11. Mackie, *Feminism in Modern Japan*, 77; Mackie, *Creating Socialist Women*, 48, 73.

12. For the actual texts of debates between Yosano Akiko, Hiratsuka Raichō, and Yamakawa Kikue, see Kouchi, *Shiryō bosei hogo ronsō*. For a brief description of each woman's philosophy and her position in the "motherhood protection debate," see Shimada, *Nihon no feminizumu*, 23–118. For English sources on the debate, see Rodd, "Yosano Akiko and the Taishō Debate over the 'New Woman,'" 189–98; Molony, "Equality versus Differences," 124–29.

13. See, in particular, Kagawa Toyohiko, "Nyonin bunmei no kaifuku" [The return of women's civilization]; Nogami Toshio, "Gendai seikatsu to danjo ryōsei no sekkin" [Modern life and the approaching of both sexes]; Fujikawa Yū, "Shintaijō yori mitaru joshi kaihō mondai" [Women's liberation issue from a physical standpoint], all in *Kaizō*, April 1920, 174–75, 181–84, 187–98, 215–21.

14. Mackie, *Creating Socialist Women*, 49–50, 79–80; Suzuki, *Yamakawa Kikue*, 28–29, 38–42, 47–48.

15. Yosano Akiko, "Bosei henchō wo haisu" [I reject maternalism] (February 1916); "Nihon fujin no tokusyoku" [The characteristic of Japanese women] (January 1917), both in Yosano, *Yosano Akiko zenshū*, 9:193, 266–67.

16. Hiratsuka Raichō, "Sanjisū seigen no mondai" [The birth control issue] (1916); "Hinin no kahi wo ronzu" [Debating the pros and cons of contraception] (September 1917), both in Hiratsuka, *Hiratsuka Raichō chosakushū*, 2:238–42, 335–40.

17. Yamada, *Katei no shakaiteki igi*, 373–74.

18. Marie Stopes visited Japan in 1907 for a scientific mission to study botany for a year and a half at Tokyo Imperial University. The Japanese felt familiarity with Stopes when she later became famous for her birth control activism.

19. Hiratsuka, "Hinin no kahi wo ronzu," 2:337.

20. Yamakawa Kikue, "Tasanshugi no noroi" [The curse of pronatalism], "Josei kaihō to sanji chōsetsu mondai" [Women's liberation and the birth control problem], "Sanji seigen mondai" [The birth control problem], "Sanji seigen ron

to shakai shugi" [Birth control theory and socialism], "Hinin zehi ni tsuite hutatabi Ishikawa Sanshirō-shi ni atau" [Once again refuting Mr. Ishikawa Sanshirō's opinion regarding contraception], all in Yamakawa, *Yamakawa Kikue shū*, 2:202–5, 210–16, 231–33, 235–36, 285, 287–93.

21. In earlier days, Japanese socialists in general rejected Malthusianism and neo-Malthusianism. Katayama Sen advocated emigration, instead of birth control or abstinence, as a solution to Japan's overpopulation problem. Katayama, "Jinkō zōka to rōdōsha" [Population increase and laborers], *Nihonjin*, March 1902, 18–22; Ōta, *Nihon sanji chōsetsu hyakunenshi*, 86–109.

22. Yamakawa Hitoshi, "Sanji chōsetsu to shin-Marusasushugi" [Birth control and neo-Malthusianism], *Kaizō*, October 1920, 95–99.

23. The article was simultaneously published in *Birth Control Review* (June, July, August 1921). In *Kaizō*, the article appeared in its original English version, accompanied by a Japanese translation.

24. Taeuber, *The Population of Japan*, 41, 231–33.

25. Fujime Yuki highlights the activism of midwife Shibahara Urako, who started to help local women suffering from multiple pregnancies during the aftermath of World War I before the term "birth control" was widely known. See Fujime, *Sei no rekishigaku*, 136–39.

26. L. Gordon, *A Social History*, 187.

27. The American birth control movement had close connections with socialism long before Margaret Sanger became politically active. One of the first activists in the United States to publicly and politically challenge the prohibition of birth control in the mid-nineteenth century was a small group of "utopian socialists," whose philosophy later inspired the proponents of "voluntary motherhood." These ideas emerged as a response to the changes in social order caused by capitalism—the disintegration of the family and the rise of poverty—but they were not intended to overturn conventional social norms and orders. For details on birth control discussions and activism in the nineteenth-century United States, see L. Gordon, *A Social History*, 72–115.

28. Kennedy, *Birth Control in America*, 11; L. Gordon, *A Social History*, 215.

29. Sanger, *My Fight for Birth Control*, 46–55.

30. Kennedy, *Birth Control in America*, 24.

31. Ishimoto, *Facing Two Ways*, 97.

32. Ibid., 77–86.

33. Many early socialists in late nineteenth-century Japan, most of whom were intellectual social reformers, supported parliamentarism and emphasized pacifism and internationalism. After the Russo-Japanese War, a new brand of socialists challenged the validity of Christian socialists' parliamentarism and instead called

for more radical "direct action." As a result, the socialist movement split into a number of factions—mainly into Christian socialists and anarcho-syndicalists. See Scalapino, *The Early Japanese Labor Movement*, 18–21.

34. Ichioka, *The Issei*, 3; Ichioka, "A Buried Past," 3; Fowler, *Japanese and Chinese Immigrant Activists*, 36–38.

35. The High Treason Case of 1910 was a purported plot to assassinate Emperor Meiji, which led to a mass arrest of socialists and anarchists and the execution of twelve alleged conspirators. The case is also known as the Kōtoku Incident (*Kōtoku jiken*), named after the principal culprit, Kōtoku Shūsui, who was also prosecuted. It is said that the government had used—or even fabricated—the incident as a pretext to round up radicals.

36. Prominent socialists who gathered in New York City around this time included Leon Trotsky, Nikolai Bukharin, V. Volodarsky, Alexandra Kollontai, Louis Fraina, and Louis Boudin. Some non-Asian Comintern leaders held Orientalist prejudice toward Asian socialists as "backward," "alien," and "childlike" and accorded them only secondary status within the international socialist movement. See Fowler, *Japanese and Chinese Immigrant Activists*, 22–23, 71–72.

37. Before the Japanese Socialist Study Group, Katayama formed the Japanese Labor Association of New York City, whose primary aim was "to exert its influence over the Japanese servants [domestic workers] and get them better employment," as he considered their occupation "degrading to [the] character and personality of Japanese." However, the organization existed only on paper with a handful of members and sympathizers, mostly wealthy merchants and professionals. See Sen Katayama, "A Japanese Working Men's Association in N.Y.," *Heimin*, August 1918, 4.

38. Scalapino, *The Japanese Communist Movement*, 8; Fowler, *Japanese and Chinese Immigrant Activists*, 36–39.

39. Smedley's socialist connections later led her to live in various countries, including Germany, Russia, and China, but she continued to assist Sanger's birth control cause after she moved from New York City by writing about birth control and establishing birth control clinics in these countries. See Smedley's correspondence with Sanger in reel 10, Margaret Sanger Papers, Library of Congress, Washington, DC (hereafter MSP-LC).

40. Agnes Smedley, "Babies and Imperialism in Japan," *Birth Control Review* (hereafter *BCR*), June 1919, 6–8; Smedley, "Young Japan for Birth Control," *BCR*, July 1919, 9.

41. Yosano Akiko, "Hitori no onna no techō" [A woman's diary], *Taiyō*, August 1916, 31.

42. Agnes Smedley, "The Awakening of Japan," *BCR*, March 1920, 6–8.

43. Yamakawa Kikue accused Yosano Akiko of "insulting" socialists, when

Yosano, in another column on *Taiyō*, compared "the misinterpreted argument of equal distribution of wealth" advocated by "the early radical socialists" to some extreme egalitarians who might indiscriminately appeal for equal types of job distribution to women and men. Yamakawa's response prompted Yosano to clarify her position that she was not a "champion of the capitalist class" and to admit that she had used an inappropriate example. For the public correspondence between Yamakawa and Yosano, see Yosano, "Danjo no honshitsuteki byōdōkan" [Fundamental egalitarianism between men and women]; Aoyama (Yamakawa) Kikue, "Yosano Akiko-shi ni atau" [To Ms. Yosano Akiko]; Yosano, "Aoyama Kikue-shi ni kotau" [Responding to Ms. Aoyama Kikue]; Yamakawa, "Futatabi Yosano Akiko-shi ni" [Again to Ms. Yosano Akiko], in Kouchi, *Shiryō bosei hogo ronsō*, 51–77.

44. Ishigaki, *Amerika hōrō yonjūnen*.
45. Margaret Sanger, "Margaret Sanger in Japan," *BCR*, June 1922, 103.
46. Ishizaki, "Seishoku no jiyū to sanji chōsetsu undō," 97.
47. This was the impression that Sanger and Ishimoto themselves had about the incident. Sanger, *Autobiography*, 320; Katō, *Katō Shizue*, 52–53; Hopper, *A New Woman of Japan*, 23.
48. Sanger, *Autobiography*, 325.
49. "Our Undesired Emigrant," *New York Times*, February 20, 1922, 7; "The Missionary Idea," *Los Angeles Times*, February 22, 1922, II4.
50. Sanger, *My Fight for Birth Control*, 243–44.
51. Newspaper clippings reporting Sanger's Japan visit in box 234, MSP-LC.
52. Yamamoto, "Sangā joshi kazoku seigenhō hihan" [Critique of Mrs. Sanger's family limitation methods], in Yamamoto, *Yamamoto Senji zenshū*, 3:27.
53. Although he did not organize any major socialist activity while in Canada, Yamamoto was listed on the socialist blacklist of the Japanese consul. Once back in Japan, he studied at Dōshisha University, Kyoto University, and then the Tokyo Imperial University. While at Tokyo Imperial University, he joined the Tōdai New Man Society (Tōdai shinjinkai), a left-wing student organization inspired by the spirit of "Taishō Democracy" and by various socialist activities. In 1920, Yamamoto began his master's studies in biology at Kyoto University, while lecturing both at Dōshisha and Kyoto Universities. In 1921, he conducted a survey of his students' views on sex education and distributed the results to other scholars and solicited comments. Sasaki, *Yamamoto Senji*, 150–67; Yasuda Tokutarō, "Kyū-'Yamamoto Senji senshū' kaisetsu" [Commentary on the former edition of the collected works of Yamamoto Senji], in Yamamoto, *Yamamoto Senji zenshū*, 7:489, 587–88; Frühstück, *Colonizing Sex*, 85–86. For the historical and social context surrounding the Tōdai New Man Society, see Umeda, *Shakai undō to shuppan bunka*, 31–89.

54. Yamamoto, "Sangā joshi kazoku seigenhō hihan," 3:27; Yasudaō, "Kyū-Yamamoto Senji zenshū kaisetsu," 7:458.

55. Yamamoto, "Sangā-shiki hinin senden no zehi" [Debating the Sanger method of birth control propaganda], in Yamamoto, *Yamamoto Senji zenshū*, 3:20.

56. Historian Michael Adas uses the case of Perry's expedition to illustrate US technological imperialism. Adas, *Dominance by Design*, 5, 8.

57. Ibid., 27.

58. Yasuda, "Kyū-'Yamamoto Senji senshū' kaisetsu," 7:510.

59. "Sa-fujin no Yokohama-chaku" [Mrs. S arrives in Yokohama], *Hokuriku*, March 12, 1922; "Kyō gogo sanji kara Sa-fujin no kōen" [Mrs. S's lecture starts from 3 p.m. today], *Yomiuri shinbun*, March 14, 1922; "Sukkirishita kuroi fuku de Sa-fujin ga danjō ni" [Mrs. S in an elegant black dress takes the stage], *Yomiuri shinbun*, March 15, 1922; "Kibishī jinmon no ato Sa-fujin yatto jōriku" [After harsh interrogation, Mrs. S finally comes onshore], *Asahi shinbun*, March 11, 1922.

60. "Ninki wo atsumete raichō shita Sangā-fujin to aisoku Guranto" [Mrs. Sanger and her beloved son Grant arrive in Japan and attract popularity], *Yomiuri shinbun*, March 11, 1922; "Sanji seigen no Sangā-fujin rainichi" [Birth control advocate Mrs. Sanger arrives in Japan], *Tokyo nichi nichi shinbun*, March 11, 1922; "Nyūkyō shita Sangā-fujin" [Mrs. Sanger arrives in Japan], *Asahi shinbun*, March 12, 1922.

61. Johnson, "Margaret Sanger and the Birth Control Movement in Japan," 64.

62. Yasuda, "Kyū-'Yamamoto Senji senshū' kaisetsu," 7:509.

63. Yamamoto, "Sangā joshi kazoku seigenhō hihan," 3:20, 27.

64. Yosano Akiko, "Saikin no zakkan" [Miscellaneous thoughts on recent events], *Myōjō*, June 1922, 129.

65. For example, *Shufu no tomo* carried a report of Sanger's press meeting in 1922 and featured many articles on the actual experiences of "success and failure" of birth control methods. In April 1922, *Fujin sekai* ran a special issue on "The Pros and Cons of Birth Control," in which Ishimoto Shizue and prominent female physician Yoshioka Yayoi exchanged opposing views in regard to what birth control would mean to Japan at the time.

66. The first and only issue of *Shō-kazoku* carried articles advocating birth control from various perspectives: neo-Malthusian, medical, economic, and social. This and subsequent birth control magazines, however, avoided description of specific birth control techniques for fear of censorship and police crackdown.

67. Baron Keikichi Ishimoto, "The Population Problem in Japan," *BCR*, January 1923, 10, 19; Abe Isoo, "The Birth Control Movement in Japan," *BCR*, January 1923, 9, 17, and *BCR*, April 1925, 102, 125–26; Keikichi Ishimoto, "Japan and

America," *BCR*, October 1925, 288–89; I. Nitobe, "Food and Population in Japan," *BCR*, December 1928, 342–43.

68. Yasuda, "Kyū-'Yamamoto Senji senshū' kaisetsu," 7:510.

69. Frühstück, *Colonizing Sex*, 133.

70. Yamamoto maintained a cooperative and amiable relationship with the proletarian female members of the Osaka Birth Control Study Society. Fujime, "Yamasen no jidai no josei tachi," 7.

71. Yamamoto, "Sangā-joshi kazoku seigenhō hihan," 3:27, 70–71, 74, 86; Yamamoto, "Ōbei ni okeru chōsetsu" [Birth control in Europe and America], in Yamamoto, *Yamamoto Senji zenshū*, 3:582–83; Yamamoto, "Sanji chōsetsu, ketsuron, sono igo" [Birth control, conclusion, and thereafter], in Yamamoto, *Yamamoto Senji zenshū*, 3:601.

72. Yamamoto to Sanger, April 1923, in Yamamoto, *Yamamoto Senji zenshū*, 7:145.

73. Sanger to Yamamoto, August 30, 1923, in ibid., 7:177–78.

74. Sanger to Yamamoto, January 5, 1924; Sanger to Yamamoto, May 25, 1926, in ibid., 7:201, 288. Sanger also notified Yamamoto that she had not received the money order that Yamamoto had sent her for the cost of pessaries he ordered, and reminded him to renew his subscription to *Birth Control Review*.

75. Yamamoto, "Kokusai sanji chōsetsu sōdōmei yume monogatari" [International confederation for birth control fantasy], in ibid., 3:176–80.

76. According to Yamamoto's own statistics, among those who joined the Study Society during the first year and responded to his questionnaire, the majority (66.9 percent) were from the working class, 16.9 percent from the middle class, and 2.8 percent from the upper class. The questionnaire also showed that most of them practiced birth control for economic reasons (53.5 percent). Another 23.4 percent cited health reasons, including the poor health of the wife (19.2 percent), husband (1.4 percent), or both (0.5 percent), and genetic reasons (2.3 percent). Yamamoto, "Sanji seigen to musan kaikyū" [Birth control and the proletariat], in ibid., 3:218–22.

77. Ōta, *Nihon sanji chōsetsu hyakunenshi*, 147, 314–18; Yasuda, "Kyū-'Yamamoto Senji senshū' kaisetsu," 7:511–13.

78. Yamamoto, "Sangā joshi kazoku seigenhō hihan," 3:23, 55.

79. Yamamoto to Sanger, April 1923, in Yamamoto, *Yamamoto Senji zenshū*, 7:145.

80. "For Healthier and Happier Babies," *Japan Today and Tomorrow* (1930), 103, box 235, MSP-LC. For information about the Japanese Union for Birth Control and the Eugenic Counseling Office, see also Frühstück, *Colonizing Sex*, 138; Fujime, *Sei no rekishigaku*, 260–63.

81. Ishimoto, *Facing Two Ways*, 373.

82. Kato, *A Fight for Women's Happiness*, 74; Johnson, "Margaret Sanger and the Birth Control Movement in Japan," 82–86.

83. Ishimoto to Florence Rose, April 13, 1934, box 8 (filmed), Margaret Sanger Papers, Sophia Smith Collection, New Hampton, MA (hereafter MSP-SSC).

84. Ishimoto, *Facing Two Ways*, 371.

85. Koyama Sakae to Margaret Sanger, October 17, 1931, and March 26, 1932, reel 18, MSP-LC. Sanger declined the offer to market Koyama's pessaries in the United States unless they were "found to be better adapted for general use than any other [pessaries] now in use." She nonetheless recommended Koyama's pessaries to birth control leaders to be tested on a mass scale in India and asked Koyama to send "a gross of these pessaries" to her contact in India. Sanger to Koyama, April 30, 1932; Koyama to Sanger, May 5, 1932; Sanger to Koyama, September 19, 1935; Koyama to Sanger, October 21, 1935, all on reel 18, MSP-LC.

86. Letter from Ishimoto to Sanger, June 1, 1932, reel 56; Ishimoto to Florence Rose, March 20, 1936, reel 18, both in MSP-LC.

87. Chesler, *Woman of Valor*, 373.

88. Ōta, *Sanji chōsetsu hyakunenshi*, 331–33, 338–39. For examples of contraceptive methods promoted and sold by proletarian advocates, see "Danzen attōteki! Kono kyōkyū nedan wo miro!" [Absolutely cheap! See this offered price!], *Puro BC nyūsu*, extra edition, June 24, 1931, 1; Iwasaki Motoko, "Ishimoto-fujin no ronsetsu ni bakusu" [Refuting Mrs. Ishimoto's article], *Sanji seigen undō*, September 1933, 12.

89. According to the 1950 survey, 9.2 percent started practicing contraception before the war (–1936), 8.8 percent during the war (1937–44), and 71.5 percent after the war (1945–). Population Problems Research Council, the Mainichi Newspapers, *Family Planning in Japan*, 106; Honda, *Public Opinion Survey on Birth Control in Japan*, 33–34.

90. Honda, *Public Opinion Survey on Birth Control in Japan*, 35; Taeuber, *The Population of Japan*, 246.

91. Intellectual leaders played a vital part in the early labor movement in Japan, and political action—establishing a "proletarian party" and participating in parliamentarism—became important in the era of universal male suffrage. See Scalapino, *Early Japanese Labor Movement*, 237–38.

92. Letter from Ishimoto to Yamamoto, October 4, 1922, in Yamamoto, *Yamamoto Senji zenshū*, 7:125.

93. Yamamoto to Sanger, April 1923, in ibid., 7:148.

94. Miyahara Shinobu, interview with Katō Shizue, "Mazu nani yori mo hinin wo" [First and foremost, use birth control], *Agora*, June 1983, 173; Shidzue

Ishimoto, "News from Japan," *BCR*, January 1923, 7. Yamamoto noted that he ridiculed Sanger in front of his male medical audience to "satisfy [their] nationalistic pride," but he personally admitted that Sanger was a well-educated woman with a sincere interest in pursuing scientific knowledge. For example, he praised Sanger's books as scientifically sound and relatively free from the typical characteristics of women's writings, which, he claimed, tended to resort to emotions and redundantly repeat general knowledge or plain facts. Yamamoto to Sanger, April 1923, in Yamamoto, *Yamamoto Senji zenshū*, 7:148; Yamamoto, "Sangā-joshi kazoku seigenhō hihan," in ibid., 3:85.

95. Yamamoto to Sanger, April 1923, in ibid., 7:148; Yamamoto, "Sangā-joshi kazoku seigenhō hihan," in ibid., 3:69.

96. Ōta, *Nihon sanji chōsetsu hyakunenshi*, 157.

97. Ishizaki, "Seishoku no jiyū to sanji chōsetsu undō," 100.

98. In 1924, Yamamoto changed the title of his journal, *Sanji chōsetsu hyōron* [Birth control review], to *Sei to shakai* [Sex and society], as he felt the need to broaden the topics beyond solely birth control. Despite such adjustments, it became difficult, both politically and financially, to continue the journal, and Yamamoto ceased its publication in May 1926. Meanwhile, Yamamoto became increasingly preoccupied with other political struggles after he was elected to the Diet. For Yamamoto's commentary on the transition, see "'Sanji chōsetsu hyōron' kara 'Sei to shakai' e" [From birth control review to sex and society], *Sei to shakai* (September–November 1925), in Yamamoto, *Yamamoto Senji zenshū*, 3:366–401.

99. Frühstück, *Colonizing Sex*, 150–51; Fujime, *Sei no rekishigaku*, 263–65.

100. Nihon sanji chōsetsu fujin renmei, "Nyūsu hakkō no aisatsu" [Message on the publication of the news], *Sanji chōsetsu nyūsu*, May 5, 1934, 1.

101. National leaders found it important to equip women with proper scientific knowledge in health so that they would produce physically fit children. Japan Women's College (JWC) was at the forefront of eugenic education for women, where a number of leading scholars in eugenics taught, including Naruse Jinzō, Ōsawa Kenji, and Nagai Hisomu. Hiratsuka Raichō was a graduate of the school. For details about JWC's eugenic education, see Sitcawich, "Eugenics in Imperial Japan."

102. See, for example, Yamakawa, "Hiratsuka Akiko-shi e: Shin-fujin kyōkai ni kansuru shokan" [To Ms. Hiratsuka Akiko: Thoughts on the new woman's association], *Fujin kōron*, April 1921; Hiratsuka, "Musan seitō to fusen undō" [The proletarian party and the suffrage movement], "Musan seitō to musan fujin dantai" [The proletarian party and the proletarian women's group] (1927), both in Hiratsuka, *Hiratsuka Raichō chosakushū*, 4:273–75; "Fusen undōsha e" [To suffragists] (1928), in Hiratsuka, *Hiratsuka Raichō chosakushū*, 5:20–27; Yosano Akiko,

"Musansha no reimeiki" [The predawn of the proletariat] (March 1928), "Musan shijo no hōkō" [The direction of proletarian children] (March 1928), both in Yosano, *Yosano Akiko zenshū*, 11:149–52, 198–202.

103. "Pro-BC katsudō hōkoku" [Activity report of proletarian birth control], *Sanji seigen undō*, September 1931, 2, 15–16. The women organizers included Nakane Akino, Iwasaki Motoko, and Katayama Masa. Prominent proletarian novelists, such as Akita Ujaku and Matsuda Tokiko, gave speeches at the inaugural meeting of the Proletarian Birth Control Union. Matsuda Tokiko later wrote about the birth control activities of the group in *Joseisen*.

104. Iwasaki, "Ishimoto-fujin no ronsetsu ni bakusu," 8–12.

105. Kutsumi, "Naze ni wareware wa hantai shitaka," 53.

106. "Pro-BC katsudō hōkoku," 2.

107. "Hakon no higeki wo sukuu kekkon eisei sōdanjo" [Marriage health consultation saves couples from the tragedy of divorce], *Rafu shimpō*, January 8, 1933.

108. "Fujin e no fukuin" [A gospel for women], *Rafu shimpō*, November 7, 1932.

109. Uesugi Haruko, "Chinomigo wo hotte hataraki ni deneba naranu watashi no nayami" [My distress of having to leave my newborn child and work outside], *Zaibei rōdō shinbun*, October 10, 1934.

110. Yamakawa Kikue, "Sanji chōsetsu ka: Umihōdai, shinihōdai ka" [Birth control or uncontrolled childbirths and deaths], *Sandē mainichi* [Sunday daily], April 2, 1923, in Yamakawa, *Yamakawa Kikue shū*, 3:105–11. Other socialist women expressed similar views about birth control. For example, Kamichika Ichiko supported birth control as a *temporary* defensive measure until the achievement of the "proletariat nation," where women could bear as *many* children as they wish. Kamichika, "Puroletaria kaihō ni okeru sanji seigen" [Birth control and the liberation of the proletariat], *Sanji seigen undō*, September 1931, 6–7.

111. Margaret Sanger, "Birth Control—Past, Present, and Future," *BCR*, June 1921, 12.

112. Margaret Sanger, "Woman's Power and Birth Control," *Kaizō*, April 1922, 147–57. See Sanger's draft of this article on reel 130, MSP-LC.

113. Ishimoto, *Facing Two Ways*, 353; Katō, *A Fight for Women's Happiness*, 67.

114. Ishimoto, *Facing Two Ways*, 351–58.

CHAPTER TWO

1. Margaret Sanger, "Woman and War," *BCR*, June 1917, 5.

2. Another internationally renown feminist visited the country in 1923 on her way back from Europe: Jane Addams, the American leader of the peace movement. Although Addams's visit did not attract the same degree of publicity that Sanger's did, Addams was enthusiastically greeted by Japanese women's groups

Notes to Chapter Two 237

as the "Mother of Peace." Both Sanger and Addams represented an intellectual trend of Wilsonian internationalism among liberal reformers of the interwar period. Iinuma, "A History of the Women's Peace Association of Japan," 39.

3. Iriye, *Global Community*, 31.

4. For historical studies on women's relationship with militarism, see Enloe, *Does Khaki Become You?*; Mackie, "Motherhood and Pacifism in Japan."

5. Rupp, *Worlds of Women*, 14–29; Rupp, "Constructing Internationalism," 1574–75.

6. Rupp, *Worlds of Women*, 75. As Mari Yoshihara's *Embracing the East* demonstrates, Western women had used the "Orient" as a source of inspiration since the late nineteenth century to articulate alternative national and gender identities in their art and literary works.

7. For Asian women's agency in international gatherings, see Ogawa, "American Women's Destiny, Asian Women's Dignity"; Yasutake, *Transnational Women's Activism*.

8. For the history of the IPR, see Akami, *Internationalizing the Pacific*; Yamaoka, *The Institute of Pacific Relations*; Holland, *Remembering the Institute of Pacific Relations*.

9. The record of the proceedings of the first PPWC included the list of delegates from Australia (sixteen representatives), Canada (one), China (seven), Fiji (one), Hawaii (ninety-one), India (one), Japan (eighteen), New Zealand (seventeen), Philippine Islands (two), Samoa (three), and the United States (twenty-seven), as well as twenty more "accredited visitors." Pan-Pacific Women's Conference, *Women of the Pacific*.

10. For studies on the PPWA, see Paisley, *Glamour in the Pacific*; Hooper, "Feminism in the Pacific," 367–78; Yasutake, "Han-Taiheiyō fujin kyōkai," 67–82; Woollacott, "Inventing Commonwealth and Pan-Pacific Feminism," 81–104; Epstein, "Linking a State to the World," 92–153.

11. WCTU leaders Gauntlet Tsuneko and Yajima Kajiko attended the Eighth Conference of the International Women's Suffrage Alliance in Geneva in 1920. The first Japanese group that attended the Third WILPF Congress in Vienna in 1921 included Nitobe Mariko, daughter of Christian humanist Nitobe Inazō, and Tsuda Umeko, founder of Tsuda College. Upper- and middle-class Christians dominated the Japanese Women's Peace Association, which was founded in 1921 and officially became affiliated with the WILPF in 1924.

12. Paisley, *Glamour in the Pacific*, 9.

13. Rupp, "Constructing Internationalism," 1577–78; Yasutake, "Han-Taiheiyō fujin kyōkai," 78; Epstein, "Linking a State to the World," 120–21. At the first PPWC in Hawaii in 1928, several elementary school teachers managed to attend after persuading reluctant elite women's leaders, including Gauntlet and

Inoue, and soliciting financial support from business moguls, such as Mitsui, Mitsubishi, and Sumitomo. While they believed that their inability to speak English should not be a source of embarrassment, at the actual conference these female teachers seemed more like observers rather than active participants, whereas the elite Japanese delegates presented their own speeches on education, politics, and health. The leader of the Female Teachers' Association and the first female school principal in Tokyo, Kiuchi Kyō, narrated her efforts to realize the plan to send a group of female teachers in her autobiography, *Kyōiku ichiro*, 133–37.

14. Rupp, *Worlds of Women*, 85.

15. Paisley, "Linking a State to the World," 31–32, 131. Mark Cohen, a New Zealand parliamentarian and a pivotal figure in the conceptualization of the PPWA, hoped that the PPWC would serve as a venue to share his country's experience in maternal and child welfare with the rest of the Pacific countries. Akiyama, *Han-Taiheiyō Tōnan Ajia fujin kyōkai rokujūnenshi*, 11; Jane Addams, presidential address, in Pan-Pacific Women's Conference, *Women of the Pacific*, 14.

16. Addams, in Pan-Pacific Women's Conference, *Women of the Pacific*, 14.

17. Rupp, *Worlds of Women*, 154.

18. "Resolution Passed by National Board, Women's International League for Peace and Freedom," January 15, 1934, box 49 (unfilmed), MSP-SSC.

19. Margaret Sanger, "War and Population," address given at Tokyo YMCA on March 14, 1922, *BCR*, June 1922, 107.

20. Sanger, diary, March 7, 1922, box 78 (filmed), MSP-SSC.

21. Sanger, "The New Women of Japan," 2, reel 130, MSP-LC.

22. Sanger, diary, March 10, 1922; Sanger, "Margaret Sanger in Japan," *BCR*, June 1922, 101.

23. Sanger, "The New Women of Japan," 7–8, 13–14, 16.

24. Sanger, diary, March 25, 1922; Sanger, *Autobiography*, 331.

25. Yasutake, *Transnational Women's Activism*, 33.

26. Sanger, "The New Women of Japan," 9–13; Sanger, *My Fight for Birth Control*, 249–50; Sanger, *Autobiography*, 330.

27. Sanger, diary, March 18, 1922; Sanger, *My Fight for Birth Control*, 248.

28. Sanger, "The New Women of Japan," 2.

29. For example, Yamakawa introduced the activism of socialist women in Sekirankai (Red Wave Society), who participated in the May Day demonstration and organized public gatherings to discuss women's issues. In the end, however, she admitted that their campaigns had been largely ineffective because the group was still small and powerless to withstand police persecution—not because they were simply voiceless or passive. "Woman in Modern Japan," 3–4.

30. Two of Yamakawa Kikue's articles on women in Japan in *Shakai-shugi kenkyū* (January and September 1922), translated into English, appear in Mary Ritter Beard Papers (folder 21, box 2) of the Sophia Smith Collection at Smith

College. For Beard's observation of Japanese women, see Mary Beard, "The New Japanese Woman," *Woman Citizen*, January 12, 1924, 10, 28-29; Beard, *A Woman Making History*, 25–26; Hopper, *A New Woman of Japan*, 33.

31. Sanger, "The New Women of Japan," 9–15.

32. Sanger, diary, March 20, 1922.

33. As an example of these "radical changes" in Japan, Sanger referred to the abolition of Article 5 of the Public Peace Police Law, which allowed women to attend political assemblies. This historical event, she insisted, was *not* "a sign that the women of Japan are aggressively determined to enter the field of politics" but instead indicated "the decay of the traditional and feudal ideas concerning woman among the younger generation of Japanese men." In fact, as historians have pointed out, the law was modified in 1922 largely because men in the government found it increasingly useful to mobilize women in public campaigns. At the same time, as Yamakawa also described, women, both socialist and bourgeois, actively participated in this political campaign. Sanger nonetheless chose to overlook or ignore this information. Sanger, "New Women of Japan," 15; Mackie, *Feminism in Japan*, 60; Garon, *Molding Japanese Minds*, 123–26; Yamakawa, "Woman in Modern Japan," 2–3.

34. Sanger, diary, March 19, 1922; Sanger, *Autobiography*, 331.

35. Sanger, "New Women of Japan," 11, 13.

36. Ibid., 16–17; Sanger, *Autobiography*, 331.

37. Margaret Sanger, "Margaret Sanger in Japan," *BCR*, May 1922, 1; Margaret Sanger, "Birth Control in China and Japan," speech at Carnegie Hall, New York, October 30, 1922, reel 128, MSP-LC.

38. Douglas, *Margaret Sanger*, 164; Sanger, diary, March 10, 1922.

39. Ishimoto, *Facing Two Ways*, 260–62; Katō, *Aru josei seijika no hansei*, 65–67; Hopper, *A New Woman of Japan*, 34.

40. For Ishimoto's description of her husband's "sudden reversion of attitude," see *Facing Two Ways*, 192–93, 299–300.

41. As a result of police persecution and internal divisions, by the 1930s early aristocratic sympathizers had mostly removed themselves from socialist activities in Japan. In her political biography of Nagai Ryūtarō, Sharon Minichiello highlights this intellectual trend in interwar Japan: "Scratch a reformist and find a nationalist." Minichiello, *Retreat from Reform*, 7.

42. Katō, *Aru josei seijika no hansei*, 73–77; Hopper, *A New Woman of Japan*, 48.

43. William B. Feakins to Margaret Sanger, May 3, 1932, reel 18, MSP-LC.

44. Feakins to Sanger, June 29, 1932, reel 56, MSP-LC.

45. Memo for press release from William B. Feakins, Inc., "Japanese Baroness to Lecture Here," October 19, 1932, reel 56, MSP-LC.

46. William B. Feakins, Inc., "Japanese Baroness to Lecture Here"; Feakins

to Sanger, June 29, 1932, reel 56, MSP-LC; "Partial List of Names and Affiliations of Guests Attending Tea in Honor of Baroness Ishimoto, Friday, Nov. 11, 1932," reel 56, MSP-LC.

47. Katō Shizue, diary, March 18, 1938, in Katō, *Saiai no hito Kanjū e*, 120.

48. When the California Birth Control Committee tried to plan a formal reception after Ishimoto's public lecture, her "manager in New York" threatened to cancel her contract because they were getting so many requests for Ishimoto that such unpaid invitation would "[take] off the sharp edge so to speak of her paid public appearances." While her hosts criticized the manager's act as "simply commercializing the Baroness," they had no choice but to cancel their formal reception and instead "confidentially" plan a private dinner party. Gladys Smith, "RE: Reception for Baroness Ishimoto," December 26, 1936, reel 38, MSP-LC.

49. Memo from Gladys Smith to Bernice Wickham, February 13, 1937, reel 38, MSP-LC.

50. Memo from Gladys Smith to Bernice Wickham, "Baroness Shidzue Ishimoto, Los Angeles, California," January 20–26, 1937, reel 38, MSP-LC.

51. See for example, "Peace by Birth Control," *Pittsburgh Press*, July 16, 1933, box 235, MSP-LC; "Facing Two Ways, by Baroness Ishimoto," *New York Times*, September 15, 1935, BR19; William B. Feakins Inc., press release, folder 9, box 31 (unfilmed), MSP-SSC.

52. Rose C. Feld, "A Woman of Old and New Japan," *New York Times*, August 25, 1935, BR5.

53. Katō, *Aru josei seijika no hansei*, 83–85.

54. "Baroness Ishimoto Finds Americans 'Childish' on Birth Control Question," *Atlanta Constitution*, February 21, 1938, box 235, MSP-LC.

55. Mildred Adams, "A Japanese Feminist," *Woman Citizen*, January 10, 1925, folder 22, box 2, Mary Ritter Beard Papers, Sophia Smith Collection (hereafter MBP-SSC).

56. John Chamberlain, "Books of the Times," *New York Times*, August 28, 1935, 15.

57. Marianne Beth, "The Woman Movement in Europe," in National Council of Women of the United States, *Our Common Cause, Civilization*, 97; "Woman's Advance Told at Congress," *New York Times*, July 19, 1933, 19.

58. Introduction by Chairman Louise Y. Robison, in National Council of Women of the United States, *Our Common Cause, Civilization*, 88.

59. Introductions by Lena Madesin Phillips and Louise Y. Robison, in ibid., 8, 88.

60. Ishimoto, "The Woman Movement in the Far East"; Ishimoto's comments on panel "Security against War," both in ibid., 93–94, 706.

61. Ishimoto, "The Woman Movement in the Far East," 90.

62. Ishimoto, *Facing Two Ways*, 372.
63. Paisley, *Glamour in the Pacific*, 49–51.
64. Ogawa, "American Women's Destiny," 311–13.
65. Katō, *Aru josei seijika no hansei*, 79.
66. Ishimoto, *Facing Two Ways*, 293–95.
67. Ibid., 371.
68. "Japanese Baroness Here to Talk Birth Control," *Washington Times*, June 29, 1933, box 235, MSP-LC.
69. Ishimoto, *Facing Two Ways*, 370.
70. "Peace by Birth Control Is Advocated by Baroness," *New York World Telegram*, June 23, 1933, 22 (emphasis added).
71. Ishimoto's comments on panel "Security against War," in National Council of Women of the United States, *Our Common Cause, Civilization*, 705.
72. Ibid., 705–6.
73. Ibid., 706.
74. "Nihon no Sangā, Ishimoto-fujin tobei" [Sanger of Japan, Mrs. Ishimoto goes to America], *Nichibei jihō*, September 14, 1932; "Wasei Sangā Ishimoto-fujin raichū su" [Sanger of Japan, Mrs. Ishimoto arrives in New York], *Nichibei jihō*, November 9, 1932.
75. Haru Matsui (Ishigaki Ayako), "Baroness Ishimoto—End or Beginning?" *China Today*, October 1935, 21.
76. Ishimoto, *Facing Two Ways*, 214–18.
77. After the eruption of the Sino-Japanese War, Ishimoto wrote an article for Japanese audiences asserting the need to study and discuss the essence and roles of Japanese women as "supporters of Japanese men in the process of creating a new cultural order in East Asia" as well as models for "Chinese women under the Wang regime now officially recognized by our country." (A puppet government led by Wang Jingwei was established in 1940 under the protection of the Empire of Japan, in opposition to the Western-supported Chiang Kai-shek regime.) Ishimoto later explained that the essay was "conveniently used by the military to enlist women to the war effort" and that this was the only way she could write to "escape the government's denouncement." The essay, "The Way of Japanese Women: Re-examining the Beauty of Japanese Women," was originally carried in *Kagaku pen* (January 1941). It was later reproduced with Ishimoto's added comments in Katō, *Hitosuji no michi*, 183–95.
78. The WCTU strongly supported the anti-VD campaign. The petition never passed, however, because it targeted only men as disease carriers. For details on this campaign, see Mackie, *Feminism in Modern Japan*, 59; Garon, *Molding Japanese Minds*, 104–5, 131–32; Fujime, *Sei no rekishigaku*, 319–20; Sitcawich, "Eugenics in Imperial Japan," 143–201.

79. Hiratsuka Raichō, "Han-Taiheiyō fujin kaigi to Nisshi mondai" [The Pan-Pacific Women's Conference and the Sino-Japanese problem] (1928), in Hiratsuka, *Hiratsuka Raichō chosakushū*, 5:68–70. Some historians see Gauntlet's apology as a potential for women's international pacifism amid nationalist hostilities. See Rupp, *Worlds of Women*, 119; Paisley, *Glamour in the Pacific*, 133.

80. When Gauntlet was elected president of the PPWA at the 1934 meeting, the Chinese delegates voted against her and angrily expressed their objection to the decision. Ogawa, "American Women's Destiny," 335–40; Iinuma, "A History of the Women's Peace Association of Japan," 58, 73–74; Gauntlett, *Shichijūshichi-nen no omoide*, 146.

81. Katō, *Aru josei seijika no hansei*, 109–11; Katō, *Aisuru "Nihon" e no yuigon*, 117–18. Equally as shocking as these pictures, she recalled, was the response of her fellow suffragist feminists, who dismissed Ishimoto's concerns, claiming that it was "normal" that such cruelty occurred in times of war. Ishimoto's descriptions of this incident, however, appear only in her memoirs published much later in her life, suggesting that they may have been affected and dramatized by her postwar rapprochement with former Asian "enemies."

82. Ishimoto to Gladys Smith, February 23, 1938, reel 19, MSP-LC.

83. Ishimoto to Florence Rose, July 5, 1938, reel 19, MSP-LC.

84. "Shorter Notices: *Wheat and Soldiers*," *The Nation*, August 5, 1939, 154; Clifton Fadiman, "What Price Bonzai?," *New Yorker*, May 27, 1939, 98–99; T. A. Bisson, "Japanese Soldier," *Saturday Review of Literature*, June 3, 1939, 5.

85. Katō, diary, August 6, 1939, in Katō, *Saiai no hito Kanjū e*, 306–7; Baroness Shidzué Ishimoto, foreword to Hino, *Wheat and Soldiers*; S. T. Williamson, "A Japanese Soldier Comes Home from the China War," *New York Times*, June 4, 1939, BR2.

86. Katō, *Saiai no hito Kanjū e*, 306–8; Mary Beard to Dorothy Brush, June/July 1947, folder 7, box 2, MBP-SSC.

87. Ishimoto to Dorothy Brush, August 4, 1939, folder 8, box 31 (unfilmed); Ishimoto to Sanger, May 24, 1941, box 20 (filmed), MSP-SSC.

88. Ogawa, "American Women's Destiny," 354–67.

89. Moore, *The Quest for Peace*, 97.

90. Women's Peace Association in Japan, *Population Problem in Japan*, 1–2, 9, 10, 24–25, 26.

91. Penington, "Trends of Discussion on the Various Topics," 32.

92. Lo, "Economic Reconstruction in China since 1927," 407, 413.

93. Penington, "Trends of Discussion on the Various Topics," 31.

94. Sasha Davidson, "Round Table Summary," in Pan-Pacific Women's Association, *Women of the Pacific*, 75; Pennington, "Trends of Discussion on the Various Topics," 32.

95. Women's Peace Association in Japan, *Population Problem in Japan*, 3–5.

96. Marie M. Keesing, "Outline to Guide Group Study during the Year Preceding the Conference," in Pan-Pacific Women's Association, *Women of the Pacific*, 73; Paisley, *Glamour in the Pacific*, 155.

97. Ishimoto, *Facing Two Ways*, 243.

98. "Baroness Ishimoto Held," *New York Times*, December 29, 1937, 3; "Baroness Ishimoto Released from Jail," *New York Times*, December 30, 1937, 3; "Baroness Left Cold by Prison in Tokyo," *New York Times*, January 1, 1938, 4; "Japan Asked to Free Political Prisoners," *New York Times*, March 18, 1938, 7.

99. The military used the WCTU's support to promote heroic images of strict moral discipline among the soldiers abroad, while in reality sexual exploitation ran rampant. See Ogawa, "American Women's Destiny," 376–78; Garon, *Molding Japanese Minds*, 140–44.

100. The conception of this legislation derived from the women's suffrage movement. Representatives from liberal and socialist groups formed the Women's League for the Promotion of the Motherhood Protection Act (Bosei hogohō seitei sokushin fujin renmei) in 1934. For details, see Mackie, *Feminism in Modern Japan*, 105; Takeda, *The Political Economy of Reproduction in Japan*, 80; Garon, *Molding Japanese Minds*, 142.

101. Fujime, *Sei no rekishigaku*, 320–21; Mackie, *Feminism in Japan*, 107.

CHAPTER THREE

1. Fred Hogue, "Social Eugenics," *Los Angeles Times*, February 19, 1939, H23.
2. Fred Hogue, "Social Eugenics," *Los Angeles Times*, February 26, 1939, J23.
3. Kevles, *In the Name of Eugenics*, 122–28, 164–73.
4. Ibid., 88.
5. Hogue, "Social Eugenics," February 26, 1939.
6. Lovett, *Conceiving the Future*, 80–81.
7. Bederman, *Manliness and Civilization*, 201.
8. Ross, "The Causes of Race Superiority," 67–89.
9. Ross, *The Old World in the New*, 299–300.
10. Grant, *The Passing of the Great Race*, 80–82.
11. Eugenics Record Office director Charles Davenport contended that heredity determined the characteristics of new immigrants, who were "darker in pigmentation, smaller in stature, more mercurial . . . more given to crimes of larceny, kidnapping, assault, murder, rape, and sex-immorality." Kevles, *In the Name of Eugenics*, 45–47.
12. The inventor of the Binet-Simon test, French psychologist Alfred Binet, did not envision the test to be used for eugenic purposes. He believed that heredity in no way predetermined intelligence. He used the test to classify the levels of children with cognitive disabilities and then developed mental and physical exercises to raise these students' intelligence levels. It was mainly through the work of

American psychologist Henry Goddard that the test was transformed into a tool to determine the supposedly innate—and therefore unchangeable—mental capacity of children. See Black, *War against the Weak*, 76–77.

13. For details about Theodore Roosevelt's views about imperialism and evolutionism, see Bederman, *Manliness and Civilization*, 170–215; Burton, "Theodore Roosevelt's Social Darwinism," 1–16. The idea of racial hierarchy permeated popular culture through educational media, such as world fairs, circuses, and museums. See, for example, Baker, *From Savage to Negro*, 54–80; Davis, *The Circus Age*, 128–36; Teslow, "Reifying Race," 53–76. For studies on white men's obsession with manliness and primitive virility as seen in American popular culture, see Gorn, *The Manly Art*; Deloria, *Playing Indian*.

14. For studies on the link between evolutionary ideas about race and US imperialist endeavors in the Philippines, see Anderson, *Colonial Pathologies*; Kramer, *The Blood of Government*.

15. Dyer, *Theodore Roosevelt and the Idea of Race*, 135–41; Sinkler, *The Racial Attitudes of American Presidents*, 320–31.

16. The topic of the previous issue (July 1909) was "Race Improvement in the United States," in which contributors discussed the pressing concern for "race degeneration" and the eugenic measures to prevent it.

17. Rowell, "Chinese and Japanese Immigrants," 3–10; MacArthur, "Opposition to Oriental Immigration," 19–26; Burnett, "Misunderstanding of Eastern and Western States regarding Oriental Immigration," 37–48.

18. Stoddard, *The Rising Tide of Color*, 263.

19. Ibid., 267–68.

20. Ibid., 12, 218; Stoddard, *The Revolt against Civilization*, 11, 177, 218, 237. The scenario of the colored revolt against white dominance, according to Stoddard's theory, was as follows: Among the colored races, the "Orientals"—the Japanese and possibly the Chinese—were the most dangerous, as they remained independent of white control but had rapidly learned to adopt white man's science, technology, and customs. The yellow race then could form a "brown-yellow" alliance—the "brown" race referring to areas of Pan-Islamism, including India, Iran, Arabistan, and Turkestan. The "black" man in Africa and the "red" man in Latin America had no intrinsic ability to stand up on his own but had always been susceptible to external influences. Thus, unless the white race kept a firm grip on the lands in Africa and Latin America, these peoples could easily yield to the "brown-yellow" alliance.

21. Stoddard, *The Rising Tide of Color*, 162–66. By the 1920s, biologists and social scientists, represented by Franz Boas and other anthropologists at Columbia University, started to stress the environmental malleability of (European) immigrants instead of the strictly hereditarian model proposed by older eugenicists. At

the same time, they accepted the classification of human beings into "three primary stocks": the Caucasoid, the Mongoloid, and the Negroid. See Barkan, *The Retreat of Scientific Racism*, 76–90; Ludmerer, *Genetics and American Society*, 126–27; Benedict, *Race*, 50–53.

22. Jacobson, *Whiteness of a Different Color*, 91–96. Nell Painter, in *The History of White People*, also identifies some other stages of the "enlargement of American whiteness" in American history, including the inclusion of Irish and Germans in the late nineteenth century and the Mexicans after World War II.

23. US Congress, "An Act Supplementary to the Acts in Relation to Immigration," sess. II, chap. 141, *U.S. Statutes at Large* 18 (March 3, 1875), 477.

24. For the local politics behind the passage of the Land Law, see Azuma, *Between Two Empires*, 62–66.

25. Governor William Stephens's letter to Secretary of State Bainbridge Colby, June 19, 1920, in California State Board of Control, *California and the Oriental*, 12.

26. V. S. McClatchy worked for the Japanese Exclusion League of California while carrying anti-Japanese articles on his own paper, the *Sacramento Bee*, until he sold it to his brother in 1923. He then began to devote much of his energy to the exclusion movement, setting up his own organization, the California Joint Immigration Committee (CJIC). For personal accounts of how these anti-Japanese campaigns played out in the field and affected Japanese farmers, see Matsumoto, *Farming the Home Place*, 30–42.

27. Statements of James D. Phelan and V. S. McClatchy, in US Congress, House Committee on Immigration and Naturalization, *Percentage Plans for Restriction of Immigration*, 183–207, 237–68. For more details on their views, see Phelan, "The Japanese Evil in California," 323–28; McClatchy, "Japanese in the Melting-Pot," 29–34.

28. Anti-Japanese California Senator J. M. Inman called this the "picture bride evil." J. M. Inman, "Japanese Aggression," *Forum*, January 1921, 1.

29. McClatchy's statement, in US Congress, House Committee on Immigration and Naturalization, *Percentage Plans for Restriction of Immigration*, 251.

30. Phelan's statement, in ibid., 192.

31. James D. Phelan, *Merced County Sun*, July 11, 1919, quoted in Matsumoto, *Farming the Home Place*, 32.

32. Stoddard, *The Rising Tide of Color*, 236, 251, 280, 287–89.

33. Stephens's letter, in California State Board of Control, *California and the Oriental*, 7–15.

34. Ibid., 12.

35. California State Board of Control, *California and the Oriental*, 37–41, 147; Gulick, "Japanese in California," 63.

36. California State Board of Control, *California and the Oriental*, 41.

37. "The Jap Menace in California," *Los Angeles Times*, July 25, 1920, II1.

38. Izumi Hirobe, in *Japanese Pride, American Prejudice*, examines the campaigns by clergymen and businessmen to grant quotas for Japanese immigrants after the passage of the 1924 Immigration Act. Akira Iriye, in *Power and Culture*, also demonstrates that US and Japanese diplomats continued to share economic interests and cultural aspirations during the war period.

39. See, for example, Gulick, "Japanese in California," 55–69; Matthews, "Racial Prejudice Un-American," 69–72; Parsons, "The Anti-Japanese Agitation from a Business Man's Standpoint," 72–74; Kanzaki, "Is the Japanese Menace in America a Reality?," 88–97.

40. Earl S. Parker, "The Real Yellow Peril," *Independent*, May 7, 1921, 475.

41. US Congress, House of Representatives, *Japanese Immigration*.

42. Gulick, "Japanese in California," 67.

43. Ibid., 55; Stoddard, "The Japanese Question in California," 46.

44. Ichioka, "Early Japanese Immigrant Quest for Citizenship," 1–2, 12, 16–17.

45. For example, the 1917 Immigration Act barred immigration for "all idiots, imbeciles, feebleminded persons, epileptics, insane persons . . . [and] persons of constitutional psychopathic inferiority." Black, *War against the Weak*, 188.

46. For details of the First International Eugenics Conference, see Eugenics Education Society, *Problem in Eugenics*; Krementsov, *International Science between the World Wars*, 16–17.

47. During the Second Congress held in New York in 1921, Charles Davenport orchestrated the renaming and broadening of the International Eugenics Committee into a Permanent International Commission of Eugenics. In its 1923 meeting, the commission ratified an "Ultimate Program," devised by the American Eugenics Society, whose aim was to promote research, education, administrative measures, and legislation for the "conservation of the race." In 1925, the commission renamed itself once again as the International Federation of Eugenic Organizations. For details, see Eugenics Research Association, "Report of Subcommittee on Ultimate Program," 73–80.

48. Historian Nancy Stepan illustrates the gap in views and ideas about eugenics, particularly over notions of race, between American eugenicists and the Latin American counterparts. See Stepan, *The Hour of Eugenics*, 171–95.

49. Connelly, *Fatal Misconception*, 61; Black, *War against the Weak*, 239.

50. See, for example, Eugenics Research Association, "Eugenical Interests in Japan," 45; Eugenics Research Association, "Eugenics in India," 2.

51. Sitcawich, "Eugenics in Imperial Japan," 215–18. Eugenic ideas were imported into Japan in the late nineteenth century during the Meiji government's Westernization process. Eugenics further gained momentum as a movement in the mid-1920s and 1930s, as journalists and scientists gathered and established eu-

genics journals and associations. For the history of eugenics and biology in Japan, see Suzuki Zenji, *Nihon no yūseigaku*; Suzuki Zenji, *Baiorojī kotohajime*.

52. Matsumura, "Seibutsugakujō yori mitaru sanji seigen," 29.

53. Tanaka, "Yūseigaku kara mita hainichi mondai," 39–46.

54. Matsumura, *Shinka to shisō*, 301–27. In fact, up until the early 1930s, British neo-Malthusian Harold Cox and Margaret Sanger proposed formation of what they called the International League of Low Birth Rate Nations. Harold Cox, "A League of Low Birth Rate Nations," in Sanger, *Sixth International Neo-Malthusian and Birth Control Conference*, 2:151–52; Sanger, "A Plan for Peace," *BCR*, April 1932, 106.

55. See, for example, Matsumura, "Seibutsugakujō yori mitaru sanji seigen," 49; Dohi, "Hyakunengo no Ōshūjin to Beikokumin," 6; Ikeda, "Yūseigakuteki shakai kairyō to yūseigaku kenkyūjo," 12–16.

56. Disease control and eradication, in fact, were integral to colonial expansionism. While the British developed official public health programs in colonial areas through the London School of Tropical Medicine and Colonial Office, private organizations, such as the RF, led the American efforts in this field in the prewar decades. For the history of the London School of Tropical Medicine, see Haynes, *Imperial Medicine*.

57. For details on the RF's early endeavors in public health in the US South and across the world, see Farley, *To Cast Out Disease*.

58. After he retired from the Division of Studies, Embree continued to pursue his interest in interracial relations through his directorship at the Rosenwald Fund, a group that made appropriations to agencies working in the area of African American welfare. He also wrote a book embracing the diverse racial composition of the United States, *Brown America: The Story of a New Race* (1931), and an introduction to an anthology, *Human Biology and Racial Welfare* (1930), that included articles on the biology of race relations by leading scientists and eugenicists, including Charles Davenport, Raymond Pearl, and Edwin Conklin.

59. Gerald Jonas, in his book on the RF's involvement in modern sciences, features Edwin Embree and his short-lived projects in the Division of Studies. He notes that the RF trustees in the end rejected Embree's proposal on human biology and documents the aborigine project in Australia as the only project in his proposal that survived. According to Jonas, even this project eventually terminated before they could actually do anything. Yet my research at the Rockefeller Archives Center shows that Embree did get approval from the trustees on some human biology projects, at least until 1927, and many of the projects in the Pacific materialized to some extent. See Jonas, *The Circuit Riders*, chaps. 16, 17.

60. Embree had already been to Japan in 1922 as part of the RF investigations into the possibilities of assisting medical and nursing education there.

61. Edwin Conklin to Edwin Embree, August 21, 1925, folder 45, box 7, series 609, record group (RG) 1.1 Rockefeller Foundation Archives (hereafter RFA), Rockefeller Archive Center, Sleepy Hollow, New York (hereafter RAC).

62. Edwin R. Embree, "Japanese Notes," Family Journal No. 8, February 24, 1926, RG 1.1, folder 35, box 4, series 100, RFA, RAC.

63. Embree, diary, June 3, 1925, reel 2, RG 12.1, RFA, RAC. Raymond Pearl's scientific investigation into the matter of differential fertility convinced him that active measures should be taken to teach simple methods of birth control to the "colored group" and foreign born whose fertility resembled the "animal pattern." See, for example, Pearl, "Variation in Parity of Women Bearing Children in the U.S.," 88.

64. Embree, diary, January–February 1926.

65. Embree, "Japan, the Miraculous," Family Journal No. 7, February 15, 1926, folder 35, box 4, series 100, RG 1.1, RFA, RAC.

66. Conklin, *The Direction of Human Evolution*, 40–46; Conklin, "Feminism and the New Woman," 304.

67. Edwin G. Conklin and Edwin R. Embree, "Report of the State of the Biological Sciences in Japan," April 16, 1926, folder 45, box 7, series 609, RG 1.1, RFA, RAC.

68. Conklin, *The Direction of Human Evolution*, 51.

69. Embree, "Japan, the Miraculous."

70. Conklin to Embree, August 3, 1926, folder 45, box 7, series 609, RG 1.1, RFA, RAC.

71. Yasuda Tokutarō, "Kyū-'Yamamoto Senji senshū' kaisetsu," in Yamamoto, *Yamamoto Senji zenshū*, 7:561–62.

72. Embree, diary, April 21, May 24, 1926.

73. There was also a plan to send an American scholar to Keio University in Tokyo, but in the end they failed to recruit a suitable biologist to assume the role. "Japan, Visiting Professors," folder 370, box 40, series 100D, RG 1.1, RFA, RAC.

74. LeBlanc, "Specific Vital Indices for Japan, 1925," 198–213; LeBlanc, "Some Aspects of Paternity in Sendai, Japan," 508–22. The first volume of the journal also included an article by Charles Davenport ("Do Races Differ in Mental Capacity?"), one by Warren S. Thompson ("Natural Selection on the Processes of Population Growth"), and a number of articles by other biologists/population scientists on the "Negro" population in the United States.

75. LeBlanc, "Sidelights on the Population Problem in Japan," 408–20.

76. For an analysis of Edwin Conklin's critique of early eugenics and his emphasis on individual opportunity and responsibility to overcome hereditary limitation and challenges, see Cooke, "Duty or Dream?," 365–84. For details on Ray-

mond Pearl's transition from eugenics to population control, see Allen, "Old Wine in New Bottles."

77. The Carnegie Institution, another patron of the Eugenics Record Office, had long been suspicious of the eugenics studies conducted at the office and finally convened an internal committee to inspect its facilities in 1929. In 1935, it formally assembled a new advisory committee of scientists, which concluded that the work was "unsatisfactory for the study of human genetics." Kevles, *In the Name of Eugenics*, 199; Black, *War against the Weak*, 388–89.

78. Embree, diary, September 28, October 16–17, 1926.

79. For the new biology program, the "Science of Man" agenda, developed under Max Mason's leadership, see Kay, *The Molecular Vision of Life*, 39–50.

80. Edwin Black reveals the flow of RF money to eugenics research in Nazi Germany in the name of genetics, brain research, or social biology. Black, *War against the Weak*, 296, 313.

81. Jonas, *The Circuit Riders*, 130.

82. Thompson, "Race Suicide in the United States," 97–146; Thompson, "Race Suicide in the United States," *BCR*, August 1920, 9–10; September 1920, 9–10; October 1920, 10–11; November 1920, 14; January 1921, 16; February 1921, 9–12; March 1921, 11–13.

83. Thompson, "Eugenics as Viewed by a Sociologist," 11–23.

84. Ross, *Changing America*, 37. See also Szreter, "The Idea of Demographic Transition," 663; Hodgson, "Demography as Social Science," 7.

85. Thompson, "Population," 959–75. In his later writings, in fact, Thompson classified Japan in Group B.

86. Thompson, *Danger Spots*, 13.

87. Ibid., 16–17, 82–83, 138, 299, 327. Lothrop Stoddard, by the time he had published another book on a similar subject in 1935, no longer saw a possibility of a clear-cut race war that he had predicted in 1920. Instead, he argued that Asia was increasingly "Balkanized," as China and Korea showed stern resistance to Japanese control. Stoddard, *Clashing Tides of Color*, 11–12.

88. For an insider's account on the institutional development of population studies, see Notestein, "Reminiscences," 67–85.

89. Condliffe, *Problems of Food and Population in the Pacific Area*; Yamaoka, *The Institute of Pacific Relations*, 3. For a detailed historical analysis on the IPR, see Akami, *Internationalizing the Pacific*.

90. Warren S. Thompson to Joseph H. Willits, September 24, 1942, folder 4555, box 533, series 200, RG 1.2, RFA, RAC. Thompson initially proposed to the RF to publish the book within a year, but it was actually published after the war. See Thompson, *Population and Peace in the Pacific*.

91. Notestein, "Reminiscences," 73–74. Some of the early results of these studies on international demography were presented at the 1944 annual meeting of the Milbank Memorial Fund.

92. Raymond Pearl, "The Differential Birth Rate," in Sanger, *The Sixth International Neo-Malthusian and Birth Control Conference*, 2:19.

93. Conklin, *Heredity and Environment in the Development of Men*, 430, 439–40, 484–85. Conklin expressed similar views about feminism and birth control in "Feminism and the New Woman," 302, 304.

94. Stoddard, *The Rising Tide of Color*, 306; Stoddard, *The Revolt against Civilization*, 236–68. Nativists in the immigration exclusion movement also frequently preached pronatalism for white women in California. See, for example, "Urges a Baby Bounty Fund: Preacher's Radical Remedy for 'Yellow Peril,'" *Los Angeles Times*, September 15, 1919, II1.

95. Sanger, "Limitations of Eugenics" (1921), reel 130, MSP-LC.

96. Sanger, *My Fight for Birth Control*, 289–90 (emphasis in original); Sanger, "Address of Welcome," in Sanger, *The Sixth International Neo-Malthusian and Birth Control Conference*, 1:4–5.

97. Sanger, *Woman and the New Race*, 30–46. In this book, Sanger briefly mentioned the numbers of colored people—the Negroes, Indians, and Chinese—in the American population, but her subsequent discussion on the "foreign stock" concerned exclusively the white immigrants from Europe. The Margaret Sanger Papers collections contain some newspaper scraps on the anti-Japanese movement, suggesting that Sanger was well aware of the debates on Japanese birth rates in California. One article started with a sensational heading: "The Real 'Yellow Peril' Is a Woman: Japanese Birth Rate in California Is Alarming" (June 3, 1921), introducing V. S. McClatchy's statement in the hearings of the House Committee on Immigration. Another article, "The Japs—a Suggestion," called out to the readers: "Birth Control! Particularly in California," *Saturday Evening Star*, n.d., box 234, MSP-LC.

98. Sanger, *Autobiography*, 374; Sanger, *The Pivot of Civilization*, 181.

99. For example, Paul Popenoe, "Birth Control and Eugenics," *BCR*, April–May 1917, 6; Lothrop Stoddard, "Population Problems in Asia," *BCR*, December 1921, 10–12; Raymond Pearl, "The Menace of Population Growth," *BCR*, March 1923, 65–67; Pearl, "The Differential Birth Rate," *BCR*, October 1925, 278–79, 300. Popenoe was not necessarily sympathetic to Sanger's birth control cause, referring to Sanger and her supporters as "a lot of sob sisters, grandstand players and anarchists." Chesler, *Woman of Valor*, 217.

100. Black, *War against the Weak*, 136. Sanger also pushed for the American Birth Control League's merger with the American Eugenics Society (AES), but the core members of the AES declined this partnership. Madison Grant explained

their decision: "When we organized the Eugenic Society, it was decided that we could keep clear of Birth Control, as it was a feminist movement and would bring a lot of unnecessary enemies." The AES finally endorsed birth control in 1934. Madison Grant's letter to Leon F. Whitney, April 15, 1928, quoted in Black, *War against the Weak*, 139–40.

101. Stoddard, "Population Problems in Asia," 101.

102. Margaret Sanger, "Introduction," in Sanger, *The Sixth International Neo-Malthusian and Birth Control Conference*, 1:v–xi.

103. Sanger compiled and published the papers in four volumes according to the following topics: "International Aspects of Birth Control," "Problems of Overpopulation," "Medical and Eugenic Aspects of Birth Control," and "Religious and Ethical Aspects of Birth Control."

104. W. E. B. Du Bois, who claimed that the "quality" rather than "quantity" of the black race was more important to its survival, later supported Sanger's efforts to establish birth control services in black neighborhoods in the 1930s. Chesler, *Woman of Valor*, 296, 388.

105. H. H. Laughlin, "Birth Control and Eugenics," in Sanger, *The Sixth International Neo-Malthusian and Birth Control Conference*, 3:233.

106. Pearl, "The Differential Birth Rate," 2:28.

107. Margaret Sanger, "Foreword," in Sanger, *The Sixth International Neo-Malthusian and Birth Control Conference*, 2:6.

108. Cox, "A League of Low Birth Rate Nations," 2:147; Ferdinand Goldstein, "War and Overpopulation," in Sanger, *The Sixth International Neo-Malthusian and Birth Control Conference*, 2:154.

109. Warren S. Thompson, "Overpopulation and Migration as Causes of War, Part I," *BCR*, May 1925, 153. Thompson also quoted Edward Ross: "Overcrowded Asia will become a menace to the rest of the world unless at the time the Asiatics are shown the means of checking disease and preserving life, they are also made acquainted with the necessity and technique of family limitations." Thompson, "Overpopulation and Migration as Causes of War, Part II," *BCR*, June 1925, 172.

110. Warren Thompson, "Population Growth and International Relations," draft written in December 1930; opening speech by chairman Henry Pratt Fairchild, American Conference on Birth Control and National Recovery, January 15–17, 1934, reel 125, MSP-LC.

111. Thompson, "Overpopulation and Migration as Causes of War, Part II," 173, 189.

112. Raymond Pearl presented his famous biological theory that the population of all living organisms—including humans, yeasts, and fruit flies—grew according to an "S-shaped logistic curve." Pearl, "The Biology of Population Growth," in Sanger, *Proceedings of the World Population Conference*, 22–38. For de-

tails on the controversy over the logistic curve theory, see Ramsden, "Carving up Population Science," 857–99.

113. Connelly, *Fatal Misconception*, 68–74.

114. Hodgson, "Ideological Origins of the Population Association of America," 2–3, 20–21, 23–24; Notestein, "Reminiscences," 70–71. Warren Thompson, a major leader in population studies, was not on the list of invitees to the 1931 meeting, but he was elected as second vice president of the association the following year.

115. Chesler, *Woman of Valor*, 203.

116. "Editorial," in Sanger, *The Selected Papers of Margaret Sanger*, 423–24.

117. Dr. Konikow's speech in "Discussion," in American Birth Control Conference, *Birth Control*, 87.

118. Specifically, Margaret Sanger recommended that the government "keep the doors of immigration closed to the entrance of certain aliens whose condition is known to be detrimental to the stamina of the race," as stated in the 1924 law, and meanwhile "apply a stern and rigid policy of sterilization and segregation" to "certain dysgenic groups in our population." Sanger, "A Plan for Peace," *BCR*, April 1932, 106.

119. "News from Margaret Sanger," September 6, 1937, reel 19, MSP-LC; Birth Control Clinical Research Bureau, "Release for Morning and Evening Papers, Thursday, September 23, 1937," reel 38, MSP-LC; "Mrs. Sanger Assails 'Population' Nations: She Cites Japan as a Present Aggressor That Has Refused to Limit Its Births," *New York Times*, September 23, 1937.

120. Margaret Sanger, "The War and Birth Control," n.d., reel 131, MSP-LC.

CHAPTER FOUR

1. Katō Shizue to Margaret Sanger, May 19, 1949; Sanger to Katō, June 13, 14, 1949; Katō to Sanger, June 28, 1949, all in S30, MSP-SS.

2. Douglas MacArthur to LeRoy J. Hess, June 17, 1950, GS(B) 01272–01276, GHQ/SCAP Records, National Diet Library, Tokyo, Japan (hereafter NDL).

3. "SCAP's declared policy of 'benevolent neutrality' on the population question in general, and on birth control in particular" is mentioned, for example, in Roger Evans, "Population: Japan—Dr. Teru Togasaki," March 7, 1949, folder 3113, box 464, series 609, RG 2; Marshall C. Balfour, diary, November 28, 1946, box 14, RG 12.1, both in RFA, RAC.

4. For details on the US Catholics' crusade against the eugenics movement during the first half of the twentieth century, see Leon, *An Image of God*; Rosen, *Preaching Eugenics*, 10–21, 139–64.

5. "Ripe for Reds: World Birth Growth Held Top Problem," *Los Angeles Times*, February 29, 1952, C1; Kingsley Davis, "The Other Scare: Too Many Peo-

ple," *New York Times*, March 15, 1959, SM13. The term "explosion" and its implicit association with the atomic bomb had often been used in American public discourses on the global population problem since the 1950s. See, for example, "Population Curb Held Key to Peace: Lack of Control Is Deadlier Than Atomic Bomb, Planned Parenthood Group Hears," *New York Times*, October 25, 1951, 42; Robert Trumbull, "Asian Population Held 'Explosive': Birth Control Drives Urged at Tokyo Meeting of Social Scientists," *New York Times*, December 2, 1958, 12; Robert Trumbull, "Exploding Population: *Too Many Asians*, by John Robbins," *New York Times*, November 8, 1959, BR16; Ehrlich, *The Population Bomb*.

6. Stewart Alsop, "No Nation Is an Island," *Washington Post*, May 4, 1949, 13; "East's Teeming Millions Communist If Not Fed," *Bcon*, November 29, 1948.

7. Schenck, "Natural Resources Problem in Japan," 367, 372.

8. Sams, *Medic*, 183–85.

9. Ōta, *Nihon sanji chōsetsu hyakunenshi*, 359–60; Oakley, "The Development of Population Policy in Japan," 173, 359; Sams, *Medic*,186.

10. "Speaker Urges Birth Rate Drop," *Stars and Stripes*, December 4, 1948.

11. Even though he was "severely beaten and starved while in the toils of the Jap," Gordon claimed that he held "no personal grudge against the Japs for their actions against us." In fact, Gordon was later featured in a number of newspapers as an example of American tolerance and Christian forgiveness. "Former Prisoner Favors Jap Birth Rate Curb," *Los Angeles Times*, October 15, 1945, 5; "Time and Yule Alter a Yank's Revenge Theme: Forgives Cruel Guards of War Prison," *Chicago Daily Tribune*, December 25, 1958, 8; "Hatred of War Guards Changes to Goodwill: American Hunts Down Tormentors in Japan, Then His Quest Ends in Friendly Meeting," *Los Angeles Times*, December 25, 1958, 10; Harold Blake Walker, "Hate and Bitterness Keep Us Out of Tune," *Chicago Daily Tribune*, January 24, 1960, F32.

12. Oakley, "The Development of Population Policy in Japan," 353.

13. "Jap Sterilizing Plan Proposed," *Los Angeles Times*, February 27, 1945, 6; Alida Campbell, "Johnson's Suggestion," *Washington Post*, March 4, 1945, B4; "The Right to Reproduce," *New Leader*, March 1945, 16.

14. For the full text of the "Geneticists' Manifesto," see "Plan for Improving Population Drawn by Famed Geneticists," *Science News Letter*, August 26, 1939, 131–33. The "left eugenicists," as Diane Paul calls them, also rejected the "extreme environmentalism" of Soviet geneticists, Lysenkoism, and sought to defend an objective "middle-ground" between the two politically motivated extremes. Paul, "Eugenics and the Left," 567–90.

15. These biologists, however, did not reject scientific research into heredity and human (racial) differences per se. Rather, they insisted that their role was to treat human differences as "facts which call for understanding and interpretation,

not as qualities to be either condemned or praised." Dunn and Dobzhansky, *Heredity, Race, and Society*, 17, 101.

16. Herbert Passin, check sheet from Public Opinion and Sociological Research, J. A. Greene, November 7, 1946, PHW 04824, GHQ/SCAP Records, NDL.

17. Crawford F. Sams, "Bill for Eugenic Protection Law," June 25, 1948; Harry G. Johnson, "Bill for Eugenics Protection," May 21, 1948, both in PHW 01178, GHQ/SCAP Records, NDL; Matsubara, "The Enactment of Japan's Sterilization Laws," 196–97.

18. Civil Censorship Detachment, Press, Pictorial, Broadcast Division, "Censorship Treatment of Birth Control," March 24, 1947, CIS 02702, GHQ/SCAP Records, NDL.

19. Norgren, *Abortion before Birth Control*, 90–91.

20. Ethel Weed of the Civil Information and Education Section was responsible for this project, while the PHW contributed "technical advice."

21. Sams, *Medic*, 273n11.

22. Oakley, "The Development of Population Policy in Japan," 185–88.

23. Crawford F. Sams, memorandum to E. M. Almond, "Population in Japan," July 29, 1948, folder 5, box 1, series 600, RG 1.2, RFA, RAC.

24. M. C. Balfour, "Preliminary Note on the R. F. Population (Public Health and Demography) Reconnaissance in the Far East," January 1949, 5–6, folder 9, box 2, series 600, RG 1.1, RFA, RAC.

25. Roger Evans, "Population: Japan—Dr. Teru Togasaki," March 7, 1949, folder 3113, box 464, series 609, RG 2, RFA, RAC.

26. Letters from Warren S. Thompson to Roger F. Evans, January 14, 1943, January 28, 1943, folder 4555; Evans interview with Thompson, March 14, 1944; letter from Evans to Thompson, May 16, 1944, folder 4556; Thompson to Evans, May 30, 1946; Evans to Thompson, June 3, 1946, folder 4557, all in box 533, series 200, RG 1.2, RFA, RAC.

27. Excerpt from Dr. R. B. Watson's Shanghai Diary, December 2, 1947, folder 4, box 1, series 600, RG 1.2, RFA, RAC; Charles B. Fahs, "Comments on Japan and Suggestions for Rockefeller Foundation Policy There," January 26, 1948, folder 22, box 3, series 600, RG 1.2, RFA, RAC.

28. John D. Rockefeller III to John D. Rockefeller Jr., "RE: Birth Control," March 17, 1934, folder 1, box 1, series K, RG 2, Office of the Messrs. Rockefeller (hereafter OMR), Rockefeller Family Archives, RAC.

29. Harr and Johnson, *The Rockefeller Century*, 462. Arthur Packard, since he joined the RF office in 1929, had also been involved in providing financial support to various birth control/ family planning/ eugenics organizations in the United States.

30. By 1947, John D. Rockefeller Jr. had also decided that there was "no reason why we should continue to make the gift [to the Planned Parenthood Federation

of America] anonymous." Memorandum by Arthur Packard, January 30, 1947; Kenneth Rose to Packard, April 10, 1947, folder 32, box 4, RG 2, OMR, RAC.

31. Roger F. Evans, "Notestein—Population—Orient," June 3, 1948, folder 4, box 1, series 600, RG 1.2, RFA, RAC. The International Health Division's work in China was forced to close in early 1949, as Shanghai was about to fall to the Red Army. Farley, *To Cast Out Disease*, 270.

32. G. K. Strode diary excerpt, December 2–3, 12, 1947, folder 4, box 1, series 600, RG 1.2, RFA, RAC.

33. Memorandum, June 14, 1948, folder 310, box 57, series 900, RG 3.2, RFA, RAC.

34. Civil Information and Education, "Conference on Problems of Public Health and Demography in Far East," September 14, 1948, CIE (B) 01750, GHQ/SCAP Records, NDL; Connelly, *Fatal Misconception*, 136; Hopper, *A New Woman of Japan*, 225–27.

35. Civil Information and Education, "Conference on Problems of Public Health and Demography in Far East"; Balfour, "Preliminary Note on the R. F. Population (Public Health and Demography) Reconnaissance in the Far East," 7; Oliver R. McCoy, diary, October 2, 1948, box 83, RG 12.1, RFA, RAC.

36. McCoy, diary, April 21, 1949.

37. Ibid., March 12, 15, May 12, July 27, August 1, 5, 9, 15, 1949.

38. McCoy to Balfour, April 27, 1949, folder 3113, box 464, series 609, RG 2, RFA, RAC; McCoy, diary, March 29, June 26, 1949. Other sections of SCAP, such as the Civil Intelligence Section and the Civil Information and Education Section, also furnished SCAP with information on the Japanese responses to birth control through public opinion surveys and Japanese publications on birth control. Civil Censorship Detachment Special Report, "Japanese Reaction to Birth Control," May 27, 1949, PHW 01240; Civil Censorship Detachment, "Publications of Possible Interest to Natural Resources Section," September 27, 1949, CIS 02702; public opinion reports by the Japanese Public Opinion Survey Report Institute, March 8, 1949, CIE (B) 07795; public opinion reports by Shinbun yoron chōsa renmei (Association for Newspaper Public Opinion Survey), April 11–14, 1949, CIE (C) 06457; public opinion survey on birth control, November 16, 1949, CIE (B) 07780, all in GHQ/SCAP Records, NDL.

39. James Y. Matsumoto to Margaret Sanger, February 19, 1950, S31 (series 2) (microfilm), MSP-SSC.

40. P. K. Whelpton, "Population Problems," memorandum, June 13, 1949, folder 7, box 3, Daniel B. Luten Jr. Papers, Hoover Institution Archives, Stanford University, Stanford, California (hereafter Luten Papers).

41. McCoy to Balfour, June 20, 1950, folder 3354, box 501, series 609, RG 2, RFA, RAC.

42. John Dower calls the Occupation's position between 1949 and 1951 "the

hard Cold War policy," as US officials called for a coordinated policy to contain communism. Dower, "Occupied Japan and the Cold War in Asia," 175–76, 179; Dower, *Embracing Defeat*, 526.

43. For the Japanese MHW's description of Thompson's controversy, see Koseishō jinkō mondai kenkyūjo [Ministry of Health and Welfare, Institute of Population Problems], "Sansei oyobi imin mondai wo chūshin to suru Tamusonhakase no hatsugen to sono hankyō" [Dr. Thompson's statement on birth control and immigration problems and responses to it], in Ogino, Matsubara, and Saito, *Sei to seishoku no jinken mondai shiryō shūsei*,10:37–41.

44. McCoy, diary, May 16, 1949.

45. Roger F. Evans, "Controversial Parts of the Summary and Conclusions of the SCAP-Ackerman Report," April 10, 1950, 3, folder 3354, box 501, series 609, RG 2, RFA, RAC. For details on the controversy over Ackerman's report, see folder 2, 17, 21, box 1, folder 13, box 3, Luten Papers; Oakley, "The Development of Population Policy in Japan," 248–60.

46. McCoy to Balfour, February 17, 1950, folder 3354, box 501, series 609, RG 2, RFA, RAC.

47. Daniel B. Luten to K. Miyashita, March 15, 1950, folder 8, box 1, Luten Papers.

48. Francis Scott Smyth to Chester Barnard, January 20, 1949, folder 3113, box 464, series 609, RG 2, RFA, RAC.

49. Roger Evans, "Population: Japan—Dr. Teru Togasaki," March 7, 1949, folder 3113, box 464, series 609, RG 2, RFA, RAC.

50. Roger Evans, "Japan: Population—Professor Warren S. Thompson," May 16, 1949, folder 3113, box 464, series 609, RG 2, RFA, RAC.

51. Irene Taeuber was later sent to Japan in August 1952 for an individual mission supported by the RF to gather more data and field information to complete her book *The Population of Japan*. Taeuber's own field notes as well as reviews of Taeuber's work reveal a mix of respect and uneasiness among Japanese male intellectuals toward Taeuber and her comprehensive and influential study on Japanese demographic history. Irene Taeuber to Roger Evans, November 22, 1952, folder 4594, box 388, series 200, RG 1.1; Irene Taeuber, "Population Research in Japan— Some Preliminary Reflections," January 26, 1953, folder 4595, box 388, series 200, RG 1.1, RFA, RAC; Ueda Tsunetaka, preface to the Japanese translation of *The Population of Japan*; Minami, "Toibā no mita Nihon no jinkō," 7:225; Minokuchi, "Toibā-cho, Nihon no jinkō," 75.

52. Margaret Sanger to G. Douglas MacArthur, October 25, 1945, folder 1, box 41, Planned Parenthood Federation of America (PPFA) Papers, SSC.

53. Ethel B. Weed to Margaret Sanger, November 15, 1945, folder 1, box 41, PPFA Papers, SSC.

54. Katō Shizue to Margaret Sanger, May 19, 1949, C08 (Collected Document Series) (microfilm), MSP-SSC.

55. Meanwhile, McCoy welcomed Sanger's introduction of Dr. Abraham Stone to send him information and formulas of contraceptive foam powders. Sanger to McCoy, July 6, 1949; McCoy to Sanger, July 25, 1949; P. K. Whelpton to Abraham Stone, August 9, 1949; Sanger to McCoy, August 31, 1949, all in S30, MSP-SSC. McCoy to Sanger, September 19,1949; McCoy to Stone, September 19, 1949, both in S31, MSP-SSC.

56. Japanese birth control supporters wrote a petition, approached SCAP officials, and gained support from some Japanese high officials to overturn the decision to deny Sanger's entry, to no avail. Sanji seigen fukyūkai, "Petition to General MacArthur, May 1951," in Ogino, Matsubara, and Saito, *Sei to seishoku no jinken mondai shiryō shūsei*, 11:209.

57. SCAP also denied a visa for Katō Shizue to visit the United States during the Occupation. Katō's friend Mary Beard believed that the possibility for recognition and admiration that Katō might attract—whereas other Japanese visitors came with the "avowed purpose of studying and observing our ways"—must have frightened US authorities. Mary Beard to Ethel Weed, December 3, 1950, folder 15, box M39, MBP-SSC.

58. "Mrs. Sanger Barred by MacArthur from Birth Control Talks in Japan," *New York Times*, February 13, 1950, 1; "Too Many Babies? Japan Tried All Out Birth Control," *Newsweek*, May 8, 1950, cover, 42–43. See also "Mrs. Sanger's Visa," *Washington Post*, February 15, 1950, 10; "MacArthur Aides Ban Birth Control," *Los Angeles Times*, February 13, 1950, 16.

59. MacArthur to Reverend LeRoy J. Hess, June 17, 1950, GS(B) 01272–01276, GHQ/SCAP Records, NDL.

60. Tentler, *Catholics and Contraception*, 136–37; Mehta, "Family Planning Is a Christian Duty."

61. Lucille K. MacDonald to MacArthur, May 28, 1950; Kingsland Camp to MacArthur, March 18, 1950, both in GS(B) 01272–01276, GHQ/SCAP Records, NDL.

62. Sarah C. Hill to MacArthur, May 2, 1950, GS(B) 01272–01276, GHQ/SCAP Records, NDL. For the battles over birth control legislation in Massachusetts, see McGreevy, *Catholicism and American Freedom*, 229–31.

63. Johnson, "Margaret Sanger and the Birth Control Movement in Japan," 104.

64. US Bureau of the Census, *Historical Statistics of the United States*, 8, 389.

65. For the development of the American Catholic Church in the mid-1940s and 1950s, see McGreevy, *Parish Boundaries*, 79–84; McCartin, *Prayers of the Faithful*, 42–70.

66. Katō, *Aru josei no hansei*, 162–63.

67. Jacobs, *America's Miracle Man in Vietnam*, 78–81.

68. McGreevy, *Parish Boundaries*, 64. At a time when Catholics were still associated with authoritarian regimes in Italy, Spain, Portugal, and Austria, anticommunism, according to John McGreevy, "eas[ed] Catholic acceptance in liberal circles." For more on American Catholics' new focus on democracy and freedom in the context of anticommunism, see McGreevy, *Catholicism and American Freedom*, 194, 211; Schultz, *Tri-faith America*, 73–74; McNamara, *A Catholic Cold War*, 167.

69. Roger F. Evans, "Rough Notes on RF Mission Conference with General Sams," October 1, 1948, 3, folder 6, box 1, series 600, RG 1.2, RFA, RAC.

70. Crawford Sams to Kenneth Colegrove, February 20, 1950, PHW 04821, GHQ/SCAP Records, NDL.

71. "Circular Airgram to All American Diplomatic and Consular Offices," January 31, 1952, FSP 1983, Records of the Foreign Service Posts of the State Department, NDL.

72. Roger F. Evans, "Summary Report of RFE's Round-the-World Trip Emphasizing South and South-East Asia and Japan," September 24–December 12, 1950, 6, folder 3, box 1, series 600, RG 1.2, RFA, RAC.

73. United Press Staff Correspondence by Rutherford Poats, 1949, folder 9, box 67 (unfilmed), MSP-SSC.

74. Frank Notestein, "Preliminary Reconnaissance in Public Health and Demography in the Far East," 5–7, 15, 17, folder 7, box 1, series 600, RG 1.2, RFA, RAC.

75. Sams, *Medic*, 183, 186, 188; Crawford F. Sams to Balfour, January 10, 1951, folder 3629, box 543, series 609, RG 2, RFA; statement by Balfour in National Academy of Sciences (hereafter NAS), "Conference on Population Problems held at Williamsburg Inn, Williamsburg, VA," afternoon session, June 21, 1952, 65, folder 720, box 85, series 1.5, RG 5, John D. Rockefeller III Papers (hereafter JDRIII Papers), Rockefeller Family Archives, RAC.

76. Sams, *Medic*, 43; excerpts from letters of Irene Taeuber, November 18, 1952, folder 4594, box 388, series 200, RG 1.1; Roger F. Evans, "Japan: Population—Professor Warren S. Thompson," May 16, 1949, folder 3113, box 464, series 609, RG 2, RFA, RAC.

77. McCoy, diary, December 30, 1949, June 8, 1950; Evans, "Japan: Population—Professor Warren S. Thompson"; statement by Paul Henshaw in NAS, "Conference on Population Problems," morning session, June 21, 1952, 55–56; Juitsu Kitaoka to Balfour, March 14, 1950, folder 3353, box 501, series 609, RG 2, RFA, RAC; Katō, *Aru josei seijika no hansei*, 115.

78. McCoy to Balfour, April 27, 1949, folder 3113, box 464, series 609, RG 2, RFA, RAC; McCoy, diary, May 10, 1949.

79. For his prewar and wartime studies on race, see Koya, *Minzoku seibutsugaku*; Koya, *Kokudo, jinkō, ketsueki*; Koya, *Kindaisen to tairyoku, jinkō*; Koya, *Nihon minzoku konseishi*.

80. Koya, "Chūken kaikyū wa zetsumetsu ka," 2–5; Koya, *Kōgakukyū no techō kara*, 67; Koya Yoshio, "Minzoku tōtaron" [Theory of racial extinction], *Kagakuken*, September 1948, 10.

81. SCAP feared that under Nobechi's directorship, the IPH could revert to a nationalistic organization after the termination of the US Occupation. It is not clear, however, what exactly made him "subversive." The forced resignation of Nobechi left a negative impression about Sams among the Japanese in the IPH, including Koya. Balfour to George K. Strode, January 31, 1947; R. B. Watson to Strode, September 12, 1947, folder 18, box 3, series 609, RG 1.1, RFA, RAC; Koya, *Kōgakukyū*, 72–73.

82. McCoy, diary, March 23, April 16, April 28, May 3, May 10, June 25, July 6, 1949.

83. Koya had told McCoy beforehand that he wished to see the "rustic" lives of the US "frontiers" and study the race relations there. Whether or not Koya's personal opinion had any effect on SCAP's planning of the trip, it conveniently coincided with their strategy to promote birth control through Japanese initiative. Koya, *Kōgakukyū*, 101.

84. In 1940, *Life Magazine* featured the newly established state-sponsored birth control program in South Carolina. "Birth Control: South Carolina Uses It for Public Health," *Life*, May 1940, 64–68.

85. See Brown, "Purity and Danger in Color," 101–31; Tera W. Hunter, "Tuberculosis as the 'Negro Servants' Disease,'" in Hunter, *To 'Joy My Freedom*, 187–218; Lombardo and Dorr, "Eugenics Medical Education, and the Public Health Service," 291–316; Tapper, "An 'Anthropathology' of the 'American Negro,'" 263–89.

86. The Rockefeller Sanitary Commission for the Eradication of Hookworm Disease, active between 1909 and 1914, was one of the first public health endeavors in the South. After the Sanitary Commission closed down, the International Health Board took over its role. While these early efforts had only limited success in actually eradicating diseases, one legacy of the Sanitary Commission, as John Ettling points out, was that it helped develop the network of state and local public health agencies and stimulated the "public-health awakening" in the South. Ettling, *The Germ of Laziness*, 220–21. See also Farley, *To Cast Out Disease*, 29–31; Fee, *Disease and Discovery*, 17–18.

87. L. Gordon, *A Social History*, 330.

88. Don Wharton, "Birth Control: The Case for the State," *Atlantic Monthly*, 1939, 465.

89. D. Williams, *Every Child a Wanted Child*, 146–48; Schoen, *Choice and Coercion*, 60.

90. Koya , "Zaisen yonjūnenkan no naichi Nihonjin hanshokuryoku," 1:183–84; Koya Yoshio et al., "Chōsen ni okeru naichijin ijūsha oyobi Chōsenjin no shusseiryoku ni tsuite," 201–2; Koya, *Kokudo, jinkō, ketsueki*, 131.

91. Koya, like many other Japanese eugenicists, had studied and accepted the racialized theories about the "nature" of African Americans presented by American eugenicists such as Charles Davenport. See Koya, *Minzoku seibutsugaku*, 73; Koya, *Kokudo, jinkō, ketsueki*, 137–38.

92. Larson, *Sex, Race, and Science*, 93; Schoen, *Choice and Coercion*, 44. The targets of prewar eugenics/birth control programs, including sterilization, were mainly white immigrant women, with the purpose of protecting white female sexuality and motherhood. See Kline, *Building a Better Race*, 59.

93. Koya, *Kōgakukyū*, 124–26.

94. Koya, *Tengoku Amerika, jigoku Amerika*, 126–28; Koya, *Kōgakukyū*, 148–50.

95. Koya, *Tengoku*, 133–38; Koya, *Kōgakukyū*, 156–61.

96. Koshiro, *Trans-Pacific Racisms*.

97. Koya, *Tengoku*, 133–37; Koya, *Kōgakukyū*, 157–60.

98. For a historical analysis of the infantilization of Japanese in American political and cultural discourses after the war, see Shibusawa, *America's Geisha Ally*.

99. Okazaki Ayanori to Roger F. Evans, December 15, 1950; George W. Bonheim to Evans, December 22, 1950, folder 3354, box 501, series 609, RG 2, RFA, RAC; Irene B. Taeuber to Marshall Balfour, January 11, 1951, folder 3630, box 344, series 609, RG 2, RFA, RAC.

100. Gamble to Sanger, February 20, 1951, folder 3097, box 196, Clarence James Gamble Papers, Francis A. Countway Library of Medicine, Boston, Massachusetts (hereafter CGP); Balfour to McCoy, September 18, 1951, folder 44, box 6, series 609, RG 1.2, RFA, RAC.

101. McCoy, diary, December 30, 1949; Kitaoka to Balfour, March 14, 1950, folder 3353, box 501, series 609, RG 2, RFA, RAC.

102. Gamble to Sanger, February 20, 1951, folder 3097, box 196, CGP.

103. In her letter to Gamble, Sanger praised that his "'silent partner' work helping the Japanese [was] most encouraging and hopeful." Sanger to Gamble, March 21, 1951, folder 3097, box 196, CGP.

104. McCoy, diary, June 8, November 28, 1950.

105. Koya, "Atarashī jinko genshō to sono taisaku," 3–7. With the help and advice of American scholars, Koya published his findings in various academic journals in the United States, including the *Milbank Memorial Fund Quarterly*,

Eugenical News, and *Population Studies*. Under the auspices of the Population Council, he later compiled his major studies into a book, *Pioneering in Family Planning*.

106. D. Williams, *Every Child a Wanted Child*, 81–103.

107. Ibid., 129–30.

108. Schoen, *Choice and Coercion*, 47–49. See also Rodrique, "The Black Community and the Birth Control Movement," 146–49; McCann, *Birth Control Politics in the United States*, 160–64.

109. Clarence J. Gamble to Mrs. Rinehart, November 1, 1939, folder 3, box 39; Division of Negro Service, PPFA, June 23, 1942, folder 8, box 39 (unfilmed), MSP-SSC.

110. Clarence Gamble to Warren Thompson, June 17, 1949; Thompson to Gamble, July 14, 1949; Gamble to McCoy, September 29, 1949, folder 1530, box 94, CGP; McCoy to Gamble, September 29, 1949, folder 3113, box 464, series 609, RG 2, RFA, RAC.

111. Warren Thompson to Daniel Luten, July 20, 1949, folder 17; Thompson to Luten, August 30, 1949, folder 10; Katō Shizue to Daniel Luten, October 22, 1949, folder 6, all in box 1, Luten Papers.

112. McCoy, diary, May 9, June 2, 1950.

113. Gamble to McCoy, May 24, 1950, Gamble to Sams, June 22, 1950, folder 1531, box 94, CGP; McCoy, diary, June 2, 1950.

114. McCoy to Balfour, December 6, 1950, folder 3354, box 501, series 609, RG 2; Balfour to McCoy, October 5, 1951, folder 3629, box 543, series 609, RG 2; Irene B. Taeuber to Balfour, February 15, 1951, folder 3630, box 344, series 609, RG 2, RFA, RAC.

115. Gamble to Katō, September 26, 1949, S31, MSP-SSC.

116. McCoy to Balfour, December 6, 1950, folder 3354, box 501, series 609, RG 2, RFA, RAC.

117. McCoy, diary, January 17, 1950. Many birth controllers who worked with him were frequently frustrated by his "noncommittal" style of "supporting a worthwhile venture and then withdrawing" abruptly. McCoy, diary, May 14, 1954; Balfour to McCoy, Apr 24, 1953, folder 278, box 43, series 609, RG 2, RFA, RAC.

118. Gamble to Katō, January 6, 1950; Gamble to McCoy, January 19, 1950, folder 1531, box 94; Gamble to Katō, March 3, 1950, folder 3096, box 195, CGP.

119. Koya, "The Program for Family Planning in Japan," 2; D. Williams, *Every Child a Wanted Child*, 215, 220–21, 341.

120. Gamble to Koya, December 6, 1951, folder 1535; Gamble to Koya, February 7, 1952, folder 1538, box 94, CGP.

121. Reed, *The Birth Control Movement and American Society*, 296; Toyoda, "Sengo Nihon no bāsu kotorōru undō to Kureransu Gyanburu," 62.

122. Koya to Gamble, December 24, 1951, folder 1531, box 94; Koya, "The Acceptability of Some Contraceptive Methods in Japan," folder 1579, box 97, CGP.

123. Koya and Koya, "Prevention of Unwanted Pregnancies in a Japanese Village," 167–70; Koya, *Kōgakukyū*, 226–28.

124. Gamble to Katō, January 6, 1950, folder 1531, box 94, CGP.

125. Gamble to Koya, December 6, 1951, folder 1535, box 94, CGP; McCoy, diary, December 3, 1951, December 10, 1953.

126. The numbers of reported induced abortions from 1949 to 1964 were as follows: 1949: 246,104; 1950: 489,111; 1951: 638,350; 1952: 798,193; 1953: 1,068,066; 1954: 1,143,059; 1955: 1,170,143; 1956: 1,159,288; 1957: 1,122,316; 1958: 1,128,231; 1959: 1,098,853; 1960: 1,063,256; 1961: 1,035,329; 1962: 985,351; 1963: 955,092; 1964: 878,748. The actual numbers of abortions are believed to be two to three times higher than the official records. "Statistics concerning Eugenic Protection," in Minoru Muramatsu, "Medical Aspects of the Practice of Fertility Control," in Kunii, *Basic Readings on Population*, 115.

127. Muramatsu, "Action Programs of Family Planning in Japan," 68.

128. Ōta, *Nihon sanji chōsetsu hyakunenshi*, 373–74, 377.

129. McCoy, diary, March 21, 1952.

130. Connelly, *Fatal Misconception*, 137.

131. Pascal K. Whelpton, "Lessening the Future Increases in the Ratio of Population to Natural Resources," June 13, 1949, PHW 01299, GHQ/SCAP Records, NDL.

132. Marshall C. Balfour and Marston Bates, "Special Report to the Board of Scientific Directors of the Int'l Health Division of the Rockefeller Foundation, Human Ecology (Population)," November 4, 1949, folder 312, box 57, series 900, RG 3.1; Balfour, diary, October 4, 1949, box 14, RG 12.1, RFA, RAC.

133. Balfour to McCoy, June 27, 1951, folder 3629, box 543, series 609, RG 2, RFA, RAC.

134. Warren Weaver, November 28, 1949, folder 310, box 57, series 900, RG 3.2, RFA, RAC.

135. Weaver, "Human Ecology," January 1, 1952; Weaver, diary, January 2, 1952, folder 116, box 20, series 200, RG 2, RFA, RAC.

136. "Conference on Population Problems, List of Attendants," folder 116, box 20, series 200, RG 2, RFA, RAC.

137. See, for example, statement by Thompson in NAS, "Conference on Population Problems," morning session, June 21, 1952, 14–16.

138. Balfour et al., *Public Health and Demography in the Far East*, 118.

139. Luten to P. K. Whelpton, November 17, 1949, folder 14, box 1; Luten, "Population," October 8, 1948, folder 5, box 2; Luten, "Review of Book, 'Popula-

tion and Peace in the Pacific,' by Warren S. Thompson," October 5, 1948, folder 5, box 2; Warren Thompson, "A Population Policy for Japan," March 30, 1949, folder 3, box 3, all in Luten Papers. For further contemporary analysis on the revised demographic theory based on the Japanese experience, see Taeuber, "Japan's Demographic Transition Re-examined," 28, 39; Taeuber, "Manpower Utilization and Demographic Transition," 21.

140. Szreter, "The Idea of Demographic Transition," 669.

141. "Conference on Population Problems, Summary Report," June 20–22, 1952, 2–3, folder 4, box 1, series K, RG 2, OMR, RAC.

142. Taeuber, "Manpower Utilization and Demographic Transition," 19, 24.

143. Adas, *Dominance by Design*, 245.

144. Luten, "Population," October 8, 1948, folder 5, box 2, Luten Papers.

145. Dorothy Nortman, introductory review in Koya, *Pioneering in Family Planning*, 4, 6, 9, 10 (emphasis added).

146. Thompson, "The Need for a Population Policy in Japan," 27; Notestein, "Preliminary Reconnaissance in Public Health and Demography in the Far East," 14; NAS, "Conference on Population Problems," morning session, June 21, 1952, 33, 42–45.

147. Statement by Marshall Balfour in NAS, "Conference on Population Problems," morning session, June 20, 1952. For the development of Western-led public health projects in developing countries from the prewar to postwar periods, see Packard, "Visions of Postwar Health and Development," 93–115.

148. Briggs, "Mother, Child, Race, Nation," 179–200.

149. Notestein, "Preliminary Reconnaissance in Public Health and Demography in the Far East," 12.

150. Irene B. Taeuber, "Population Research in Japan: Some Preliminary Reflections," folder 4595, box 388, series 200, RG 1.1, RFA, RAC; "Conference on Population Problems, Summary Report," 8.

151. Marshall Balfour, "Notes on Conference on Population Problems," July 17, 1952, 33, folder 116, box 20, series 200, RG 2.

152. Taeuber and Eldridge, "Some Demographic Aspects of the Changing Role of Women," 24–34.

153. Statement by Balfour in NAS, "Conference on Population Problems," morning session, June 21, 1952, 48.

154. According to Crawford Sams, "In the mind of the average Oriental abortion or even infanticide is not a moral question. That is a part of their philosophy; that human life is cheap." Sams, *Medic*, 187; McCoy to Balfour, May 28, 1951, and Sams to Balfour, January 10, 1951, both in folder 3629, box 543, series 609, RG 2, RFA, RAC. A study conducted by Koya Yoshio, however, confirmed the possible

harmful effects of (multiple) abortions on women's physical and mental health. See Koya, "A Study of Induced Abortion in Japan and Its Significance," in Koya, *Pioneering in Family Planning*, 74.

155. McGreevy, *Catholicism and American Freedom*, 226.

156. Despite this enthusiastic resolution, Marshall Balfour was still concerned whether any possible action would follow the meeting at Williamsburg, as he heard a rumor that "JDR might be advised by public relations against support of population study and fertility control." Balfour, diaries, September 29–30, 1952, box 14, RG 12.1, RFA, RAC.

157. "Conference on Population Problems, Summary Report," 8–9.

158. Chesler, *Woman of Valor*, 426–27.

159. Curt L. Heymann, "The 'Culmination' of Margaret Sanger's Life Work," *Los Angeles Times*, December 21, 1952, B5.

CHAPTER FIVE

1. Japanese elites started to use the phrase *gyaku tōta* in the 1930s as the country expanded its empire. In particular, Koya Yoshio warned that the spread of neo-Malthusianism and birth control philosophy among the educated class was a cause of *gyaku tōta*. See "Chūken kaikyū wa zetsumetsu ka," 2–5. *Gyaku tōta* was similar to the American argument of "race suicide" yet quite different in terms of its notion of race. Whereas the source of racial degeneration in American discourses was the invasion of "inferior" races from outside, Japanese eugenic discourses rarely included the impact of non-Japanese (including other Asian peoples) on the Japanese racial body. Instead, the source of *gyaku tōta* came from within: the lower-class Japanese. For more on eugenics in wartime Japan in relation to population policies, see Chung, *Struggle for National Survival*; Oguma, *A Genealogy of 'Japanese' Self-Images*, 203–36.

2. Postwar magazines and newspapers during the Occupation of Japan cited in this chapter are from the Gordon Prange Collection at the University of Maryland, College Park; NDL; and other individual university libraries at the University of Tokyo, Harvard University, and Stanford University.

3. Garon, *Molding Japanese Minds*, 152.

4. A number of scholars have examined the EPL, but most of them focus on the law's provisions on abortion and sterilization, presumably because the birth control provision was eliminated in the first draft. Through the process of revisions, however, the EPL would have a crucial role in implementing birth control policies throughout Japan. On the abortion and sterilization policies, see Coleman, *Family Planning in Japanese Society*; Norgren, *Abortion before Birth Control*; Matsubara, "Enactment of Japan's Sterilization Laws in the 1940s," 187–201.

5. The *New York Times* reported each of these developments in population

policies in Japan immediately after the war. See, for example, "Birth Control Planned for the Shrunken Japan," *New York Times*, October 28, 1945, 5; "Birth Control Opposed by Welfare Head," *New York Times*, December 16, 1945, 3. See also Takeda, *The Political Economy of Reproduction in Japan*, 84; Oakley, "The Development of Population Policy in Japan," 222–23; Ōta, *Nihon sanji chōsetsu hyakunenshi*, 367–68.

6. Jinkō mondai kenkyūkai, *Shin-jinkō seisaku kihon hōshin ni kansuru kengi* [Proposal on the basic principles of the new population policy] (November 1946), in Ogino, Yoko, and Hikaru, *Sei to seishoku no jinken mondai shiryō*, 25:125–26 (emphasis added); Yoshioka Yayoi, "Shokuryō to sanji seigen" [Food and birth control], *Shin josei*, October 1946, 22–23.

7. Statement by Katō Shizue, "Kōsei iinkai gijiroku" [Minutes of the Health and Welfare Committee meeting], no. 35, Shūgiin [House of Representatives], 1st sess., December 1, 1947, http://kokkai.ndl.go.jp/SENTAKU/syugiin/001/0790/00112010790035a.html.

8. Ōta, *Datai kinshi to yūsei hogo hō*, 164–66; Hopper, *A New Woman of Japan*, 220.

9. Katō, "Mazu nani yorimo hinin wo," 173–74.

10. Taniguchi and Fukuda, *Yūsei hogo hō kaisetsu*, 83–85; Ōta, *Datai kinshi to yūsei hogo hō*, 163, 168–71.

11. Taniguchi and Fukuda, *Yūsei hogo hō kaisetsu*, 89.

12. Jinkō mondai kenkyūjo, "Yūsei hogo hōan ni taisuru kentō kekka yōshi" [Result on the study of the Eugenic Protection Bill], October 31, 1947, in Ogino, Yoko, and Hikaru, *Sei to seishoku no jinken mondai shiryō*, 25:176–77; check sheet, Government Section to Public Health and Welfare Section, "Draft Legislation," May 8, 1948, PHW 01178, GHQ/SCAP Records, NDL; McCoy, diary, October 2, 1948, box 83, RG 12.1, RFA, RAC.

13. See Taniguchi's explanation of Article 28 of the EPL, which forbade sterilization outside cases stipulated in the law. Taniguchi, however, did note that in the near future he planned to include birth control instruction as part of the general services of the Eugenic Marriage Consultation Offices. Taniguchi and Fukuda, *Yūsei hogo hō kaisetsu*, 71, 76.

14. Statement by Katō, "Kōsei iinkai gijiroku." Katō frequently made eugenic arguments in magazines and newspapers, calling out to Japanese women that it was in their hands to create "uniformly fine" (*tsubu zoroi*) Japanese citizens rather than the "overproduction of inferior bodies" (*sosei ranzō*). As "negative" examples, she referred to "races that propagate like rabbits," such as Puerto Ricans, Indians, Egyptians, and American blacks. See, for example, Katō Shizue, "Sanji seigen no imi" [The meaning of birth control], *Tōsei minpō*, June 1946, 5; Katō, "Sanji seigen wa naze shuchō sareru ka" [Why we advocate birth control], *Fujin gahō*, April

1946, 18–19; Katō, "Jinkō to sanji seigen" [Population and birth control], *Hataraku fujin*, October 1946, 19; Katō, "Sanji seigen wa ze ka hi ka" [Pros and cons of birth control], *Keizai*, February 1947, 28–29; Katō, "Sanji seigen wa naze hitsuyō ka" [Why we need birth control], *Fujin kōron*, March 1947, 28–32; Katō, "Shinsei nihon no tameni: Sanji seigen jisshi no kyūmu" [For New Japan: Urgent need to practice birth control], *Katei yomimono*, April 1948, 18; Katō, *Sanji seigen to fujin*, 8, 11–12.

15. Matsubara, "The Enactment of Japan's Sterilization Laws in the 1940s," 191–92, 197; Frühstück, *Colonizing Sex*, 177–84; Fujino, *Nihon fashizumu to yūsei shisō*, 439–59; Fujime, *Sei no rekishigaku*, 343–77.

16. The law covered not only congenital malformations and physical disorders but a long list of "hereditary" mental disorders, including schizophrenia, depression, sexual perversion, and criminality. See Taniguchi and Fukuda, *Yūsei hogo hō hayawakari*, 9; Taniguchi, *Yūsei hogo hō shōkai*, 7–11.

17. Taniguchi and Fukuda, *Yūsei hogo hō kaisetsu*, 7, 36–37, 61.

18. In a meeting with SCAP and RF representatives, Katō attributed the passage of the EPL, which included birth control guidance, to her own initiative and the strong backing of other women members. She did not mention the male physicians' co-optation of the bill. Katō's statement, in "Conference on Problems of Public Health and Demography in Far East," September 14, 1948, CIE (B) 01750, GHQ/SCAP Records, NDL.

19. Before this second revision, doctors were apparently reluctant to apply for permission to the Eugenic Protection Committee. Not only did the procedure require extra time, but it also demanded an additional "processing fee" to be paid to public health centers. See discussions of obstetricians and gynecologists regarding the EPL in "Yūsei hogo hō, sanpu seido, sanfujinka kyōju hō ni tsuite" [Eugenic Protection Law, maternity policy, and pedagogy on obstetrics], *Rinshō fujinka sanka*, July 1950, 288–94; "Yūsei hogo hō wo meguru mondai, sono 1" [Problems surrounding the Eugenic Protection Law, part 1], *Sōgō igaku*, April 15, 1949, 14–21; "Yūsei hogo hō wo meguru mondai, sono 2" [Problems surrounding the Eugenic Protection Law, part 2], *Sōgō igaku*, May 1, 1949, 16–20.

20. Taniguchi, *Yūsei hogo hō shōkai*, 23–27.

21. "Yami no onna ya mekake nimo tekiyō, kaisei yūsei hogo hō" [Revised Eugenic Protection Law applies to women of the night and mistresses too], *Ikai kōron*, July 1949, 23; Abe Yūkichi, "Yūsei hogo hō ni tsuite" [On the Eugenic Protection Law], *Shakai jigyō*, September 1949, 25; Uehara Kotarō, "Yūsei kekkon to kokumin yūsei hogo hō" [Eugenic marriage and the national Eugenic Protection Law], *Seimei*, January 1949, 5.

22. Koya Yoshio, "Yūsei mondai to shite no jinkō mondai" [Population problem as a eugenic issue], *Fujin no seiki*, August 1949, 8; Koya, "Wagakuni saikin

no jinkō ninshin chūzetsu ni tsuite" [Population and abortion in Japan today], *Rinshō fujinka sanka*, November 1952, 494.

23. Takahashi, *Shōkai kaisei yūsei hogo hō*, 8–15.

24. See, for example, Andō Kakuitsu, "Jinkō ninshin chūzetsuhō to jinkō funinhō (danshuhō) no jōshiki" [Common knowledge on abortion law and sterilization law], *Shufu no tomo*, March 1947, 60–65; "Dono hininhō ga ichiban iika" [Which birth control method is the best?], *Shufu no tomo* October 1948, 34–35; Andō Kakuitsu and Ōno Hiroshi, "Hinin to ninshin" [Birth control and pregnancy], *Shufu no tomo*, July 1949, 69; "Anzan, ninshin, hinin daitokushū" [Special issue on easy labor, pregnancy, and birth control], *Shufu no tomo*, January 1951, 193–224; Andō Kakuitsu, Yamamoto Sugi, and Tachi Minoru, "Sanji seigen wo dōsuru" [What to do with birth control], *Shufu no tomo*, September 1951, 88–99; "Tadashī ninshin chōsetsu kyōhon" [Guidebook on proper birth control], *Fujokai*, supplementary volume, April 1949, 4–24.

25. See, for example, Nagai Hisomu, preface to Takeuchi, *Yūsei kekkon*.

26. Ikeda, "Kokuritsu yūsei sōdnjo secchi no kyūmu," 18–31.

27. Fujime, *Sei no rekishigaku*, 260–63; Fujino, *Nihon fashizumu*, 107–8, 173–74; Sitcawich, "Eugenics in Imperial Japan," 272–75, 282; Takeda, *The Political Economy of Reproduction*, 81–82.

28. See, for example, Ikeda, "Kekkon shitewa naranu hito," 2–11; Ikeda, "Yūsei undō ni taisuru hantairon," 10–23; Dohi, "Hyakunengo no ōshūjin to beikokujin," 5–7; Tayui, "Amerika ni okeru ishihakujakusha ni taisuru yūseigakuteki danshujutsu," 13–18.

29. Suzuki, *Yūseigaku*, 150–62. It is noteworthy that the largest eugenic organization, the Japan Racial Hygiene Association, adopted the German term *Rassen-hygiene* rather than the more widely employed term *Yūseigaku*, which had a direct influence from Gordonian genetics. The choice reflected a shift from the Anglo-American eugenics to German racial hygiene among eugenics leaders in Japan in the 1930s.

30. In the United States, the first heredity clinic was opened at the University of Michigan in 1940. The following year, another major clinic, the Dight Institute, was established at the University of Minnesota. See Porter, "Evolution of Genetic Counseling in America," 22–25. In 1930 Paul Popenoe, leader of the eugenics movement in California, opened the American Institute of Family Relations. The institute provided counseling on eugenics and family heritage to both engaged and married couples, but its services dealt more broadly with sex and motherhood *after* marriage. See Kline, *Building a Better Race*, 141–49; Stern, *Eugenic Nation*, 155–73.

31. Fujino, *Nihon fashizumu*, 335; Takeda, *The Political Economy of Reproduction*, 82; Sitcawich, "Eugenics in Imperial Japan," 302–4.

32. Kōseishō yūsei kekkon sōdanjo, *Kekkon no susume*. See also, Kōseishō yobōkyoku, *Kokumin yūsei zukai*, 62–63.

33. Takeuchi, *Yūsei kekkon*, 6. SCAP's internal memo on the EPL noted Takeuchi Shigeyo's view that the purpose of the law was to prevent "race selection" and "not for general birth control." SCAP, Civil Affairs Section, "Eugenics Protection Law, 1947–1951," file 2803, RG331, Archives II Reference Section (Military), National Archives at College Park, Maryland.

34. Nagai, *Shin kekkon dokuhon*, 262–65; Nagai, *Minzoku no unmei*, 98–99; Nagai Hisomu, "Kiken na sanji seigen" [Danger of birth control], *Maru*, June 1949, 78–80.

35. For the history of the EMCO in Mitsukoshi, Ginza, operated by the Tokyo metropolitan government, see Tōkyōto kekkon sōdanjo, *Tōkyōto kekkon sōdanjo gojūnen no ayumi*.

36. Yamagiwa Yoshiko, "Pātī kōsai kara risō no kekkon e" [From dating to ideal marriage], *Fujin kurabu*, December 1947, 30; Yamada Eiji, "Yūsei kekkon sōdanjo" [Eugenic marriage consultation office], *Iden*, August 1948, front matter; Yamagiwa, "Kekkon wa dorehodo kagakuteki de aru beki ka" [How scientific should marriage be?], *Iden*, May 1950, 12–20.

37. Investigative agencies, called *kōshijo*, have been widely used, although in behind-the-scenes ways, for background checks on the "bloodlines" (*kettō*) of individuals for marriage arrangement or labor recruitment. Since the proto-historic era (AD 200–300), a clear differentiation existed between "well-bred" people (*ryōmin*) and innately "polluted" people (*senmin*) in indigenous discourses. In response to the Meiji government's attempt to abolish the inherited class system to present a "civilized" image to the Western powers, the investigative agency system emerged to fulfill the traditional needs for status distinction. Urbanization and "democratization" of Japan after the war simultaneously increased the demands for *kōshijo*. The system still exists today despite criticisms that it is discriminatory. See Hayashida, "Identity, Race and the Blood Ideology of Japan," 183–200.

38. Mihira Harumichi, "Kekkonnan wo ikani kaiketsu subekika" [How to solve the problems of getting married], *Kibō*, July 1946, 5; "Kekkon e: Watashi no kōsō wa kouda" [This is my vision of marriage], *Ōita gōdō shinbun*, May 3, 1948; Yamagiwa Yoshiko, "Pātī kōsai kara risō no kekkon e," 31; Katō Shizue, Moriyama Yutaka, and Kanzaki Kiyoshi, "Sanji chōsetsu no kihon mondai wo megutte" [Basic issues over birth control], *Fujin no seiki*, August 1949, 113.

39. Katō Shizue and Tanaka Kōtarō, "Teisō wo megutte" [Discussion on chastity], *Josei kaizō*, April 1947, 29–30.

40. See, for example, Tanaka Yoshimaro, "Yūsei kekkon" [Eugenic marriage], *Iden*, March 1955, 7; Yuasa Akira, "Kōfuku wo motarasu idengaku" [Genetics

brings happiness], *Iden*, October 1958, 23; Yamagiwa, "Kekkon wa dore hodo kagakuteki de aru beki ka," 19.

41. For the prewar antiprostitution campaign among Japanese moral reformers, including women's groups, Christian groups, and the bureaucrats of the Home and Education Ministries, see Garon, *Molding the Japanese Mind*, 88–114. For the government's measure against venereal diseases before World War II, see Frühstück, *Colonizing Sex*, 35–49.

42. Koya, *Minzoku seibutsugaku*, 10. The wartime government's attitude toward VD is illustrated in Kōseishō yobōkyoku ed., *Kokumin yūsei zukai*, 65–79.

43. For social and historical contexts surrounding *pan-pan* girls in Occupied Japan, see Dower, *Embracing Defeat*, 123–39.

44. Koya Yohio, "Sei kagaku mandan: Sei dōtoku to yūseigaku" [Rambling talk on sexual science: Sexual morality and eugenics], *Kagakuken*, May 1947, 43; Takeuchi, *Yūsei kekkon*, 30–34; Uehara, "Yūsei kekkon to kokumin yūsei hogo hō," 5; Moriyama Yutaka, "Dare ni mo wakaru iden no hanashi" [Genetics for dummies], *Shufu to seikatsu*, September 1949, 113.

45. See, for example, Koya Yoshio's and Yoshioka Yayoi's remarks in "Atarashī kekkon rinri" [New marriage ethics], *Seikatsu kagaku*, December 1946, 8–9; Katō Shizue, Majima Kan, and Oka Hidemichi, "Sanji chōsetsu wa naze histuyō ka" [Why we need birth control], *Fujin kōron*, March 1947, 33.

46. See, for example, Katō and Tanaka, "Teisō wo megutte," 33; Katō, Majima, and Oka, "Sanji chōsetsu wa naze histuyō ka," 28, 34; Katō, "Sanji seigen wa ze ka hi ka" [Pros and cons of birth control], *Hōsō*, June 1946, 6; Nomiyama Fuji, "Rokkuferā-shi to kataru" [Dialogue with Mr. Rockefeller], *Katei shūhō*, October 1947, 8–9. Gregory Pflugfelder demonstrates how the concept of "civilized morality" in Meiji Japan served to marginalized acts of "male-male sexuality" as "barbarous" and "immoral" practices of the past. Once sexologists of the early twentieth century started to discover that these practices were still thriving in modern societies, they relabeled "same-sex love" as a "disease of civilization," which needed to be "treated" properly. See Pflugfelder, *Cartographies of Desire*, 193–285.

47. Ōbayashi Satoru, "Sekai no haha: Wakaki hi no Sangā fujin" [Mother of the world: Mrs. Sanger in her youth], *Nihon P.T.A.*, July 1949, 30.

48. Reproductive issues have been an integral part of the so-called New Life Movement, initiatives promoted by government offices, women's groups, and corporations since the late 1940s. The programs were aimed largely at women to improve the environment and health of family life, which national leaders believed affected men's performance in the workplace. Although they were based on conservative gender roles, they also provided "scientific" and "modern" knowledge and skills for women. See A. Gordon, "Managing the Japanese Household," 245–83.

49. Kawakami Riichi, "Jinrui ni okeru idenbyō no chishiki to kekkon no gōrika" [Knowledge on genetic diseases and the rationalization of marriage in humankind], *Kagakuken*, September 1948, 18–19; Kawakami, "Josei to iden" [Women and genetics], *Shin joen*, December 1947, 10–13.

50. Kida Fumio, "Kekkon sōdan to kekkaku" [Marriage consultation and tuberculosis], *Iden*, August 1948, 30–35; Tanaka, "Yūsei kekkon," 5–8; Komai Taku, "Yūsei sōdan no keiken kara" [From my experience of eugenic consultation], *Iden*, March 1955, 9–11.

51. Yoshimasu Shūfu, "Yūseihō to minzoku eisei" [Eugenics law and racial hygiene], *Iden*, August 1948, 27; Yoshimasu, "Yūsei kekkon" [Eugenic marriage], *Kagakuken*, June 1948, 27–32; Tanaka Yoshimaro, "Yūsei kekkon" [Eugenic marriage], *Iden*, March 1955, 5. For the state of science and technology in postwar Japan, see Nakayama, Goto, and Yoshioka, *A Social History of Science and Technology in Contemporary Japan*.

52. Tanaka, "Yūsei kekkon," 6; Yoshimasu, "Yūseihō to minzoku eisei," 29.

53. Kida Fumio, "Sanji chōsetsu to iden kankyō no mondai" [The issue of birth control and genetic environment], *Fujin no seiki*, August 1949, 57; Takeuchi Shigeyo, "Kindaijin no kekkon" [Marriage for modern people], *Iden*, August 1948, 7.

54. Robertson, "Blood Talks," 208.

55. Tanaka Kokki, "Genbakushō wa iden suru ka" [Whether radiation sickness will be transmitted], *Iden*, July 1954, 4–8; Yamaura Atsushi and Fukuda Itoko, "Josei to iden" [Women and genetics], *Iden*, November 1948, 13. A group of American scientists representing the Atomic Bomb Casualty Commission (ABCC), formed in 1947 by the US National Academy of Sciences, studied the genetic effects of radiation on atomic bomb victims. Some leading Japanese geneticists also cooperated in the research. For the ABCC, see Lindee, *Suffering Made Real*.

56. Kawakami, "Josei to iden," 10; Date Gen, "Musume to tsuma to haha no eisei hyakka zenshū: Kekkon-hen" [Encyclopedia on hygiene for daughters and mothers: Marriage edition], *Shufu to seikatsu*, supplementary booklet, February 1951, 30. Scientists and medical professionals made similar arguments during the war. See, for example, Takeuchi Shigeyo, "Rikō na tsuma wo tore" [Marry a smart woman], in Ishida and Takano, *Kekkon shin-taisei*, 386–87.

57. Coined by C. H. Waddington in 1942, scientists in the 1940s and 1950s—when the physical nature of genes and their roles in heredity was not fully understood—used epigenetics to explain how genes might interact with their surroundings to produce a phenotype. The concept reemerged in the 1990s with varying meanings, but in 2008 scientists made a consensual definition of epigenetic traits as "stably heritable phenotypes resulting from changes in a chromosome without

alterations in the DNA sequence." Berger et al., "An Operational Definition of Epigenetics," 781–83.

58. See, for example, Kida, "Sanji chōsetsu to iden kankyō no mondai," 44–49; Kida, "Yūsei hogo hō wo meguru idenkan to tōtakan no saikentō" [Reconsidering the concepts of genetics and selection in the Eugenic Protection Law], *Rinshō fujinka sanka*, April 1949, 13–17; Kida, *Chie no okureta kodomo no igaku*, 97–130; Kida, *Jōzu na ikuji, heta na ikuji*, 20–42. Kida Fumio was head of the Japanese genetics team of the ABCC and biology professor at Kumamoto University. Kida wrote and counseled widely on genetics and constitutional predisposition. Because of his emphasis on environmental influences, his fellow Japanese scientists often labeled him as a follower of Lysenkoism, a popular biological theory in the Soviet Union known for its emphasis on acquired characteristics through environmental reforms. Kida, of course, was not alone in his attention to the interaction between genetics and environment. In February 1949, for example, *Iden* ran a feature issue on "Education and Genetics."

59. Yamaura and Fukuda, "Josei to iden," 10–13.

60. Katō Shizue, "Sangā-fujin ni tsuite: Kekkon to sansei" [About Mrs. Sanger: Marriage and birth control], *Iden*, August 1948, 46–48.

61. Yamagiwa, "Kekkon wa dorehodo kagakuteki de aru beki ka," 12–20.

62. Robertson, "Biopower," 341.

63. "Kekkonnan jidai: Dōshitara kekkon dekiruka" [Difficult time for marriage: How to get married], *Fujin seikatsu*, March 1949, 46; Yamagiwa, "Pātī kōsai kara risō no kekkon e," 30.

64. Yamada, "Yūsei kekkon sōdanjo."

65. Kawakami Riichi, "Yūsei kekkon to iden" [Eugenic marriage and genetics], *Seikatsu bunka*, May 1948, 16; Katō, Moriyama, and Kanzaki, "Sanji chōsetsu no kihon mondai wo megutte," 98; Yamada, "Yūsei kekkon sōdanjo"; Yamagiwa, "Kekkon wa dore hodo kagakuteki de aru beki ka," 18. For examples of readers' questions to medical consultants on birth control in matrimonial magazines, see "Risōteki hininhō" [Ideal method of birth control], *Kibō*, January 1947, 12; "Sanji seigen no kahi" [Pros and cons of birth control], *Kibō*, February 1947, 20.

66. Takeda Hiroshi, "Kekkon sōdanjo wa shinyō dekiru ka" [Can you trust marriage consultation centers?], *Josei kaizō*, February 1949, 64.

67. Civil Censorship Detachment Special Report, "Japanese Reaction to Birth Control," May 27, 1949, PHW 01240, GHQ/SCAP Records, NDL.

68. George Cooper, the North Carolina health official famous for his birth control programs, confessed in a private letter that these black women "represent[ed] the lowest class of midwives, and also [that] their work [was] among the lowest and most sordid class of our population." Quoted in Schoen, *Choice and Co-*

ercion, 27. For the history of midwives in the United States, see Borst, *Catching*; Litoff, *American Midwives*. As an exception to this trend, Mary Breckinridge, an American public health nurse with British training in midwifery, established the Frontier Nursing Service (FNS) in 1925 and provided nurse-midwifery service mainly to white women in the rural Appalachian Mountains. Breckinridge tactically raised money for the FNS by claiming to help the Anglo-Saxon Protestant stock to thrive and distancing its work from the antimodern image of "granny" midwives. For details on the FNS and the history of nurse-midwifery, see Ettinger, *Nurse-Midwifery*.

69. Congratulatory message by Major Grace Elizabeth Alt, *Hoken to josan*, February 1947, 3; Enid Mathison, "Josanpu no sekinin" [The responsibility of midwives], *Hoken to josan*, September 1947, 3.

70. Ryder and Oishi, *Sengo Nihon no kango kaikaku*, 81–82; Ōbayashi, *Josanpu no sengo*, 5–23, 225–41; Kayo, *Nihon josanpushi kenkyū*, 38–41; Kaneko, "Kangoshoku, hakui no tenshi no chii kōjō," 171–80. US officials tried to dissuade the opposing midwives by pointing out that male physicians essentially had controlled the previous Japanese Midwives' Association, thus making the new integrated organization appear more democratic and female oriented. M. Elizabeth Pickens, "Report of Meeting Held on 24 June 1947," June 25, 1947, PHW 01371, GHQ/SCAP Records, NDL.

71. Emiko Ochiai argues that the first "reproductive revolution" occurred *before* the Meiji Restoration, during the late Tokugawa period, when a new discourse to regulate reproduction emerged as local villages and domains suffered from depopulation and a consequent decrease in tax revenue. For the prewar history of midwives in Japan, see Ochiai, "The Reproductive Revolution at the End of the Tokugawa Period," 187–215; Rousseau, "Enduring Labors"; Terazawa, "Gender, Knowledge, and Power."

72. Rousseau, "Enduring Labors," 211–12, 255.

73. For midwife Shibahara Urako's birth control activism in Osaka during the 1920s and 1930s, see Fujime, "One Midwife's Life," 247–53, 273–76.

74. Katō Shizue, "Dai-gokai kokusai kazoku keikaku kaigi ni kanshite" [About the fifth international conference on planned parenthood], *Josanpu zasshi*, June 1955, 14–15.

75. Taniguchi Yasaburō, "Jinkō seisaku to josanpu" [Population policy and midwives], *Hoken to josan*, November 1948, 3–4.

76. Ishigaki Junji, "Josanpu wa dōsureba ima no kukyō kara sukuwareru ka" [How can midwives escape from current hardship?], *Josanpu zasshi*, January 1952, 7–9; Moroyama Yutaka, "Jutai chōsetsuhō 1" [Contraceptive method, part 1] *Hoken to josan*, March 1949, 3; Andō Kakuichi, "Josanpu no kongo ni kitai suru mono" [What is expected of midwives from now], *Josanpu zasshi*, February 1952,

26–27; Obata Korekiyo, "Jutai chōsetsu mondai wa jūbun na kōryo ga histsuyō" [The birth control issue needs deliberate consideration], *Josanpu zasshi*, April 1952, 38–39; Kuji Naotarō, "Josanpu no chii kōjō wo netsubō" [Strongly desiring the improvement of midwives' status], *Josanpu zasshi*, May 1952, 40–41.

77. Takeuchi Shigeki, "Josanpu no inai Amerika no bunben" [Childbirth in America without midwives], *Josanpu zasshi*, February 1952, 6–9; Ishigaki Junji, "Mōdo Karen obasan no koto" [About Mrs. Karen Mode], *Josanpu zasshi*, March 1952, 26; Muramatsu Minoru, "Amerika no josanpu" [Midwives in America], *Josanpu zasshi*, August 1952, 38–41; Saeki Riichirō, "Josanpu ni atau" [To midwives], *Josanpu zasshi*, January 1952, 9; Shinohara Kōzō, "Nihon no josanpu" [Midwives in Japan], *Hoken to josan*, January 1954, 6–7; Ojima Nobuo, "Amerika no josanpu jijō" [The situation of midwives in America], *Hoken to josan*, February 1956, 23.

78. Smith, *Sick and Tired*, 118–48.

79. Koya later confessed that he thought that the midwives were "somewhat jealous" of the part nurses might play in birth control instruction. Oliver McCoy, diary, April 25, 1952, box 83, RG 12.1, RFA, RAC.

80. Obata, "Jutai chōsetsu mondai wa jūbun na kōryo ga histsuyō," 38; Taniguchi Yasaburō, "Yūsei hogo hō no kaisei to jutai chōsetsu no aratana hōkō" [The revision of the Eugenic Protection Law and the new direction of birth control], *Josanpu zasshi*, July 1952, 28–30; Ōbayashi Michiko, "Sengo no gyōsei shudō no jutai chōsetsu" [State-led birth control after the war], *Josanpu zasshi*, September 1987, 85.

81. Organizers were initially concerned whether they could recruit enough "body models" for the demonstrations, but in most cases they had no trouble finding women who voluntarily offered to assume the role for a per diem allowance—and even at a lower cost than they had expected. "Jutai chōsetsu to josanpu" [Birth control and midwives], *Hoken to josan*, June 1953, 17–21; Yokoyama Fuku, "Ugoki" [Trends], *Hoken to josan*, September 1952, 34–35; Sudō Ryōichi, "Jutai chōsetsu mondai no sonogo" [The birth control issue thereafter], *Josanpu zasshi*, November 1952, 7.

82. Sonoda Susano, "Jutai chōsetsu sidōsha kōshūkai wo oete" [Completing the birth control instruction training course], *Hoken to josan*, March 1953, 34.

83. "Jutai chōsetsu to josanpu" [Birth control and midwives], *Hoken to josan*, June 1953, 24–25; "Jutai chōsetsu shidō no jissai" [The practice of birth control instruction], *Hoken to josan*, September 1955, 16; "Jutai chōsetsu shidōin no tachiba" [The standpoint of birth control case workers], *Josanpu zasshi*, August 1953, 44–45; "Ankēto: Jutai chōsetsu jisshi shidōin ni tsuite" [Survey on birth control case workers], *Josanpu zasshi*, December 1954, 56–59; Suzuki Takako, "Ankēto ni yoysete" [Accompanying the survey], *Josanpu zasshi*, January 1955, 62.

84. Yokoyama Fuku, "Watashi no pēji: Kokkai no uchi soto" [My page: The

Diet from within and without], *Hoken to josan*, February 1954, 34; Yokoyama, "Watashi no pēji: Kokkai no uchi soto," *Hoken to josan*, May 1954, 27–29; Yokoyama, "Watashi no pēji: Josanpu-kai uchi to soto," [My page: Association of midwives from within and without], *Hoken to josan*, June 1955, 25–29; Yokoyama, "Josanpu no genjō to shōrai" [The present situation and future of midwives], *Josanpu zasshi*, January 1955, 53.

85. Yokoyama Fuku, "Watashi no pēji" [My page], *Hoken to josan*, October 1955, 35; Taniguchi Yasaburō, "Yūsei hogo hō no ichibu kaisei to yakujihō" [Partial revision of the Eugenic Protection Law and the Pharmaceutical Law], *Josanpu zasshi*, December 1955, 6–7; Fukushima Akinori, "Yūsei hogo hō no kaisei ni tsuite" [On the revision of the Eugenic Protection Law], *Josanpu zasshi*, December 1955, 10–13.

86. Yokoyama Fuku, "Kokkai e no michi" [Road to the Diet], *Hoken to josan*, June 1953, 4–5; Yokoyama, "Saikin no josanpu-kai" [Association of midwives recently], *Hoken to josan*, December 1953, 21–22; Sonoda, "Jutai chōsetsu shidōsha kōshūkai wo oete," 34.

87. The class-based prejudice was sometimes directed specifically toward Koreans living in Japan. For example, one midwife described the "animal-like" behavior of her Korean clients. "Jutai chōsetsu shidō no jissai," 26.

88. Sonoda, "Jutai chōsetsu sidōsha kōshūkai wo oete," 34; Arai Asae, "Jutai chōsetsu: Machi no hyōjō" [Birth control: Expressions on the streets], *Hoken to josan*, June 1953, 26–27.

89. Matsui Asano, "Kyōsei yūsei shujutsu wo okonawaseru made" [The process of inducing forced sterilization], *Hoken to josan*, June 71953, 33–35. A midwife Upper House Diet member, Tanaka Tatsu, submitted a recommendation to the Diet on August 12, 1947, *before* the Eugenic Protection Bill was proposed, that they insert a clause on the National Eugenic Law to allow local mayors, doctors, nurses, and midwives to be able to report the Eugenic Protection Committee for forced sterilization of those with severe hereditary diseases. Tanaka Tatsu, "Kokumin yūsei hō chū ni ichijō sōnyū ni kansuru kengian" [Proposal to insert a clause to the National Eugenic Law], August 12, 1946, in Ogino, Yoko, and Hikaru, *Sei to seishoku no jinken mondai shiryō shūsei*, 25:120.

90. Reminiscences of midwife birth control instructors quoted in Ōbayashi, "Sengo no gyōsei shudō no jutai chōsetsu," 90.

91. Suzuki Takako, "Jutai chōsetsu no tadashī nerai" [The proper purpose of birth control], *Josanpu zasshi*, October 1954, 36–37.

92. Hashimoto, "Josanpu mo doryoku shimashitayo," 141–43; Ōbayashi, "Sengo no gyōsei shudō no jutai chōsetsu," 90.

93. Ishigaki, "Josanpu wa dōsureba ima no kukyō kara sukuwareru ka," 7; Kuji, "Josanpu no chii kōjō wo netsubō," 40–41; Ishigaki Junji, "Yūsei hogo hō kaisei saru" [Eugenic Protection Law revised], *Josanpu zasshi*, July 1952, 49.

94. "Yūsei hogo hō, sanpu seido, sanfujinka kyōju hō ni tsuite," 294–95.
95. "Jutai chōsetsu shidō no jissai," 5.
96. Smith, *Sick and Tired*, 118–48.
97. In 1947, 92 percent of all births in Japan were attended by midwives, but by 1975 more than 90 percent of births took place in hospitals and were attended by doctors. Coleman, *Family Planning in Japanese Society*, 47.
98. The council also sponsored Margaret Sanger's visit to Japan in 1952 and published the Japanese translation of Irene B. Taeuber's *The Population of Japan*.
99. Population Problems Research Council, the Mainichi Newspapers (hereafter PPRC), *Family Planning in Japan: Opinion Survey by the Mainichi Newspapers*, 98.
100. In 1950, the rates of practicing contraception according to the husband's occupation were 11.5 percent for blue-collar workers and 25.9 percent for white-collar workers. According to the wife's educational levels, the rates were 13.0 percent for those with less than nine years of schooling, 32.4 percent for those with ten to twelve years, and 36.0 percent for those with more than thirteen years. In the 1955 survey, the rates were 25.4 percent for farmers and fishermen; 35.8 percent for laborers; 37.4 percent for those engaged in commerce and industry; 39.7 percent for salaried workers, and 41.0 percent for the self-employed. The rates according to the wife's educational levels were 28.2 percent for those less than nine years of education; 46.1 percent for ten years; and 47.8 percent for more than thirteen years. Yōichi Okazaki, "Family Planning," in PPRC, *Family Planning in Japan*, 99–102.
101. Koya, "Family Planning among Japanese on Public Relief," in Koya, *Pioneering in Family Planning*, 57.
102. PPRC, *The Population and Society of Postwar Japan*, 176, 183, 190, 195, 202.
103. Okazaki, "Family Planning," 112–13.
104. Ibid., 117; PPRC, *The Population and Society of Postwar Japan*, 183, 189, 195, 202.
105. PPRC, *The Population and Society of Postwar Japan*, 174–79, 185, 191, 197, 204.
106. Ōbayashi, "Sengo no gyōsei shudō no jutai chōsetsu," 88. See also Katō, Moriyama, and Kanzaki, "Sanji chōsetsu no kihon mondai wo megutte," 98.
107. McCoy, diary, December 30, 1949, June 8, 1950; Juitsu Kitaoka to Marshall Balfour, March 14, 1950, folder 3353, box 501, series 609, RG 2; excerpts from letters of Irene Taeuber, November 18, 1952, folder 4594, box 388, series 200, RG 1.1; Roger F. Evans, "Japan: Population, Professor Warren S. Thompson," May 16, 1949, folder 3113, box 464, series 609, RG 2, all in RFA, RAC.
108. The correlation between the spread of contraception and the rise of abortions is proven in Koya Yoshio's abortion study. See Koya, "Why Induced Abortions in Japan Remain High," in Koya, *Pioneering in Family Planning*, 80.

109. According to the study made by Aoki Hisao of the Institute of Population Problems, Ministry of Health and Welfare, the ratio between averted births by contraception and by induced abortion in 1955 was 3 to 7. In 1965, the ratio was 7 to 3, the exact opposite of the results in 1955. Minoru Tachi, "Introduction," in PPRC, *Family Planning in Japan*, 9, 11.

110. Okazaki, "Family Planning," 120–21.

111. Koya, "A Study of Induced Abortion in Japan and Its Significance," in Koya, *Pioneering in Family Planning*, 74.

112. Ishikawa Fumiko, Furusawa Yuriko, and Tanabe Hiroko to Margaret Sanger, May 15, 1959, S55, MSP-SSC.

113. Sanger to Dorothy Brush, July 14, 1959, S55, MSP-SSC.

CHAPTER SIX

1. Scholars have revealed the use of Puerto Rican women as guinea pigs for testing oral contraceptives. See, for example, Briggs, *Reproducing Empire*, 109–41; Ramirez de Arellano and Seipp, *Colonialism, Catholicism, and Contraception*, 105–23; May, *America and the Pill*, 29–31; Asbell, *The Pill*, 141–55.

2. Michael Adas examines Cold War modernization projects as part of America's expansionism and "civilizing mission" using technological prowess. His work, however, like most studies on the modernization theory, does not include a discussion on contraceptive technology. See Adas, *Dominance by Design*, 219–79.

3. Ishimoto Shizue to Margaret Sanger, March 8, 1931, box 5 (filmed), MSP-SSC.

4. Koya Yoshio to Sanger, January 31, 1953, S40, MSP-SSC.

5. XYZ, "Sekai kazoku keikaku kaigi ni shussekishita shitennō," 24.

6. Majima Kan to Sanger, February 11, 1953, S40, MSP-SSC.

7. Sanger to Koya, January 27, 1953; Sanger to Katō, February 3, 1953, both in S40, MSP-SSC.

8. Sanger to Vera Houghton, December 18, 1953, S42, MSP-SSC.

9. Clarence Gamble to Sanger, March 16, 1953, S41, MSP-SSC; Toyoda, "Sengo Nihon no bāsu kontorōru undō to Kurarensu Ganburu," 59.

10. Sanger to Katō, February 4, 1954; Sanger to Koya, February 4, 1954, both in S42, MSP-SSC.

11. Koya to Sanger, March 11, March 24, 1954, S43, MSP-SSC.

12. Sanger to Koya, March 29, 1954, S43, MSP-SSC.

13. Sanger to Katō, October 7, 1952, quoted in Hopper, *A New Woman of Japan*, 248.

14. For Sanger's interview with the Japanese American magazine *Scene*, see Masamori Kojima to Chieko Hata, September 24, 1954; Hata to Sanger, February 7, 1955; Sanger to Hata, February 16, 1955, all in S46, MSP-SSC. For Sanger's

radio interview with "Town Crier," see "Town Crier, Margaret Sanger; Radio Interview," January 3, 1953, S83, MSP-SSC.

15. Kamijō Aiichi to Sanger, April 13, 1954, S43, MSP-SSC; Johnson, "Margaret Sanger and the Birth Control Movement in Japan," 151–65.

16. May, *America and the Pill*, 21–29; Watkins, *On the Pill*, 26–28.

17. Rock, *The Time Has Come*, 18–21; Briggs, *Reproducing Empire*, 132–33.

18. Clarence Gamble had ventured onto the island since the 1930s to spread simple methods of contraception to Puerto Rican women. Gamble insisted on using simple and cheap methods of contraception such as the salt-and-sponge method, foam and jellies, and sterilization in Japan, Puerto Rico, and India over more effective and safer—although more expensive and complex—devices such as diaphragms. Sanger, anxious not to offend Gamble and negate his previous work in these regions, wrote to Gamble, pleading that he not "discourage this [pill] experiment." In the end, Gamble himself became involved in some of the pill experiments, although not committedly, in Puerto Rico as well as in Japan. See Briggs, *Reproducing Empire*, 102–7, 152–53; May, *America and the Pill*, 29–30; Ramírez de Arellano and Seipp, *Colonialism, Catholicism, and Contraception*, 45–56, 103–4, 117–21; Sanger to Gamble, April 15, 1954, S43, MSP-SSC.

19. Sanger to Pincus, March 18, March 29, 1954, S43, MSP-SSC.

20. Sanger to Koya, March 31, 1954, S43, MSP-SSC.

21. Sanger to McCormick, April 16, 1954, S43, MSP-SSC.

22. Koya to Sanger, June 21, 1954; Sanger to J. Ozawa, June 25, 1954, both in S43, MSP-SSC.

23. Sanger to Muramatsu Minoru, August 16, 1954; Matsuba Michio to Sanger, August 27, 1954; Katherine McCormick to Gregory Pincus, August 12, 1954; Yamazaki Eiichi to Gregory Pincus, September 8, 1954, all in S44, MSP-SSC.

24. Ishikawa Masaomi to Monserrate Anselmi, February 28, 1954; Ishikawa to Sanger, February 28, 1954, both in S46, MSP-SSC.

25. Koya to Sanger, July 8, 1954, C10, MSP-SSC.

26. Koya to Sanger, October 24, 1954, C10, MSP-SSC.

27. Sanger to Koya, July 12, 1954; Sanger to Koya, July 13, 1954, both in S44, MSP-SSC.

28. Nihon kazoku keikaku renmei, *Jinkō kajō to kazoku keikaku*, 1.

29. Sanger to Kitaoka Juitsu, February 2, 1955; Sanger to Vera Houghton, February 18, 1955, both in S46, MSP-SSC.

30. Nihon kazoku keikaku renmei, *Jinkō kajō to kazoku keikaku*, 2–3; Sanger to Koya, January 15, 1954, S42, MSP-SSC; Sanger to Kitaoka, May 5, 1955, S47, MSP-SSC.

31. In response, Roma Rau and Thompson contended that overpopulation was suggested as "only one of the important probable causes of war" and that the

phrase was not meant to attack any particular country. In the end, the resolution containing the original sentence stating the connection between overpopulation and war was passed by a small margin of 79 to 74 votes. Nihon kazoku keikaku renmei, *Jinkō kajō to kazoku keikaku*, 6, 285; International Planned Parenthood Federation, *Report of the Proceedings*, 15, 259–60.

32. Sanger, "To My Friends and the American Sponsors of the Fifth International Conference on Planned Parenthood in Tokyo, Japan," November 5, 1955, S48, MSP-SSC.

33. Gregory Pincus, "Some Effects of Progesterone and Related Compounds upon Reproduction and Early Development in Mammals"; Abraham Stone and Herbert S. Kupperman, "The Effects of Progesterone on Ovulation"; Masaomi Ishikawa, Fujii Kyushiro, Furusawa Yoshio, Kobayashi Takashi, Magara Masanao, Matsuba Michio, Matsumoto Seiichi, Takashima Tatsuo, and Takeuchi Sigeki, "Report on the Control of Fertility by Oral Progesterone," all in International Planned Parenthood Federation, *Report of the Proceedings*, 175–87.

34. Solly Zuckerman, "Summing Up Research into Biological Methods of Controlling Fertility," in International Planned Parenthood Federation, *Report of the Proceedings*, 212.

35. Asbell, *The Pill*, 135. To overcome the image of "illegitimacy" and establish their work as a scientific discipline, reproductive scientists in the mid-twentieth century tried to distinguish themselves from birth control advocates and instead stressed basic research and scientific methods. See Clarke, *Disciplining Reproduction*.

36. Pincus to Sanger, February 2, 1953; Sanger to Koya, February 11, 1956; Sanger to Pincus, February 14, 1956; Koya to Sanger, February 16, 1956; Sanger to Pincus, February 25, 1956, all in S49, MSP-SSC.

37. Sanger to Koya, July 22, 1957; Koya to Sanger, August 1, 1957, both in S52, MSP-SSC.

38. Clarence Gamble to Sanger, November 18, 1954, S45, MSP-SSC.

39. Duka and DeCherney, *From the Beginning*, 82.

40. Pincus to Koya, October 18, 1957, S52, MSP-SSC; Rice-Wray, "Field Study with Enovid as a Contraceptive Agent," 78–85.

41. For Pincus's pill experiments in Puerto Rico, see also Watkins, *On the Pill*, 32; Reed, *The Birth Control Movement*, 360–61; Asbell, *The Pill*, 147–48; Briggs, *Reproducing Empire*, 137–39; Ramirez de Arellano and Seipp, *Colonialism, Catholicism, and Contraception*, 115–17.

42. Vital, Health, and Social Statistics Division, Statistics and Information Department, Minister's Secretariat, Ministry of Health, Labour and Welfare, Japan, "Summary of Vital Statistics (Rates)," September 5, 2013, http://www.mhlw.go.jp/english/database/db-hw/populate/dl/02.pdf.

43. Sanger to Gamble, March 29, 1956, S49; Sanger to Koya, August 30, 1956, S50; Sanger to Katō, August, 1956, S50; Koya to Sanger, October 8, 1956, S50; Majima to Sanger, February 28 and February, 1957, S51, all in MSP-SSC.

44. Margaret Sanger, "Planned Parenthood: A Cultural Civilization Will Bring World Peace," in International Planned Parenthood Federation, *Report of the Proceedings*, 6.

45. Hiroko Tanabe, "My Personal Views on Planned Parenthood in Japan," 1959, S56, MSP-SSC.

46. Clarence Gamble to Vera Houghton, February 8, 1955, S46, MSP-SSC.

47. Koya to Sanger, November, 1956, S50, MSP-SSC.

48. Koya to Rufus S. Day, January 8, 1958, S53, MSP-SSC.

49. Koya to Vera Houghton, November 2, 1958, S54, MSP-SSC. With the support of Oliver McCoy and the RF, Koya himself conducted and published a study on sterilization in Japan for the international audience. Koya et al., "A Survey of Health and Demographic Aspects of Reported Female Sterilizations," 368–92.

50. For example, the use of Sampoon, a vaginal foam tablet, yielded satisfactory results in Koya's case study but was a complete failure when family planning workers used it in the so-called Khanna Study, launched in 1953 in India. This was a method that Clarence Gamble had supported since his birth control experiments in North Carolina. Population Council, "India," 4–7; Williams, *Every Child a Wanted Child*, 221; Koya, *Kōgakukyū*, 226–28; Koya, *Pioneering in Family Planning*, 171; Koya and Koya, "The Prevention of Unwanted Pregnancies," 170.

51. Bogue, "Hypothesis for Family Planning," 6; Frank W. Notestein, keynote address, in Muramatsu and Harper, *Population Dynamics*, 6.

52. See this view expressed, for example, in Notestein, "Preliminary Reconnaissance," 23; Balfour et al., *Public Health and Demography in the Far East*, 119–20.

53. Taeuber, "Japan's Demographic Transition Re-examined," 39.

54. There were some population controllers who preferred to disseminate male methods of contraception, specifically condoms, as a simple and inexpensive method for the masses in India. Dudley Kirk, a demographer at the Population Council, allegedly felt that a "feminist bias" was subverting family planning programs in the developing world. See Chesler, *Woman of Valor*, 451.

55. Minoru Muramatsu, "Problem in Procuring Contraceptive Materials in a Rural Area in Japan," in Koya, *Pioneering in Family Planning*, 150–65.

56. Notestein, "Preliminary Reconnaissance," 23.

57. Frank W. Notestein, keynote address, in Muramatsu and Harper, *Population Dynamics*, 10; NAS, "Conference on Population Problems, Summary Report," 5, folder 720, box 85, series 1.5, RG 5, JDRIII Papers, RAC; Notestein, "Preliminary Reconnaissance," 23.

58. The government avoided the discussion to legalize IUDs and left them under the supervision and discretion of individual doctors. See Norgren, *Abortion before Birth Control*, 120.

59. Ōta, *Nihon sanji chōsetsu hyakunenshi*, 398; Japan Birth Control Institute, "Contraceptive Gadgets in Japan," 31, 40; Doi, "Intrauterine Ring," 1–2; Kondo, "Intrauterine Contraceptive Method," 3–4.

60. Watkins, *On the Pill*, 70–71; Nagelberg, "Promoting Population Policy," 181–86.

61. Japan Birth Control Institute, "Contraceptive Gadgets in Japan," 40.

62. Population Council, "Report on Intra-uterine Contraceptive Devices," 11–12 (emphasis added).

63. Chesler, *Woman of Valor*, 272, 446, 451.

64. For the same reason—the presumption that women in poor countries lacked the necessary skills and conditions—international population control agencies discouraged the use of diaphragms and other barrier methods. L. Gordon, *The Moral Property of Women*, 336.

65. Marsh and Ronner, *The Fertility Doctor*, 200–201.

66. Asbell, *The Pill*, 159, 166; May, *America and the Pill*, 32–34; Watkins, *On the Pill*, 32.

67. Pincus to Sanger, August 25, 1959, S55, MSP-SSC. Sanger continued to use her Japanese network to arrange clinical experiments for Enovid in Japan as late as 1960. In her letter to Pincus, she suggested that he contact Majima Kan, although there is no further record showing that such arrangement actually took place. Sanger to Pincus, May 5, 1960, S57, MSP-SSC.

68. Pincus to Vera Houton, November 8, 1958; Houton to Pincus, November 17, 1958, both in S54, MSP-SSC.

69. Pincus to Sanger, August 25, 1959, S55, MSP-SSC; Marks, *Sexual Chemistry*, 242.

70. Marks, *Sexual Chemistry*, 105–6; Marsh and Ronner, *The Fertility Doctor*, 196; May, *America and the Pill*, 31.

71. For a feminist critique of the dangers of new contraceptives, see L. Gordon, *Birth Control in America*, 421–27.

72. Norgren, *Abortion before Birth Control*, 107–29.

73. For a sociological analysis of the contradictory reproductive policies in Japan after the 1950s—a "progressive" abortion law combined with "conservative" contraceptive regulations—see ibid., 108–13; Coleman, *Family Planning in Japanese Society*, 34–41.

74. Norgren, *Abortion before Birth Control*, 120.

75. Sanger to Koya, July 12, 1954, S44; Koya to Sanger, July 8, 1954, C10, both in MSP-SSC.

76. Koya, *Kōgakukyū*, 172, 186, 206.

77. Norgren, *Abortion before Birth Control*, 111.

78. Minoru Muramatsu, "Medical Aspects of the Practice of Fertility Control," in Kunii, *Basic Readings*, 111.

79. Frederick Osborn to Vera Houghton, March 7, 1957; Frederick Osborn to Margaret Sanger, April 3, 1957, both in S51, MSP-SSC. The locations of the ICPP conference, from the first to the ninth, were as follows: Stockholm (1946); Cheltenham, England (1948); Bombay (1952); Stockholm (1953); Tokyo (1955); New Delhi (1959); Singapore (1963); Santiago, Chile (1967); Brighton, England (1973). Suitters, *Be Brave and Angry*.

80. State Department circular, December 2, 1959, quoted in Connelly, *Fatal Misconception*,187.

81. Sanger, "Population Planning: Program of Birth Control Viewed as Contributing to World Peace," *New York Times*, January 3, 1960. In her letter to Majima Kan, Sanger also expressed resentment toward her own government for not giving "one dollar to the Birth Control Movement." Sanger to Majima, March 15, 1954, S43, MSP-SSC.

82. Connelly, *Fatal Misconception*, 198–99; L. Gordon, *The Moral Property of Women*, 289.

EPILOGUE

1. Sanger, personal note, date unknown, folder 7, box 95 (filmed), MSP-SSC.

2. Gaimushō (Ministry of Foreign Affairs of Japan), "Kokusai kazoku keikaku renmei (IPPF) kyoshutsukin" (IPPF contributions), 2012, http://www.mofa.go.jp/mofaj/annai/yosan_kessan/kanshi_kouritsuka/gyosei_review/h24/h23jigyo/pdfs/117.pdf; IPPF, "Financial Statements 2016," 17, 32, http://www.ippf.org/sites/default/files/2017-06/FinancialReport_2016.pdf.

3. Connelly, *Fatal Misconception*, 353.

4. Committee on Foreign Affairs, *The Mexico City Policy/Global Gag Rule*, 25, 32; Goldberg, *The Means of Reproduction*, 161–62.

5. For details on how these international organizations ended up supporting sterilization and other coercive programs in India and China, see Connelly, *Fatal Misconception*, 276–326.

6. Armstrong Williams, "Righteous Indignation: The Essence of Hypocrisy on Abortion," *Washington Times*, July 16, 2012, A8; Glenn Kessler, "Fact Checker: Herman Cain on Abortion," *Washington Times*, November 6, 2011, A7; Deborah Simmons, "Can We Talk: Time to Blunt Pro-Choicers' New 'Initiative,'" *Washington Times*, May 23, 2011, A14; Editorial, "Planned Parenthood Targets Blacks," *Washington Times*, August 25, 2008, A14.

7. For details on the Christian Right campaigns against population control/

family planning programs abroad since the 1980s, see Buss and Herman, *Globalizing Family Values*, 56–79. For the black nationalists' campaign against birth control, see Nelson, *Women of Color and the Reproductive Rights Movement*, 85–111.

8. Ellen Barry and Celia W. Dugger, "India Is Changing Its Decade-Long Reliance on Female Sterilization," *New York Times*, February 21, 2016, A8.

9. Public controversy erupted in June 2014 after some male members of the Tokyo Metropolitan Assembly made derogatory remarks against a female member, who spoke in favor of increased support for working mothers and infertile women. As she took the podium and started speaking, a council member shouted out, "Why don't you get married first?" and "Can't you even bear a child?," as jeering filled the assembly hall. Joyce Gelb offers a commentary on the incident in the broader context of sexism in contemporary Japanese society, in an interview article by Seana K. Magee, "U.S. Academic Hopes Tokyo Metropolitan Assembly Heckling Will Lead to Change," *Japan Times*, August 12, 2014.

10. Kōsei rōdō shō, "Jinkō dōtai tōkei geppō nenkei (gaisū) no gaikyō" [Fact sheet on demographics, monthly report of annual total (estimate)], 2016, http://www.mhlw.go.jp/toukei/saikin/hw/jinkou/geppo/nengai16/dl/gaikyou28.pdf.

11. "Nihon wa chūzetsu tengoku: Beikoku e no senden no tegami" [Japan is an abortion paradise: Advertising letter to the United States], *Asahi shinbun*, March 7, 1967, evening edition, 11; Uematsu Tadashi, "Datai tengoku Nihon" [Abortion paradise Japan], *Toki no hōrei*, April 1967, 9; "Aoi me ga urayamu datai tengoku Nippon" [Abortion paradise Japan, envied by blue-eyed women], *Shūkan bunshun*, April 17, 1967, 46–47; "Nijūbyō ni hitori no gōhō satsujin: Kaigai ni todoroku datai tengoku Nippon" [Legal murder every twenty seconds: Abortion paradise Japan disturbs the world], *Shūkan gendai*, March 20, 1960, 78–81. Although the antirevision forces were able to stop the attempts at removing the economic reasons clause, in 1990 the MHW did move up the ban on abortion from twenty-four to twenty-two weeks. Gelb, *Gender Policies in Japan and the United States*, 95–96.

12. There had been repeated left-wing attempts since the early 1970s among disability rights activists and feminists to revise the EPL, but nothing significant materialized until the 1990s. See Norgren, *Abortion before Birth Control*, 65–81; Gelb, *Gender Policies in Japan and the United States*, 96–97.

13. Gelb, *Gender Policies in Japan and the United States*, 100.

14. The guideline requires pill users to visit a doctor every three months for a pelvic examination, whereas in the United States and Europe, an annual examination is the standard. The national health insurance does not cover the costs for the pill, and women may also need to pay for the frequent doctor visits, consultations, and examinations. The added costs have further made oral contraceptives unattractive and inaccessible to many Japanese women. The current guideline, re-

vised and adopted in 2005 by the Japan Society of Obstetrics and Gynecology, the Japan Association of Obstetricians and Gynecologists, the Japan Society for Reproductive Medicine, the Japanese Society for AIDS Research, the Japanese Society for Sexually Transmitted Infections, and the Japan Family Planning Association, is available at Nihon sanka fujinka gakkai, ed., "Tei-yōryō keikō hininyaku no shiyō ni kansuru gaidorain" [Guideline on the use of low-dose oral contraceptive drug], December 2005, http://www.jsognh.jp/common/files/society/guide_line.pdf. All of the nine committee members who examined the guideline are male representatives for the listed associations.

15. Shimizu Keihachiro, "Shōshika taisaku no kimete wa 'Yūsei hogohō' no haishi da" [Key measure against declining-birth-rate crisis is to repeal the Eugenic Protection Law], *Gekkan Nihon*, October 2005, 56–59.

16. Investigative journalist Michelle Goldberg refers to France and Sweden as examples of developed countries that have relatively high fertility as a result of a rich array of public policies that assist childbearing and rearing. Goldberg, *The Means of Reproduction*, 217–18.

17. Gretchen Livingston and D'Vera Cohn, "U.S. Birth Rate Falls to a Record Low; Decline Is Greatest among Immigrants," *Pew Social & Demographic Trends*, November 29, 2012, http://www.pewsocialtrends.org/2012/11/29/u-s-birth-rate-falls-to-a-record-low-decline-is-greatest-among-immigrants/1/; Sam Roberts, "A Generation Away, Minorities May Become the Majority in U.S.," *New York Times*, August 14, 2008, A1; Sabrina Tavernise, "Whites Account for under Half of Births in U.S.," *New York Times*, May 17, 2012, A1; Sam Roberts, "For Whites, More Deaths Than Births, Data Shows," *New York Times*, June 13, 2013, A16.

18. For sterilization abuses in the US South and in California in the 1960s and 1970s, see Nelson, *Women of Color*, 119–69; Schoen, *Choice and Coercion*, 75–138; Littlewood, *The Politics of Population Control*, 79–132; Ordover, *American Eugenics*, 179–94; McCann, *Birth Control Politics in the United States*, 135–73; Stern, "Sterilized in the Name of Public Health," 1128–38.

19. Corey G. Johnson, "Many Women in State Prisons Sterilized without Required OK," *San Francisco Chronicle*, late edition, July 7, 2013, A1; "Echoes of Eugenics," *Los Angeles Times*, July 12, 2013, A14.

20. Jeffrey Passel and D'Vera Cohn, "Unauthorized Immigrant Population: National and State Trends, 2010," *Pew Research Hispanic Center*, February 1, 2011, http://www.pewhispanic.org/2011/02/01/iii-births-and-children/.

21. Janell Ross, "The Myth of the 'Anchor Baby' Deportation Defense," *Washington Post*, August 20, 2015.

22. Hawaii is the popular destination for "birth tourism" for a growing number of Japanese women. While some celebrities' birth experiences in Hawaii (*hawai shussan*) have been featured in the media since the early 2000s, the number of

such births in total seems negligible. For examples of media stories about *hawai shussan*, see Hayashi Manami, "Nijū kokuseki nerai kaigai shussan ni hashiru: Oyano kenkoku to dasan" [Choosing to give birth abroad for dual citizenship: Parents' hatred of their country and calculations], *Yomiuri weekly*, April 7, 2002, 125–27; "Amerika kokuseki wo umitai" [Why they want to give birth in America], *Asahi shinbun weekly AERA*, July 9, 2001, 12–16.

23. During the Republican presidential nomination campaign in 2015, Jeb Bush's comment linking the term "anchor babies" to "Asian people" sparked outrage from Asian American politicians. Alex Altman, "Jeb Bush Bungles 'Anchor Baby' Explanation," *Time*, August 24, 2015; Alan Rappeport, "Jeb Bush's Choice of Words Upsets Asian-Americans," *New York Times*, August 25, 2015.

24. National Center for Health Statistics, Center for Disease Control and Prevention (CDC), "Table A. Births by Place of Occurrence and Residence," *The Public Use Natality File—2015 Update*, ftp://ftp.cdc.gov/pub/Health_Statistics/NCHS/Dataset_Documentation/DVS/natality/UserGuide2015.pdf; National Center for Health Statistics, CDC, "Table B. Births by State of Occurrence and Residence," in *Documentation of the Detail Natality Tape File for 2000 Data*, ftp://ftp.cdc.gov/pub/Health_Statistics/NCHS/Dataset_Documentation/DVS/natality/Nat2000doc.pdf. Annual reports of vital statistics, including birth data, are available at Centers for Disease Control and Prevention, "Vital Statistics Data Available Online," accessed May 19, 2017, http://www.cdc.gov/nchs/data_access/Vitalstatsonline.htm.

25. Riggan, "G12 Country Regulations," 6–7.

26. Colen, "Like a Mother to Them," 78.

27. For the impact of ART on Euro-American concepts of motherhood and kinship, see May, *Barren in the Promised Land*, 213–17; Strathern, "Displacing Knowledge," 346–63.

Bibliography

MANUSCRIPT AND ARCHIVAL SOURCES
Francis A. Countway Library of Medicine, Boston, Massachusetts
  Gamble, Clarence James, Papers (CGP)
Hoover Institution Library and Archives, Stanford University, Stanford, California
  Luten, Daniel B., Jr., Papers (Luten Papers)
  Sams, Crawford F., Papers
Library of Congress, Manuscript Division, Washington, DC
  Sanger, Margaret, Papers (MSP-LC)
National Archives at College Park, Maryland
  Archives II Reference Section (Military), Textual Archives Services Division
National Diet Library (NDL), Tokyo, Japan
  Modern Japanese Political History Materials Room (Kensei shiryō shitsu)
  Newspaper Reading Room (Shinbun shiryō shitsu)
Rockefeller Archive Center, Sleepy Hollow, New York (RAC)
  Embree, Edwin, Papers
  Rockefeller, John D., III, Papers, Rockefeller Family Archives (JDRIII)
  Rockefeller Foundation Archives (RFA)
  Office of the Messrs. Rockefeller, Rockefeller Family Archives (OMR)
Sophia Smith Collection, Women's History Archives at Smith College, Northampton, Massachusetts
  Beard, Mary Ritter, Papers (MBP-SSC)
  Planned Parenthood Federation of America Papers (PPFA Papers)
  Sanger, Margaret, Papers (MSP-SSC)
University of Maryland, College Park, Maryland
  The Gordon W. Prange Collection

NEWSPAPERS AND MAGAZINES

Agora
Asahi shinbun (Asahi newspaper)
Asahi shinbun weekly AERA
Atlantic Monthly
Bcon
Birth Control Review
Chicago Daily Tribune
China Today
Chokugen (Plain talk)
Chūō kōron (Central review)
Forum
Fujin gahō (Women's illustrated magazine)
Fujin kōron (Women's review)
Fujin kurabu (Women's club)
Fujin no seiki (Women's century)
Fujin seikatsu (Women's lives)
Gekkan Nihon (Japan monthly)
Hataraku fujin (Working women)
Heimin (Commoner)
Heimin shinbun (Commoner's news)
Hoken to josan (Health and midwifery)
Hokuriku
Hōsō (Broadcast)
Iden (Genetics)
Ikai kōron (Medical review)
Independent
Japan Times
Josanpu zasshi (Midwives' magazine)
Josei kaizō (Women's reconstruction)
Kagakuken (Scientific sphere)
Kaizō (Reconstruction)
Katei no yomimono (Home reader)
Katei shūhō (Home weekly)
Keizai (Economics)
Kibō (Hope)
Life
Los Angeles Times
Maru (Circle)

Minzoku eisei (Racial hygiene)
Myōjō (Morning star)
The Nation
New Leader
New York Times
New Yorker
Newsweek
Nichibei jihō (Japanese American commercial weekly)
Nihon P.T.A. (Japan P.T.A.)
Nihonjin (Japanese)
Ōita gōdō shinbun (Ōita associated newspaper)
Pew Research Hispanic Center
Pew Social & Demographic Trends
Puro BC nyūsu (Proletariat birth control news)
Rafu shimpo (Los Angeles daily Japanese news)
Rinshō fujinka sanka (Clinical obstetrics and gynecology)
San Francisco Chronicle
Sanji chōsetsu nyūsu (Birth control news)
Sanji seigen undō (Birth control movement)
Saturday Review of Literature
Science News Letter
Seikatsu bunka (Lifestyle)
Seikatsu kagaku (Family and consumer science)
Seimei (Life)
Shakai jigyō (Social enterprise)
Shin joen (New women's circle)
Shin josei (New women)
Shufu no tomo (Housewives' friend)
Shufu to seikatsu (Housewives and family life)
Shūkan bunshun (Bunshun weekly)
Shūkan gendai (Modern weekly)
Sōgō igaku (General medicine)
Stars and Stripes
Taiyō (Sun)
Time
Toki no hōrei (Law of the times)
Tokyo nichi nichi shinbun (Tokyo daily news)
Tōsei minpō (Tosei news)
Woman Citizen

Yomiuri shinbun (Yomiuri news)
Yomiuri weekly
Zaibei rōdō shinbun (Japanese workers in America)

PUBLICATIONS

Adas, Michael. *Dominance by Design: Technological Imperatives and America's Civilizing Mission*. Cambridge, MA: Harvard University Press, 2006.

Akami, Tomoko. *Internationalizing the Pacific: The United States, Japan, and the Institute of Pacific Relations in War and Peace, 1919–45*. New York: Routledge, 2003.

Akiyama Tsune. *Han-Taiheiyō Tōnan Ajia fujin kyōkai rokujūnenshi* [Sixty-year history of the Pan-Pacific and Southeast Asia Women's Association]. Tokyo: Domesu shuppan, 1993.

Allen, Garland E. "Old Wine in New Bottles: From Eugenics to Population Control in the Work of Raymond Pearl." In *The Expansion of American Biology*, edited by Keith Rodney Benson, Jane Maienschein, and Ronald Rainger, 231–61. New Brunswick, NJ: Rutgers University Press, 1991.

American Birth Control Conference. *Birth Control: What It Is, How It Works, What It Will Do: The Proceedings of the First American Birth Control Conference Held at the Hotel Plaza, New York, November 11, 12, 1921*. New York: Birth Control Review, 1922.

Anderson, Warwick. *Colonial Pathologies: American Tropical Medicine, Race, and Hygiene in the Philippines*. Durham, NC: Duke University Press, 2006.

Asbell, Bernard. *The Pill: A Biography of the Drug That Changed the World*. New York: Random House, 1995.

Auslin, Michael R. *Pacific Cosmopolitans: A Cultural History of U.S.-Japan Relations*. Cambridge, MA: Harvard University Press, 2011.

Azuma, Eiichiro. *Between Two Empires: Race, History, and Transnationalism in Japanese America*. New York: Oxford University Press, 2005.

Baker, Lee D. *From Savage to Negro: Anthropology and the Construction of Race, 1896–1954*. Berkeley: University of California Press, 1998.

Balfour, Marshall C., Roger F. Evans, Frank W. Notestein, and Irene B. Taeuber. *Public Health and Demography in the Far East: Report of a Survey Trip, September 13–December 13, 1948*. New York: Rockefeller Foundation, 1950.

Bannister, Robert C. *Social Darwinism: Science and Myth in Anglo-American Social Thought*. Philadelphia: Temple University Press, 1979.

Barkan, Elazar. *The Retreat of Scientific Racism: Changing Concepts of Race in Britain and the United States between the World Wars*. Cambridge: Cambridge University Press, 1992.

Beard, Mary Ritter. *A Woman Making History: Mary Ritter Beard through Her Letters*, edited by Nancy F. Cott. New Haven, CT: Yale University Press, 1991.

Bederman, Gail. *Manliness & Civilization: A Cultural History of Gender and Race in the United States, 1880–1917*. Chicago: University of Chicago Press, 1995.

Benedict, Ruth. *Race: Science and Politics*. New York: Viking Press, 1945.

Berger, Shelley L., Tony Kouzarides, Ramin Shiekhattar, and Ali Shilatifard. "An Operational Definition of Epigenetics." *Genes and Development* 23, no. 7 (2009): 781–83.

Black, Edwin. *War against the Weak: Eugenics and America's Campaign to Create a Master Race*. New York: Four Walls Eight Windows, 2003.

Bogue, Donald. "Hypothesis for Family Planning Derived from Recent and Current Experience in Asia." *Studies in Family Planning* 1, no. 3 (1964): 6–9.

Borst, Charlotte G. *Catching Babies: The Professionalization of Childbirth, 1870–1920*. Cambridge, MA: Harvard University Press, 1995.

Briggs, Laura. "Mother, Child, Race, Nation: The Visual Iconography of Rescue and the Politics of Transnational and Transracial Adoption." *Gender & History* 15, no. 2 (2003): 179–200.

———. *Reproducing Empire: Race, Sex, Science, and U.S. Imperialism in Puerto Rico*. Berkeley: University of California Press, 2002.

Brown, JoAnne. "Purity and Danger in Color: Notes on Germ Theory and the Semantics of Segregation." In *Heredity and Infection: The History of Disease Transmission*, edited by Jean-Paul Gaudillière and Ilana Löwy, 101–31. New York: Routledge, 2001.

Burnett, Albert G. "Misunderstanding of Eastern and Western States regarding Oriental Immigration." *Annals of the American Academy of Political and Social Science* 34, no. 2 (1909): 37–48.

Burton, David. "Theodore Roosevelt's Social Darwinism and Views on Imperialism." In *Race and U.S. Foreign Policy from 1900 through World War II*, edited by Michael L. Krenn, 1–16. New York: Garland Publishing, 1998.

Buss, Doris, and Didi Herman. *Globalizing Family Values: The Christian Right in International Politics*. Minneapolis: University of Minnesota Press, 2003.

California State Board of Control. *California and the Oriental: Japanese, Chinese and Hindus*. Sacramento: California State Print Office, 1920.

Chesler, Ellen. *Woman of Valor: Margaret Sanger and the Birth Control Movement in America*. New York: Simon & Schuster, 1992.

Choy, Catherine Ceniza. *Empire of Care: Nursing and Migration in Filipino American History*. Durham, NC: Duke University Press, 2003.

Chung, Yuehtsen Juliette. *Struggle for National Survival: Eugenics in Sino-Japanese Contexts, 1896–1945*. New York: Routledge, 2002.

Clarke, Adele. *Disciplining Reproduction: Modernity, American Life Sciences, and "The Problems of Sex."* Berkeley: University of California Press, 1998.

Coleman, Samuel. *Family Planning in Japanese Society: Traditional Birth Control in a Modern Urban Culture.* Princeton, NJ: Princeton University Press, 1983.

Colen, Shellee. "'Like a Mother to Them': Stratified Reproduction and West Indian Childcare Workers and Employers in New York." In *Conceiving the New World Order: The Global Politics of Reproduction*, edited by Faye D. Ginsburg and Rayna Rapp, 78–102. Berkeley: University of California Press, 1995.

Condliffe, John Bell, ed. *Problems of Food and Population in the Pacific Area: Preliminary Syllabus for Round Table Discussion, Hangchow Conference, October 21 to November 4, 1931.* Honolulu: Institute of Pacific Relations, 1931.

Conklin, Edwin Grant. *The Direction of Human Evolution.* New York: C. Scribner's Sons, 1921.

———. "Feminism and the New Woman: Their Eugenical Significance." *Eugenics* 3, no. 8 (1930): 302, 304.

———. *Heredity and Environment in the Development of Men.* Princeton, NJ: Princeton University Press, 1915.

Connelly, Matthew James. *Fatal Misconception: The Struggle to Control World Population.* Cambridge, MA: Belknap Press of Harvard University Press, 2008.

Cooke, Kathy J. "Duty or Dream? Edwin G. Conklin's Critique of Eugenics and Support for American Individualism." *Journal of the History of Biology* 35, no. 2 (2002): 365–84.

Cooper, John Milton, Jr. "American Sphinx: Woodrow Wilson and Race." In *Jefferson, Lincoln, and Wilson: The American Dilemma of Race and Democracy*, edited by John Milton Cooper Jr. and Thomas J. Knock, 145–62. Charlottesville: University of Virginia Press, 2010.

Cowdry, Edmund Vincent, ed. *Human Biology and Racial Welfare.* New York: P. B. Hoeber, 1930.

Davenport, Charles. "Do Races Differ in Mental Capacity?" *Human Biology* 1, no. 1 (1929): 70–89.

Davidann, Jon Thares. *Cultural Diplomacy in U.S.-Japanese Relations, 1919–1941.* New York: Palgrave Macmillan, 2007.

Davis, Janet M. *The Circus Age: Culture & Society under the American Big Top.* Chapel Hill: University of North Carolina Press, 2002.

Deloria, Philip Joseph. *Playing Indian.* New Haven, CT: Yale University Press, 1998.

Dikötter, Frank. *Imperfect Conceptions: Medical Knowledge, Birth Defects and Eugenics in China.* New York: Columbia University Press, 1998.

Dohi Keizō. "Hyakunengo no Ōshūjin to Beikokumin" [Europeans and Americans one-hundred years later]. *Yūseigaku* [Eugenics] 3, no. 2 (1926): 5–7.

Doi, Jun. "Intrauterine Ring." *Japan Planned Parenthood Quarterly* 4, no. 1 (1953): 1–2.

Douglas, Emily Taft. *Margaret Sanger: Pioneer of the Future*. New York: Holt, Rinehart and Winston, 1969.

Dower, John W. *Embracing Defeat: Japan in the Wake of World War II*. New York: W. W. Norton, 1999.

———. "Occupied Japan and the Cold War in Asia." In *Japan in War and Peace: Selected Essays*, by John W. Dower, 155–207. New York: W. W. Norton, 1993.

———. *War without Mercy: Race and Power in the Pacific War*. 7th ed. New York: Pantheon Books, 1993.

Duka, Walter E., and Alan H. DeCherney. *From the Beginning: A History of the American Fertility Society, 1944–1994*. Birmingham, AL: American Fertility Society, 1994.

Dunn, Leslie Clarence, and Theodosius Dobzhansky. *Heredity, Race, and Society*. New York: Penguin Books, 1946.

Dyer, Thomas G. *Theodore Roosevelt and the Idea of Race*. Baton Rouge: Louisiana State University Press, 1980.

Ehrlich, Paul R. *The Population Bomb*. New York: Ballantine Books, 1968.

Embree, Edwin Roger. *Brown America: The Story of a New Race*. New York: Viking Press, 1931.

Enloe, Cynthia H. *Does Khaki Become You? The Militarisation of Women's Lives*. Boston: South End Press, 1983.

Epstein, Alexandra. "Linking a State to the World: Female Internationalists, California, and the Pacific, 1919–1939." PhD diss., University of California, Santa Barbara, 2003.

Ettinger, Laura Elizabeth. *Nurse-Midwifery: The Birth of a New American Profession*. Columbus: Ohio State University Press, 2006.

Ettling, John. *The Germ of Laziness: Rockefeller Philanthropy and Public Health in the New South*. Cambridge, MA: Harvard University Press, 1981.

Eugenics Education Society. *Problem in Eugenics: Report of Proceedings of the First International Eugenics Congress Held at the University of London, July 24th to 30th, 1912*. London: Eugenics Education Society, 1913.

Eugenics Research Association. "Eugenics in India." *Eugenical News* 7 (January 1922): 2.

———. "Eugenical Interests in Japan." *Eugenical News* 7 (March 1922): 45.

———. "Report of Sub-committee on Ultimate Program to be Developed by the Eugenics Society of the United States of America." *Eugenical News* 8 (August 1923): 73–80.

Farley, John. *To Cast Out Disease: A History of the International Health Division*

of the Rockefeller Foundation (1913–1951). New York: Oxford University Press, 2004.
Fausto-Sterling, Anne. "Gender, Race, and Nation: The Comparative Anatomy of 'Hottentot' Women in Europe, 1815–1817." In *Deviant Bodies: Critical Perspectives on Difference in Science and Popular Culture*, edited by Jennifer Terry and Jacqueline Urla, 19–48. Bloomington: Indiana University Press, 1995.
———. *Myths of Gender: Biological Theories about Women and Men*. New York: Basic Books, 1985.
Federici, Silvia. *Caliban and the Witch*. New York: Autonomedia, 2004.
Fee, Elizabeth. *Disease and Discovery: A History of the Johns Hopkins School of Hygiene and Public Health, 1916–1939*. Baltimore: Johns Hopkins University Press, 1987.
Fishkin, Shelley Fisher. "Crossroads of Cultures: The Transnational Turn in American Studies." *American Quarterly* 57, no. 1 (2005): 17–57.
Foucault, Michel. *Discipline and Punish: The Birth of the Prison*. New York: Pantheon Books, 1977.
———. *The History of Sexuality: An Introduction*. Vol. 1. New York: Pantheon Books, 1978.
Fowler, Josephine. *Japanese and Chinese Immigrant Activists: Organizing in American and International Communist Movements, 1919–1933*. New Brunswick, NJ: Rutgers University Press, 2007.
Franks, Angela. *Margaret Sanger's Eugenic Legacy: The Control of Female Fertility*. Jefferson, NC: McFarland, 2005.
Frühstück, Sabine. *Colonizing Sex: Sexology and Social Control in Modern Japan*. Berkeley: University of California Press, 2003.
Fujime Yuki. "One Midwife's Life: Shibahara Urako, Birth Control, and Early Shōwa Reproductive Activism." In *Gender and Japanese History*, edited by Haruko Wakita, vol. 1, *Religion and Customs/The Body and Sexuality*, 304–20. Osaka: Osaka University Press, 1999.
———. *Sei no rekishigaku: Kōshō seido, dataizai taisei kara baishun bōshihō, yūsei hogo hō taisei e* [The history of sex: From the system of state-regulated prostitution and criminal abortion to the system of antiprostitution law and eugenic protection law]. Tokyo: Fuji shuppan, 1997.
———. "Yamasen no jidai no josei tachi" [Women during the age of Yamasen]. *Yamasen* 10 (2004): 7.
Fujino Yutaka. *Nihon fashizumu to yūsei shisō* [Fascism and eugenics in Japan]. Kyoto: Kamogawa shuppan, 1998.
Garon, Sheldon M. *Molding Japanese Minds: The State in Everyday Life*. Princeton, NJ: Princeton University Press, 1997.

Gauntlett Tsune. *Shichijūshichinen no omoide: Denki Gantoretto Tsuneko* [Seventy-seven years of memory: Biography of Gauntlett Tsuneko]. Tokyo: Ōzorasha, 1989.
Gelb, Joyce. *Gender Policies in Japan and the United States: Comparing Women's Movements, Rights, and Politics.* Gordonville, VA: Palgrave Macmillan, 2003.
Goldberg, Michelle. *The Means of Reproduction: Sex, Power, and the Future of the World.* New York: Penguin Press, 2009.
Gordon, Andrew. "Managing the Japanese Household: The New Life Movement in Postwar Japan." *Social Politics* 4, no. 2 (1997): 245–83.
Gordon, Linda. *The Moral Property of Women: A History of Birth Control Politics in America.* Urbana: University of Illinois Press, 2007.
———. *Woman's Body, Woman's Right: A Social History of Birth Control in America.* New York: Grossman, 1976.
———. *Woman's Body, Woman's Right: Birth Control in America.* Rev. and updated. New York: Penguin Books, 1990.
Gorn, Elliott J. *The Manly Art: Bare-Knuckle Prize Fighting in America.* Ithaca, NY: Cornell University Press, 1986.
Grant, Madison. *The Passing of the Great Race; or, The Racial Basis of European History.* New York: Charles Scribner's Sons, 1916.
Gray, Madeline. *Margaret Sanger: A Biography of the Champion of Birth Control.* New York: Richard Marek Publishers, 1979.
Gulick, Sidney L. "Japanese in California." *Annals of the American Academy of Political and Social Science* 93 (January 1921): 55–69.
Haraway, Donna Jeanne. *ModestWitness@SecondMillennium.FemaleManMeets OncoMouse: Feminism and Technoscience.* New York: Routledge, 1997.
———. *Primate Visions: Gender, Race, and Nature in the World of Modern Science.* New York: Routledge, 1989.
Harding, Sandra G. *Whose Science? Whose Knowledge? Thinking from Women's Lives.* Ithaca, NY: Cornell University Press, 1991.
Harr, John Ensor, and Peter J. Johnson. *The Rockefeller Century.* New York: Scribner, 1988.
Hashimoto Haruko. "Josanpu mo doryoku shimashitayo" [Midwives made efforts too]. In *Yoakemae no wakai kikansha: Nihon kazoku keikaku kyōkai 15-nen no ayumi* [Locomotive before dawn: The fifteen-year course of the Japan Family Planning Association], edited by Nihon kazoku keikaku kyōkai, 141–43. Tokyo: Nihon kazoku keikaku kyōkai, 1969.
Hayashida, Cullen Tadao. "Identity, Race and the Blood Ideology of Japan." PhD diss., University of Washington, 1976.
Haynes, Douglas Melvin. *Imperial Medicine: Patrick Manson and the Conquest of Tropical Disease.* Philadelphia: University of Pennsylvania Press, 2001.

Hino, Ashihei. *Wheat and Soldiers*. Translated by Shidzue Hirota Ishimoto. New York: Farrar & Rinehart, 1939.

Hiratsuka Raichō. *Hiratsuka Raichō chosakushū* [Collected works of Hiratsuka Raichō]. Tokyo: Ōtsuki shoten, 1983.

Hirobe, Izumi. *Japanese Pride, American Prejudice: Modifying the Exclusion Clause of the 1924 Immigration Act*. Stanford, CA: Stanford University Press, 2001.

Hodgson, Dennis. "Demography as Social Science and Policy Science." *Population and Development Review* 9, no. 1 (1983): 1–34.

———. "The Ideological Origins of the Population Association of America." *Population and Development Review* 17, no. 1 (1991): 1–34.

Holland, William L. *Remembering the Institute of Pacific Relations: The Memoirs of William L. Holland*. Tokyo: Ryukei Shyosha, 1995.

Honda, Chikao. *Public Opinion Survey on Birth Control in Japan*. Tokyo: Population Problems Research Council, Mainichi Newspapers, 1952.

Hooper, Paul F. "Feminism in the Pacific: The Pan-Pacific and Southeast Asia Women's Association." *Pacific Historian* 20, no. 4 (1976): 367–78.

Hopper, Helen M. *A New Woman of Japan: A Political Biography of Katō Shidzue*. Boulder, CO: Westview Press, 1995.

Hoskins, Janet, and Viet Thanh Nguyen, eds. *Transpacific Studies: Framing an Emerging Field*. Honolulu: University of Hawaii Press, 2014.

Hunter, Jane. *The Gospel of Gentility: American Women Missionaries in Turn-of-the-Century China*. New Haven, CT: Yale University Press, 1984.

Hunter, Tera W. *To 'Joy My Freedom: Southern Black Women's Lives and Labors after the Civil War*. Cambridge, MA: Harvard University Press, 1997.

Ichioka, Yuji. "A Buried Past: Early Issei Socialists and the Japanese Community." *Amerasia Journal* 1, no. 2 (1971): 1–25.

———. "The Early Japanese Immigrant Quest for Citizenship: The Background of the 1922 Ozawa Case." *Amerasia Journal* 4, no. 2 (1977): 1–22.

———. *The Issei: The World of the First Generation Japanese Immigrants, 1885–1924*. New York: Free Press, 1988.

Iinuma, Takeko. "A History of the Women's Peace Association of Japan: The Japanese Section of the Women's International League for Peace and Freedom in the Period before World War II." Master's thesis, Sarah Lawrence College, 1988.

Ikeda Shigenori. "Kekkon shitewa naranu hito" [Those who should not get married]. *Yūsei undō* [Eugenics movement] 2, no. 9 (1927): 2–11.

———. "Kokuritsu yūsei sōdnjo secchi no kyūmu" [Urgent need to establish a national eugenic consultation office]. *Yūsei undō* 2, no. 12 (1927): 18–31.

———. "Yūsei undō ni taisuru hantairon" [Opposing view on the eugenics movement]. *Yūsei undō* 4, no. 7 (1929): 10–23.

———. "Yūseigakuteki shakai kairyō to yūseigaku kenkyūjo" [Eugenic social improvement and a eugenics institution]. *Yūsei undō* 4, no. 10 (1929): 12–16.

International Planned Parenthood Federation, ed. *Report of the Proceedings: The Fifth International Conference on Planned Parenthood, 24–29 October 1955, Tokyo, Japan*. London: International Planned Parenthood Federation, 1955.

Iriye, Akira. *Cultural Internationalism and World Order*. Baltimore: Johns Hopkins University Press, 1997.

———. *Global Community: The Role of International Organizations in the Making of the Contemporary World*. Berkeley: University of California Press, 2002.

———. "The Internationalization of History." *American Historical Review* 94, no. 1 (1989): 1–10.

———. *Power and Culture: The Japanese-American War, 1941–1945*. Cambridge, MA: Harvard University Press, 1981.

Ishida Hirohide and Takano Zenichirō. *Kekkon shin-taisei* [New marriage system]. Tokyo: Seijisha, 1941.

Ishigaki Eitarō. *Amerika hōrō yonjūnen* [Forty years of roaming in America]. Tokyo: Chūō kōronsha, 1952.

Ishimoto, Shidzue Hirota. *Facing Two Ways: The Story of My Life*. New York: Farrar & Rinehart, 1935.

Ishizaki Nobuko. "Seishoku no jiyū to sanji chōsetsu undō: Hiratsuka Raichō to Yamamoto Senji" [Reproductive freedom and the birth control movement: Hiratsuka Raichō and Yamamoto Senji). *Rekishi hyōron* [Historical review] 503 (1992): 92–107.

Jacobs, Seth. *America's Miracle Man in Vietnam: Ngo Dinh Diem, Religion, Race, and U.S. Intervention in Southeast Asia, 1950–1957*. Durham, NC: Duke University Press, 2004.

Jacobson, Matthew Frye. *Whiteness of a Different Color: European Immigrants and the Alchemy of Race*. Cambridge, MA: Harvard University Press, 1998.

Japan Birth Control Institute. "Contraceptive Gadgets in Japan." *Japan Planned Parenthood Quarterly* 2, no. 3–4 (1951): 31, 40.

Johnson, Malia Sedgewick. "Margaret Sanger and the Birth Control Movement in Japan, 1921–1955." PhD diss., University of Hawaii, 1987.

Jonas, Gerald. *The Circuit Riders: Rockefeller Money and the Rise of Modern Science*. New York: Norton, 1989.

Kaneko Mitsuru. "Kangoshoku, hakui no tenshi no chii kōjō" [Nursing profession, improving the status of angels in white gowns]. In *Senryōka no Nihon fujin seisaku: Sono rekishi to shōgen* [Japanese women's policies during the Occupation: Its history and testimonies], edited by Nishi Kiyoko, 169–82. Tokyo: Domesu shuppan, 1985.

Kanzaki, Kiichi. "Is the Japanese Menace in America a Reality?" *Annals of the American Academy* 93 (January 1921): 88–97.

Kato, Shidzue. *A Fight for Women's Happiness: Pioneering the Family Planning Movement in Japan.* Tokyo, Japan: Japanese Organization for International Cooperation in Family Planning, 1984.

Katō Shizue. *Aisuru "Nihon" e no yuigon* [A will to my beloved Japan]. Tokyo: Shoen shinsha, 1995.

———. *Hitosuji no michi* [A straight journey]. Tokyo: Dabiddosha, 1956.

———. *Katō Shizue: Aru josei seijika no hansei* [Katō Shizue: Life of a woman]. Tokyo: Nihon tosho sentā, 1997.

———. *Saiai no hito Kanjū e: Katō Shizue nikki* [To my most beloved Kanju: Katō Shizue's diary]. Tokyo: Shinyōsha, 1988.

———. *Sanji seigen to fujin* [Birth control and women]. Tokyo: Yomiuri shinbunsha, 1946.

Kay, Lily E. *The Molecular Vision of Life: Caltech, the Rockefeller Foundation, and the Rise of the New Biology.* New York: Oxford University Press, 1993.

Kennedy, David M. *Birth Control in America: The Career of Margaret Sanger.* New Haven, CT: Yale University Press, 1970.

Kevles, Daniel J. *In the Name of Eugenics: Genetics and the Uses of Human Heredity.* New York: Knopf, 1985.

Kida Fumio. *Chie no okureta kodomo no igaku* [Medical study on intellectually disabled children]. Tokyo: Maki shoten, 1950.

———. *Jōzu na ikuji, heta na ikuji: Jutai kara nyūgaku made* [Good parenting, bad parenting: From conception to preschool]. Fujin gahōsha, 1955.

Kiuchi Kyō. *Kyōiku ichiro: Han-Taiheiyō fujin kaigi ni resshite* [Road to education: Attending the Pan-Pacific Women's Conference]. Tokyo: Ōzorasha, 1989.

Kline, Wendy. *Building a Better Race: Gender, Sexuality, and Eugenics from the Turn of the Century to the Baby Boom.* Berkeley: University of California Press, 2001.

Kondo, Hajime. "Intrauterine Contraceptive Method." *Japan Planned Parenthood Quarterly* 4, no. 1 (1953): 3–4.

Kōseishō yobōkyoku [Ministry of Health and Welfare, Department of Disease Prevention], ed. *Kokumin yūsei zukai* [Illustrated guide to national eugenics]. Tokyo: Kokumin yūsei renmei, 1941.

Kōseishō yūsei kekkon sōdanjo [Ministry of Health and Welfare, Eugenic Marriage Consultation Office]. *Kekkon no susume* [Advice on marriage]. Tokyo: Kokumin yūsei renmei, 1941.

Koshiro, Yukiko. *Trans-Pacific Racisms and the U.S. Occupation of Japan.* New York: Columbia University Press, 1999.

Kouchi Nobuko, ed. *Shiryō bosei hogo ronsō* [Collected documents on the motherhood protection debate]. Tokyo: Domesu shuppan, 1984.

Koya Yoshio. "Atarashī jinko genshō to sono taisaku: Moderu-mura no kenkyū" [The new population phenomenon and its countermeasures: A study of three rural villages]. *Nihon iji shinpō* [Japan medical journal] 37, no. 1439 (1951): 3–7.

———. "Chūken kaikyū wa zetsumetsu ka: Shin-Marusasushugi no shinjun no kiki" [Will the middle class go extinct: Crisis of the spread of neo-Malthusianism]. *Yūseigaku* 7, no. 8 (1930): 2–5.

———. "Five-Year Experiment on Family Planning among Coal Miners in Joban." *Population Studies* 13, no. 2 (1959): 157–63.

———. *Kindaisen to tairyoku, jinkō* [Modern wars, physical fitness, and population]. Tokyo: Sōgensha, 1944.

———. *Kōgakukyū no techō kara* [From an old scholar's diary]. Tokyo: Nihon kazoku keikaku kyōkai, 1970.

———. *Kokudo, jinkō, ketsueki* [National land, population, blood]. Tokyo: Asahi shinbunsha, 1941.

———. *Minzoku seibutsugaku* [Race biology]. Tokyo: Kōyō shoin, 1938.

———. *Nihon minzoku konseishi* [Comprehensive history of the Japanese race]. Tokyo: Nisshin shoin, 1944.

———. *Pioneering in Family Planning: A Collection of Papers on the Family Planning Programs and Research Conducted in Japan.* Tokyo: Japan Medical Publishers, 1963.

———. "The Program for Family Planning in Japan." *Eugenical News* 38, no. 1 (1953): 1–3.

———. "A Study of Induced Abortion in Japan and Its Significance." *Milbank Memorial Fund Quarterly* 32, no. 3 (1954): 282–93.

———. *Tengoku Amerika, jigoku Amerika* [Heaven America, hell America]. Tokyo: Deidō shuppansha, 1951.

———. "Zaisen yonjūnenkan no naichi Nihonjin hanshokuryoku" [Fertility of Japanese immigrants for forty years in Korea]. In *Minzoku kagaku kenkyū* [Studies on racial science], edited by Hayashi Haruo and Koya Yoshio, 1:183–84. Tokyo: Asakura shoten, 1943.

Koya Yoshio, Kumazawa Kiyoshi, Enishi Jinyoshi, and Amagishi Toshisuke. "Chōsen ni okeru naichijin ijūsha oyobi Chōsenjin no shusseiryoku ni tsuite" [Fertility of Japanese immigrants and Koreans in Korea]. In *Minzoku kagaku kenkyū*, edited by Hayashi Haruo and Koya Yoshio, 1:185–203. Tokyo: Asakura shoten, 1943.

Koya, Yoshio, Minoru Muramatsu, Sakito Agata, and Naruo Suzuki. "A Survey of Health and Demographic Aspects of Reported Female Sterilizations in Four

Health Centers of Shizuoka Prefecture, Japan." *Milbank Memorial Fund Quarterly* 33, no. 4 (1955): 368–92.

Koya, Yoshio, and Tomohiko Koya. "The Prevention of Unwanted Pregnancies in a Japanese Village by Contraceptive Foam Tablets." *Milbank Memorial Fund Quarterly* 38, no. 2 (1960): 167–70.

Kramer, Paul A. *The Blood of Government: Race, Empire, the United States, & the Philippines.* Chapel Hill: University of North Carolina Press, 2006.

Krementsov, Nikolai L. *International Science between the World Wars: The Case of Genetics.* New York: Routledge, 2005.

Kühl, Stefan. *The Nazi Connection: Eugenics, American Racism, and German National Socialism.* New York: Oxford University Press, 1994.

Kunii, Chojiro, ed. *Basic Readings on Population and Family Planning in Japan.* Tokyo: Japanese Organization for International Cooperation in Family Planning, 1976.

Kutsumi Fusako. "Naze ni wareware wa hantai shitaka: Sōdōmei taikai ni teishutsu sareshi BC-an" [Why we opposed the birth control proposal submitted to the Federation of Labor convention]. *Sanji chōsetsu hyōron* 4 [Birth control review] (May 1925): 53.

Larson, Edward J. *Sex, Race, and Science: Eugenics in the Deep South.* Baltimore: Johns Hopkins University Press, 1995.

Latham, Michael E. *Modernization as Ideology: American Social Science and "Nation Building" in the Kennedy Era.* Chapel Hill: University of North Carolina Press, 2000.

LeBlanc, Thomas J. "Sidelights on the Population Problem in Japan." *Human Biology* 4, no. 3 (1932): 408–20.

———. "Some Aspects of Paternity in Sendai, Japan." *Human Biology* 2, no. 4 (1930): 508–22.

———. "Specific Vital Indices for Japan, 1925." *Human Biology* 1, no. 2 (1929): 198–213.

Lee, Erika, and Naoko Shibusawa. "What Is Transnational Asian American History? Recent Trends and Challenges." *Journal of Asian American Studies* 8, no. 3 (2005): vii–xvii.

Leon, Sharon M. *An Image of God: The Catholic Struggle with Eugenics.* Chicago: University of Chicago Press, 2013.

Lindee, M. Susan. *Suffering Made Real: American Science and the Survivors at Hiroshima.* Chicago: University of Chicago Press, 1994.

Litoff, Judy Barrett. *American Midwives, 1860 to the Present.* Westport, CT: Greenwood Press, 1978.

Littlewood, Thomas B. *The Politics of Population Control.* Notre Dame, IN: University of Notre Dame Press, 1977.

Lo, Wei-Djen Djang. "Economic Reconstruction in China since 1927." *Mid-Pacific Magazine* 47, no. 5 (1934): 407–13.

Lock, Margaret M. *Encounters with Aging: Mythologies of Menopause in Japan and North America*. Berkeley: University of California Press, 1993.

Lombardo, Paul A., and George M. Dorr. "Eugenics Medical Education, and the Public Health Service: Another Perspective on the Tuskegee Syphilis Experiment." *Bulletin of the History of Medicine* 80 (2006): 291–316.

Longino, Helen E. *Science as Social Knowledge: Values and Objectivity in Scientific Inquiry*. Princeton, NJ: Princeton University Press, 1990.

Lovett, Laura L. *Conceiving the Future: Pronatalism, Reproduction, and the Family in the United States, 1890–1938*. Chapel Hill: University of North Carolina Press, 2007.

Lublin, Elizabeth Dorn. *Reforming Japan: The Woman's Christian Temperance Union in the Meiji Period*. Vancouver: University of British Columbia Press, 2010.

Ludmerer, Kenneth M. *Genetics and American Society: A Historical Appraisal*. Baltimore: Johns Hopkins University Press, 1972.

MacArthur, Walter. "Opposition to Oriental Immigration." *Annals of the American Academy of Political and Social Science* 34, no. 2 (1909): 19–26.

Mackie, Vera C. *Creating Socialist Women in Japan: Gender, Labour, and Activism, 1900–1937*. Cambridge: Cambridge University Press, 1997.

———. *Feminism in Modern Japan: Citizenship, Embodiment, and Sexuality*. Cambridge: Cambridge University Press, 2003.

———. "Motherhood and Pacifism in Japan, 1900–1937." *Hecate* 14, no. 2 (1988): 28–49.

Marchetti, Gina. *Romance and the "Yellow Peril": Race, Sex, and Discursive Strategies in Hollywood Fiction*. Berkeley: University of California Press, 1993.

Marks, Lara. *Sexual Chemistry: A History of the Contraceptive Pill*. New Haven, CT: Yale University Press, 2001.

Marsh, Margaret, and Wanda Ronner. *The Fertility Doctor: John Rock and the Reproductive Revolution*. Baltimore: John Hopkins University Press, 2008.

Martin, Emily. *The Woman in the Body: A Cultural Analysis of Reproduction*. Boston: Beacon Press, 1987.

Matsubara, Yoko. "The Enactment of Japan's Sterilization Laws in the 1940s: A Prelude to Postwar Eugenic Policy." *Historia Scientiarum* 8, no. 2 (1998): 187–201.

Matsuda Tokiko. *Joseisen* [The line of women]. Tokyo: Akebi shobō, 1995.

Matsumoto, Valarie J. *Farming the Home Place: A Japanese American Community in California, 1919–1982*. Ithaca, NY: Cornell University Press, 1993.

Matsumura Shōnen. "Seibutsugakujō yori mitaru sanji seigen" [Birth control from a biological standpoint]. *Yūsei undō* 5, no. 1 (1930): 20–50.

———. *Shinka to shisō* [Evolution and thoughts]. Tokyo: Dai-Nihon yūbenkai, 1927.

Matthews, Mark A. "Racial Prejudice Un-American." *Annals of the American Academy* 93 (January 1921): 69–72.

May, Elaine Tyler. *America and the Pill: A History of Promise, Peril, and Liberation.* New York: Basic Books, 2010.

———. *Barren in the Promised Land: Childless Americans and the Pursuit of Happiness.* New York: Basic Books, 1995.

McCann, Carole R. *Birth Control Politics in the United States, 1916–1945.* Ithaca, NY: Cornell University Press, 1994.

McCartin, James P. *Prayers of the Faithful: The Shifting Spiritual Life of American Catholics.* Cambridge, MA: Harvard University Press, 2010.

McClatchy, Valentine S. "Japanese in the Melting-Pot: Can They Assimilate and Make Good Citizens?" *Annals of the American Academy of Political and Social Science* 93 (January 1921): 29–34.

McGreevy, John T. *Catholicism and American Freedom: A History.* New York: W. W. Norton, 2003.

———. *Parish Boundaries: The Catholic Encounter with Race in the Twentieth-Century Urban North.* Chicago: University of Chicago Press, 1996.

McNamara, Patrick H. *A Catholic Cold War: Edmund A. Walsh, S.J., and the Politics of American Anticommunism.* New York: Fordham University Press, 2005.

Mehta, Samira K. "'Family Planning Is a Christian Duty': Religion, Population Control, and the Pill in the 1960s." In *Devotions and Desires: Histories of Sexuality and Religion in the Twentieth-Century United States*, edited by Gillian Frank, Bethany Moreton, and Heather White. Chapel Hill: University of North Carolina Press, forthcoming.

Mihalopoulos, Bill. *Sex in Japan's Globalization, 1870–1930: Prostitutes, Emigration and Nation-Building.* London: Pickering & Chatto, 2011.

Minami Ryōzaburō. "Toibā no mita Nihon no jinkō" [The population of Japan as seen by Taeuber]. In *Keizai shutaisei kōza* [Rekishi II] [Economic independence course, history II], edited by Arisawa Hiromi, Higashihata Seiichi, and Nakayama Ichirō, 7:224–46. Tokyo: Chūō kōronsha, 1960.

Minichiello, Sharon. *Retreat from Reform: Patterns of Political Behavior in Interwar Japan.* Honolulu: University of Hawaii Press, 1984.

Minokuchi Tokijirō. "Toibā-cho, Nihon no jinkō" [Review of *The Population of Japan* by Taeuber]. *Hitotsubashi ronsō* [Hitotsubashi review] 41, no. 3 (1959): 70–75.

Molony, Barbara. "Equality versus Differences: The Japanese Debate over 'Motherhood Protection,' 1915–50." In *Japanese Women Working*, edited by Janet Hunter, 124–29. New York: Routledge, 1993.

Moore, Eleanor M. *The Quest for Peace, as I Have Known It in Australia.* Melbourne: Wilke, 1948.
Morris, Charles R. *American Catholic: The Saints and Sinners Who Built America's Most Powerful Church.* New York: Times Books, 1997.
Mosse, George L. *Nationalism and Sexuality: Respectability and Abnormal Sexuality in Modern Europe.* New York: H. Fertig, 1985.
Muramatsu, Minoru. "Action Programs of Family Planning in Japan." In *Population Dynamics: International Action and Training Programs; Proceedings of the International Conference on Population, May, 1964, the Johns Hopkins School of Hygiene and Public Health,* edited by Minoru Muramatsu and Paul A. Harper, 67–75. Baltimore: Johns Hopkins University Press, 1965.
Muramatsu, Minoru, and Paul A. Harper, eds. *Population Dynamics: International Action and Training Programs; Proceedings of the International Conference on Population, May, 1964, the Johns Hopkins School of Hygiene and Public Health.* Baltimore: Johns Hopkins University Press, 1965.
Nagai Hisomu. *Minzoku no unmei* [The fate of a race]. Tokyo: Muramatsu shoten, 1948.
———. *Shin kekkon dokuhon* [New guide to marriage]. Tokyo: Izumo shobō, 1950.
Nagelberg, Judith. "Promoting Population Policy: The Activities of the Rockefeller Foundation, the Ford Foundation and the Population Council, 1959–1966." PhD diss., Columbia University, 1985.
Nakayama, Shigeru, Kunio Goto, and Hitoshi Yoshioka, eds. *A Social History of Science and Technology in Contemporary Japan.* Vol. 1. Melbourne: Trans Pacific Press, 2001.
National Council of Women of the United States. *Our Common Cause, Civilization.* New York: National Council of Women of the United States, 1933.
Nelson, Jennifer. *Women of Color and the Reproductive Rights Movement.* New York: New York University Press, 2003.
Newman, Louise Michele. *White Women's Rights: The Racial Origins of Feminism in the United States.* New York: Oxford University Press, 1999.
Nihon kazoku keikaku kyōkai. *Yoakemae no wakai kikansha: Nihon kazoku keikaku kyōkai 15-nen no ayumi.* Tokyo: Nihon kazoku keikaku kyōkai, 1969.
Nihon kazoku keikaku renmei [Family Planning Federation of Japan]. *Jinkō kajō to kazoku keikaku: Dai-gokai kokusai kazoku keikaku kaigi gijiroku* [Overpopulation and family planning: Proceedings of the Fifth International Conference on Planned Parenthood]. Tokyo: Dai-gokai kokusai kazoku keikaku kaigi jimukyoku, 1956.
Norgren, Christiana A. E. *Abortion before Birth Control: The Politics of Reproduction in Postwar Japan.* Princeton, NJ: Princeton University Press, 2001.

Notestein, Frank W. "Reminiscences: The Role of Foundations, the Population Association of America, Princeton University and the United Nations in Fostering American Interest in Population Problems." *Milbank Memorial Fund Quarterly* 49, no. 4 (1971): 67–85.

Oakley, Deborah Jane Hacker. "The Development of Population Policy in Japan, 1945–1952, and American Participation." PhD diss., University of Michigan, 1977.

Ōbayashi Michiko. *Josanpu no sengo* [Midwives after the war]. Tokyo: Keisō shobō, 1989.

Ochiai, Emiko. "The Reproductive Revolution at the End of the Tokugawa Period." In *Women and Class in Japanese History*, edited by Hitomi Tonomura, Anne Walthall, and Haruko Wakita, 187–215. Ann Arbor: Center for Japanese Studies, the University of Michigan, 1999.

Ogawa, Manako. "American Women's Destiny, Asian Women's Dignity: Trans-Pacific Activism of the Woman's Christian Temperance Union, 1886–1945." PhD diss., University of Hawaii, 2004.

Ogino Miho, Matsubara Yōko, and Saitō Hikaru, eds. *Sei to seishoku no jinken mondai shiryō shūsei* [Collected documents of human rights issues on sex and sexuality]. Tokyo: Fuji shuppan, 2000.

Oguma, Eiji. *A Genealogy of "Japanese" Self-Images*. Translated by David Askew. Melbourne: Trans Pacific Press, 2002.

Ong, Aihwa. *Flexible Citizenship: The Cultural Logics of Transnationality*. Durham, NC: Duke University Press, 1999.

Ordover, Nancy. *American Eugenics: Race, Queer Anatomy, and the Science of Nationalism*. Minneapolis: University of Minnesota Press, 2003.

Ōta Tenrei. *Datai kinshi to yūsei hogo hō* [Abortion ban and the Eugenic Protection Law]. Tokyo: Keieisha kagaku kyōkai, 1967.

———. *Nihon sanji chōsetsu hyakunenshi* [Centennial history of birth control in Japan]. Tokyo: Shuppan kagaku sōgō kenkyūjo, 1976.

Packard, Randall. "Visions of Postwar Health and Development and Their Impact on Public Health Interventions in the Developing World." In *International Development and the Social Sciences: Essays on the History and Politics of Knowledge*, edited by Frederick Cooper and Randall Packard, 93–115. Berkeley: University of California Press, 1997.

Painter, Nell Irvin. *The History of White People*. New York: W. W. Norton, 2010.

Paisley, Fiona. *Glamour in the Pacific: Cultural Internationalism and Race Politics in the Women's Pan-Pacific*. Honolulu: University of Hawaii Press, 2009.

Pan-Pacific Women's Association. *Women of the Pacific: A Record of the Proceedings of the Fourth Triennial Conference of the Pan Pacific Women's Association, Held in Vancouver, Canada, July 1937*. Vancouver, BC: Pan Pacific Women's Association, 1937.

Pan-Pacific Women's Conference. *Women of the Pacific: Being a Record of the Proceedings of the First Pan-Pacific Women's Conference Which Was Held in Honolulu from the 9th to the 19th of August 1928*. Honolulu: Pan-Pacific Union, 1928.

Parsons, Reginald H. "The Anti-Japanese Agitation from a Business Man's Standpoint." *Annals of the American Academy* 93 (January 1921): 72–74.

Paul, Diane B. "Eugenics and the Left." *Journal of the History of Ideas* 45, no. 4 (1984): 567–90.

Pearl, Raymond. "Variation in Parity of Women Bearing Children in the U.S. Birth Registration Area in 1930: Part I." *Human Biology* 9, no. 1 (1937): 65–98.

Pease, Donald E. "Introduction: Re-mapping the Transnational Turn." In *Reframing the Transnational Turn in American Studies*, edited by Winfried Fluck, Donald E. Pease, and John Carlos Rowe, 1–48. Hanover, NH: Dartmouth College Press, 2011.

Penington, Frances. "Trends of Discussion on the Various Topics." In *Report of the Australian Delegation and the Functions of the Round Table and Other Information for Delegates*, edited by Julia Rapke and Frances Penington, 30–38. Melbourne: Australian Pan-Pacific Women's Conference, 1937.

Pflugfelder, Gregory M. *Cartographies of Desire: Male-Male Sexuality in Japanese Discourse, 1600–1950*. Berkeley: University of California Press, 1999.

Phelan, James D. "The Japanese Evil in California." *North American Review* 210, no. 766 (1919): 323–28.

Poovey, Mary. *Making a Social Body: British Cultural Formation, 1830–1864*. Chicago: University of Chicago Press, 1995.

Population Council. "India: The India-Harvard-Ludhiana Population Study." *Studies in Family Planning* 1, no. 1 (1963): 4–7.

———. "Report on Intra-uterine Contraceptive Devices." *Studies in Family Planning* 1, no. 3 (1964): 11–12.

Population Problems Research Council, the Mainichi Newspapers, ed. *Family Planning in Japan: Opinion Survey by the Mainichi Newspapers*. Tokyo: Japanese Organization for International Cooperation in Family Planning, 1972.

———. *The Population and Society of Postwar Japan: Based on Half a Century of Surveys on Family Planning*. Tokyo: Population Problems Research Council, 1994.

Porter, Ian H. "Evolution of Genetic Counseling in America." In *Genetic Counseling: A Monograph of the National Institute of Child Health and Human Development*, edited by Herbert Augustus Lubs and Felix F. De la Cruz, 17–34. New York: Raven Press, 1977.

Ramirez de Arellano, Annette B., and Conrad Seipp. *Colonialism, Catholicism, and Contraception: A History of Birth Control in Puerto Rico.* Chapel Hill: University of North Carolina Press, 1983.

Ramsden, Edmund. "Carving Up Population Science: Eugenics, Demography and the Controversy over the 'Biological Law' of Population Growth." *Social Studies of Science* 32, no. 5–6 (2002): 857–99.

Reed, James. *The Birth Control Movement and American Society: From Private Vice to Public Virtue.* Princeton, NJ: Princeton University Press, 1984.

Rice-Wray, Edris. "Field Study with Enovid as a Contraceptive Agent." In *Proceedings of a Symposium on 19-nor Progestational Steroids*, edited by G. D. Searle & Co., 78–85. Chicago: Searle Research Laboratories, 1957.

Riggan, Kristen. "G12 Country Regulations of Assisted Reproductive Technologies." *Dignitas* 16, no. 4 (2009): 6–7.

Robertson, Jennifer. "Biopower: Blood, Kinship, and Eugenic Marriage." In *A Companion to the Anthropology of Japan*, edited by Jennifer Robertson, 327–54. Malden, MA: Blackwell Publishing, 2005.

———. "Blood Talks: Eugenic Modernity and the Creation of New Japanese." *History and Anthropology* 13, no. 3 (2002): 191–216.

Rock, John. *The Time Has Come: A Catholic Doctor's Proposals to End the Battle over Birth Control.* New York: Alfred A. Knopf, 1963.

Rodd, Laurel Rasplica. "Yosano Akiko and the Taishō Debate over the 'New Woman.'" In *Recreating Japanese Women, 1600–1945*, edited by Gail Lee Bernstein, 189–98. Berkeley: University of California Press, 1991.

Rodrique, Jessie M. "The Black Community and the Birth Control Movement." In *Passion and Power: Sexuality in History*, edited by Kathy Lee Peiss, Robert A. Padgug, and Christiana Simmons, 138–56. Philadelphia: Temple University Press, 1989.

Rosen, Christine. *Preaching Eugenics: Religious Leaders and the American Eugenics Movement.* New York: Oxford University Press, 2004.

Rosenberg, Emily S. *Spreading the American Dream: American Economic and Cultural Expansion, 1890–1945.* New York: Hill & Wang, 1982.

Ross, Edward Alsworth. "The Causes of Race Superiority." *Annals of the American Academy of Political and Social Science* 18 (July 1901): 67–89.

———. *Changing America: Studies in Contemporary Society.* New York: Century, 1912.

———. *The Old World in the New: The Significance of Past and Present Immigration to the American People.* New York: Century, 1914.

Rousseau, Julie M. "Enduring Labors: The 'New Midwife' and the Modern Culture of Childbearing in Early Twentieth Century Japan." PhD diss., Columbia University, 1998.

Rowell, Chester H. "Chinese and Japanese Immigrants: A Comparison." *Annals of the American Academy of Political and Social Science* 34, no. 2 (1909): 3–10.

Rupp, Leila J. "Constructing Internationalism: The Case of Transnational Women's Organizations, 1888–1945." *American Historical Review* 99, no. 5 (1994): 1571–1600.

———. *Worlds of Women: The Making of an International Women's Movement.* Princeton, NJ: Princeton University Press, 1997.

Russett, Cynthia. *Sexual Science: The Victorian Construction of Womanhood.* Cambridge, MA: Harvard University Press, 1989.

Ryder Shimasaki Reiko and Ōishi Sugino. *Sengo Nihon no kango kaikaku: Fūin wo tokareta GHQ bunsho to shōgen ni yoru kenshō* [Reforming nursing in postwar Japan: Examination of declassified GHQ documents and testimonies]. Tokyo: Nihon kango kyōkai shuppankai, 2003.

Sams, Crawford F. *Medic: The Mission of an American Military Doctor in Occupied Japan and Wartorn Korea.* Armonk, NY: M. E. Sharpe, 1998.

Sanger, Margaret. *Margaret Sanger: An Autobiography.* New York: W. W. Norton, 1938.

———. *My Fight for Birth Control.* New York: Farrar & Rinehart, 1931.

———. *The Pivot of Civilization.* New York: Brentano's, 1922.

———, ed. *Proceedings of the World Population Conference, Held at the Salle Centrale, Geneva, August 29th to September 3rd, 1927.* London: E. Arnold, 1927.

———. *The Selected Papers of Margaret Sanger.* Urbana: University of Illinois Press, 2002.

———, ed. *The Sixth International Neo-Malthusian and Birth Control Conference.* New York: American Birth Control League, 1925.

———. *Woman and the New Race.* New York: Brentano's, 1920.

Sasaki Toshiji. *Yamamoto Senji.* Kyoto: Chōbunsha, 1974.

Satō Kayo. *Nihon josanpushi kenkyū: Sono igi to kadai* [Study on the history of midwifery in Japan: Its significance and challenges]. Tokyo: Higashi-Ginza shuppansha, 1997.

Sawayama, Mikako. "The 'Birthing Body' and the Regulation of Conception and Childbirth in the Edo Period." *U.S.-Japan Women's Journal* 24 (2003): 10–34.

Scalapino, Robert A. *The Early Japanese Labor Movement: Labor and Politics in a Developing Society.* Berkeley: Institute of East Asian Studies, University of California, 1983.

———. *The Japanese Communist Movement, 1920–1966.* Berkeley: University of California Press, 1967.

Schenck, Hubert G. "Natural Resources Problem in Japan." *Science* 108, no. 2806 (1948): 367–72.

Schiebinger, Londa L. *Nature's Body: Gender in the Making of Modern Science.* Boston: Beacon Press, 1993.

Schoen, Johanna. *Choice and Coercion: Birth Control, Sterilization, and Abortion in Public Health and Welfare.* Chapel Hill: University of North Carolina Press, 2005.

Schultz, Kevin M. *Tri-faith America: How Catholics and Jews Held Postwar America to Its Protestant Promise.* New York: Oxford University Press, 2011.

Shibusawa, Naoko. *America's Geisha Ally: Reimagining the Japanese Enemy.* Cambridge, MA: Harvard University Press, 2006.

Shimada Akiko. *Nihon no feminizumu: Genryū to shite no Akiko, Raichō, Kikue, Kanoko* [Feminism in Japan: Akiko, Raichō, Kikue, Kanoko as the origins]. Tokyo: Hokuju shuppan, 1996.

Shu, Yuan, and Donald E. Pease, eds. *American Studies as Transnational Practice: Turning toward the Transpacific.* Hanover, NH: Dartmouth College Press, 2015.

Sievers, Sharon L. *Flowers in Salt: The Beginnings of Feminist Consciousness in Modern Japan.* Stanford, CA: Stanford University Press, 1983.

Sinkler, George. *The Racial Attitudes of American Presidents, from Abraham Lincoln to Theodore Roosevelt.* Garden City, NY: Doubleday, 1971.

Sitcawich, Sumiko Otsubo. "Eugenics in Imperial Japan: Some Ironies of Modernity, 1883–1945." PhD diss., Ohio State University, 1998.

Smith, Susan L. *Sick and Tired of Being Sick and Tired: Black Women's Health Activism in America, 1890–1950.* Philadelphia: University of Pennsylvania Press, 1995.

Stepan, Nancy. *"The Hour of Eugenics": Race, Gender, and Nation in Latin America.* Ithaca, NY: Cornell University Press, 1991.

Stern, Alexandra Minna. *Eugenic Nation: Faults and Frontiers of Better Breeding in Modern America.* Berkeley: University of California Press, 2005.

———. "Sterilized in the Name of Public Health: Race, Immigration, and Reproductive Control in Modern California." *American Journal of Public Health* 95, no. 7 (2005): 1128–38.

Stewart-Steinberg, Suzanne. *The Pinocchio Effect: On Making Italians 1860–1920.* Chicago: University of Chicago Press, 2007.

Stoddard, Lothrop. *Clashing Tides of Color.* New York: Charles Scribner's Sons, 1935.

———. "The Japanese Question in California." *Annals of the American Academy* 93 (January 1921): 42-47.

———. "Population Problems in Asia." In *Birth Control: What It Is, How It Works, What It Will Do: The Proceedings of the First American Birth Control Conference Held at the Hotel Plaza, New York, November 11, 12, 1921*, edited by American Birth Control Conference, 94–101. New York: Birth Control Review, 1922.

———. *The Revolt against Civilization: The Menace of the Under Man.* New York: Charles Scribner's Sons, 1922.

———. *The Rising Tide of Color against White World-Supremacy.* New York: Charles Scribner's Sons, 1920.

Strathern, Marilyn. "Displacing Knowledge: Technology and the Consequences for Kinship." In *Conceiving the New World Order: The Global Politics of Reproduction,* edited by Faye D. Ginsburg and Rayna Rapp, 346–63. Berkeley: University of California Press, 1995.

Suitters, Beryl. *Be Brave and Angry: Chronicles of the International Planned Parenthood Federation.* London: International Planned Parenthood Federation, 1973.

Surkis, Judith. *Sexing the Citizen: Morality and Masculinity in France, 1870–1920.* Ithaca, NY: Cornell University Press, 2006.

Suzuki Sadami. *Yūseigaku yori miru sekushuaritī: Ansorojī* [Sexuality from the lens of eugenics: Anthology]. Tokyo: Yumani shobō, 2007.

Suzuki Yūko. *Yamakawa Kikue: Hito to shisō* [Yamakawa Kikue: Character and thoughts]. Tokyo: Rōdō daigaku, 1989.

Suzuki Zenji. *Baiorojī kotohajime: Ibunka to deatta Meijijintachi* [The dawn of biology: The Meiji people's encounter with different cultures]. Tokyo: Yoshikawa kōbunkan, 2005.

———. *Nihon no yūseigaku: Sono shisō to undō no kiseki* [Eugenics in Japan: Trajectory of thoughts and movements]. Tokyo: Sankyō shuppan, 1983.

Szreter, Simon. "The Idea of Demographic Transition and the Study of Fertility Change: A Critical Intellectual History." *Population and Development Review* 19, no. 4 (1933): 659–701.

Taeuber, Irene Barnes. "Japan's Demographic Transition Re-examined." *Population Studies* 14, no. 1 (1960): 28–39.

———. "Manpower Utilization and Demographic Transition: Japan, Manchuria, Taiwan." *Asian Survey* 1, no. 3 (1961): 19–25.

———. *The Population of Japan.* Princeton, NJ: Princeton University Press, 1958.

Taeuber, Irene B., and Hope T. Eldridge. "Some Demographic Aspects of the Changing Role of Women." *Annals of the American Academy of Political and Social Science* 251 (May 1947): 24–34.

Takahashi Katsuyoshi. *Shōkai kaisei yūsei hogo hō* [Detailed commentary on the revised Eugenic Protection Law]. Tokyo: Chūgai igakusha, 1952.

Takeda, Hiroko. *The Political Economy of Reproduction in Japan: Between Nation-State and Everyday Life.* London: RoutledgeCurzon, 2005.

Takeuchi Shigeyo. *Yūsei kekkon* [Eugenic marriage]. Tokyo: Manyō shuppansha, 1949.

Tanaka Yoshimaro. "Yūseigaku kara mita hainichi mondai" [Anti-Japanese problem from the perspective of eugenics]. *Yūseigaku* 2, no. 6 (1925): 39–46.

Taniguchi Yasaburō. *Yūsei hogo hō shōkai* [Detailed commentary on the Eugenic Protection Law]. Kumamoto: Nihon bosei hogoi kyōkai, 1952.
Taniguchi Yasaburō and Fukuda Masako. *Yūsei hogo hō hayawakari* [Easy guide to the Eugenic Protection Law]. Tokyo: Nihon bosei hogoi kyōkai, 1949.
———. *Yūsei hogo hō kaisetsu* [Commentary on the Eugenic Protection Law]. Tokyo: Kenshinsha, 1948.
Tapper, Melbourne. "An 'Anthropathology' of the 'American Negro': Anthropology, Genetics, and the New Racial Science, 1940–1952." *Social History of Medicine* 10 (1997): 263–89.
Tayui Sōsei. "Amerika ni okeru ishihakujakusha ni taisuru yūseigakuteki danshujutsu" [Eugenic sterilization to the feebleminded in America]. *Yūseigaku* 6, no.9 (1929): 13–18.
Tentler, Leslie Woodcock. *Catholics and Contraception: An American History.* Ithaca, NY: Cornell University Press, 2004.
Terazawa, Yuki. "Gender, Knowledge, and Power: Reproductive Medicine in Japan, 1790–1930." PhD diss., University of California, Los Angeles, 2002.
Teslow, Tracy Lang. "Reifying Race: Science and Art in Races of Mankind at the Field Museum of Natural History." In *The Politics of Display: Museums, Science, Culture*, edited by Sharon Macdonald, 53–76. New York: Routledge, 1998.
Thompson, Warren Simpson. *Danger Spots in World Population*. New York: A. A. Knopf, 1929.
———. "Eugenics as Viewed by a Sociologist." *Monthly Labor Review* 18 (February 1924): 11–23.
———. "Natural Selection on the Processes of Population Growth." *Human Biology* 1, no. 4 (1929): 501–13.
———. "The Need for a Population Policy in Japan." *American Sociological Review* 15, no. 1 (1950): 25–33.
———. "Population." *American Journal of Sociology* 34, no. 6 (1929): 959–75.
———. *Population and Peace in the Pacific*. Chicago: University of Chicago Press, 1946.
———. "Race Suicide in the United States." *American Journal of Physical Anthropology* 3 (1920): 97–146.
Tipton, Elise K. "Birth Control and the Population Problem in Prewar and Wartime Japan." *Japanese Studies* 14, no. 1 (1994): 54–64.
———. "Ishimoto Shizue: The Margaret Sanger of Japan." *Women's Historical Review* 6 (1997): 337–55.
Tōkyōto kekkon sōdanjo. *Tōkyōto kekkon sōdanjo gojūnen no ayumi* [Fifty-year course of Tokyo Marriage Consultation Office]. Tokyo: Tōkyōto kekkon sōdanjo, 1985.

Toyoda Maho. "Sengo Nihon no bāsu kontorōru undō to Kureransu Gyanburu: Dai gokai kokusai kazoku keikaku kaigi no kaisai wo chūshin ni" [Birth control movement in postwar Japan and Clarence Gamble: Focusing on the hosting of the Fifth International Conference on Planned Parenthood]. *Jendā shigaku* [Modern history] 6 (2010): 55–70.

Tyrrell, Ian. "Reflections on the Transnational Turn in United States History: Theory and Practice." *Journal of Global History* 4 (2009): 453–74.

Umeda Toshihide. *Shakai undō to shuppan bunka: Kindai Nihon ni okeru chiteki kyōdōtai no keisei* [Social movements and the publishing culture: Formation of intellectual communities in modern Japan]. Tokyo: Ochanomizu shobō, 1998.

US Bureau of the Census. *Historical Statistics of the United States, Colonial Times to 1970*. Washington, DC: US Government Printing Office, 1975.

US Congress, House Committee on Foreign Affairs. *The Mexico City Policy/ Global Gag Rule: Its Impact on Family Planning and Reproductive Health*. Hearing before the Committee on Foreign Affairs, House of Representatives, 110th Cong., 1st sess., October 31, 2007. Washington, DC: US Government Printing Office, 2008.

US Congress, House Committee on Immigration and Naturalization. *Japanese Immigration*. Hearings before the Committee on Immigration and Naturalization, House of Representatives, 66th Cong., 2nd sess. Washington, DC: Government Printing Office, 1921.

———. *Percentage Plans for Restriction of Immigration*. Hearings before the Committee on Immigration and Naturalization, 66th Cong., 1st sess. Washington, DC: Government Printing Office, 1919.

Watkins, Elizabeth Siegel. *On the Pill: A Social History of Oral Contraceptives, 1950–1970*. Baltimore: Johns Hopkins University Press, 1998.

Wexler, Laura. *Tender Violence: Domestic Visions in an Age of U.S. Imperialism*. Chapel Hill: University of North Carolina Press, 2000.

Williams, Doone. *Every Child a Wanted Child: Clarence James Gamble, M.D. and His Work in the Birth Control Movement*. Boston: Harvard University Press for the Francis A. Countway Library of Medicine, 1978.

Williams, William Appleman. *The Tragedy of American Diplomacy*. Cleveland, OH: World Publishing, 1959.

Women's Peace Association in Japan. *Population Problem in Japan: Fourth Pan-Pacific Women's Conference in Vancouver, July 12–24, 1937*. Tokyo: Toppan, 1937.

Woollacott, Angela. "Inventing Commonwealth and Pan-Pacific Feminism: Australian Women's International Activism in the 1920s–30s." In *Feminism and Internationalism*, edited by Mrinalini Sinha, Donna Guy, and Angela Woollacott, 81–104. Oxford: Blackwell Publishers, 1999.

XYZ. "Sekai kazoku keikaku kaigi ni shussekishita shitennō" [Frankly introducing Japanese delegates]. *Japan Planned Parenthood Quarterly* 4, no. 1 (1953): 24–25.

Yamada Waka. *Katei no shakaiteki igi* [Social significance of the family]. Tokyo: Kindai bunmeisha, 1922.

Yamakawa Kikue. "Woman in Modern Japan: VI. The Woman's Movement." *Shakai-shugi kenkyū* [Studies of socialism] 6, no. 2 (1922): 1–5.

———. *Yamakawa Kikue shū* [Collected works of Yamakawa Kikue]. Tokyo: Iwanami shoten, 1981.

Yamamoto Senji. *Yamamoto Senji zenshū* [Collected works of Yamamoto Senji], edited by Sasaki Toshiji. Tokyo: Chōbunsha, 1979.

Yamaoka, Michiyo, ed. *The Institute of Pacific Relations: Pioneer International Non-governmental Organization in the Asia-Pacific Region*. Tokyo: Institute of Asia-Pacific Studies, Waseda University, 1999.

Yasutake Rumi. "Han-Taiheiyō fujin kyōkai no setsuritsu to senkanki no katsudō" [The formation of the Pan-Pacific Women's Association and its activities between the wars]. *Dōshisha Amerika kenkyū* [Doshisha American studies] 45 (2009): 67–82.

———. *Transnational Women's Activism: The United States, Japan, and Japanese Immigrant Communities in California, 1859–1920*. New York: New York University Press, 2004.

Yosano Akiko. *Yosano Akiko zenshū* [Collected works of Yosano Akiko]. Vol. 9. Tokyo: Bunsendō shoten, 1972.

Yoshihara, Mari. *Embracing the East: White Women and American Orientalism*. Oxford: Oxford University Press, 2003.

Yuh, Ji-Yeon. *Beyond the Shadow of Camptown: Korean Military Brides in America*. New York: New York University Press, 2004.

Index

Abe Isoo, 31, 41, 44, 50
abortion: anti, 212–13, 214–16; as backup of contraceptive failure, 207; criminal law against, 14, 22, 156–57, 227n6; feminist advocacy for, 23, 216; health risks, 206; increase in Japan, 143, 149, 178; legalization of, 9, 154–58, 162–63, 214; physicians' control over, 157, 168, 174, 206; midwives performing, 168–69, 180
Ackerman, Edward, 127, 193
Adas, Michael, 38, 146
Addams, Jane, 60, 73, 236n2
adoption, 147, 219
African Americans, 90, 96, 135–37, 140, 168–69, 170, 174
Alien Land Law, 91, 96
Amano Kageyasu, 198
American Birth Control League, 68, 110, 113, 250n100
American Eugenics Society, 83, 87, 108, 110, 246n47, 250n100
American Medical Association, 9
assisted reproductive technology (ART), 219–20
atomic bomb, 166, 173, 253n5, 270n55

Balfour, Marshall, 124, 144, 148–49
Beard, Mary Ritter, 65, 68, 70, 78

birth control: conception of term, 12, 29; movement in Japan, 41–53; movement in US, 28–29, 229n27; as solution to overpopulation, 26, 36, 41, 72, 85, 101, 111, 112, 120, 127, 145. *See also* contraceptives; eugenics, birth control movement and
Birth Control Federation of America, 140
birth rates: and contraceptive use, 197, 201; crisis of low (*shōshika*), 197, 206, 214–16; decline among whites, 83, 85, 86, 108, 217; decline in Japan, 18, 119, 143, 146, 148, 153, 161, 178, 182, 200, 207; differential, 83–84, 96, 100–4, 108, 110, 113–14, 135–36, 217; of immigrants, 92–95, 121, 217; international agreement on, 98; in relation to death rates, 105, 131; transition, 17, 161; of the "unfit," 98, 164
birth tourism, 218

California, 31–32, 52–53, 61, 70, 84, 91–96, 109, 217
capitalism: anti, 25, 28; US/Western, 12, 19, 21, 54
Catholic Church: and anticommunism, 118, 130, 258n68; countries, 196, 216; opposition to birth control, 70, 117–

Catholic Church (*continued*) 20, 126, 127, 129–30, 209. *See also* Christianity
Catt, Carrie Chapman, 68, 73
China, 34, 58, 213, 216, 218; imperialist invasions in, 2, 7, 75–76, 84, 102; overpopulation in, 105, 107, 120, 124, 125, 143. *See also* Sino-Japanese War
Chinese Exclusion Act, 89, 96
Christianity: of internationalist women, 57, 59–60; of Japanese intellectuals, 30, 31, 63; missionaries, 61; views on birth control, 129. *See also* Catholic Church
Cold War, 6, 13, 16; and birth control policies in Japan, 118, 126–28, 130, 212; and global population control, 181, 198, 199; *See also* communism; modernization, projects; modernization, theory
Condoms, 10, 18, 47, 164, 207, 208, 279n54
Contraceptives: experiments, 142, 181–82, 200–4; female-oriented, 10, 183, 200–3; legal approval (Japan), 122, 202, 206; methods, 18, 45, 47–48, 207–8; practicing rate, 48, 175–76, 179; sales of, 51, 171–72; state regulations against (US), 122, 129, 139, 189, 203. *See also* Comstock Law; Ordinance Regulating Harmful Contraceptive Devices; Pharmaceutical Law; *names of specific contraceptives*
colonialism: anti, 7, 12; European, 6, 7, 55, 118, 131; Japanese, 23, 76, 133; legacy of, 213
communism: anti, 118, 130, 212; Chinese, 198; Japan and India as bulwarks against, 126, 150, 182, 198, 199; Japanese, 31; Soviet, 118, 131, 198; and uncontrolled fertility, 16
Comstock Law, 9, 15, 29, 42, 47, 60, 122
Conklin, Edwin, 99–103, 108, 140
Cooper, George M., 135, 136–37, 140, 142, 271n68

Davenport, Charles, 97, 98, 110, 113, 243n11, 246n47, 260n91
Davis, Kingsley, 108, 145
democracy: in Japan, 33, 100, 119, 120, 159, 163, 165, 231n53; US, 95, 119, 130, 131; and women's enslavement, 55
demographic transition theory, 104–5, 145–47, 199, 207
demography. *See* population studies
Dower, John, 223n2, 224n10, 255n42
Draper, William, 209
Du Bois, W. E. B., 111, 251n104

Eisenhower, Dwight, 209
Ellis, Havelock, 21, 29, 111
Embree, Edwin R., 99–103, 247nn58–59
Enovid, 196, 203–4, 280n67. *See also* oral contraceptives
eugenic marriage (*yūsei kekkon*), 152, 159–60, 162–63, 165–66
Eugenic Marriage Consultation Office (EMCO), 46, 125, 143, 152, 161–63, 167, 176
Eugenic Protection Law (EPL), 9; American interest in, 121, 125; drafting of, 154–56; name change, 215–16; provisions on abortion and sterilization, 156–58, 162–63, 166, 168, 178; provisions on birth control, 133, 137, 143, 162, 170; revisions, 143, 158, 170–71, 214–15. *See also* Maternal Protection Law
eugenics: anti-immigration and, 83–84, 87–91, 96, 243n11; birth control movement and, 2–4, 7–8, 20–21, 48, 60, 85, 108–14, 140, 213; Japanese interest in Western, 98–99, 102, 235n101, 246n51; legislations, 50–51, 82, 96; mainline, 84, 103, 107, 109, 113; negative, 109, 114; positive, 109, 113; public health and, 99, 135; reform, 84, 109; transnational network of, 16–17, 97. *See also* Nazi, genocide
Eugenics Record Office, 87, 99, 249n77
Evans, Roger F., 123, 124, 131
expansionism: colonial, 247n56; Japanese, 2, 15, 23, 57, 69, 70, 73, 76, 79, 84, 119; US, 13, 276n2

Factory Law, 23, 63
Fairchild, Henry Pratt, 111, 113, 120
Family Planning Federation of Japan (FPFJ), 185, 186, 192, 197–98, 199, 211

feminism: anti, 108–9, 251n100; in Japan, 23–25; marginalization in reproductive policies and research, 202, 215–16; positions on birth control, 21, 25–26, 51–53, 60, 66, 72, 80–81, 205–6; and socialism, 10, 28, 29, 40, 65; transnational/international activism, 5, 56, 58, 221. *See also* Orientalism, feminist
fertility. *See* birth rates
Ford Foundation, 12, 209. *See also* NGO
Freedom and People's Rights Movements, 21, 22
Freud, Sigmund, 21
fukoku kyōhei, 22
Fukuda Masako, 155

Gamble, Clarence J.: birth control work in North Carolina, 135; birth control work in Puerto Rico, 277n18; involvement in birth control programs in Japan, 139–42, 185, 197, 198; Pathfinder Fund, 213
Garon, Sheldon, 153
Gauntlet (Yamada) Tsuneko, 59, 77, 80
G. D. Searle and Company, 196, 203–4
General Headquarters (GHQ). *See* SCAP
genetics. *See* EMCO; eugenic marriage; eugenics
Gentlemen's Agreement, 88, 92, 93
Germany, 36, 90, 97, 132, 161, 165. *See also* Nazi
Goldman, Emma, 23–24, 29
Gordon, Linda, 3, 27, 135
Grant, Madison, 87, 89, 96, 101
Greenwich Village (New York), 19, 27, 28, 32, 34
Gulick, Sidney L., 94, 95
gyaku tōta, 152–55, 157–59, 164, 167, 169, 172, 264n1

High Treason Case, 31
Hiratsuka Raichō, 23–26, 77, 235n101
Hogue, Fred, 83, 85

Ichikawa Fusae, 81, 154, 160
Ikeda Shigenori, 160
immigration: exclusionist policies, 80, 91, 96, 100, 106, 109, 114; as solution to overpopulation, 84, 112, 145, 229n21; and (supposed) high fertility, 85–87, 92–94, 96, 104, 217–19; and transnationalism, 8–9. *See also* eugenics, and anti-immigration; Japanese Americans
imperialism, 6, 213; anti-, 20, 33–34, 84, 103; Japanese, 51, 69, 74–78; US, 7, 12, 13, 88, 131, 132, 147, 182, 205, 232n56; women and, 10, 15, 58. *See also* colonialism; expansionism
India: anti-Americanism, 193, 205, 213; birth control projects in, 182, 199, 200, 203, 207, 234n85, 279n54; government support of birth control, 198, 209; overpopulation in, 105, 120, 145; participation in international eugenics/birth control efforts, 97, 110, 150, 188, 192, 194; surrogacy in, 219; US exclusion of immigrants from, 96
industrialization: as factor for fertility decline, 18, 100, 105, 120, 145, 147; in Japan, 20, 23, 30–31, 34, 64–65, 75,79, 102
infertility, 189, 194, 214, 219
Institute of Pacific Relations (IPR), 58, 106–7
Institute of Public Health (IPH), 123, 125, 132–33, 137, 169, 173, 190, 197
International Conference on Planned Parenthood (ICPP): Third (Bombay), 150, 181, 183, 184–85; Fifth (Tokyo), 183, 192–95; Sixth (New Delhi), 199, 204
International Conference on Population and Development (Cairo), 215
International Congress of Women, 58, 71–72, 75
International Council of Women (ICW), 58, 60
Internationalism: conflict between nationalism and, 79–80; liberal, 7, 11–12, 56, 120; Pacific-centered, 58; Wilsonian, 7, 42, 55, 114, 237n2
International Neo-Malthusian and Birth Control Conference: Fifth (London), 34, 110; Sixth (New York), 44, 81, 110–11, 113

International Planned Parenthood Federation (IPPF), 150, 181, 185, 199, 211–13
intrauterine devices (IUDs), 5, 18, 200, 202, 203, 206, 207, 208
Iriye, Akira, 7, 55–56
Ishigaki Ayako, 76, 226n28
Ishigaki Eitarō, 32, 34
Ishihama Atsumi, 202
Ishimoto Keikichi, 30–34, 68, 71
Ishimoto Shizue, 2, 4, 5, 10, 56–57, 61, 81–82; birth control activism in Japan, 40–41, 46–47, 49–50, 54, 160; exposure to socialism, 29–30; first meeting with Sanger, 19, 32, 34; US visits, 58, 67–76. Works: *Facing Two Ways* (autobiography), 70, 76–77, 83; translation of *Wheat and Soldiers*, 78

Jacobson, Matthew, 90
Japan: government support of global population control/family planning, 198, 209, 212; as leader in Asia, 8, 16, 79, 199, 215. *See also* colonialism, Japanese; expansionism, Japanese; imperialism, Japanese; nationalism, Japanese
Japan Association for Maternal Welfare, 206, 215
Japan Birth Control Federation, 50, 51
Japanese Americans: anti-, 42, 61, 84, 88–96; positions on birth control, 52–53; proposal to sterilize, 121; in SCAP, 126; and socialism, 31–32. *See also* immigration, exclusionist policies
Johnson, Albert, 91, 96, 113
Johnson, Lyndon, 209
Johnson-Reed Immigration Act (1924), 84, 90, 91, 96, 97, 98, 106
josei mondai, 22, 24–25

Kaizō, 24, 25, 26–27, 53
Kaizō Publishing Company, 34, 36, 37, 40, 44–45
Katayama Sen, 31–32, 34, 53, 229n21, 230n37
Katō Kanjū, 41, 117
Katō Shizue: as Diet member, 9, 154–57, 169, 187, 206; inviting Sanger to Japan, 117, 128–29; in the media, 166, 184–85, 265n14; relationship with US activists, 125, 141, 197, 257n57; role in the FPFJ, 185, 197–98, 211. *See also* Ishimoto Shizue
Kawakami Riichi, 165
Kennedy, John F., 209
Key, Ellen, 21, 23–24, 25
Kida Fumio, 165, 271n58
Kitaoka Juitsu, 125, 139, 141, 154
Koshiro, Yukiko, 138
Kōtoku Shūsui, 31, 230n35
Koyama Sakae, 47
Koya Yoshio: birth control experiments (including the Three Village Studies), 139–42, 146, 185, 187, 189, 200, 201; eugenics research, 133, 136, 164, 216; role in the FPFJ, 185, 186, 197, 199; role in pill project, 189–92, 195–96, 206–207; trip to the US South, 133–38; work as MHW official, 132–33, 154, 158, 170, 180, 183–84

Laughlin, Harry, 96, 98, 111, 113
LeBlanc, Thomas J., 102, 103
Liberal Democratic Party (LDP), 154, 156, 157, 158
liberalism, 6–7, 12–13, 224n9; in Japan, 30–31; limits of, 4–5, 76. *See also* internationalism
Luten Jr., Daniel B., 141

MacArthur, Douglas, 117, 121, 127, 128, 129, 130, 139
Mainichi Newspaper Company, 150; surveys, 48, 174–77
Majima Kan, 41, 50, 125, 183–84, 185, 197, 198
Malthusianism, 15, 27, 53, 106, 223n3. *See also* neo-Malthusianism
Manchuria, 45, 68, 146; Japanese military invasion into, 51, 69, 74–77, 79, 80, 102, 107, 111
Maternalism, 23, 82
Maternalist pacifism, 56, 57, 60, 61, 69, 74, 77

Maternal Protection Law, 215–16
McClatchy, V. S., 92, 95
McCormick, Katherine Dexter, 188, 191, 194, 203
McCoy, Oliver, 123, 124, 125, 127, 129, 132, 133, 141
Meiji period: government's reproductive policies, 22, 169; intellectual thoughts during, 31, 63; population increase during, 41
Midwives: as birth control case workers, 142, 143, 152–53, 158, 167, 169–74, 176, 180, 189; in Japan (prewar), 168–69, 229n25; in the US, 169–70, 174, 180, 272n68
Milbank Memorial Fund, 107, 108, 112, 150
Ministry of Health and Welfare of Japan (MHW): birth control policies, 122, 142–43, 160, 170, 186, 207; Institute of Population Problems, 154; Progesterone Committee, 190–91, 195–96; Round-Table Conference on Population Problems, 133, 154. *See also* Koya Yoshio
Mississippi, 134, 135, 136
modernization: in Japan, 21–22, 31, 38, 162; projects, 182, 199; theory, 13, 146, 200
motherhood protection: 23, 77, 82; debate (*bosei hogo ronsō*), 24–25
Muller, Hermann. J., 121, 145
Muramatsu Minoru, 138

Nagai Hisomu, 154, 160, 163, 235n101
National Eugenic Law, 155, 156, 157, 160, 274n89
nationalism: and birth control, 4, 57, 114–15; and the female body, 15–16; Japanese, 38, 105, 197; and war, 7, 56–57, 75, 79. *See also* imperialism; internationalism
Nazi: eugenic genocide, 16, 118, 121, 126, 130, 152, 163, 215; sterilization law, 157, 160
neo-Malthusianism, 3, 5, 120, 212, 223n3; British, 109; in Japan, 20–21, 26–27,

42; Sanger as authority in, 27, 36, 38, 54
New Life Movement, 269n48
New Women's Association, 77, 160
Nitobe Inazō, 30, 41, 63
nongovernmental organizations (NGOs), 12, 84, 103, 209, 212, 213
North Carolina, 134–35, 136–37, 140, 217
Notestein, Frank: 108, 113, 141, 145, 201, 202; as part of RF Far East Mission, 124, 143, 149

obstetrician-gynecologists. *See* physicians
Ogawa, Manako, 73, 79
oral contraceptives (the pill): in the context of overpopulation, 5, 18, 181, 189, 203; legal approval, 203–4, 206, 207, 208, 215–16; progesterone experiments, 188–92, 194–97, 206; research as international science, 194, 204; side effects, 191, 196–97, 205
Ordinance Regulating Harmful Contraceptive Devices, 45, 47
Orientalism: expressed by American intellectuals and officials, 101, 131, 230n36; expressed by Sanger, 62–63, 66–67; feminist, 57, 58, 62, 68; against Ishimoto, 70–74
Osaka, 40, 42, 43, 46, 49
Osaka Birth Control Society, 43, 46, 50, 52
Osborn, Fairfield, 145
Osborn, Frederick, 107–8, 113, 145, 149, 209
Ōta Tenrei, 155, 184, 185, 202

Page Act, 91
Paisley, Fiona, 59, 73
Pan-Pacific Women's Association (PPWA), 59
Pan-Pacific Women's Conference (PPWC): in Honolulu (1928), 58–59, 60, 77; in Vancouver (1937), 79–81
Pearl, Raymond, 100, 102, 103, 108, 111, 113; scientific studies, 248n63, 251n112; working with Sanger, 109, 110, 112, 114, 186

Perry, Commodore Matthew C., 20, 38
pessaries (diaphragms), 45, 46–47, 202, 277n18, 280n64. *See also* United States v. One Package of Japanese Pessaries
pharmaceutical companies, 205, 206
Pharmaceutical Law, 122, 125, 157, 171
Phelan, James D., 92, 95
physicians: control over childbirth, birth control, and abortion, 14, 50, 156–57, 158, 168, 169, 206, 214–15, 283n14; control over legislation, 154, 156, 158, 170, 171; providing birth control guidance, 52–53, 125, 167, 176, 180; relationship with midwives, 153, 168, 169–70, 173–74; supporting the birth control movement, 36, 41, 43, 45, 46, 47, 64, 66, 69
picture brides, 92, 94. *See also* Japanese Americans, anti-
Pincus, Gregory Goodwin, 188–89, 191, 194–97, 204
Planned Parenthood Federation of America, 133, 145, 150, 188, 254n30
Popenoe, Paul, 109, 113, 267n30
Population Association of America, 112–13
population control: from birth control to, 12, 115; global, 12–13, 143–49, 181–82, 198–205, 213; Western/white scheme against the East/colored races, 36, 119, 136, 205, 213; to women's rights, 212, 215
Population Council, 144, 149, 150, 202
Population Problems Research Council. *See* Mainichi Publishing Company, surveys
population studies, 84, 103, 106–8, 111, 112–13, 138, 150
Princeton Office of Population Research (OPR), 107–8, 138
pronatalism: of American eugenicists, 108–9, 113, 115; contemporary, 216, 219; of the Japanese government, 35, 47, 76, 81, 133, 160, 169, 226n28
prostitution: anti, 82, 91; licensed, 22–23, 73; as target of eugenic policies, 158, 164, 167, 170
public health: centers, 122, 133; and colonialism, 247n56; nurses as case workers, 137, 142, 170, 176; state programs in the US South, 135–36. *See also* Rockefeller Foundation, public health efforts
Public Health and Welfare Section (PHW), 120, 122, 123, 125, 128, 133. *See also* SCAP
Public Peace Police Law, 22, 35, 239n33
Public Peace Preservation Law, 35, 50
Puerto Rico, 189–90, 192, 196, 203, 204, 205, 277n18

race: mixture, 88, 99, 135, 136; scientific theories on, 87–88, 121, 244n21; war, 88, 89, 224n10, 249n87. *See also* eugenics
race suicide, 85–86, 88, 89, 90, 104, 108, 109, 111, 140
radicalism. *See* socialism
rhythm method, 207, 208
Rock, John, 189, 195, 203, 204
Rockefeller Foundation (RF): conservative position on birth control, 131, 144, 150; Far East Mission, 124–25, 143, 145, 146; Human Biology Commission, 99–103; public health efforts, 12, 99, 123, 147, 259n86; sending SCAP consultants, 123, 128, 149; support of eugenics research, 84, 97, 99, 103, 107; support of global population control programs, 12, 209
Rockefeller III, John D., 124, 144, 147, 209
Roosevelt, Theodore, 7, 88
Ross, Edward, 86–87, 88, 89, 104, 113
Rupp, Leila, 58, 60
Russell, Bertrand, 34, 111
Russian revolution, 6, 26, 30, 32, 90
Russo-Japanese War, 38, 88, 89, 223n2
ryōsai-kenbo, 22–23, 25

Sams, Crawford F., 120, 121–23, 125–26, 130, 133, 148
Sanger, Margaret: death, 211; denial of visa to Japan, 35, 117–18, 128–30; domestic legislative efforts, 47, 209; exclusion from professional meetings and

research, 112–13, 145, 150, 203; Japanese views on, 26–27, 37–40; media portrayal of, 151, 163, 165, 167; organizing the ICPP, 192–94; the pill project, 181, 188–92, 193–96; racist projects, 140, 213; relationship with eugenicists, 85, 109–14, 224n6; relationship with Japanese activists, 41–47, 197–98; socialist associations, 19–20, 28–29, 32, 63, 114; view on immigration, 109, 114; 1922 visit to Japan, 1–2, 34–40; 1952 visit to Japan, 150, 151, 153; 1957 visit to Japan, 179–80. Works: *Autobiography*, 1, 29, 66; *Birth Control Review*, 29, 33, 34, 41, 43, 55, 104, 109, 111, 113; *Family Limitation*, 42, 49; *Woman and the New Race*, 26, 250n97; *Woman Rebel*, 29

Schoen, Johanna, 140
Scripps Foundation, 106, 150
Seitō, 23–24
sexuality: Asian, 15, 88; female, 9–16; and morality, 23, 26, 49, 64, 153, 155, 164–65; regulation of, 22–23, 173; education (sexology), 28–29, 37, 43, 44. *See also* prostitution
Sino-Japanese War: of 1894–95, 31, 38; of 1937–45, 69, 77–78, 80, 241n77
Smedley, Agnes, 32–34, 230n39
sterilization: coerced, 121, 122, 154, 173, 217; law in Germany, 157, 160, 165; laws in Japan, 83, 154–58, 162, 168, 173; laws in the US, 98, 160, 165; used in global population control, 18, 199, 207. *See also* EPL, provisions on abortion and sterilization
Stoddard, Lothrop, 89, 95, 96, 101, 106, 109, 110; *The Rising Tide of Color against White World-Supremacy*, 89–90, 92
Stopes, Marie, 26, 29, 44
stratified reproduction, 219
socialism: in Japan, 21, 24–27, 30–31, 35, 68, 229n33; transnational activities in New York, 27–28, 32–34; women's views, 51–53, 65. *See also* feminism, and socialism
Socialist Party: Japan, 154–58; US, 28, 29

Supreme Command for the Allied Powers (SCAP): anticommunism, 130; "benevolent neutrality," 118, 120, 126, 141, 143, 156; rejection of Sanger's visa, 117, 128–29; roles in reproductive policies in Japan, 119, 121–23, 125–28, 132, 133, 139, 157, 168. *See also* MacArthur, Douglas; PHW

Tachi Minoru, 138, 154
Taeuber, Irene B., 124, 128, 145, 146, 148; *The Population of Japan*, 108, 256n51
Taishō period, 20, 30, 35; "black ship of," 35, 38, 151
Takeuchi Shigeyo, 160, 162, 170
Taniguchi Yasaburō, 156, 169, 170, 171
Thomas, Dorothy Swaine, 128, 145
Thompson, Warren: *Danger Spots in World Population*, 104–6; institutional support, 106–7, 123; as SCAP consultant, 123, 141, 149, 159, 193; in support of birth control, 111–12, 115, 127, 131, 137–38, 145, 147, 159
Tokyo: birth control movement in, 40–41, 46, 49, 50, 51, 52; ICPP in, 181, 183–85, 192–95, 198; Ishimoto in, 30, 72; RF projects in, 99, 123, 124; Sanger in, 34, 40, 189–90, 211
transnationalism, 3–5, 8, 11–12, 224n7, 225n16. *See also* eugenics, transnational network of; feminism, transnational/international; immigration, and transnationalism; socialism, transnational activities in New York
Tsurumi Yūsuke, 30, 69

United Nations, 12, 130, 150; Population Fund, 213; Women's Conference (Beijing), 215
United States: government position on global population control/reproductive health, 209–10, 212; superiority in science and technology, 8, 13, 38, 193, 200. *See also* capitalism, US; democracy, US; expansionism, US; imperialism, US

United States v. One Package of Japanese Pessaries, 9, 47, 122

venereal disease (VD), 23, 29, 60, 115, 163–64, 166; legislative campaign for marriage restriction against men with, 77, 82, 160
Versailles Conference (Paris Peace Conference), 90, 91
voluntary motherhood, 21, 57, 85, 109, 229n27

Washington Naval Conference, 35–36
Watumull, G. J., 197
Whelpton, Pascal K., 106, 123, 126, 137–38, 143, 145, 147, 149
Williamsburg Conference on Population Problems, 144–49
Wilson, Woodrow, 7, 115, 224n9, 225n15. See also internationalism, Wilsonian
Woman's Christian Temperance Union (WCTU), 59, 73, 79, 82, 241n78
Women's International League for Peace and Freedom (WILPF), 58, 60, 77, 237n11
World Population Conference (Geneva), 112, 186

World War I: anti-imperialism/internationalism/liberalism after, 19, 20, 27, 55, 58, 111, 225n15; antiradicalism during, 29, 31; as crisis in European nationalism/colonialism, 7, 58, 90; and population, 26, 27, 36, 111
World War II: continuity before and after, 5–6, 120–21, 124, 133, 162. See also nationalism, and war; race, war; Sino-Japanese War, of 1937–45

Yamada Waka, 24, 25
Yamagiwa Yoshiko, 163, 167
Yamakawa Hitoshi, 26–27, 41
Yamakawa Kikue, 41, 49, 125; socialist views, 24, 25–26, 53, 65, 230n43
Yamamoto Senji: as leader of the proletariat birth control movement, 40, 42–43, 45–46, 49–50, 184; political radicalism, 102, 231n53; views on Sanger, 37–38, 40, 43–44
Yellow Peril, 2, 15, 84, 89, 92, 95, 102, 105, 108
Yokoyama Fuku, 170, 171, 172, 206
Yomiuri Newspaper Company, 117, 128
Yosano Akiko, 24, 25, 33–34, 40, 230n43
Yoshioka Yayoi, 60, 66, 160

The authorized representative in the EU for product safety and compliance is:
Mare Nostrum Group
B.V Doelen 72
4831 GR Breda
The Netherlands

www.ingramcontent.com/pod-product-compliance
Lightning Source LLC
Chambersburg PA
CBHW032055230426
43662CB00035B/422